The Pauline Letters

The Pauline Letters

A Rhetorical Analysis

David Oliver Smith

Foreword by Robert M. Price

RESOURCE *Publications* · Eugene, Oregon

THE PAULINE LETTERS
A Rhetorical Analysis

Copyright © 2022 David Oliver Smith. All rights reserved. Except for brief quotations in critical publications or reviews, no part of this book may be reproduced in any manner without prior written permission from the publisher. Write: Permissions, Wipf and Stock Publishers, 199 W. 8th Ave., Suite 3, Eugene, OR 97401.

Resource Publications
An Imprint of Wipf and Stock Publishers
199 W. 8th Ave., Suite 3
Eugene, OR 97401

www.wipfandstock.com

PAPERBACK ISBN: 978-1-6667-4456-9
HARDCOVER ISBN: 978-1-6667-4457-6
EBOOK ISBN: 978-1-6667-4458-3

JUNE 3, 2022 7:34 AM

Contents

Foreword by Robert M. Price | vii

    1   Literary Structures in the Pauline Letters | 1

    2   Using Literary Structures To Detect Interpolation | 18

PART I   THE UNDISPUTED LETTERS

    3   Letter To The Romans | 33

    4   First Letter To The Corinthians | 108

    5   Second Letter To The Corinthians | 185

    6   Letter To The Galatians | 227

    7   Letter To The Philippians | 255

    8   First Letter To The Thessalonians | 269

    9   Letter To Philemon | 285

    10   Literary Units Of Paul | 291

PART II   THE DEUTERO-PAULINE LETTERS

    11   Second Letter To The Thessalonians | 297

    12   Letter To The Colossians | 303

    13   Letter To The Ephesians | 315

    14   First Letter To Timothy | 332

    15   Second Letter To Timothy | 344

    16   Letter To Titus | 350

    17   Conclusion | 356

Bibliography | 359

Foreword

DAVID OLIVER SMITH'S LATEST astonishing book is tantamount to the most recent in a series of brilliant doctoral dissertations that he didn't bother submitting to committees who are not competent to judge them. But one can at least hope such scholars will avail themselves of his findings for their own work. By applying his expertise in the analysis of the ancient compositional technique of chiasm-crafting (expressing one's thoughts in an artful ABBA pattern, i.e., arriving at the end of a thought and recognizing it as one's familiar starting point, not a circular argument, but a tightening verbal lasso), Smith has provided a helpful piece of rhetorical technology for the study of the Pauline Epistles. Specifically, his method, demonstrated herein, is like a surgical laser replacing a blunt scalpel.

This simile is an apt one because in question is the authenticity/integrity of these New Testament texts in cases where proposed interpolations have been detectable by internal evidence, since, if actually secondary, these new patches must have been added to the old wineskins in that early period from which manuscript copies, useful for textual criticism, have not survived. (Where did they end up? Lining a monastery's garbage can, like Codex Sinaiticus's pages? As kindling for somebody's campfire like some of the Nag Hammadi codices? Or suffocating behind a Geniza wall like the Damascus Document?) Since no one can call these witnesses to the stand to testify, we are reduced to weighing circumstantial evidence: do the available copies betray their fraudulence by an anachronism, as when Woody Allen's "reporting" on "the Scrolls" noted the doubts of some scholars because of the appearance of the word "Oldsmobile" in the text? Or does this or that passage read like an interloper clumsily intruding into the otherwise smooth flow of the argument? Is the vocabulary suddenly uncharacteristic compared with the ostensible author's habitual usage elsewhere, as when Romans chapters 9-11 speak of "Israel" whereas the rest of Romans has "Jews"?

Many scholars, like Bart Ehrman, seem to grow quite uneasy when one proposes an interpolation unattested by manuscript evidence. This can be ironic, since Ehrman is quick to stress the dubiety of the received text because of the many (usually trivial) variants but resists the obvious implication that these might be taken for iceberg tips denoting a vaster mass of textual corruption hidden below the surface. And he evidences no scruples when it comes to the controversial text of the *Testimonium*

Flavianum, making strategic cuts unattested by the (unavailable) autographic original. The motive underlying this double standard would seem to be to afflict the comfortable believers in verbal inspiration (to whose ranks he once belonged) while comforting mainstream critics who do not relish going so far as to question the existence of an unattested Jesus lest they be ousted from the SBL Magisterium.

David Oliver Smith has provided an important supplementary test for Pauline authenticity which often tends to confirm the results of previous methods. Other times it casts doubt on older interpolation hypotheses. One relishes the prospect of the spectacle of competing refutations and counter-defenses among the scholars thus implicated. But it's not just entertaining; what better way to increase the magnification on the problem passages? Not to mention evaluating one competing methodology over against others! Yes, it's a mind game, but isn't that equally true of the whole large-scale enterprise? And David Oliver Smith may very likely be declared MVP!

*

How are we to account for the compositional intricacies spotlighted by "Dr." Smith (if he doesn't mind the due recognition)? Is it possible that Paul, dictating his missives, just naturally spoke in reiterative sum-ups before moving on to the next topic? Many people have the habit of repeating themselves in case what they said may not have been sufficiently clear, or for emphasis. That might be what's going on in the Epistles, though the result would not likely be as polished. And the remaining possibility is that these "letters" are far from what we are meant to think them. Who would write actual, personal, casual letters, even dealing with important matters, with such exacting complexity? I think of what Austin Farrer said about Mark's gospel: the more literary, the less historical. The more artifice went into it, the more artificial is the result.

The Dutch Radical Critics of a bolder time ventured that these "letters" were instead treatises cast in letter form simply as a literary device. This meant not only that the actual author of them was not a historical apostle named Paul, but also that, equally, the ostensible recipients were not a bunch of half-educated sectarians in Corinth, Philippi, or Thessalonica. A.D. Loman indicated the absurdity of taking the addressees of Galatians literally: if it were really Paul writing to the "historical Galatians," it would be like Hegel lecturing to New Guinea savages! Accordingly, just imagine these rude rustics savoring the complexity of Paul's chiasmic structures! In fact, how many of *us*, with all our boasted sophistication, ever even noticed it?

Some gospel scholars (apologists) try to exploit the studies of anthropologists Albert Lord and Milman Parry, contending that the faithfulness of the oral performers of the Jesus traditions, previous to their literary petrification in Matthew, Mark, Luke, and John, was just like that of Balkan balladeers who could recite long verse epics without benefit of a written script. The many differences in detail among the gospels were merely the accidental variations endemic to oral performance. Well, not only did the recorded recitations prove so fluid and flexible that every performance

Foreword

was really a new "original" (hence very far from the near-inerrant standard of accuracy the apologists sought to vindicate for the gospels); the whole model purposely ignored the intricate patterns of variation on which Redaction Criticism is based: just coincidence! Nothing to see here! Move along! This is just the same embarrassment those face who minimize, much less just ignore, the fine tuning David Oliver Smith demonstrates in the Pauline texts. In genuine letters, Paul would never have poured such skill and effort into them just for the sake of style. Moreover, his ancient readers could never have noticed it, much less appreciated it.

So who *did* write them, and *for* whom? That remains to be seen, but I take a cue from Philip R. Davies's conclusion that the Old Testament "histories" had to have been produced by an elite class of educated scribes, and for their colleagues. We must ask, again, who else was in a position to research and write them? Who even had access to them once written? Not a bunch of dawn-to-dusk olive farmers and shepherds, that's for sure. They had no copies available to them either at home or in the motel room nightstand! They were lucky to hear contextless, near-unintelligible snatches of these texts, read without a PA system, on the occasional feast day. "What did he say? Blessed are the cheese-makers?"

David Oliver Smith is, so to speak, one of those scribes. He shows himself adept at fathoming hidden secrets of the biblical text, secret even though hidden in plain sight. And he certainly has more secrets to reveal. The wonder of it is that he remains firmly rooted in visible reality, never tempted to repair to high-flown kabbalistic fantasies or mystagogical allegories. He is instead a particularly sharp-eyed detective, spotting clues and fingerprints the less-astute have missed.

ROBERT M. PRICE
Good Friday, 2022

1

Literary Structures in the Pauline Letters

Rhetorical Analysis

SCHOLARS HAVE LONG THOUGHT that Paul's letters found in the canon had been redacted by later church leaders in order to get Paul's imprimatur for their ideas.[1] In fact, William O. Walker Jr. in his seminal *Interpolations in the Pauline Letters* is of the opinion that *a priori* it should be expected that Paul's letters contain non-Pauline interpolations.[2] Winsome Munro states, "It strains credulity to assume interpolations did not take place."[3] Pauline scholars generally agree that seven of the letters attributed to Paul were actually written by him.[4] These letters are typically referred to as Paul's "undisputed" letters. A minority of scholars follows the opinion of F.C. Baur that only Romans, 1 Corinthians, 2 Corinthians and Galatians, known as the *hauptbriefe*, are original to Paul.[5] Much has been written by Pauline scholars with regard to exactly which part of the Pauline text is original and which parts are later interpolations. Scholars have heretofore proposed ninety-seven interpolations into Paul's seven undisputed letters.[6] The other six letters that claim to be authored by Paul, 2 Thessalonians, Colossians, Ephesians, 1 Timothy, 2 Timothy and Titus, the "Deutero-Pauline" letters, are generally regarded by Pauline scholars as total forgeries.[7]

In the debate regarding forged letters of Paul and interpolation into the undisputed letters, traditional scholarship investigates whether the text under consideration seems to interrupt the context of the surrounding text, contains atypical vocabulary

---

1. Ehrman, *Corruption of Scripture,* 321. Walker, *Interpolations*.

2. Walker, *Interpolations,* 43.

3. Munro, "Interpolations," 161–68.

4. These are Romans, 1 Corinthians, 2 Corinthians, Galatians, Philippians, 1 Thessalonians, and Philemon; Ehrman, *Forged,* 93.

5. Britannica.com/biography/Ferdinand-Christian-Baur.

6. Walker, *Interpolations,* 16–19; O'Neill, *Romans;* O'Neill, *Galatians*. Of the ninety-seven interpolations proposed by Pauline scholars, rhetorical analysis agrees totally or partially with eleven, cannot dispute three, disagrees with eighty-three, and proposes twenty-four additional interpolations.

7. Ehrman, *Forged,* 93.

or grammatical forms, whether there is contradictory text elsewhere in the subject letter, and whether the subject passage is missing or located in a different place in early manuscripts.[8] These are all relevant discussions by Pauline scholars in coming to their conclusions with regard to interpolations and forgeries, and that data provides important clues as to whether different texts may have been written by different authors.

This work presents an additional tool that can be utilized to detect possible interpolated passages and forgeries. This tool will be referred to as "rhetorical analysis." Rhetorical analysis can also be used to confirm or refute proposed interpolations that have been suggested by scholars using the traditional methods. Rhetorical analysis is akin to analysis of vocabulary, grammatical forms and other elements of style. It involves analyzing the literary structures contained in letters allegedly written by Paul. Scholars have heretofore mostly ignored the structures of Paul's literary units as contained in his letters. A careful examination of Paul's work reveals parallelisms, especially repeated words, phrases, and abstract concepts he used to structure his literary units.

Paul made extensive use of parallelism in his letters. Parallelism in rhetoric is a literary device in which coordinate ideas are arranged in phrases, sentences, and paragraphs that balance one element with another of equal importance and similar wording. The repetition of sounds, meanings, and structures serves to order, emphasize, and point out relationships.[9] Paul used repetition of words and phrases, repetition of grammatical forms, repetition of abstract concepts stated differently, and contrasting statements, all sub-categories of the literary device parallelism. He deftly used these to emphasize and drive home the points he was attempting to make. Parallelism was a main attribute of his rhetoric. As one reads Paul's letters, he cannot help but notice Paul's repeated phrases.

Pauline scholars have noted Paul's use of parallelisms,[10] but little attention seems to have been paid to the systematic structural use of parallelisms in the letters. While Paul used all types of parallelism in his undisputed letters, the focus herein will be on the sub-category of repetition, particularly the repetition of words, phrases and abstract concepts. Careful examination of these repeated words, phrases, and concepts can be used to discover the structure, including the beginning and the ending of Paul's literary units. For purposes of this analysis a parallelism is not necessarily merely a repeated word, phrase, or abstract concept, although the vast majority are in that category. The relationship of the parallelism could be of opposites (Heaven and Earth), synonyms (sin and immorality) or complementary concepts (faith and forgiveness). The relationship could be a question and the answer or an epithet and the target. An interesting aspect of Paul's parallelisms is that occasionally in a chiastic structure the matching language in a particular stich will form a chiasm within the

8. Walker, *Interpolations*, 63–90.
9. https://www.britannica.com/art/parallelism-literature-and-rhetoric.
10. Lund, *Chiasmus*, 142–43.

chiastic structure. For instance, in the chiastic structure of Rom 6:1–23 "died to sin" (*apethanen tē hamartia*) in v. 6:10 is matching language with "sin to death" (*hamartias eis thanaton*) in v. 6:16. The only way a reader would recognize the chiasm is by realizing that they form a stich in a chiastic structure. This is done a number of times in the undisputed letters. After the parallel text has been identified, a further determination is made whether a particular section of text is a unified literary unit with the repeated words and phrases arranged in a chiastic structure, a parallel structure, a hybrid structure, or a common prose structure devoid of parallelisms. Some Pauline structures actually have both a chiastic and a parallel structure overlapping each other.

Once a determination of the extent and structure of the literary units has been accomplished, a comparison can be made of these structures among the letters in order to determine whether a consistent pattern of literary structures can be identified as those of a single author. If a structure can be identified as being consistent with other structures found in Paul's letters, additional text that has been inserted into the unit unbalancing and disrupting the original flow of the structure can be detected. In addition, some entire letters can be identified as not containing typical Pauline structures, rendering them total forgeries.

While Pauline scholars are certainly aware of Paul's parallelisms, it appears that no systematic analysis of that element of Paul's style has been performed. Several scholars have noted that chiasms can occasionally be found in the Pauline corpus.[11] They then used the chiastic structures they discovered as an exegetical tool. It has apparently gone unnoticed that Paul divided his letters into literary units and defined them by using the parallels of which he was so fond. The method of rhetorical analysis used herein is a chapter-by-chapter analysis. Of course, Paul did not organize his letters into chapters. However, he did organize his letters. He discussed one subject, came to a conclusion and then shifted to another subject. Rhetorical analysis reveals that Paul structured the separate topics and sub-topics in his letters into separate literary units using chiastic, parallel, hybrid chiastic/parallel, and dual chiastic/parallel structures, setting the topics and sub-topics apart.

The majority of the literary structures that are identified herein and contained in Paul's seven undisputed letters encompass entire chapters. This validates the work of Stephen Langdon in the thirteenth century when he divided the books of the Bible into chapters.[12] When dividing Paul's letters into chapters, Bishop Langdon would have naturally decided to end a chapter and begin a new chapter when one topic was completed and a new topic begun. If Paul used chiastic, parallel, or hybrid literary structures, it would be natural for him to have organized separate topics in his letters into separate literary structures. As Bishop Langdon divided them and are found in the canon, there are sixty-one chapters in Paul's undisputed letters. Rhetorical analysis

---

11. Lund, *Chiasmus*, 142–43; Thomson, *Chiasmus*; Bailey, *Structure*; Welch, "Chiasmus," 211–249; Slusser, "Pauline Writings?"

12. Metzger, New Testament, 347.

shows that only one chapter, 1 Cor 8, is not in Paul's customary style. While 1 Cor 8 does contain repeated words and phrases, they are not arranged in any systematic pattern that Paul typically used. The repeated words and phrases found in 1 Cor 8 are similar to the chaotic type of repetition found in Ephesians. The conclusion is that the entire chapter is an interpolation. The fact that 1 Cor 8 contradicts 1 Cor 10:19–33 lends weight to the conclusion that it is an interpolation.

Thirty-five chapters of the authentic sixty found in the undisputed letters, or 58 percent of them, have a single literary structure that encompasses the entire chapter. One literary structure encompasses two chapters, Rom 12–13. In the sixty chapters rhetorical analysis identified a total of ninety-eight separate literary structures. Thirty-eight of them are solely chiastic, forty of them are solely parallel, thirteen have both a chiastic and a parallel structure, five structures are a hybrid mix of parallel and chiastic, and two structures encompassing Rom 4 and 2 Cor 2 have an unusual "progressive parallel" structure.

For those chapters in Paul's letters that contain more than one literary structure, it would be understandable that Bishop Langdon did not want to separate out fifty or a hundred words as a separate chapter. He quite sensibly chose to divide the letter at the end of the second, third, or fourth structure where Paul completed a thought. With six relatively short structures, 1 Cor 7 contains the most structures of any chapter in Paul's undisputed letters. In addition to the single literary unit of Rom 12–13, Gal 1:18–2:1 and Phil 1:7–2:4 are the only two other instances in the undisputed letters where a literary unit begins in one chapter and ends in another. There are also two instances in Colossians and one in Ephesians.

Chiastic Structure

A chiastic structure, also called a "chiasm" or "chiasmus," is a literary construction wherein words, phrases, or concepts in the first half of the literary unit are repeated in exact reverse order in the second half. These are also called "ring structures" and "concentric structures." For example, Mark 10:31: "But many first will be last, and the last, first." The significant word order is "first, last; last, first." This is a short, simple, small chiastic structure. A famous chiasm from John F. Kennedy's Inaugural Address is "Ask not what your country can do for you, rather, ask what you can do for your country."

Except for the italicized font a chiasm is typically diagramed as follows:

  A Ask not what *your country*
    B *can do*
      C for *you*
      C' ask what *you*
    B' *can do*
  A' for *your country*.

Each matching pair A, A'; B, B'; and C, C' is called a "stich" and each half is a "hemistich." Throughout this work the parallel or matching words, phrases, or concepts will be shown in italicized font as presented above to facilitate recognition by the reader. Also in this work the term "A stich" means both hemistiches, A and A', of a chiastic or parallel structure, or all elements, A, A,' A," A,'" of a multi-element parallel stich. However, the term "A hemistich" means only the first half of the A stich.

With experience it is relatively simple to detect the chiasmus as in the above example when exact words or phrases are placed in reverse order in a composition. However, in New Testament scripture often the author intends that two abstract concepts be recognized by the reader as being parallel or a matched pair. In these cases a subjective element enters the analysis. Treatises on chiastic structure go into great detail setting forth rules to follow in order to identify a chiastic structure and reduce the subjective element. In attempting to make the identification of chiastic structures rigorous, these scholars probably obscure some chiastic structures that were intended by the ancient authors.

Scholars have heretofore noted chiastic structures in Paul's letters.[13] Nils Lund in his 1942 work, *Chiasmus in the New Testament* identifies chiasmi at 1 Cor 6:12–14,[14] 1 Cor 5:2–6,[15] 1 Cor 9:19–22,[16] 1 Cor 11:8–12,[17] 2 Cor 1:3–5,[18] the overall structure of 1 Cor 7,[19] a large structure encompassing 1 Cor 11:34b—14:40,[20] Eph 5:22–33,[21] Eph 6:1–4,[22] Eph 6:5–9,[23] Col 1:3–9a,[24] the overall conceptual structure of Philemon,[25] and Rom 11:33–36.[26] Lund elucidates two different kinds of chiasmus. One, he matches words and phrases in short, one to four-verse passages, and two, he finds structural chiasmi in long passages, but the matches in the structural chiasmi are conceptual

---

13. Lund, *Chiasmus*; Thomson, *Chiasmus*; Bailey, *Structure*; Welch, "Chiasmus," Slusser, "Pauline Writings?"

14. Lund, *Chiasmus*, 145.

15. Lund, *Chiasmus*, 146.

16. Lund, *Chiasmus*, 147.

17. Lund, *Chiasmus*, 148.

18. Lund, *Chiasmus*, 150.

19. Lund, *Chiasmus*, 151.

20. Lund, *Chiasmus*, 164. Rhetorical analysis shows that canonical 1 Cor 12–14 is actually out of order and that the original section written by Paul was 1 Cor 12, 14, 13, with 1 Cor 14:1a coming at the end of the literary unit 1 Cor 13:1–14:1a.

21. Lund, *Chiasmus*, 148.

22. Lund, *Chiasmus*, 201.

23. Lund, *Chiasmus*, 202.

24. Lund, *Chiasmus*, 207.

25. Lund, *Chiasmus*, 219.

26. Lund, *Chiasmus*, 222. Rhetorical analysis finds that Rom 11:33–36 is an interpolation.

themes, not in repeated words and phrases. In both cases he is using the chiasmus as an exegetic tool to assist in determining the meaning of that portion of the letter.

In *Chiasmus in the Pauline Epistles* Ian Thompson detects chiasmi at Eph 1:3–10,[27] Eph 2:11–22,[28] Gal 5:13–22,[29] Col 2:6–19,[30] and Rom 5:12–21.[31] Thompson also uses the chiasmus to assist in exegesis.[32] It was not the intention of either Lund or Thompson to utilize the structures they discovered to detect possible interpolated passages or identify a consistent corpus wide Pauline literary characteristic. Since an interpolation in all likelihood disrupts Paul's original structure, they were, in fact, encumbrances to Lund and Thompson in detecting chiasmi. Their endeavors in using chiasmus to assist in exegesis are interesting and elucidate the writing style of Paul. The analysis of Paul's letters presented herein has a different focus and will detect literary structures that the others did not report.

Recognizing Chiastic Structures

As stated above nearly half of the literary structures in Paul's undisputed letters have a chiastic structure. Because of the balanced nature of the structure, these provide the best opportunities to detect interpolations that disrupt the balance. The following set of principles sets out the parameters of the process of identifying a chiastic structure of a literary unit that encompasses a chapter or a substantial portion of a chapter in Paul's letters. First Corinthians 7:20–24 will be used to illustrate these principles. Below the diagram of the entire unit is a table showing only the matching text.

A 7:20 *Let each one remain* in that calling *wherein he was called*.
  B 7:21a Were you called as a *slave*? Do not care about it.
    C 7:21b But if *you can become free*, rather take advantage.
      D 7:22a For he that was *called* in the *Lord* being a *slave* is the *Lord's freed* man.
      D' 7:22b Likewise he that was *called* being *free* is *Christ's slave*.
    C' 7:23a *You were bought with a price*.
  B' 7:23b Do not become *slaves* of men.
A' 7:24 Brothers, *let each one remain wherein he was called*, with God.[33]

---

27. Thompson, *Chiasmus*, 46–69.
28. Thompson, *Chiasmus*, 84–115.
29. Thompson, *Chiasmus*, 116–151. Rhetorical analysis identifies Gal 5:14–36 as having a chiastic structure.
30. Thompson, *Chiasmus*, 152–185.
31. Thompson, *Chiasmus*, 186–212. Rhetorical analysis identifies the entire chapter of Rom 5 as having a chiastic structure.
32. Thompson, *Chiasmus*, 41–45.
33. The translation of all the Pauline letters herein is by the author hereof.

1 Cor 7:20–24 Chiastic Structure Table

A 7:20—let each one remain . . . wherein he was called	A' 7:24—let each one remain . . . wherein he was called
B 7:21a—slave	B' 7:23b—slaves
C 7:21b—you can become free	C' 7:23a—you were bought with a price
D 7:22a—called . . . Lord being a slave . . . Lord's freed	D' 7:22b—called . . . Christ's slave . . . free

Principles

1. A chiastic structure of a Pauline literary unit exists when there are words, phrases, or concepts found in the first half of the literary unit that are repeated in the second half of the unit in the exact reverse order from those found in the first half. In the table above the verses are in numerical order in the left hand column, but in the right hand column the verse numbers are in reverse numerical order, reflecting that the repetitions in second half are in reverse order from the first half. In 1 Cor 7:20–24 it can easily be seen that, with the exception of the C stich, exact words and/or phrases found in the first half have been repeated in reverse order in the second half of the structure. Clearly Paul intentionally created this effect for this section of 1 Cor 7.

2. The parallel word, phrase, or concept found in the second half of the literary unit may be the exact opposite of its counterpart found in the first half, e.g., "life" matching "death," "righteousness" matching "sinfulness," etc. In 1 Cor 7:20–24 above in the C stich "you can become free" has the opposite connotation of "you were bought with a price." However, ironically, being bought with a price is what sets one free, christologically speaking; therefore, the reader can be sure Paul intended that match.

3. The words in a repeated phrase may be in a different order in the second half from that found in the first half, e.g., "Heaven and Earth" is parallel to "Earth and Heaven." This is the situation in the D stich of 1 Cor 7:20–24 ("called" "slave" "freed" in the D hemistich versus "called" "free" "slave" in the D' hemistich).

4. When the exact same word or phrase is used in both the first half and the second half of a literary unit, the reader can easily discern that there is a chiastic match; however, as mentioned above, matching an abstract concept in the first half to another abstract concept found in the second half introduces a subjective element. Reasonable minds can differ on whether two abstract concepts are in fact parallel, and it may depend on the context and the mindset of the reader. As

discussed, there is a question in the C stich as to whether Paul intended to match "you can become free" with "you were bought with a price."

5. If there are several stiches containing words and/or phrases in the first half and these words or phrases are repeated in exact reverse order in the second half, and in the midst of such exact word or phrase repetitions, there appears to be a tenuous repetition of an abstract concept in the appropriate order, such tenuous concept repetition should be considered as an additional stich. Once again, this is the situation with the C stich. Since it falls between the repetitions of the identical words "slave" in the B stich and "called," "slave," and "free" in the D stich, it is probable that Paul intended the match shown above for the C stich.

6. Each stich in a chiastic structure is usually balanced. There should be roughly the same number of Greek words and/or syllables in each hemistich of a particular stich. Different stiches in the same chiastic structure may vary in number of Greek words. That is, the B stich may contain many more Greek words than the C stich. A long multisyllabic word balances several short words. In 1 Cor 7:20–24 the A hemistich of the A stich contains nine Greek words, and the A' hemistich contains ten. The B hemistich contains five Greek words, while the B' hemistich contains four. The C hemistich contains eight Greek words, but the C' hemistich only contains 2; however, one of the words in the C' hemistich has five syllables. The D hemistich contains nine Greek words, and the D' hemistich contains seven. There are literary units in the undisputed letters wherein several hemistiches in one half of the unit have many more words than the hemistiches in the other half of the unit, but no interpolation can be detected. These are rare.

7. First Thessalonians 2:19–20 is the only chiastic structure of the fifty-one found in the undisputed letters wherein the center stich contains only one hemistich. This is a special case because of the wording of the center hemistich about Jesus coming to Earth, a main theme of 1 Thessalonians. All other chiastic structures have a two-hemistich center stich. The center stich of a chiastic structure is typically the theme of the chiastic structure. The center D stich of the chiastic structure of 1 Cor 7:20–24 has two hemistiches, and it is the theme of the unit.

Parallel Structure

There are slightly more parallel literary structures in Paul's letters than there are chiastic structures. Lund observed that there are parallel structures in Paul's letters.[34] Paul constructed two different types of parallel structures. The most common contains repeated words, phrases, and concepts in an A, A'; B, B'; C, C'; etc., pattern. He also

---

34. Lund, *Chiasmus*, 141–225.

constructed several units with an A, B, C; A,' B,' C,'; etc., structure. Frequently there will be more than two elements in a single stich, such as A, A'; B, B'; C, C,' C,'' C'''.

Parallel structures are more easily discerned than chiastic structures because the matching words or phrases are closer to each other. As with chiastic structures, parallel structures are generally balanced. When there are more than two occurrences of a matching phrase in a stich, as in the below A stich, they will be referred to as "elements." The parallel hemistiches or elements should contain approximately the same number of Greek words. Galatians 1:1–17 is a typical Pauline parallel structure.

> A 1:1 Paul, an apostle not from men nor through man but through *Jesus Christ* and *God the father*, the one raising him from the dead,
> A' 1:2 and all the brothers that are with me to the churches of Galatia. 1:3 Grace to you and peace from *God our father* and the *Lord Jesus Christ*,
> A" 1:4 who gave *himself* for our sins so that he might deliver us out of this presently evil age according to the will of our *God and father*, 1:5 to whom be the glory for ever and ever. Amen.
>> B 1:6 I am astonished that you are so quickly deserting from the one who called you in the grace of *Christ* to a *different gospel*;
>> B' 1:7 which is not *another one*, only some who trouble you and would *pervert the gospel* of *Christ*.
>>> C 1:8 But even if we or an angel from Heaven, should *preach a gospel to you* other than the one which we preached to you *let him be accursed*.
>>> C' 1:9 As we have said before, so I now say again, if anyone *preaches to you any gospel* other than that which you received *let him be accursed*.
>>>> D 1:10 For am I now seeking the approval of *men* or of God? Or am I striving to please *men*? If I were pleasing *men*, I would not in any way be a servant of *Christ*.
>>>> D' 1:11 For I make known to you, *brothers*, regarding the gospel which was preached by me, that it is not according to *man*. 1:12 For neither did I receive it from *man* nor was I taught it, but through revelation of *Jesus Christ*.
>>>>> E 1:13 For you have heard of *my former way of life in Judaism*, that beyond measure *I persecuted* the church of God, and was *destroying* it.
>>>>> E' 1:14 And *I advanced in Judaism* beyond many of my contemporaries among my countrymen, being more *exceedingly zealous* for the traditions of my fathers.
>>>>>> F 1:15 And when it pleased God, who selected me from my mother's womb and *called me* through his grace,
>>>>>> F' 1:16 to reveal his son in me that *I might preach him* among the Gentiles, I did not immediately consult with flesh and blood.
>>>>>>> G 1:17a Nor did *I go up to Jerusalem* to them that were apostles before me.

G' 1:17b But *I went away into Arabia.*

G" 1:17c And again *I returned to Damascus.*

Gal 1:1-17 Parallel Structure Table

A 1:1—Jesus Christ . . . God the father	A' 1:2-3—Lord Jesus Christ . . . God our father		A" 1:4-5—himself . . . our God and father
B 1:6—Christ . . . different gospel	B' 1:7—Christ . . . another one . . . pervert the gospel		
C 1:8—preach a gospel to you . . . let him be accursed	C' 1:9—preaches to you any gospel . . . let him be accursed		
D 1:10—men . . . men . . . men . . . Christ	D' 1:11-12—man . . . man . . . brothers . . . Jesus Christ		
E 1:13—my former way of life in Judaism . . . I persecuted . . . destroying	E' 1:14—I advanced in Judaism . . . exceedingly zealous		
F 1:15—called me	F' 1:16—I might preach him		
G 1:17a—I go up to Jerusalem	G' 1:17b—I went away into Arabia		G" 1:17c—I returned to Damascus

In the A stich this analysis determines that there are three elements based on the repetition of "God" and "father" and a reference to Jesus. In the table for the B stich the repeated words found in the B hemistich are placed in the table cell in the order they are found in the text. However, for the B' hemistich the repeated words are placed in the table cell in the same order they are found in the B hemistich, so that both cells appear as much alike as possible for comparison. This procedure will be followed throughout this work. Presumably in the E stich Paul intended that "I persecuted" be parallel to "I advanced" in that both are actions that Paul took. It is also presumed that "destroying" is intended to be parallel to "exceedingly zealous" since one would need to be exceedingly zealous to destroy churches. In the F stich "called me" was determined to be parallel to "I might preach him" because preaching is the objective of the calling. Paul was called to preach. Paul's literary structures are quite often symmetrical. The initial A stich and the final G stich both contain three elements, while all the stiches in between contain two hemistiches.

First Corinthians 4:9-13 is an example of the other type of parallel structure found in Paul's letters. In addition, it contains an inclusio, which is an attribute that is found in twelve of Paul's parallel structures. An inclusio is present when the two hemistiches of the A stich introduce and conclude a parallel structure. An inclusio provides a definite division between structures. Paul made clear divisions between his literary units.

A 4:9 For I think God has proclaimed us apostles last as *men condemned to death*. For we have become *a spectacle to the world*, both to angels and to men.
  B 4:10a We are *fools* for Christ's sake, but you are *wise* in Christ.
    C 4:10b We are *weak*, but you are *strong*.
      D 4:10c You are *honored*, but we are *despised*.
  B' 4:11a Even to the present hour we both *hunger*, and *thirst*,
    C' 4:11b and are *naked*, and are *mistreated*,
      D' 4:11c and are *homeless*. 4:12a And we *grow weary working* these hands.
  B" 4:12b Being *reviled*, we *bless*.
    C" 4:12c Being *persecuted*, we *endure*.
      D" 4:13a Being *slandered*, we *encourage*.
A' 4:13b As *the scum of the Earth*, we have become the *refuse of all things* until now.

1 Cor 4:9–13 Parallel Structure Table

A 4:9—men condemned to death . . . a spectacle to the world		A' 4:13b—refuse of all things . . . the scum of the Earth	
B 4:10a—fools . . . wise	B' 4:11a—hunger . . . thirst	B" 4:12b—reviled . . . bless
C 4:10b—weak . . . strong	C' 4:11b—naked . . . mistreated	C" 4:12c—persecuted . . . endure
D 4:10c—honored . . . despised	D' 4:11c—homeless . . . grow weary working	D" 4:13a—slandered . . . encourage

In this structure each stich has three parallel elements except the A stich which is an inclusio that sets off and defines the structure. It was mentioned above that in a chiastic structure the center stich defines the unit. In parallel units with inclusios, the inclusio defines the unit. In this structure it is the construction of the phrases that are parallel and not the repetition of exact words as is typical in Paul's structures. The parallels are travails of the apostles Paul and Apollos. The first B, C, D group tells how Paul and Apollos are considered to have flawed characters. The second B, C, D group tells how they physically suffer. The third B, C, D group tells how they overcome abuse. Note that the versification is clumsy. If the versifier had appreciated Paul's parallel literary unit, verse 4:12 would begin with "Being reviled" and verse 4:13 would begin after "encourage." Robert Estienne, a French printer, is credited with the versification of the Bible in 1551 that was generally accepted.[35] To properly represent the author's intent, each new hemistich or element should be a separate verse. The problem is that reasonable minds can disagree on where to end one hemistich and begin another, although the process should not be random. Such a division should occur at the end of a sentence or clause, consistent with the balance principle.

---

35. Smith, "Chapters and Verses," 46–47.

Hybrid Chiastic/Parallel Structures

The hybrid chiastic/parallel structure has parallel aspects and chiastic aspects. Usually the chiastic portion matches the beginning and ending of the literary unit while the parallel portion is in the center of the unit. This is in keeping with Paul's love of symmetry and clearly delineating the beginning and ending of his literary units. An example of a hybrid structure is Rom 14:7-12.

> A 14:7 For no one lives to *himself*, and no one dies to *himself*.
> B 14:8a For if we live, *we live to the Lord*.
>   C 14:8b And if we die, *we die to the Lord*.
>   C' 14:8c Whether we live therefore or *die, we are the Lord's*.
>   D 14:9a For to this end Christ *died and lived*,
>   D' 14:9b that he might be Lord of both *the dead and the living*.
>   E 14:10a But you, why do you *judge* your brother?
>   E' 14:10b Or you also, why do you *condemn* your brother?
>   E" 14:10c For we will all stand before the *judgment seat* of God.
> B' 14:11 For it is written, "*As I live, says the Lord*, to me every knee shall bow, and every tongue will acknowledge God."
> A' 14:12 So then each of us will give account of *himself* to God.

Rom 14:7-12 Hybrid Structure Table

A 14:7—himself . . . himself		A' 14:12—himself	
B 14:8a—we live to the Lord		B' 14:11—as I live says the Lord	
C 14:8b—we die to the Lord		C' 14:8c—die we are the Lord's	
D 14:9a—died and lived		D' 14:9b—the dead and the living	
E 14:10a—judge	E' 14:10b—condemn		E" 14:10c—judgment seat

The A and B stiches are chiastic with "himself" matching "himself" in the A stich and "we live to the Lord" matching "I live says the Lord" in the B stich. This could be regarded as a two-element inclusio. However, the C, D, and E stiches are parallel, with three elements in the E stich. There can be no doubt that this was an intentional structure created by the author. The reverse of this structure is found in Gal 3:1-17 where there is a parallel structure of five verses followed by a chiastic structure containing eleven verses and concludes with a parallel structure of two verses.

Dual Chiastic/Parallel Structures

There are thirteen literary units in the undisputed letters where Paul designed them both with a chiastic structure and a parallel structure, an amazing feat of literary construction.[36] Such structures have been designated "dual chiastic/parallel structures." In every case the entwined structures begin and end with the same verses. In two cases the parallel structure has an inclusio where the A stich of the parallel structure is identical to the A stich of the chiastic structure. Often the center stich of the chiastic structure is also one of the parallel stiches in the parallel structure. In the majority of cases these dual chiastic/parallel structures are fairly long and encompass an entire chapter. An example of this extraordinary type of structure is 2 Cor 11:1–19.

2 Cor 11:1–19 Chiastic Structure

A 11:1 I wish that *you were bearing with me* in a little *foolishness*. But indeed you do *bear with me*.
  B 11:2 For I am jealous as to you with a godly jealousy. For *I have given you in marriage* to one husband, a pure virgin to present to *Christ*.
    C 11:3 But I fear, lest by any means as the *serpent deceived Eve in his craftiness your minds might be corrupted* from the simplicity and the purity in Christ.
      D 11:4 For if *he who is coming proclaims another Jesus* whom we did not proclaim, or you receive a different spirit, which you did not receive, or a different gospel, which you did not accept, you are bearing it well.
        E 11:5 For I conclude that *I am inferior in nothing* to the *most chief apostles*.
          F 11:6 But though I am unpolished in speech, yet *I am not in knowledge*. But in every way we have revealed this to you in all things.
            G 11:7 Or did I commit a sin in humbling myself so that you might be exalted, because *I gratuitously proclaimed to you the gospel of God*?
              H 11:8 *I robbed other churches*, having received support for the ministry to you. 11:9a And when I was present with you and was in need, *I did not burden anyone*.
              H' 11:9b For *the brothers coming from Macedonia, fully supplied my need*. And in everything *I kept from being a burden to you*, and so will I keep.
            G' 11:10 The *truth of Christ is in me* so that this boasting of mine will not be obstructed in the regions of Achaia.
          F' 11:11 Why? Because I do not love you? God knows I do. 11:12a But what I do that I will do so that *I might cut off the opportunity*

---

36. A similar construction is found in The Gospel of Mark, although not in the construction of a single pericope. The Prologue, Mark 1:2–14, forms a parallel structure with the Epilogue, Mark 15:39–16:8. These two sections of Mark also form a chiastic structure. See Smith, *Unlocking*, 28–73.

E' 11:12b from *those who desire an opportunity*. That in what they are boasting they might be found *as we are*.

D' 11:13 For such as *these are false apostles*, deceitful workers, *disguising themselves as apostles of Christ*.

C' 11:14 And no wonder; for even *Satan disguises himself* as an *angel of light*. 11:15 It is no great thing therefore if his *ministers also disguise themselves* as ministers of righteousness, whose end shall be according to their works.

B' 11:16 I say again no one should think I am a fool. But if so, *receive me* as a fool that I also may boast a little. 11:17a What I am saying, I am not saying according to the *Lord*,

A' 11:17b but in *foolishness*, in this confidence of boasting. 11:18 Since many boast according to the flesh, I will boast also. 11:19 For being wise *you bear fools gladly*.

2 Cor 11:1-19 Chiastic Structure Table

A 11:1—were bearing with me . . . foolishness . . . bear with me	A' 11:17b-19—you bear fools . . . foolishness
B 11:2—I have given you in marriage . . . Christ	B' 11:16-17a—receive me . . . Lord
C 11:3—Serpent deceived Eve in his craftiness . . . your minds might be corrupted . . . Christ	C' 11:14-15—Satan disguises himself . . . ministers also disguise themselves . . . angel of light
D 11:4—he who is coming . . . proclaims another Jesus	D' 11:13—these are false apostles . . . disguising themselves as apostles of Christ
E 11:5—I am inferior in nothing . . . most chief apostles	E' 11:12b—as we are . . . those who seek an opportunity
F 11:6—I am not in knowledge	F' 11:11-12a—I might cut off the opportunity
G 11:7—I gratuitously proclaimed to you the gospel of God	G' 11:10—the truth of Christ is in me
H 11:8-9a—I robbed other churches . . . I did not burden anyone	H' 11:9b—the brothers coming from Macedonia fully supplied my need . . . I kept from being a burden to you

Both the A and A' hemistiches contain "foolishness." The A hemistich contains "bearing with me" and "bear with me" while the A' hemistich contains "you bear fools." The B stich matches "I have given you in marriage" with "receive me," a match of opposites—giving you and receiving me. The B stich also matches "Christ" with "Lord." The C stich matches "serpent deceived Eve in his craftiness" with "Satan disguises himself," "Christ" with "angel of light," and "your minds might be corrupted" with "ministers also disguise themselves." The D stich matches "he who is coming" in the D hemistich with "false apostles" in the D' hemistich emphasizing the D hemistich text, "proclaims another Jesus." The second D stich match is between "proclaims another Jesus" and "disguising themselves as apostles of Christ." Obviously in Paul's mind if an apostle is proclaiming a Jesus with different attributes from Paul's Jesus, then such apostle is disguising himself as an apostle of Christ, but is not an apostle of Paul's Christ. In the E stich the match is between "I am inferior in nothing" in the first half with "as we are" in the second half since "as we are" means that Paul's opponents are boasting they are equal to Paul in stature. The second match of the E stich is between "most chief apostles" and "those seeking an opportunity." Paul is warning that the chief apostles of his opponents are coming to Corinth seeking an opportunity to reconvert Paul's proselytes in Corinth into a different Christianity. The F hemistich has "I am not in knowledge" matching "I might cut off the opportunity" in the F' hemistich with Paul in both cases bragging about his abilities and in the F' hemistich making a word play about circumcision. The G hemistich has "I gratuitously proclaimed to you the gospel of God" which matches "the truth of Christ is in me" found in the G' hemistich. The center H stich matches "I robbed other churches" and "the brothers coming from Macedonia fully supplied my need," both claiming that the Corinthians did not pay him anything. The H stich has a second parallelism with "I did not burden anyone" being parallel to "I kept from being a burden to you."

2 Cor 11:1–19 Parallel Structure

Below is the same literary unit showing the parallel structure with which Paul overlaid the chiastic structure. This structure contains parallelisms using some of the same phrases that define the chiastic structure and using others that are not included in the chiastic matches. In the parallel structure the C and H stiches each have three elements. The C stich is the third from the beginning and the H stich is the third from the end. This is another example of Paul's parallel structures having symmetry.

  A 11:1a I wish that you were *bearing with me* in a little foolishness.
  A' 11:1b But indeed you do *bear with me*.
    B 11:2 For I am jealous as to you with a godly jealousy. For I have given you in marriage to one husband, a *pure virgin to present to Christ*.
    B' 11:3 But I fear, lest by any means as the serpent deceived Eve in his craftiness, your minds might be corrupted from the *simplicity and the purity in Christ*.
      C 11:4a For if he who is coming *proclaims another Jesus, whom we did not proclaim*,
      C' 11:4b or you *receive a different spirit, which you did not receive*,
      C" 11:4c or a *different gospel, which you did not accept*, you are bearing it well.
        D 11:5 For I conclude that *I am inferior in nothing* to the most chief apostles.

D' 11:6 But though I am unpolished in speech, yet *I am not in knowledge*. But in every way we have revealed this to you in all things.

　E 11:7 Or *did I commit a sin in humbling myself* so that you might be exalted because I gratuitously proclaimed to you the gospel of God?

　E' 11:8 *I robbed other churches*, having received support for the ministry to you. 11:9a And when I was present with you and was in need I did not burden anyone.

　　F 11:9b For the brothers *coming from Macedonia* fully supplied my need; and in everything I kept from being a burden to you, and so will I keep.

　　F' 11:10 The truth of Christ is in me, so that this boasting of mine will not be obstructed *in the regions of Achaia*.

　　　G' 11:11 Why? Because I do not love you? God knows I do. 11:12a But what I do, that I will do so that *I might cut off the opportunity*

　　　G' 11:12b from *those who desire an opportunity*. That in what they are boasting they might be found as we are.

　　　　H 11:13 For such as these are *false apostles*, deceitful workers, disguising themselves as *apostles of Christ*.

　　　　H' 11:14 And no wonder; for even *Satan* disguises himself as an *angel of light*.

　　　　H" 11:15 It is no great thing therefore if his *ministers* also disguise themselves as *ministers of righteousness*, whose end shall be according to their works.

　　　　　I 11:16a *I say again*, no one should think *I am a fool*.

　　　　　I' 11:16b But if so, *receive me as a fool* that I also may boast a little. 11:17a What *I am saying*, I am not saying according to the Lord,

　　　　　　J 11:17b but in foolishness, in this *confidence of boasting*.

　　　　　　J' 11:18 Since many *boast according to the flesh*, I will boast also. 11:19 For being wise you bear fools gladly.

2 Cor 11:1-19 *Parallel Structure Table*

A 11:1a—bearing with me		A' 11:1b—bear with me	
B 11:2—pure virgin to present to Christ		B' 11:3—simplicity and the purity in Christ	
C 11:4a—proclaims another Jesus whom we did not proclaim	C' 11:4b—receive a different spirit which you did not receive		C" 11:4c—different gospel which you did not accept
D 11:5—I am inferior in nothing		D' 11:6—I am not in knowledge	
E 11:7—I commit a sin in humbling myself . . . you might be exalted		E' 11:8-9a—I robbed other churches . . . I did not burden anyone	
F 11:9b—coming from Macedonia		F' 11:10—in the regions of Achaia	

G 11:11–12a—I might cut off the opportunity		G' 11:12b—those who desire an opportunity	
H 11:13—false apostle . . . apostles of Christ	H' 11:14—Satan . . . angel of light	H" 11:15—ministers . . . ministers of righteousness	
I 11:16a—I say again . . . I am a fool		I' 11:16b–17a—I am saying . . . receive me as a fool	
J 11:17b—confidence of boasting		J' 11:18–19—boast according to the flesh	

In the A stich "bearing with me" matches "bear with me." In the B stich both halves mention "purity" and "Christ." The C stich contains three elements with a parallel construction about "another Jesus," "a different spirit," and a "different gospel." Both halves of the D stich have Paul bragging about himself. "Commit a sin" in the E hemistich matches "robbed other churches" in the E' hemistich, when Paul's meaning is that he did not sin against the Corinthians by relying on other churches to support him. Then the second match of the E stich is "you might be exalted" with "I did not burden anyone." "Burden" has the opposite connotation from "exalted." Both halves of the F stich mention the name of a Greek region, "Macedonia" and "Achaia." The G stich has Paul's word play about circumcision and the opportunists Paul opposes. All three elements of the H stich have two matching phrases "false apostle" matching "Satan" and "ministers." Then "apostle of Christ" matches "angel of light" and "ministers of righteousness." Both matching phrases in the two halves of the I stich mention "say" and "fool." Finally, both halves of the J stich mention "boasting."

It is no small feat for Paul to have constructed a literary unit having both a chiastic structure and a parallel structure. Rhetorical analysis identifies thirteen of these dual chiastic/parallel structures. This shows the sophistication of Paul's literary education. The device of using parallel constructions to establish one's premise rhetorically must have been constantly practiced in Paul's education so that it came naturally and effortlessly to him as he expounded his arguments.

2

Using Literary Structures To Detect Interpolation

Recognizing Interpolations

In analyzing Paul's undisputed letters rhetorical analysis shows that every chapter of those seven letters, except 1 Cor 8, contains at least one literary unit defined by repetition and other parallelisms, and that every literary unit has either a chiastic, parallel, both, or hybrid structure. The sixty authentic chapters in Paul's undisputed letters contain ninety-eight separate identifiable literary units. This analysis reveals that twenty-two of those structures have been disrupted with excessive verbiage in one or more passages destroying the normal balance of Paul's structures. The following pages will analyze each of the letters attributed to Paul. Part I will analyze the undisputed letters demonstrating the literary structures as composed by Paul. Part I will also analyze the interpolations revealed by the literary structure analysis, comparing this rhetorical analysis of interpolations with the analyses of Pauline scholars who have opined on putative interpolations into these seven letters. Part II will analyze the Deutero-Pauline letters using the rhetorical structure analysis method, attempting to confirm or deny whether any part of these letters were written by Paul.

Rhetorical analysis assumes that an interpolator either did not realize that he was disrupting a carefully constructed literary structure or that he did not care. If an interpolator knew that a particular part of Paul's text was a literary structure and added more text in keeping with the structure, this method would not be able to detect it. There is good reason for assuming that interpolators ignored Paul's chiastic structures. Chiastic structures are a trait of Semitic literature, found only occasionally in Greek and Latin literature.[1] Welch states that later Greek and Latin writers typically only used chiasmus as a technique within a sentence and not as a structural device as Semitic writers did.[2] This suggests that Paul was educated in a Hebrew milieu and that

---

1. Welch, "Chiasmus in Greek," 258.
2. Welch, "Chiasmus in Greek," 258.

Using Literary Structures To Detect Interpolation

chiastic structure and parallelism were second nature to him.[3] Therefore, it would be unlikely that later Greek or Roman Christians desiring to interpolate a passage into one of Paul's letters would be attuned to detecting the chiastic structure of an entire literary unit. In other words, they would not be looking for it. For some two thousand years New Testament scholars have failed to note the full extent of chiastic and parallel structures in Paul's letters because they, too, were not looking for them, and they were concentrating on the message of the letters. In addition, an interpolator would probably be more intent on expressing his ideas than in attempting to imitate Paul's style. This is the same assumption that is made by scholars when pointing out that a particular passage they believe has been interpolated contains words or grammatical constructions not usually found in Paul's letters. Scholars pointing out that a particular section does not use Pauline vocabulary and/or sentence structure are assuming that an interpolator would write a passage in his own style and was not attempting to copy Paul's style.

There are passages in the Pauline corpus that are identified herein as interpolations where the assumed interpolator apparently did make an attempt to copy Paul's style by including a number of parallel phrases. However, the interpolator did not thoroughly understand Paul's style and failed to arrange these parallel phrases in a Pauline manner. This is particularly obvious in 1 Cor 8. It also occurs in the Deutero-Pauline letters, especially Colossians and Ephesians.

A long interpolation becomes rather obvious once the surrounding literary structure with its matching repetitions and other parallelisms have been identified. Naturally, the shorter the interpolation, the more difficult it is to detect. The premise of the rhetorical analysis technique is that an interpolation destroys the balance of the parallel hemistiches or elements. In other words, the interpolated passage results in there being too much text in one of the hemistiches or elements containing no matching words, phrases, or concepts. In addition, the interpolated passage usually disrupts the train of thought of the surrounding literary unit. Once a suspected interpolation has been identified, the investigator should determine if the remaining text makes sense when the offending text is removed.

As a demonstration of how this works, the rhetorical analysis technique will be compared with the opinion of a Pauline scholar regarding an interpolation. In his book *Interpolations in the Pauline Letters*, William O. Walker Jr., has identified 1 Cor 11:3–16 as an interpolation.[4] Does the rhetorical analysis technique of detecting interpolation confirm Professor Walker's determination in this case? Interestingly, 1 Cor 11 is one of the thirteen literary units with a dual chiastic/parallel structure. In this instance the structure encompasses the entire chapter. The chiastic structure also has a paralleled center at vv. 11:23–25 as Paul relates to the Corinthians the actions of Jesus at the Last Supper as revealed to him. In this center stich the action surrounding

---

3. Thompson, *Chiasmus*, 20.
4. Walker, *Interpolations*, 91–126.

first the bread and then the cup are related in parallel form, and both structures are identical in this stich.

Below 1 Cor 11:3–16 is set off and is in parentheses because it does not seem to be part of the original chiastic structure of the chapter. Setting off in parentheses proposed interpolations will be used throughout this work.

Chiastic Structure of 1 Cor 11:1–34 Exposing an Interpolation

A 11:1 Be imitators of me even as I also am of Christ. 11:2a Now *I commend you* that you remember me in all things.

B 11:2b And hold fast the teachings as I delivered them to you.

(11:3 But I would have you know that the head of every man is Christ; and the head of the woman is the man; and the head of Christ is God. 11:4 Every man praying or prophesying having his head covered dishonors his head. 11:5 But every woman praying or prophesying with her head unveiled dishonors her head. For it is one and the same thing as if she were shaven. 11:6 For if a woman is not veiled, let her also be shorn. But if it is a shame to a woman to be shorn or shaven, let her be veiled. 11:7 For a man indeed ought not to have his head veiled, forasmuch as he is the image and glory of God. But the woman is the glory of the man. 11:8 For the man is not of the woman, but the woman of the man. 11:9 For neither was the man created for the woman, but the woman for the man. 11:10 For this cause ought the woman to have authority on her head because of the angels. 11:11 Nevertheless, neither is the woman without the man, nor the man without the woman, in the Lord. 11:12 For as the woman is of the man, so is the man also by the woman; but all things are of God. 11:13 Judge in yourselves. Is it seemly that a woman pray to God unveiled? 11:14 Does not even nature itself teach you that if a man has long hair, it is a dishonor to him? 11:15 But if a woman has long hair, it is a glory to her. For her hair is given her for a covering. 11:16 But if any man seems to be contentious, we have no such custom, neither the churches of God.)

B 11:17 But in giving you this commandment, I do not commend you. Because *you come together* not for the better but for the worse. 11:18 For first of all, when *you come together in the church* I hear that divisions exist among you, and I partly believe it.

C 11:19 For there must also be factions among you so that *those who are approved* should become evident among you.

D 11:20 Therefore, when you assemble together, it is not to *eat the Lord's supper*. 11:21 For in your eating each *one takes first his own supper*. And *this one is hungry*, and *that one is drunk*.

E 11:22a For do you not have houses in which *to eat and to drink*? Or do you despise the church of God, and you are shaming those that have nothing?

  F 11:22b What shall I say to you? Should I commend you? *In this I do not commend you.*

    G 11:23a For I received from the Lord that which also I delivered to you. That the Lord Jesus in the night in which *he was delivered up*

      HA 11:23b took *bread*, 11:24a and when he had given thanks, he broke it,

        HB 11:24b and said, "*This is my body*, which is for you.

          HC 11:24c *Do this in remembrance of me.*"

      H'A' 11:25a Likewise after supper also the *cup*,

        H'B' 11:25b *saying, "This cup is the new covenant in my blood.* As often as you drink it,

          H'C' 11:25c *do this in remembrance of me.*"

    G' 11:26 For as often as you eat this bread and drink the cup you proclaim *the Lord's death* until he should come.

  F' 11:27 Therefore whoever will eat the bread or drink the cup of the Lord in an unworthy manner will be *guilty of the body and the blood of the Lord*.

E' 11:28 But let a man prove himself, and so let him *eat of the bread, and drink of the cup*.

D' 11:29 For he that *eats and drinks, eats and drinks judgment* to himself, if he does not discern the body. 11:30 For this cause many among *you are weak and sickly*, and many *sleep*. 11:31 But if we were judging ourselves, we would not be condemned.

C' 11:32 But being judged by the Lord, we are trained so that we *may not be condemned* with the world.

B' 11:33 Therefore, my brothers, *when you come together to eat* wait one for another. 11:34a If any man is hungry, let him eat at home. So that *your coming together* not be for judgment.

A' 11:34b And the rest *I will set in order* whenever I come.

1 Cor 11:1–34 Chiastic Structure Table

A 11:1–2a—I commend you	A' 11:34b—I will set in order
B 11:17—you come together . . . you come together in the church	B' 11:34a—your coming together . . . you come together to eat
C 11:19—those who are approved	C' 11:32—we may not be condemned

D 11:20–21—eat the Lord's Supper … one takes first his own supper … this one is hungry … that one is drunk	D' 11:29–31—eats and drinks … eats and drinks judgment … you are weak … sickly
E 11:22a—to eat and to drink	E' 11:28—eat of the bread and drink of the cup
F 11:22b—in this I do not commend you	F' 11:27—guilty of the body and the blood of the Lord
G 11:23a—he was delivered up	G' 11:26—the Lord's death
HA 11:23b–24a—bread	H'A' 11:25a—cup
HB 11:24b—said this is my body	H'B' 11:25b—saying this cup is the new covenant in my blood
HC 11:24c—do this in remembrance of me	H'C' 11:25c—do this in remembrance of me

Interpolation 1 Cor 11:3–16

The interpolation interrupts the B hemistich coming between v. 11:2b and v. 11:17. As set out here the B hemistich including the interpolation contains one hundred thirty-five words while the B' hemistich contains only eleven words. By removing vv. 11:3–16 the B hemistich is reduced to twenty-two words, a more balanced stich. The B hemistich match for "your coming together" found in the B' hemistich at v. 11:34a is not near the beginning of the chapter as one would expect in a well-written chiastic structure. It is not found until the reader reaches v. 11:17 with "your coming together." Including the entirely of vv. 11:3–16 in the B hemistich would destroy the literary balance of the structure. As set out above there are thirteen Greek words in the A hemistich and seven Greek words in the A' hemistich. Therefore, vv. 11:3–16 cannot be moved into A hemistich to achieve the desirable balance. The structure simply cannot support the long text of vv. 11:3–16 as being part of the unit.

Clearly the text of vv. 11:3–16 disrupts the chiastic structure of 1 Cor 11 as originally designed by the author. As stated in the principles, a chiastic structure should be balanced. There should be roughly the same number of Greek words and syllables in the A and A' hemistiches and roughly the same number of Greek words and syllables in the B and B' hemistiches. The balance principle is achieved if vv. 11:3–16 is deleted from the text. Professor Walker's assessment is confirmed—1 Cor 11:3–16 is an interpolation.

In addition, vv. 11:3–16 interrupts Paul's train of thought. At v. 11:2 Paul says he commends the Corinthians, and then he does not say he does not commend them until v. 11:17. This would have more argumentative effect if it followed more quickly. Further, at v. 11:17 Paul says he gave the Corinthians a single commandment, but the entire sequence of vv. 11:2–17 contains six commandments: 1 hold fast Paul's teachings, 2 men should not cover their heads while praying, 3 women should cover their heads when praying, 4 if a woman is not veiled, her hair should be shorn, 5 men have authority over women, 6 men should not have long hair. Therefore, it is likely that the only commandment Paul was referring to at v. 11:17 is the one in v. 11:2 to hold fast his teachings. The others were added by an interpolator.

Interpolation 1 Cor 11:3-16 Table

Stiches	Words in first half	Words in second half	Interpolation words
B	11:2b–16–135	11:34a – 11	11:3–16–113

Parallel Structure of 1 Cor 11:1-34 Exposing the Interpolation

The parallel structure of 1 Cor 11:1-34 also reveals the interpolation, although there are parallels in the interpolation itself. The interpolator was evidently cognizant of Paul's use of repetition, but failed to notice he was separating Paul's first parallel with a one hundred and thirteen-word passage.

A 11:1 Be imitators of me, even as I also am of Christ. 11:2a Now *I commend you that you remember me in all things.*
A' 11:2b And hold fast the teachings, as I delivered them to you.

(11:3 But I would have you know that the head of every man is Christ; and the head of the woman is the man; and the head of Christ is God. 11:4 Every man praying or prophesying, having his head covered, dishonors his head. 11:5 But every woman praying or prophesying with her head unveiled dishonors her head. For it is one and the same thing as if she were shaven. 11:6 For if a woman is not veiled, let her also be shorn. But if it is a shame to a woman to be shorn or shaven, let her be veiled. 11:7 For a man indeed ought not to have his head veiled, forasmuch as he is the image and glory of God, but the woman is the glory of the man. 11:8 For the man is not of the woman, but the woman of the man. 11:9 For neither was the man created for the woman, but the woman for the man. 11:10 For this cause ought the woman to have authority on her head because of the angels. 11:11 Nevertheless, neither is the woman without the man, nor the man without the woman, in the Lord. 11:12 For as the woman is of the man, so is the man also by the woman, but all things are of God. 11:13 Judge in yourselves. Is it seemly that a woman pray to God unveiled? 11:14 Does not even nature itself teach you, that, if a man has long hair, it is a dishonor to him? 11:15 But if a woman has long hair, it is a glory to her. For her hair is given her for a covering. 11:16 But if any man seems to be contentious, we have no such custom, neither the churches of God.)

11:17a But in giving you this commandment, *I do not commend you.*
  B 11:17b Because *you come together* not for the better but for the worse.
  B' 11:18a For first of all, when *you come together* in the church,
    C 11:18b I hear that *divisions exist among you,* and I partly believe it.
    C' 11:19 For *there must also be factions among you,* so that those who are approved should become evident among you.
      D 11:20 Therefore when you assemble together, *it is not to eat* the lord's supper.
      D' 11:21a For *in your eating* each one takes first his own supper.
        E 11:21b And *this one is hungry, and that one is drunk.*
        E' 11:22a For do you not have houses in which *to eat and to drink*? Or do you despise the church of God, and you are shaming those that have nothing?
          F 11:22b What shall I say to you? *Should I commend you?*
          F' 11:22c In this *I do not commend you.*
            G 11:23a For I received from the Lord that which also *I delivered to you*
            G' 11:23b That the Lord Jesus in the night in which *he was delivered up*
              HA 11:23c took *bread,* 11:24a and when he had given thanks, he broke it,
                HB 11:24b and *said, "This is my body,* which is for you.
                HC 11:24c *Do this in remembrance of me."*
              H'A' 11:25a Likewise after supper also the *cup,*
                H'B' 11:25b *saying, "This cup is the new covenant in my blood.* As often as you drink it,
                  H'C' 11:25c *do this in remembrance of me."*
            I 11:26 For as often as *you eat this bread, and drink the cup,* you proclaim the Lord's death until he should come.
            I' 11:27 Therefore whoever shall *eat the bread or drink the cup* of the lord in an unworthy manner, shall be guilty of the body and the blood of the lord.
            I" 11:28 But let a man prove himself, and so let him *eat of the bread, and drink of the cup.*
              J 11:29 For he that eats and drinks, eats and drinks *judgment to himself,* if he does not discern the body.
              J' 11:30 For this cause many among you are weak and sickly, and many sleep. 11:31 But if we were *judging ourselves,* we would not be condemned.
              J" 11:32 But being *judged by the Lord,* we are trained, so that we may not be condemned with the world.
                K 11:33 Therefore, my brothers, *when you come together* to eat, wait one for another.

K' 11:34 If any man is hungry, let him eat at home. So that *your coming together* not be for judgment. And the rest I will set in order whenever I come.

1 Cor 11:1–34 Parallel Structure Table

A 11:1–2a—I commend you	A' 11:2b–17a—I do not commend you
B 11:17b—you come together	B' 11:18a—you come together
C 11:18b—divisions exist among you	C' 11:19—there must also be factions among you
D 11:20—it is not to eat	D' 11:21a—in your eating
E 11:21b—this one is hungry and that one is drunk	E' 11:22a—to eat and to drink
F 11:22b—shall I commend you	F' 11:22b—I do not commend you
G 11:23a—I delivered to you	G' 11:23b—he was delivered up
HA 11:23c–24a—bread	H'A' 11:25a—cup
HB 11:24b—said this is my body	H'B' 11:25b—saying this cup is the new covenant in my blood
HC 11:24c—do this in remembrance of me	H'C' 11:25c—do this in remembrance of me
I 11:26—eat this bread and drink the cup	I' 11:27—eat the bread or drink the cup	I" 11:28—eat of the bread and drink of the cup
J 11:29—judgment to himself	J' 11:30–31—judging ourselves	J" 11:32—judged by the Lord
K 11:33—when you come together	K' 11:34—your coming together	

Interpolation 1 Cor 11:3–16

The parallel structure of 1 Cor 11:1–34 also reveals the interpolation even though vv. 11:3–16 contain numerous parallels. The interpolator stuck his extra text in between "I commend you" in v. 11:2 and "I do not commend you" in v.11:17. If he had inserted it after v. 11:17a, the parallel structure would not have revealed it, but the chiastic structure would still have exposed the interpolation.

Interpolation 1 Cor 3-16 Table

Stich	Words in first half	Words in second half	Interpolation words
A	11:1–2a—12	11:2b–17a—135	113

Literary Structure Determining Lack of Interpolation

On the other hand, an interpolation proposed by Walker that is not confirmed by rhetorical analysis is 1 Cor 2:6–16.[5] Rhetorical analysis determines that 1 Cor 2:1–16 has a typical Pauline chiastic structure. If vv. 2:6–16 have been interpolated as Walker has suggested, the interpolator was extremely clever and knowledgeable about Paul's propensity for chiastic structures. The following is the chiastic structure of 1 Cor 2:1–16 as determined by rhetorical analysis:

A 2:1 And I, having come to you, brothers, did not come with excellent speech or wisdom, *proclaiming to you the testimony of God.* 2:2 For I determined not to know anything among you, save Jesus Christ, and him crucified.

  B 2:3 And I was with you in weakness, and in fear, and in much trembling. 2:4 And my speech and my preaching were not in persuasive words of wisdom, but in *demonstration of the spirit* and of power.

    C 2:5 So that your faith should not stand in the *wisdom of men,* but in the *power of God.*

      D 2:6a But *we speak wisdom* among those who are mature.

        E 2:6b yet a *wisdom not of this age,* nor of the rulers of this age, who are coming to naught.

          F 2:7a But we speak *God's wisdom in a mystery,* that has been hidden,

            G 2:7b *which God foreordained* before the ages for our glory.

              H 2:8 which *none of the rulers of this age has understood.* For had they understood it, they would not have crucified the Lord of glory.

              H' 2:9 But as it is written, *"That which eye has not seen, and ear has not heard, and has not entered into the heart of man,* God has prepared for those who love him."

            G' 2:10 For to us *God has revealed through the spirit.* For the spirit searches all things, even the depths of God.

          F' 2:11 For who among men knows the things of a man, if not the spirit of the man which is in him? So also *the things of God no one knows,* except the spirit of God.

        E' 2:12 But we received, *not the spirit of the world,* but the spirit that is from God, that we may know the things that were granted to us by God.

      D' 2:13 *Which we also speak,* not in words that man's *wisdom* teaches, but those that the spirit teaches, revealing spiritual things with spiritual words.

    C' 2:14a Now the *natural man* does not accept the things of the *spirit of God,* for they are foolishness to him.

  B' 2:14b And he cannot know them, because *they are spiritually discerned.* 2:15 But he that is spiritual judges all things, and he himself is judged by no one.

---

5. Walker, *Interpolations,* 127–146.

A' 2:16 For who has known the mind of the Lord? *Who will instruct him?* But we have the mind of Christ.

1 Cor 2:1–16 Chiastic Structure Table

A 2:1-2—proclaiming to you the testimony of God	A' 2:16—who will instruct him
B 2:3-4—demonstration of the spirit	B' 2:14b-15—they are spiritually discerned
C 2:5—wisdom of men … power of God	C' 2:14a—natural man … spirit of God
D 2:6a—we speak wisdom	D' 2:13—which we also speak … wisdom
E 2:6b—wisdom not of this age	E' 2:12—not the spirit of the world
F 2:7a—God's wisdom in a mystery	F' 2:11—the things of God no one knows
G 2:7b—which God foreordained	G' 2:10—God has revealed through the spirit
H 2:8—none of the rulers of this age has understood	H' 2:9—that which eye has not seen and ear has not heard and has not entered the heart of man

Interpolation in 1 Cor 2:1–16

If Walker is correct, the interpolator wrote his addition to Paul's letter, vv. 6–16, writing "who will instruct him" at v. 2:16 which makes a reasonably good match with Paul's words at v. 2:1–2, "proclaiming to you the testimony of God," to complete the A stich, with the concepts of instructing God and proclaiming the testimony of God being similar. In doing so Walker's purported interpolator quoted Isa 40:13, 14 in the typical Pauline manner without attribution. In addition, his interpolator created a B' hemistich writing "they are spiritually discerned" at vv. 2:14b–15 to match "demonstration of the spirit" that Paul wrote at v. 2:4. Then Walker's interpolator wrote "natural man" and "spirit of God" at v. 2:14a to match Paul's "wisdom of men and "power of God" at v. 2:5 creating a C stich. The assumed interpolator continued in an imitation of Paul creating the D – G stiches, a longer than average chiastic structure.

Walker notes eight linguistic anomalies in 1 Cor 2:2–16 that are not found in other Pauline letters.[6] It would seem more likely that Paul would use vocabulary not common to other undisputed letters than an interpolator having the presence of mind to faithfully copy Paul's style of chiastic structure. In addition, if the interpolator was astute enough to create a chiastic structure in the Pauline style where there was no chiastic structure, it does not seem reasonable to assume he would unthinkingly use vocabulary that was not Pauline. Such a scenario seems unlikely.

---

6. Walker, *Interpolations*, 138.

The Pauline Letters

Presentation

The following chapters will set out each literary structure separately. The matching words, phrases, abstract concepts, and other parallelisms will be identified, and a structure table noting the parallel/matching language follows immediately after the literary unit. As noted above the table will show the matching phrases in the order the phrases are found in the first hemistich or first element of a particular stich. A commentary section will discuss the matching language, and if there is an interpolation, an interpolation section will discuss the reasoning behind identification of the interpolation. The detection of an interpolation will be compared with that of scholars who have proposed that there have been interpolations into Paul's letters, especially those of William O. Walker Jr. and J.C. O'Neill.[7] An explanation of agreement or disagreement with their conclusions will be included.

There are several verses in the Pauline corpus that appear to be out of order. These are exposed by rhetorical analysis, with a chiastic hemistich being out of order. The investigator who charts one of Paul's literary units can immediately discern that a particular verse is out of the originally intended order. These are marked with asterisks and comment is made about them in the commentary section.

Unfortunately, some of the discussion in the commentaries defining various stiches becomes quite tedious, especially when the obvious is pointed out, for example, that "Christ Jesus" in the B hemistich matches "Christ Jesus" in the B' hemistich. However, this is needed for completeness. Some of the tedium can be alleviated if the reader will refer back to the structure table as he is reading the commentary. In discussions concerning this technique with others who are interested in Biblical exegesis, it has been noted that some can readily recognize matching language and appreciate the structure proposed while others are resistant to the concept, and express deep misgivings about whether there is, in fact, matching or parallel language, and/or whether there is any pattern to the parallel language. They seem to look at each parallelism as if it were a coincidence and do not appreciate that ten, or twenty, or a thousand coincidences describe a pattern. In addition, if the obvious matches were not expressly pointed out, the reader might have a tendency to focus on the less obvious proposed matches and disagree with them, ignoring the vast majority of matches that are obvious repetitions and other parallelisms. The fact that there are obvious matches in the same literary unit makes the less obvious matches more likely. Rhetorical analysis identifies thirty-five interpolations into the ninety-eight literary structures of Paul's undisputed letters. Therefore, most structures do not contain an interpolation detected by rhetorical analysis and are rather mundane from an interpolation standpoint. These mundane literary structures add to the evidence that Paul organized all his writings in literary structures defined by parallelisms. Some of them are interesting in themselves, demonstrating how Paul constructed his arguments. In addition, obvious

---

7. Walker, *Interpolations*; O'Neill, *Romans*; O'Neill, *Galatians*.

matches tend to disprove the opinions of scholars who have proposed a particular interpolation but have failed to take account of the obvious matches forming a literary structure.

Paul's letters as presented herein are the translation of the author of this work. In the vast majority of cases the parallelism in Greek is also present in English. Occasionally Bible translators have translated a word or phrase that destroys the parallelism existing in Greek. They also have occasionally created parallelisms in English that did not exist in Greek. An attempt has been made to avoid these pitfalls. There are some words where the normal translation into English destroys the parallelism that is obvious in Greek. For example, "righteousness" and "justification" in Greek have the same root (*dikaiosunē*) as do "gift" and "grace" (*charis*). The Greek will be noted where the parallelism is not clear in English or the Greek needs to be explained.

Part I

THE UNDISPUTED LETTERS

3

Letter To The Romans

Romans 1

ROMANS 1 CONTAINS THREE literary units, two of which have chiastic structures. The last unit, which is chiastic, reveals three interpolations, although one might consider the second and third interpolations to be a single interpolation.

Rom 1:1–6

The first literary unit in Romans is a chiastic structure containing three stiches with an A, B, A', B' parallel in the center stich.

> A 1:1 Paul, a servant of *Christ Jesus, a called* apostle, having been appointed into the gospel of God,
> > B 1:2 which he long ago *promised through his prophets* in the holy scriptures
> > > CA 1:3a concerning his *son*, who, having come from the *seed of David*
> > > > CB 1:3b *according to the flesh*,
> > > C'A' 1:4a having been declared the *son of God* in power
> > > > C'B' 1:4b *according to the spirit of holiness*, by resurrection from the dead
> > B' 1:4c Jesus Christ our Lord, 1:5a *through whom we received* grace and apostleship,
> A' 1:5b to faithful obedience among all the Gentiles, on behalf of his name. 1:6 Among whom you are also *called of Jesus Christ*.

Rom 1:1–6 Chiastic Structure Table

A 1:1—Christ Jesus a called	A'—1:5b–6 called of Jesus Christ
B 1:2—promised through his prophets	B' 1:4c–5a—through whom we received
CA 1:3a—son . . . seed of David	C'A' 1:4a—son of God
CB 1:3b—according to the flesh	C'B' 1:4b—according to the spirit of holiness

Part I | The Undisputed Letters

Commentary

Paul's letter to the Romans begins with a six verse chiastic structure. The A stich matches "Christ Jesus a called" with "called of Jesus Christ." Paul created a chiasmus within the chiastic structure, with the two matching phrases of the A stich having reverse wording (*Christou Iēsou klētos, klētoi Iēsou Christou*). In the B stich "promised through his prophets" is a parallel concept to "through whom we received" with the verb "promised" preceding "through" in the B hemistich and the verb "received" following "through" in the B' hemistich. In the B hemistich there is a promise, and in the B' hemistich there is a reception—promised and received. In the CA hemistich of the center stich "son" and "seed of David" are parallel to "son of God" found in the C'A' hemistich. Then "according to the flesh" in the CB hemistich is parallel to "according to the spirit of holiness" in the C'B' hemistich. The center C stich is parallel in this structure. Not only does the center C stich contain repetition of phrases, it contains a parallel grammatical construction. This type of chiastic structure having a parallel center stich is found here in Romans and three times in 1 Corinthians. Moreover, as typically found in Paul's letters, the center of the chiastic structure is the theme or main point of the literary unit.

Interpolation

Rhetorical analysis shows this literary unit to have a well-formed chiastic structure with reasonably balanced stiches. There are no apparent interpolations. However, J.C. O'Neill proposed that all of Rom 1:1–6 is an interpolation[1] with the exception of the first six Greek words (Paul, a servant of Christ Jesus, a called apostle) and eight Greek words in 1:5 (among all the Gentiles on behalf of his name).[2] Rhetorical analysis shows O'Neill's conclusion to be incorrect, although he makes some good points. A point against O'Neill is, as mentioned, that the A stich contains a chiasmus within the chiasmus. It is extremely unlikely that an interpolator would have created this structure. He would have had to realize that many of Paul's literary structures were chiasms and desired to faithfully imitate Paul's style in his interpolation, and then be clever enough to create the chiasm within the chiastic structure. O'Neill's interpolator would also have had to be aware that Paul created parallel centers for three chiastic structures in 1 Corinthians and decided to make this the only chiastic structure with a parallel center in Romans.

O'Neill identified vv. 1:2–5a as a creedal statement and assumed it was inserted by an interpolator. He points out that Codex Boernerianus written in the 9th century has Romans without this creedal statement.[3] O'Neill neglected to mention that

---

1. O'Neill, *Romans*, 28.
2. O'Neill, *Romans*, 28.
3. O'Neill, *Romans*, 26.

there is an abbreviated similar creedal statement at Gal 1:1: "Jesus Christ and God the father, the one raising him from the dead." There are other affinities between Romans and Galatians such as extensive discussions of Abraham; "love your neighbor" is in both letters; "Abba, Father" is in both letters along with the concept that Christians are adopted sons of God. Scholars generally agree that Galatians is an early letter and Romans is a late letter.[4] Paul may have used Galatians as a guide and decided to expand the opening creedal statement, making it into a chiastic structure with a parallel center.

O'Neill justifies eliminating all of v. 1:6 by pointing out that Paul would not have addressed the Romans as he does in v. 1:6 before he mentioned to whom the letter was written.[5] O'Neill's point is logical, but it ignores Paul's desire to form a chiastic literary unit. An author concentrating on creating a particular literary structure well might tend to ignore other conventions in order to satisfactorily complete his creation. O'Neill also justifies eliminating vv. 1:3 and 1:4 because the addition of "by resurrection of the dead" destroys the parallelism. But the parallelism is not destroyed, there is merely text following the end of the parallelism.

Rom 1:7–17

This literary unit is a parallel structure containing four stiches.

A 1:7 To all who are in Rome, beloved of *God*, called saints. Grace to you and peace from *God* our father and the *Lord Jesus Christ*.
A' 1:8 First, I thank my *God* through *Jesus Christ* concerning all of you because your faith is proclaimed throughout the entire world.
A" 1:9 For *God* is my witness, whom I serve in my spirit in the gospel of *his son*, how unceasingly I make mention of you
   B 1:10 always in my prayers imploring, if perhaps now at last I will make a successful journey *to come to you* by the will of God.
   B' 1:11 For I long *to see you*, so that I may impart to you a spiritual gift, to strengthen you. 1:12 That we may encourage each other in our faith.
   B" 1:13a Now I do not want you to be ignorant, brothers, that many times I planned *to come to you* and was hindered so far.
      C 1:13b That *I might bear some fruit with you* also even as with the other *Gentiles*. 1:14a I am a debtor both to *Greeks and to Barbarians*,
      C' 1:14b both to *the wise and to the foolish*. 1:15 So, as much as I can, *I am ready to preach the gospel to you* also *who are in Rome*.
      C" 1:16 For *I am not ashamed of the gospel*. For it is the power of God into salvation to *everyone* who has faith. To the *Jew first*, also to the *Greek*.

4. Goodacre, "Dating Game II."
5. O'Neill, Romans, 28.

D 1:17a For in it a *righteousness* of God is revealed from *faith to faith*.
D' 1:17b As it is written, "But the *righteous* shall live by *faith*."

Rom 1:7-17 Parallel Structure Table

A 1:7—God ... God ... Lord Jesus Christ	A' 1:8—God ... Jesus Christ	A" 1:9—God ... his son
B 1:10—to come to you	B' 1:11–12—to see you	B" 1:13a—to come to you
C 1:13b–14a—I might bear some fruit with you ... Gentiles ... Greeks and to Barbarians	C' 1:14b–15—I am ready to preach the gospel to you ... who are in Rome ... the wise and to the foolish	C" 1:16—I am not ashamed of the gospel .. everyone ... Jew first and also to the Greek
D 1:17a—righteousness ... faith to faith		D' 1:17b—righteous ... faith

Commentary

The second literary unit of Rom 1 is a parallel structure with the A, B, and C stiches containing three elements but the concluding D stich containing only two hemistiches. In the A stich there is a progression of "Lord Jesus Christ" following "God," to "Jesus Christ" following "God," and finally "son" following "God," with each description of Jesus becoming more abbreviated. This is significant in determining the original composition of Rom 1:1–6. O'Neill would have reduced vv. 1–6 to fourteen words. Those fourteen words would not have fit into the literary structure of 1:7–17 and would be an orphan introductory phrase not connected to any literary unit. In the undisputed letters there is only one instance noted herein where a verse was solely introductory and apparently not connected to a literary unit. That is found at 2 Cor 12:1. This is the introduction before Paul tells his story of the man who went to the third level of Heaven. It is much more likely that Paul began the letter to the Romans with a six-verse chiastic structure rather than an extremely rare dangling introductory sentence. In writing his commentary O'Neill divided Romans into sections. His first section is Rom 1:1–7[6] since he eliminated most of that section and surmises that in Paul's original letter the address to the Romans at 1:7 is at the very beginning. This makes his second section run from vv. 1:8–17.[7] Interestingly, this is the way rhetorical analysis has determined that the literary structures are divided, with the exception that it is clear v. 1:7 belongs in the second section because of the parallel language of "Lord Jesus Christ" and "God." Further, O'Neill's third section matches the literary

---

6. O'Neill, *Romans*, 25–34.
7. O'Neill, *Romans*, 34–39.

structure of vv. 1:18–32.⁸ At least in Rom 1 O'Neill agrees with rhetorical analysis on the natural division of Paul's literary units.

In the B stich there are three obviously parallel phrases "to come to you," "to see you," and "to come to you." The C stich has another nice parallel progression of "I might bear some fruit with you," progressing to "I am ready to preach the gospel to you," progressing to "I am not ashamed of the gospel." Additionally, there are two other progressions in the C stich: first "Gentiles," then "who are in Rome," then "everyone" and second "Greeks and Barbarians," then "the wise and foolish," then "the Jew first and also the Greek." Paul ends the literary unit with "righteousness . . . faith to faith" parallel to "righteous . . . faith." In v. 1:17 Paul quotes Habakkuk 2:4.

Rom 1:18–32

The final literary unit in Rom 1 is a chiastic structure containing three stiches, revealing three interpolations.

> A 1:18 For the *wrath of God* from Heaven is revealed against all *ungodliness* and *unrighteousness* of men who suppress the truth in *unrighteousness.*
> B 1:19 Because that which is *known of God is revealed in them. For God revealed it to them.*

(1:20 For his invisible things since the creation of the world are clearly seen, being perceived through the things that are made, his eternal power and divinity. That they may be without excuse. 1:21 Because that, knowing God, they glorified him not as God, neither gave thanks, but became futile in their reasoning, and their senseless heart was darkened. 1:22 Professing themselves to be wise, they became fools, 1:23 and changed the glory of the incorruptible God for the likeness of an image of corruptible man, and of birds, and four-footed beasts, and creeping things. 1:24 Therefore God gave them up in the lusts of their hearts to impurity, that their bodies should be dishonored among themselves. 1:25 For that they exchanged the truth of God for a lie, and worshipped and served the creature rather than the creator, who is blessed for ever. Amen.)

> C 1:26 For this cause God gave them up to vile passions. *For their women changed the natural use into that which is against nature.*
> C' 1:27 And likewise also *the men, leaving the natural use of the woman, burned in their lust one toward another, men with men,* working unseemliness, and receiving in themselves that retribution of their error which was inevitable.

---

8. O'Neill, *Romans*, 40–45.

> B' 1:28 And even as they *refused to have God in their knowledge, God gave them up to a depraved mind*, to do those things which are not fitting,
> A' 1:29a being filled with all *unrighteousness, wickedness, covetousness, malice.*

(1:29b full of envy, murder, strife, deceit, malevolence; gossips, 1:30 slanderers, hateful to God, insolent, arrogant, boastful, inventors of evil things, disobedient to parents, 1:31 foolish, untrustworthy, heartless, unmerciful.)

1:32a Those who do such things knowing the *ordinance of God* are worthy of death.

(1:32b not only practice them, but also approve of those who practice them.)

Rom 1:18-32a Chiastic Structure Table

A 1:18—wrath of God . . . ungodliness . . . unrighteousness . . . unrighteousness	A' 1:29-32a—ordinance of God . . . wickedness, covetousness, malice . . . unrighteousness
B 1:19—known of God is revealed in them . . . For God revealed it to them	B' 1:28—refused to have God in their knowledge . . . God gave them up to a depraved mind
C 1:26—for their women changed the natural use into that which is against nature	C' 1:27—the men leaving the natural use of women burned in their lust toward one another men with men

Commentary

This literary unit contains longer phrases in parallel than typically found in Paul's letters. There are repeated key words, but the main parallelisms Paul is trying to get across are complementary abstract concepts. In the A stich "wrath of God" in the A hemistich matches "ordinance of God." Presumably God's wrath is engendered by violation of his ordinances. Secondly, in the A stich "ungodliness" matches "wickedness, covetousness, malice." Lastly in the A stich "unrighteousness" is found twice in the A hemistich and once in the A' hemistich. The B hemistich has "known of God is revealed in them" parallel to "refused to have God in their knowledge." The relationship here is that the ungodly refuse to acknowledge what God's ordinances reveal. Secondly, in the B hemistich "for God revealed it to them" is parallel to "God gave them up to a depraved mind" in the B' hemistich. One must be depraved to refuse what God has revealed to him. The C hemistich has "for their women changed the natural use into that which is against nature" matching "the men leaving the natural use of women burned in their lust toward one another, men with men" in the C' hemistich.

Viewing Rom 1 as a whole, it begins with a three-stich chiastic structure followed by a four-stich parallel structure, ending with another three-stich chiastic structure. The entire chapter is nicely balanced and ready to embark on a new topic. The ending of a literary unit was correctly identified by Bishop Langdon when he divided Romans into chapters.

Interpolation

Rom 1:20–1:25

In this last literary unit of Rom 1 the identification of the chiastic structure of the original unit reveals three probable interpolations into the structure. O'Neil was of the opinion that the entire unit has been interpolated.[9] He pointed out that at least twenty-nine words in this literary unit are found nowhere else in Paul's writings.[10] What O'Neill did not notice is that those twenty-nine words are confined to vv. 1:20–25, 29b–31, and 32b, the passages rhetorical analysis identifies as being interpolated. This demonstrates that rhetorical analysis can be a much more finely tuned tool for detecting interpolations. Identification of the literary unit allows the investigator to retain that which Paul actually wrote rather than throwing out the baby with the bath water. P.N. Harrison proposed that vv. 1:19–2:1 has been interpolated.[11] Bultmann also thought that v.2:1 had been interpolated.[12] The next section shows that v. 2:1a is the first half of an inclusio in a parallel structure and that v. 2:1b is the B hemistich of the parallel B stich in that literary unit. The subject literary unit, vv. 1:18–32a, with the interpolations excised is a typical Pauline chiastic structure containing three stiches just as Rom 1:1–6 contains three stiches.

The interpolation in vv. 1:20–25 is revealed by the excess text in the first half of the B and C stiches. That is, the B and C hemistiches run from v. 1:19 through v. 1:26, seven full verses. While the B' and C' hemistiches only encompass vv. 1:27–28, two verses. In the B' hemistich "refused to have God in their knowledge" follows within seventeen Greek words of "men with men" found in the C' hemistich. However, in the first half of the structure, the B and C hemistiches, there are a full six verses, one hundred twelve Greek words ending in "Amen," between the matching language of the B hemistich "for God revealed it to them" and the matching language of the C hemistich, "for their women." There is clearly too much text in the first half of this structure. The hemistiches do not have the typical Pauline balance. In addition, if Rom 1:20–25 is removed the unit still makes sense. The offending passage is a disruption to Paul's argument.

9. O'Neill, *Romans*, 41.
10. O'Neill, *Romans*, 41 (note).
11. Harrison, *Paulines and Pastorals*, 79–85.
12. Bultmann, "Glossen," 197–202.

Stiches	Words in first half	Words in second half	Interpolation words
B – C	1:19–26 – 148	1:27–28–55	1:20–25–112

Rom 1:29b, 32b

There seem to be further interpolations into the structure at vv. 1:29b–31 and 1:32b. Joseph A. Fitzmeyer thinks that the entire verse 1:32 has been interpolated.[13] However "ordinance of God" in v. 1:32a is parallel to "wrath of God" found in v. 1:18 and is probably original. Apparently the same interpolator who inserted the diatribe against the unrighteous in Rom 1:20–25 added more unseemly conduct Christians should avoid at vv. 1:29b–31 and 32b. Rhetorical analysis shows that the A hemistich contains only eighteen words. However, there are forty-nine words in the A' hemistich, vv. 1:29–32, including the interpolation. In addition, vv. 1:29–31 seems to be awkwardly worded in describing various sins the unrighteous commit. By removing vv. 1:29b–31 and 32b, the A' hemistich is reduced to twenty words, nicely balanced with the A' hemistich. That confirms that vv. 1:29b–31, and 32b are also interpolated. Additionally, v. 1:32b does not quite fit into Paul's argument.

Stiches	Words in first half	Words in second half	Interpolation words
A	1:18–18	1:29–32–49	1:29b–31–20
A	1:18–18	1:29–32–49	1:32b—9

Romans 2

The second chapter of Romans is a series of parallel literary units for the most part. Two of them are defined by inclusios. Romans 2:25–29 is unique in Pauline literary units. It is a series of short chiastic and parallel units about circumcision, each encompassing about one verse.

Rom 2:1–11

The first literary unit in Rom 2 is a parallel structure defined by an inclusio.

> A 2:1a Therefore you are without excuse, O man, whoever you are that judges. For wherein *you judge another*, you condemn yourself.
> B 2:1b For you *who judges* do practice the same things. 2:2 And we know that *the judgment of God* is according to truth against *those who practice such things*.

---

13. Fitzmeyer, *Romans*, 65.

B' 2:3 And reckon you this, O man, *who judges those who practice such things* and do the same, that you shall escape the *judgment of God*?

C 2:4 Or do you despise the *riches* of his goodness and forbearance and long suffering, not knowing that the *goodness of God leads you to repentance*?

C' 2:5 But after your hardness and impenitent heart *treasures up* for yourself wrath in the day of wrath and revelation of the *righteous judgment of God 2:6 who will render to every man according to his works.*

D 2:7 To those who by *patience in good work seek for glory and honor and incorruption, eternal life.*

D' 2:8 But to those who are *factious, and disobey the truth,* but *obey unrighteousness, wrath and anger,*

E 2:9 *tribulation and anguish,* upon *every soul of man who works evil, of the Jew first, and also of the Greek.*

E' 2:10 But *glory and honor and peace* to *everyone who works good, to the Jew first, and also to the Greek.*

A' 2:11 For there is *no favoritism of persons with God.*

Rom 2:1–11 Parallel Structure with Inclusio Table

A 2:1a—you judge another	A' 2:11—no favoritism of persons with God
B 2:1b–2—who judges ... the judgment of God ... those who practice such things	B' 2:3—who judges ... the judgment of God ... those who practice such things
C 2:4—riches ... goodness of God ... leads you to repentance	C' 2:5–6—treasures up ... righteous judgment of God ... who will render to every man according to his works
D 2:7—patience in good work ... seek for glory and honor and incorruption, eternal life	D' 2:8—factions and disobey the truth ... obey unrighteousness, wrath, and anger
E 2:9—Tribulation and anguish ... every soul of man who works evil ... of the Jew first and also the Greek	E' 2:10—glory and honor and peace ... everyone who works good ... of the Jew first and also the Greek

Commentary

The first literary unit of Rom 2 is defined by an inclusio. The A stich has "you judge another" in the A hemistich parallel to "no favoritism of persons with God" in the A' hemistich. These, of course, are concepts that are diametrically opposed. If there is no favoritism, there has been no judgment. The B stich contains repetitions of three exact phrases in both hemistiches—"who judges," "the judgment of God," and "those who practice such things." After those exact phrase repetitions the C stich matches "riches" with "treasures up." Then secondly in the C stich there is a match of God's qualities with "goodness of God" parallel to "righteous judgment of God," and thirdly in the C stich, "leads you to repentance" is parallel to "who will render to every man according to his works." These last two are parallel because they are the result of the previous match: one leads to the other. The D stich matches opposites with two phrases in each hemistich: first, "patience in good work" is parallel to its opposite "factions and disobey the truth;" and second, "seek for glory and honor and incorruption, eternal life" is parallel to its opposite "obey unrighteousness, wrath, and anger." Then the final E stich has three matching phrases in each hemistich that are a mixture of opposite and complimentary phrases. "Tribulation and anguish" is opposite to "glory and honor and peace," and "every soul of man who works evil" is opposite to "everyone who works good." However, "of the Jew first and also the Greek" is exactly the same.

Interpolation

O'Neill proposed that the entire second chapter of Romans is an interpolation along with vv. 1:18–32. Walker agrees with O'Neill.[14] O'Neill thought that Rom 3 begins immediately after v. 1:17. He was of the opinion that vv. 1:18–2:29 was originally a piece of missionary literature of Hellenistic Judaism inserted into Paul's letter by an interpolator.[15] If vv. 1:18–2:29 is based upon a Hellenistic Jewish document, it must have been reworked by Paul for insertion into his letter since the literary units have typical Pauline characteristics. Romans 1:18–32 has a chiastic structure, admittedly redacted by an interpolator, but with careful analysis the chiastic structure can be discerned. Then vv. 2:1–11 has a parallel structure with an inclusio that is very much in the Pauline style. O'Neill believed that Rom 2 misunderstands Paul's reason for writing Romans.[16] However, rhetorical analysis finds the literary units in Rom 2 to be consistent with Pauline literary units throughout the undisputed letters. Romans 2:25–29 is unique in the letters, but is similar to other short chiasms and parallelisms found in 1 Corinthians and 1 Thessalonians.

Rom 2:12–16

This short structure is a three-stich parallel structure.

> A 2:12a For *as many as have sinned without law will also perish without the law.*
> A' 2:12b And *as many as have sinned under the law will be judged by the law.*
> B 2:13a For the *hearers of the law are not just* before God,
> B' 2:13b but the *doers of the law will be justified.*

14. Walker, *Interpolations*, 166–89.
15. O'Neil, *Romans*, 54.
16. O'Neill, *Romans*, 49.

C 2:14 For when Gentiles that *do not have the law* do by nature the things of the law, these, not having the law, *are the law to themselves*.

C' 2:15 Those who show the work of the *law written in their hearts*, their conscience bearing witness, and their thoughts with one another accusing or defending them 2:16 on the day when *God will judge the secrets of men*, according to my gospel, by Jesus Christ.

Rom 12-16 Parallel Structure Table

A 2:12a—as many as have sinned without law will also perish without the law	A' 2:12b—as many as have sinned under the law will be judged by the law
B 2:13a—hearers of the law are not just	B' 2:13b—doers of the law will be justified
C 2:14—do not have the law . . . are the law to themselves	C' 2:15-16—law written in their hearts . . . God will judge the secrets of men

Commentary

The second literary unit in Rom 2 has a parallel structure with three stiches. The A and A' hemistiches have almost the exact same phraseology with only a few words changed. "Without the law" in the A hemistich is changed to its opposite "under the law," and "will perish" is changed to "will be judged." In the B stich "hearers" is parallel to its opposite "doers," and "are not just" is parallel to its opposite "will be justified." The C stich continues the matching of opposites with "do not have the law" parallel to "law written in their hearts," and "are the law to themselves" is parallel to "God will judge the secrets of men." Bultmann thought that v. 2:16 had been interpolated,[17] but there seems to be a match of v. 2:16 with the end of v. 2:14. If one is the law to himself then God will judge him. It is true that the C' hemistich has forty-two words and is much longer than the C hemistich, having only nineteen words. Removing v. 2:16 would reduce the C' hemistich to twenty-five words, a much better balance. The parallel relationship between "are the law to themselves" and "God will judge the secrets of men" tips the decision in favor of retaining v. 2:16.

Rom 2:17-24

This literary structure is a parallel structure with an inclusio. The inclusio is in a format found several times in the undisputed letters wherein the inclusio A stich contains three elements, the first two being parallel at the beginning of the structure and the third element being the concluding element and completes the inclusio.

---

17. Bultmann, "Glossen," 200-01.

A 2:17 But if *you* bear the name of a *Jew*, and *rely upon the law*, and *boast in God*,
A' 2:18 and know his will, and approve the things that are excellent, being *instructed out of the law*,
  B 2:19a and are confident that you yourself are a *guide of the blind*,
  B' 2:19b a *light to those in darkness*,
    C 2:20a a *corrector of the foolish*,
    C' 2:20b a *teacher of infants*,
      D 2:20c having in the law the form of *knowledge*
      D' 2:20d and of the *truth*.
        E 2:21a You therefore that *teach another*,
        E' 2:21b do you not *teach yourself*?
          F 2:21c You that preach a man should *not steal*,
          F' 2:21d do you *steal*?
            G 2:22a You say a man should *not commit adultery*,
            G' 2:22b do you *commit adultery*?
              H 2:22c *You abhor idols*,
              H' 2:22d do *you rob temples*?
                I 2:23a You who *boast in the law*,
                I' 2:23b do you dishonor God through your *transgression of the law*?
A" 2:24 For the name of *God is blasphemed* among the *Gentiles* because of *you*, as has been written.

Rom 2:17-24 Parallel Structure with Inclusio Table

The below table is presented somewhat differently with the A element being in two separate rows: once for the parallel stich and once for the inclusio stich.

A 2:17—rely upon the law	A' 2:18—instructed out of the law
A 2:17—you … Jew … boast in God	A" 2:24—you … Gentile … God is blasphemed
B 2:19a—guide of the blind	B' 2:19b—light to those in darkness
C 2:20a—corrector of the foolish	C' 2:20b—teacher of infants
D 2:20c—knowledge	D' 2:20d—truth
E 2:21a—teach another	E' 2:21b—teach yourself
F 2:21c—not steal	F' 2:21d—steal
G 2:22a—not commit adultery	G' 2:22b—commit adultery
H 2:22c—you abhor idols	H' 2:22d—you rob temples
I 2:23a—boast in the law	I' 2:23b—transgression of the law

Commentary

This is a literary unit with a parallel structure that is defined by an inclusio. It is unusual in the Pauline letters, but the A element of the A stich is parallel to the A' element in words different from the words in the A" element. Therefore, the A element works as a parallel hemistich in an A, A'; B, B'; C, C' parallel structure, but also works as the initial hemistich in an inclusio matching different words in the concluding element.

The inclusio elements A and A" first match "you," being in both elements, secondly "Jew" matches "Gentile," and thirdly, "boast in God" matches its opposite "God is blasphemed." The A" element, v. 2:24, is a quote of Isa 52:5. The A element also matches the A' element by having "rely on the law" parallel to "instructed out of the law."

The balance of the structure, stiches B to I, is typically Pauline, matching similar concepts and opposites. The B stich matches "guide of the blind" with "light to those in darkness." The C stich matches "corrector of the foolish" with "teacher of infants." The D stich matches "knowledge" with "truth." The E stich matches "teach another" with "teach yourself." The F stich matches "not steal" with "steal." The G stich matches "not commit adultery" with "commit adultery." The H stich matches "you abhor idols" with "you rob temples." The I stich matches opposites "boast in the law" with "transgression of the law." In the first twenty-four verses of Rom 2 there are three parallel structures; however, it is clear that they are separate literary units because of the inclusios in the units encompassing vv. 2:1–11 and vv. 2:17–24. Interestingly, Rom 1 was structured chiastic – parallel – chiastic and vv. 2:1–24 is structured parallel/inclusio – parallel – parallel/inclusio. Each literary unit has a clear demarcation.

Rom 2:25–29

The final unit of Rom 2 is unique in the Pauline letters. It is a series of short chiastic and parallel structures each about one verse long based upon "circumcision."

  A 2:25a For *circumcision* indeed profits,
    B 2:25b if you be a doer of the *law*.
    B' 2:25c But if you be a transgressor of the *law*,
  A' 2:25d your *circumcision* is become uncircumcision.

  A 2:26a If therefore the *uncircumcision*
    B 2:26b keeps the *ordinances*
    B' 2:26c of the *law*,
  A' 2:26d shall not his *uncircumcision* be reckoned for circumcision?

  A 2:27a And shall not the *uncircumcision* which is by nature,

    B 2:27b if it fulfill the *law*, judge you,
A' 2:27c who with the letter and *circumcision*
    B' 2:27d are a transgressor of the *law*?

A 2:28a For he is not a *Jew who is one outwardly*;
    B 2:28b neither is that *circumcision* which is outward in the *flesh*.
A' 2:29a But he is a *Jew who is one inwardly*;
    B' 2:29b and *circumcision* is of the *heart*,

A 2:29c in the *spirit*
    B 2:29d *not in the letter*,
        B' 2:29e whose praise is *not of men*,
A' 2:29f but of *God*.

Commentary

Although this literary unit is unique, it appears to be original and not interpolated. The structures encompassing vv. 2:25–29 could be viewed as all one unit since the subject is circumcision and the law. In addition, the point of the unit comes at the end in v. 2:29. This work views the series as separate structures since there is an A, B, B,' A' chiastic structure followed by another A, B, B' A' chiastic structure. Then there is an A, B, A,' B' parallel unit followed by a second one. The series ends with an A, B, B,' A' chiastic structure that mirrors the beginning of the unit, but strangely is not a separate sentence in itself. Another reason for viewing this series as separate units is that in the fourth unit of vv. 2:28–29 "circumcision" is no longer in the A hemistich as it had been in the three previous structures.

Romans 3

Romans 3 is the first chapter wherein the entire chapter is one chiastic structure. Interestingly, vv. 3:10–18 are a series of quotes from the Old Testament, mostly from Psalms, but Paul has strung them together to form the center of this chiastic structure. This literary unit also has a parallel structure making it a dual chiastic/parallel unit where Paul has designed the unit with a chiastic structure and a parallel structure beginning and ending at the same place. The chiastic structure with ten stiches is shown first. Second to be shown is the parallel structure containing eleven stiches. The consecutive parallels in the center J stich of the chiastic structure are identical to the F stich in the parallel structure. Three interpolations are revealed.

Rom 3:1–31

Chiastic Structure

A 3:1 What advantage then has the Jew? Or what is the benefit of? 3:2 Much in every way. First of all, they were entrusted with the oracles of *God*. 3:3 For what if some *disbelieved*? Should their *lack of faith nullify the faithfulness* of God? 3:4a *May it never be.*

  B 3:4b Now let *God* be found true, but every man a liar.

    C 3:4c As it is written, that you *might be justified* in your words, and might prevail when you come into judgment.

      D 3:5 But if our *unrighteousness* exhibits the *righteousness* of God, what will we say? Is God unrighteous to inflict with wrath? (I speak after the manner of men.)

        E 3:6 May it never be. For then how shall *God* judge the world? 3:7a But if the truth of *God* through my lie abounded to his glory,

          F 3:7b why *am I also still judged as a sinner*? 3:8 And (as we are slanderously reported, and as some affirm that we say), why not let us do evil, that good may come? Whose condemnation is just.

            G 3:9 What then? Are we better? Not at all. *For we have already charged both Jews and Greeks*, that *they are all under sin*.

              H 3:10 As it is written, "None are righteous, not even one. 3:11 There are none who understand. *There are none who seek after God.*

                I 3:12 They have all turned aside, together they have become worthless. *There are none who do good*, there is not so much as one.

                  J 3:13a Their *throat* is an open sepulcher. With their *tongues* they have *used deceit.*

                  J' 3:13b The poison of asps is under their *lips.* 3:14 Whose *mouth* is full of *cursing and bitterness.*

                I' 3:15 Their feet are swift to shed blood. 3:16 Destruction and misery are in their ways; 3:17 And *they have not known the way of peace.*

              H' 3:18 *There is no fear of God* before their eyes." 3:19a But we know that what ever the law says, it speaks to those under the law;

(3:19b So that every mouth may be stopped, and all the world may be brought under the judgment of God.)

            G' 3:20 Because by the works of the law *no flesh will be justified in his sight*. For through the law comes the *knowledge of sin.*

          F' 3:21a But now apart from the law the righteousness of God has been revealed.

(3:21b being witnessed by the law and the prophets.)

>   3:22 And the righteousness of God through faith of Jesus Christ toward all those who believe; for there is no distinction; 3:23 For *all have sinned*, and fall short of the glory of God,
>
> E' 3:24 being justified freely by his grace through the redemption that is in *Christ Jesus*. 3:25a Whom *God* set forth, a propitiation, through faith, in his blood,
>
> D' 3:25b for a demonstration of his *righteousness* because of the forbearance of the sins committed beforehand, in the forbearance of God. 3:26a For the demonstration of his *righteousness* at this present time.

(3:26b that he might himself be just, and the justifier of him who has faith in Jesus. 3:27 Where then is the boasting? It has been excluded. By what manner of law? Of works? No. But by a law of faith.)

>   C' 3:28 We reckon therefore that *a man is justified* by faith apart from the works of the law.
> B' 3:29 Or is *God* of Jews only? Not of the Gentiles also? Yes, of Gentiles also.
> A' 3:30 Since indeed *God* is one, he shall justify the circumcised by *faith*, and the uncircumcised through *faith*. A' 3:31 Then do we *nullify* the law *through faith*? *May it never be*. No, we establish the law.

Rom 3:1–31 Chiastic Structure Table

A 3:1–4a—God ... disbelieved ... lack of faith ... nullify the faithfulness ... may it never be	A' 3:30–31—God ... faith ... faith ... nullify through faith ... may it never be
B 3:4b—God	B' 3:29—God
C 3:4c—you might be justified	C' 3:28—a man is justified
D 3:5—unrighteousness ... righteousness	D' 3:25b–26a—righteousness ... righteousness
E 3:6–7a—God ... God	E' 3:24–25a—Christ Jesus ... God
F 3:7b–8—am I also still judged a sinner	F' 3:21–23—all have sinned
G 3:9—for we have already charged both Jews and Greeks ... they are all under sin	G' 3:20—no flesh will be justified in his sight ... knowledge of sin
H 3:10–11—there are none who seek after God	H' 3:18–19—there is no fear of God
I 3:12—there are none who do good	I' 3:16–17—they have not known the way of peace
J 3:13a—throat ... tongue ... used deceit	J' 3:13b–15—lips ... mouth ... cursing and bitterness

Parallel Structure

A 3:1 What advantage then has the Jew? Or what is the benefit of? 3:2 Much every way. First of all, they were entrusted with the oracles of God. 3:3a For what if *some disbelieved*?

A' 3:3b Should their *lack of faith* nullify the faithfulness of God? 3:4a May it never be. Now let God be found true, but every man a liar.

  B 3:4b As it is written, that *you might be justified* in your words, and might prevail when you come into judgment.

  B' 3:5 But if our unrighteousness *exhibits the righteousness of God*, what will we say? Is God unrighteous to inflict with wrath? (I speak after the manner of men.)

    C 3:6 May it never be. For then how shall *God judge the world*? 3:7a But if the truth of God through my lie abounded to his glory,

    C' 3:7b why am *I also still judged as a sinner*? 3:8a And (as we are slanderously reported, and as some affirm that we say), why not let us do evil, that good may come?

      D 3:8b Whose *condemnation* is just. G 3:9a What then? Are we better? Not at all.

      D' 3:9b For we have *already charged* both Jews and Greeks, that they are all under sin.

        E 3:10 As it is written, "*None are righteous, not even one.* 3:11 There are none who understand. There are none who seek after God.

        E' 3:12 They have all turned aside, together they have become worthless. *There are none who do good, there is not so much as one.*

          F 3:13a Their *throat is an open sepulcher*. With their *tongues they have used deceit*.

          F' 3:13b The *poison of asps is under their lips*. 3:14 Whose *mouth is full of cursing and bitterness*.

            G 3:15 Their feet are swift to *shed blood*.

            G' 3:16 *Destruction* and misery are in their ways;

              H 3:17 And they have not known the way of peace. 3:18 There is no fear of God before their eyes." 3:19a But we know that *what ever the law says*, it speaks to those under the law;

(3:19b So that every mouth may be stopped, and all the world may be brought under the judgment of God.)

              H' 3:20 Because by the *works of the law* no flesh will be justified in his sight. For through the law comes the knowledge of sin.

                I 3:21a But now apart from the law the *righteousness of God* has been revealed,

(3:21b being witnessed by the law and the prophets.)

> I' 3:22 And the *righteousness of God* through faith of Jesus Christ toward all those who believe; for there is no distinction.
>> J 3:23 For all have sinned, and fall short of the glory of God, 3:24 being *justified freely by his grace through the redemption* that is in Christ Jesus.
>> J' 3:25a Whom God set forth, *a propitiation, through faith, in his blood,*
>>> K 3:25b *for a demonstration of his righteousness* because of the forbearance of the sins committed beforehand,
>>> K' 3:25c in the forbearance of God. 3:26a *For the demonstration of his righteousness* at this present time.

(3:26b that he might himself be just, and the justifier of him who has faith in Jesus. 3:27 Where then is the boasting? It has been excluded. By what manner of law? Of works? No. But by a law of faith.)

> L 3:28 We reckon therefore that a man is *justified by faith* apart from the works of the law. 3:29 Or is *God of Jews* only? Not *of the Gentiles* also? Yes, of Gentiles also.
> L' 3:30 Since indeed God is one, *he shall justify the circumcised by faith,* and the *uncircumcised through faith.*
>> M 3:31a Then do *we nullify the law* through faith?
>> M' 3:31b May it never be. No, *we establish the law.*

Rom 3:1–31 Parallel Structure Table

A 3:1–3a—some disbelieved	A' 3:3b–4a—their lack of faith
B 3:4b—you might be justified	B' 3:5—exhibits the righteousness of God
C 3:6–7a—God judge the world	C' 3:7b–8a—I also still judged as a sinner
D 3:8b–9a—condemnation	D' 3:9b—already charged
E 3:10–11—none are righteous, not even one	E' 3:12—there are none who do good, there is not so much as one.
F 3:13a—throat is an open sepulcher . . . tongues they have used deceit	F' 3:13b–14—poison of asps is under their lips . . . mouth is full of cursing and bitterness
G 3:15—shed blood	G' 3:16—destruction
H 3:17–19—what ever the law says	H' 3:20—works of the law
I 3:21—righteousness of God	I' 3:22—righteousness of God

J 3:23–24—justified freely by his grace through the redemption	J' 3:25a—a propitiation, through faith in his blood
K 3:25b—for a demonstration of his righteousness	K' 3:25c–26a—for the demonstration of his righteousness
L 3:28–29—justified by faith . . . God of the Jews . . . of the Gentiles	L' 3:30—he will justify the circumcised by faith . . . uncircumcised through faith
M 3:31a—we nullify the law	M' 3:31b—we establish the law

Commentary

Romans 3 is a single literary unit having a dual chiastic/parallel structure. Discerning the chiastic structure exposes three possible interpolations. The parallel structure does not reveal the interpolated passages.

CHIASTIC STRUCTURE

In the chiastic structure the A stich contains five matches. "God" is found in both hemistiches as the first match. The second and third matches of the A stich are "disbelieved" and "lack of faith" in the A hemistich matching their opposites "faith" found twice in the A' hemistich. The fourth A stich match is "nullify the faithfulness" in the A hemistich with "nullify through faith" in the A' hemistich. The final A stich match is "may it never be" contained in both hemistiches. The B stich matches "God" in both hemistiches, and the C stich matches "you are justified" with "a man is justified." Both hemistiches in the D stich contain the word "righteousness" twice, although one of the instances in the D hemistich is actually 'unrighteousness." The E stich matches "God" twice in the E hemistich with "God" once and "Christ Jesus" once in the E' hemistich.

The G stich matches "For we have already charged both Jews and Greeks" with "no flesh will be justified in his sight." The second G stich match is "they are all under sin" matching "knowledge of sin." The F stich matches "why am I judged a sinner" with "for all have sinned." The H, I, and J stiches, vv. 3:10–18, contain quotes of Ps 14:1–3, 53:1–3, 5:9, 140:3, 10:7, Prov 1:16, Isa 59:7–8 and Ps 36.1. The parallelism of "there are none that do good, no not one" at vv. 3:10, 12 is found in Ps 14:1. The H stich matches "there are none who seek after God" with "there is no fear of God." The I stich matches "there are none who do good" with "they have not known the way of peace." The center J stich contains three matches in each hemistich, "throat" matching "lips," "tongue" matching "mouth," and "used deceit" matching "cursing and bitterness."

Part I | The Undisputed Letters

Parallel Structure

The A stich of the parallel structure matches "some disbelieved" with "their lack of faith." The B stich of the parallel structure matches "you might be justified" (*dikaiōthēs*) with "exhibits the righteousness of God" (*Theou dikaiosynēn synistēsin*). The match is clearer in Greek than in English since "justified" and "righteousness" have the same root. The C stich of the parallel structure matches "God judge the world" with "I also still judged as a sinner." The D stich matches "condemnation" with "already charged." The E stich of the parallel structure begins Paul's series of quotations with "none are righteous, not even one" matching "there are none who do good, there is not so much as one." As mentioned, the F stich of the parallel structure is identical to the center J stich of the chiastic structure with "throat is an open sepulcher" in the F hemistich matching "the poison of asps is under their lips" in the F' hemistich. Then "tongues they have used deceit" in the F hemistich matches "mouth is full of cursing and bitterness."

The G stich of the parallel structure has "shed blood" matching "destruction." The H hemistich matches "what ever the law says" with "the works of the law." Both halves of the I stich contain "righteousness of God." The J hemistich has "justified freely by his grace through the redemption" matching "a propitiation through faith in his blood." In the K stich both hemistiches contain "for a demonstration of his righteousness." The L stich contains an unusual match with the L hemistich containing "justified by faith" and then separate questions asking about the "God of the Jews" and "of the Gentiles." The L' hemistich uses two separate phrases to match those three phrases, "justify the circumcised (Jews) by faith" and "uncircumcised (Gentiles) through faith." Both hemistiches discuss justifying Jews and Gentiles by faith but the construction of the sentences are different. The final M stich matches opposites, "we nullify the law" and "we establish the law."

Interpolations

O'Neill thought Rom 3 is original to Paul for the most part. He did think that vv. 3:12–18 and "to those under the law" in 3:19 had been interpolated.[18] O'Neill's putative interpolation of vv. 3:12–18 eliminates the I and J stiches of the chiastic structure, and takes away the H' hemistich of the chiastic structure. This is where Paul cleverly arranged quotes from the Old Testament to be chiastic and parallel matches. It is also where the center J stich of the chiastic structure is identical with the F stich of the parallel structure. O'Neill would have us believe that his interpolator was aware of Paul's dual chiastic/parallel structures and the fact that Paul often had the center stich of the chiastic structure as one of the stiches in the parallel structure and designed his interpolation to emulate that attribute. This is highly unlikely. O'Neill also thought that "for

---

18. O'Neill, *Romans*, 265.

a demonstration of his righteousness because of the sins committed beforehand in the forbearance of God" found in 3:25 is an interpolation.[19] However, that eliminates one instance of the two times "righteousness" matches in the D' hemistich of the chiastic structure. It is also unlikely that O'Neill was correct in that assessment.

Rom 3:19b

The H' and G' hemistiches in the chiastic structure together contain too many words. The G hemistich has fifteen words and the G' hemistich has fifteen words assuming it encompasses 3:20. There is no room in the G' hemistich to absorb any excess words from the H' hemistich. The H hemistich contains eighteen words. The H' hemistich contains thirty-two words but if all the words of v. 3:19 following "it speaks" are excised, the H' hemistich is reduced to twenty words, balancing with the eighteen words of the H hemistich.

Stiches	Words in first half	Words in second half	Words in interpolation
G—H	Rom 3:9–10–33	Rom 3:18–20–47	Rom 3:19b—12

Rom 3:21b

The second interpolation into Rom 3 is in the F' hemistich at v. 3:21. The F hemistich has twenty-nine words. However the F' hemistich contains thirty-eight words, a few too many for a usual Pauline balance. Since v. 3:26a contains the matching phrase "for a demonstration of his righteousness," it is not a candidate for excision. In addition, in the parallel structure Rom 3:21a and 3:22 both contain the phrase "the righteousness of God," therefore those phrases are probably original to Paul. The remaining phrase in v. 3:21b "being witnessed by the law and the prophets" is the likely candidate for excision. While Paul mentions "prophets" quite often, this is the only example of "law and the prophets" in the undisputed letters. This is obviously a reference to the Old Testament but it adds little to Paul's argument. Removing those seven words reduces the F' hemistich to thirty-one words, just two more than the twenty-nine words of the F hemistich. It goes without saying that the shorter the interpolation, the more difficult it is to detect. Whether or not v. 3:21b has been interpolated is a borderline case.

Stiches	Words in first half	Words in second half	Words in interpolation
F	3:7b–8–29	3:21–39	3:21b—7

---

19. O'Neill, *Romans*, 265.

Rom 3:26b–27

C. H. Talbert has proposed that vv. 3:24–26 are an interpolation.[20] Rhetorical analysis partially agrees with him. There appears to be an interpolation in the D' hemistich. The D hemistich contains nineteen words while the D' hemistich contains fifty-three words, entirely too many. The C stich is relatively balanced having the C hemistich contain thirteen words and the C' hemistich contain eight words, but the C hemistich has eight one syllable words and v. 3:4 is a quote of Ps 51:4. Therefore, the extra twenty-seven words apparently in the D' hemistich can not be part of the C' hemistich. The conclusion is that vv. 3:26b–27 has been interpolated. Romans 3:26a contains one of the instances of "righteousness" and is therefore probably original. Removing vv. 3:26b–27 reduces the D' hemistich to twenty-six words, a perfect balance with the twenty-six word D hemistich. Talbert's proposal would eliminate the second half of the D and E stiches with their matches of "righteousness," "God," and "Christ Jesus."

Stiches	Words in first half	Words in second half	Words in interpolation
C—D	3:4c–5–39	3:25b–28–61	3:26b–27–27

Romans 4

Romans 4 is an unusual literary unit by Paul. It has a progressive parallel structure. A similar unit is found at 1 Cor 2. Notice the progression of parallels from the elements in the A and B stiches to the C and D stiches and then to the E and F stiches. This unit also uses a two-stich inclusio.

Romans 4:1–25

> A 4:1 What then shall we say that Abraham, our forefather, has found according to the flesh? 4:2 For if Abraham was *justified* by works, he has reason to boast, but not toward God.
>
>> B 4:3 For what does the scripture say? And Abraham believed God, and it was *reckoned to him for righteousness*. 4:4 Now to him who works, the reward is not reckoned as of grace but as of debt.
>
> A' 4:5a But to him who does not work, but believes on him that *justifies* the ungodly,
>
>> B' 4:5b his faith is *reckoned for righteousness*. 4:6 Even as David also declares blessing upon the man, to whom God *reckons righteousness* apart from works,
>
> A" 4:7 saying, "Blessed are they whose *iniquities are forgiven*, And whose *sins are covered*.
>
>> B" 4:8 Blessed is the man to whom, the Lord *will not reckon sin*."

---

20. Talbert, "Fragment in Romans 3:24–26?"

C 4:9a Is this blessing then pronounced upon the *circumcision*,
- D 4:9b or upon the *uncircumcision* also?

B''' 4:9c For we say, to Abraham his faith was *reckoned for righteousness*.
- C' 4:10a How then was it reckoned? When he was in *circumcision*,
  - D' 4:10b or in *uncircumcision*?
- C'' 4:10c Not in *circumcision*,
  - D'' 4:10d but in *uncircumcision*.
- C''' 4:11a And he received the sign of *circumcision*,
  - D''' 4:11b a seal of the righteousness of the faith which he had while he was in *uncircumcision*. That he might be the father of all them that believe, though they be in *uncircumcision*,

B'''' 4:11c that *righteousness might be reckoned* to them.
- C'''' 4:12a And the father of *circumcision* to them who not only are of the *circumcision*,
  - D'''' 4:12b but those also who during *uncircumcision*
    - E 4:12c walk in the steps of *faith* of our father Abraham.
      - F 4:13a For not through the law was the *promise* to Abraham or to his seed that he should be heir of the world,
    - E' 4:13b but through the righteousness of *faith*.
    - E'' 4:14a For if they that are of the law are heirs, *faith* is made void,
      - F' 4:14b and the *promise* is made of none effect. 4:15 For the law works wrath; but where there is no law, neither is there transgression.
    - E''' 4:16a Therefore it is of *faith* that according to grace
      - F'' 4:16b the *promise* may be sure to all the seed, not only to that which is of the law,
    - E'''' 4:16c but also to that of the *faith* of Abraham, who is the father of us all.
      - G 4:17 As it is written, "A *father of many nations* have I made you" before him whom he believed, God, who gives life to the dead, and calls the things that are not, as though they were.
      - G' 4:18 Who in hope believed against hope, to the end that he might become a *father of many nations*, according to that which had been spoken, So shall your seed be.
    - E''''' 4:19 And without being weakened in *faith* he considered his own body now as good as dead (he being about a hundred years old), and the deadness of Sarah's womb.
      - F''' 4:20a Yet, looking to the *promise* of God, he wavered not through unbelief,
    - E'''''' 4:20b but waxed strong through *faith*, giving glory to God,
      - F'''' 4:21 and being fully assured that what he had *promised*, he was able also to perform.

B'''' 4:22 Therefore also it was *reckoned to him for righteousness*. 4:23 Now it was not written for his sake alone, that it was reckoned to him. 4:24a But for our sake also, to whom it shall be reckoned,

A''' 4:24b who believe on him that raised Jesus our Lord from the dead, 4:25 who was delivered up for our trespasses, and was raised for our *justification*.

Rom 4:1–25 Progressive Parallel Structure with Inclusio Table

A 4:1–2—justified	A' 4:5—justifies		A'' 4:7—iniquities are forgiven . . . sins are covered		A''' 4:24b–25—justification	
B 4:3–4—reckoned to him for righteousness	B' 4:5b–6—reckoned for righteousness . . . reckons righteousness	B'' 4:8—will not reckon sin	B''' 4:9c—reckoned for righteousness	B'''' 4:11c—that righteousness might be reckoned	B''''' 4:22–24a—reckoned to him for righteousness	
C 4:9a—circumcision	C' 4:10a—circumcision	C'' 4:10c—circumcision		C''' 4:11a—circumcision	C'''' 4:12a—circumcision . . . circumcision	
D 4:9b—uncircumcision	D' 4:10b—uncircumcision	D'' 4:10d—uncircumcision		D''' 4:11b—uncircumcision	D'''' 4:12b—uncircumcision	
E 4:12—faith	E' 4:13b—faith	E'' 4:14a—faith	E''' 4:16a—faith	E'''' 4:16c—faith	E''''' 4:19a—faith	E'''''' 4:20b—faith
F 4:13a—promise	F' 4:14b—promise		F'' 4:16b—promise	F''' 4:20a—promise		F'''' 4:21—promise
G 4:17—a father of many nations				G' 4:18—a father of many nations		

Commentary

The table above graphically demonstrates the progressive nature of Rom 4 with the number of elements increasing from the A stich to the E stich and then diminishing to the G stich. The E stich, the word "faith," the center post of Paul's theology, has the greatest number of elements.

This is another Pauline literary unit that extends for an entire chapter. That there is only one unit and not several in Rom 4 is evident by Paul's use of a two-element inclusio, both of which have the same root (*dikaiosune*) "righteousness" or "justification." The inclusio makes it is clear that this literary unit encompasses the entire chapter because the A element at v. 4:2 contains "was justified" and the A''' element at v. 4:25 contains "justification." Completing the two part inclusio, the B element at v. 4:3 contains "reckoned to him for righteousness" and the B'''' element at v. 4:22 has the exact same phrase. This is a quote of Gen 15:6. Romans 4:7–8 is a quote of Ps 32:1–2.

The main body of the unit is what has been denominated a progressive parallelism. That means that Paul uses a parallel style such as A, B, A', B' and then adds another parallel sequence, "circumcision" and "uncircumcision," on top of that so that there is A, B, C, D, B', C', D'. He then continues on adding E, and F, "faith" and "promise." O'Neill proposed that vv. 4:14–15 has been interpolated,[21] and he has a good point that these two verses do not seem to make sense as stated. However, they do make sense if "heirs" in v. 14a means the only heirs. In that case it does not contradict v. 16. Also from a rhetorical analysis standpoint the E'' and F' elements found in v. 4:14 seem to break up a symmetrical E, F, E'; E,'' F, E''' pattern. However, since v. 4:14 contains the words "faith" and "promise," it is more likely that vv. 4:14–15 are original to Paul. Finally, the G stich, "father of many nations" has parallel elements. The G, and G' elements are quotes of Gen 17:5. P. N. Harrison thought that vv. 4:17–19 had been interpolated.[22] If he is correct that would eliminate the G stich and the E'''' element. Rhetorical analysis cannot show that Harrison is incorrect here, only that if there were an interpolator he was astute enough to include a Pauline type parallelism in his interpolation.

Romans 5

Romans 5 is a single chiastic structure having mostly abstract concepts forming the parallelisms. There is also the use of "justified/justification" linking the end of Romans 4 with the beginning of Romans 5.

Rom 5:1–21

A 5:1 Being therefore *justified* by faith, we have peace with God through our *Lord Jesus Christ*, 5:2a through whom also we have had our access by faith into this *grace* wherein we stand.

B 5:2b And we boast in hope of the glory of God. 5:3 And not only so, but we also boast in *tribulations*. Knowing that *tribulation* produces *steadfastness*, 5:4 and *steadfastness*, *character*, and *character*, *hope*. 5:5 And hope does not put us to shame, because the love of God has been bestowed in our hearts through the Holy Spirit which was given to us.

---

21. O'Neill, J.C., *Romans*, 83.
22. Harrison, *Paulines*, 79–85.

C 5:6 For while we were yet weak, in due season *Christ died for the ungodly.* 5:7 For scarcely *will one die for a righteous man.* Perhaps for the good man some one would even dare to *die.* 5:8 But God demonstrates his love toward us in that while we were still sinners *Christ died for us.*

  D 5:9 Much more then, now *having been justified* by his blood, we will be saved from the wrath through him.

    E 5:10 For if we were hostile, we were *reconciled to God through the death of his son.* Being reconciled, we will be saved by his life much more.

      F 5:11 Now not only so but we also rejoice in God through *our Lord Jesus Christ, through whom we have now received the reconciliation.*

        G 5:12 Therefore, as through one man *sin entered into the world and death through sin. And so death passed to all men* for that all sinned.

        G' 5:13 For *until the law sin was in the world. But sin is not imputed when there is no law.*

      F' 5:14 Nevertheless, death reigned from Adam until Moses even over them who had not sinned after the likeness of Adam's transgression, *who is a figure of the coming one.*

    E' 5:15 But not as the trespass, so also is the free gift. For if by the trespass of the one the many died, much more did the grace of God and the *gift by the grace of the one man, Jesus Christ,* abound to the many.

  D' 5:16 And not as through one that sinned is the gift. For the judgment came of one to condemnation, but the free gift came of many trespasses to *justification.*

C' 5:17 For if by the trespass of the one *death* reigned through the one, much more will those who receive the abundance of grace and the *gift of justification* reign in life through the one, *Jesus Christ.* 5:18 So then as condemnation came to all men through one trespass, so also through one act of righteousness justification of life came to all men.

B' 5:19 For as through the one man's disobedience the many were made sinners, even so through the obedience of the one shall the many be made righteous. 5:20 And the *law* came in besides that the *trespass* might abound. But where *sin* abounded *grace* did abound more exceedingly.

A' 5:21 So that as sin reigned in death even so might *grace* reign through *righteousness* to eternal life through *Jesus Christ our Lord.*

Rom 5:1-21 Chiastic Structure Table

| A 5:1–2a—justified ... Lord Jesus Christ ... grace | A' 5:21—righteousness ... Jesus Christ our Lord ... grace |

B 5:2b–5—tribulations ... tribulation ... steadfastness ... steadfastness ... character ... hope	B' 5:19–20—law ... trespass ... sin ... grace
C 5:6–8—Christ died for the ungodly ... will one die for a righteous man ... die ... Christ died for us	C' 5:17–18—Jesus Christ ... act of righteousness justification of life came to all men ... death ... gift of justification
D 5:9—having been justified	D' 5:16—justification
E 5:10—reconciled to God through the death of his son	E' 5:15—gift by the grace of the one man, Jesus Christ
F 5:11—our Lord Jesus Christ through whom we have now received the reconciliation	F' 5:14—who is a figure of the coming one
G 5:12—sin entered into the world, and death through sin and so death passed to all men	G' 5:13—until the law sin was in the world but sin is not imputed when there is no law

Commentary

Romans 5 is another one-unit chapter. In v. 5:1 there is a transition from Rom 4 to Rom 5 with the use of the words "justified by faith" which is similar to "justification" at v. 4:25, the end of the literary unit for Rom 4. The chiastic structure of Rom 5 depends more on concepts and less on repeated exact phrases than typical Pauline structures. Nonetheless, the structure can be discerned. The A stich matches first "having been justified," (*dikasiōthenes*) with "righteousness" (*dikiosynēs*), second, "Lord Jesus Christ" with "Jesus Christ our Lord," and third "grace." Harrison proposed that v. 5:1 had been interpolated.[23] Clearly Harrison is incorrect. Since v. 5:1 includes three word matches with v. 5:21 to form the A stich, it is original and written by Paul.

The B stich is somewhat different in that it is the arguments in both hemistiches that are parallel. This is another form of rhetorical parallelism, but not the repetition that Paul typically uses. The B hemistich argues that tribulation produces steadfastness, steadfastness produces character, and character produces hope. In the B' stich Paul argues that the law produced sin and sin produced grace. Another unusual aspect is that the B and B' hemistiches are not quite balanced, with the B hemistich containing fifty-two words and the B' hemistich containing only thirty-eight words. However, both are longer than typical Pauline chiastic hemistiches, and the arguments made in both hemistiches have a consistent flow. There is not an interruption of Paul's train of thought as would be found if there were an interpolation.

The C stich also matches concepts more than words or phrases. "Death" is a theme in both hemistiches and Jesus's atoning sacrifice is present in both hemistiches although described differently: "Christ died for the ungodly" versus "gift of justification ... through the one Jesus Christ" and "by the one act of righteousness justification

---

23. Harrison, *Paulines*, 79–85.

of life came to all men." Leander E. Keck proposed that vv. 5:6–7 had been interpolated.[24] He would eliminate the match of Jesus's death in the C hemistich. This would leave too much unmatched text in vv. 5:17–18. However, Fitzmeyer came to his rescue fourteen years later and proposed that v. 5:17 is also an interpolation.[25] It would seem unlikely that either of them is correct. If Keck is correct, Paul had too much text in the C' hemistich. If Fitzmeyer is correct, Paul had too much text in the C hemistich. If they are both correct, the interpolator correctly analyzed the chiastic structure and placed the interpolations perfectly to blend in with Paul's existing chiastic structure. This seems to be less likely than both passages being original to Paul.

The D stich matches "having been justified" and "justification." The E stich again matches concepts with "reconciled to God through the death of his son" matching "the gift of the grace of one man, Jesus Christ. In the F stich the F hemistich has "our Lord Jesus Christ through whom we have now received the reconciliation," and in the F' hemistich there is "who is a figure of the coming one." These phrases are parallel because Jesus is referred to as an agent of salvation in both.

The G center stich equates death with the law using the intermediary of sin. The G hemistich has "sin entered into the world, and death through sin, and so death passed to all men," and the G' hemistich has "until the law sin was in the world, but sin is not imputed when there is no law." Sin is common to both hemistiches, but death is in the G hemistich and law is in the G' hemistich.

O'Neill proposed that vv. 5:12–21, the entire second half of Rom 5, is an interpolation.[26] He admires the skill of the writer, but is of the opinion Paul did not write it. Rhetorical analysis does not agree. The chiasmus is too good. True, it matches concepts rather than the usual words, phrases or opposites, but the chances are very small that an interpolator would match Paul's concepts expressed at vv. 1–11 in exact reverse order. In addition, without vv. 5:12–21 there are no parallelisms and no defined literary unit.

Romans 6

This literary unit is a chiastic structure encompassing the entire chapter revealing an interpolation at Rom 6:19b.

Rom 6:1–23

A 6:1 What shall we say then? Shall we continue in *sin* that *grace* may abound? 6:2 May it never be. We who *died to sin*, how shall we any longer live therein? 6:3 Or

---

24. Keck, "The Post-Pauline Interpretation."
25. Fitzmeyer, *Romans*, 65.
26. O'Neill, *Romans*, 96.

are you ignorant that all we who were baptized into *Christ Jesus* were baptized into his death?

  B 6:4 We were buried therefore with him through baptism to death. That like as Christ was raised from the dead through the glory of the *father* so we also might walk in *newness of life*.

    C 6:5 For if we have become united with him in the *likeness of his death*, we will be also in the likeness of his resurrection.

      D 6:6 Knowing this, that our old man was crucified together, that the *body of sin* might be done away, that we are no longer *enslaved to sin*. 6:7 For he who has died is *justified from sin*. 6:8 But if we died with Christ, we believe that we will also live with him. 6:9 Knowing that Christ having been raised from the dead dies no more. Death no more has dominion over him.

        E 6:10 For the death that he died, he *died to sin* once. But the life that he lives, he lives to God.

          F 6:11 Even so reckon also *yourselves to be dead to sin* but alive to God in Christ Jesus. 6:12 Therefore, do not let *sin reign in your mortal body* that you should obey the lusts thereof.

            G 6:13a Neither *present your body parts* to sin as *tools of unrighteousness*.
            G' 6:13b But *present* yourselves to God as alive from the dead and *your body parts as tools of righteousness* to God.

          F' 6:14 For *sin will not have dominion over you*. For you are not under law but under grace. 6:15 What then? Should we *sin because we are not under law* but under grace? May it never be.

        E' 6:16 Do you not know that to whom you present yourselves as servants for obedience, you are his servants whom you obey, whether of *sin to death*, or of obedience to righteousness?

      D' 6:17 But thanks be to God, that whereas you were *servants of sin* you became obedient from the heart to that form of teaching to where you were delivered. 6:18 And being made *free from sin* you became servants of righteousness. 6:19a I speak after the manner of men because of the infirmity of your flesh.

(6:19b For as you presented your members as servants to uncleanness and to iniquity to iniquity, even so now present your members as servants to righteousness to sanctification.)

    6:20 For when you were *slaves of sin* you were free with regard to righteousness.
    C' 6:21 What fruit then did you have at that time in the things you are now ashamed of? For the *end of those things is death*.
   B' 6:22 But now being made free from sin and having become servants to *God* you have your fruit to sanctification, and the end *eternal life*.

A' 6:23 For the wages of *sin are death*; but the *gift* of God is eternal life in *Christ Jesus* our Lord.

Rom 6:1-23 Chiastic Structure Table

A 6:1-3—sin . . . grace . . . died to sin . . . Christ Jesus	A' 6:23—sin are death . . . gift . . . Christ Jesus
B 6:4—father . . . newness of life	B' 6:22—God . . . eternal life
C 6:5—the likeness of his death	C' 6:21—the end of those things is death
D 6:6-9—body of sin . . . enslaved to sin . . . justified from sin	D' 6:17-20—servants of sin . . . slaves of sin . . . free from sin
E 6:10—died to sin	E' 6:16—sin to death
F 6:11-12—yourselves to be dead to sin . . . sin therefore reign in your mortal body	F' 6:14-15—sin shall not have dominion over you. . . sin because we are not under law
G 6:13a—present your body parts . . . as tools of unrighteousness	G' 6:13b—present . . . your body parts as tools of righteousness

Commentary

This is the fourth chapter in a row wherein there is only one literary unit for the entire chapter. Romans 6 also has a transition from Rom 5 in the use of the word "grace" (*charis*) in v. 6:1 in parallel with v. 5:21. In this chiastic structure most of the matching words and phrases contain "sin" and "death." In the A hemistich there is "died to sin" matching "sin are death" in the A' hemistich. Also in the A hemistich "grace" (*charis*) matches "gift" (*charisma*) in the A' hemistich. In English this match might be overlooked, but it is more obvious in Greek. In addition "Christ Jesus" is found in both hemistiches of the A stich. In the B stich "God" matches "father" and "newness of life" matches "eternal life." The C stich contains "death" in both hemistiches. The D stich has three phrases about sin in both hemistiches: "body of sin" matches "servants of sin," "enslaved to sin" matches "slaves of sin," and "justified from sin" matches "free from sin." In the E stich "died to sin" (*apethanen tē hamartia*) matches "sin to death" (*hamartias eis thanaton*). This is another chiasm within the chiastic matches. Both hemistiches of the F stich contain "sin" twice. The center G stich matches two phrases: "present your body parts" found in both hemistiches and "as tools of unrighteousness (or righteousness)." Also "sin" is in the G hemistich and "dead" is in the G' hemistich.

Interpolation Rom 6:19b

The A stich is somewhat unbalanced with the A hemistich containing thirty-four words and the A' hemistich containing nineteen. However, with the obvious matches at the beginning, middle and end of the A hemistich, there is no clear section that can be identified as an interpolation. There is an identifiable interpolation in the middle of the D' hemistich at v. 6:19b. Both hemistiches of the D stich contain phrases about sin three times. In addition, both hemistiches in the D stich are rather long. The D hemistich contains forty-nine words and the D' hemistich has seventy words. However, v. 6:19 does not contain the word "sin," and if everything after the end of the first sentence ending in "your flesh" (*tēs sarkos hymōn*) is removed, the two hemistiches become balanced.

Wayne H. Hagen proposed that vv. 6:13 and 19 have been interpolated.[27] With respect to v. 6:13, that verse constitutes the center G stich of the chiastic structure. Rhetorical analysis does not detect any reason to suspect that the G stich has been interpolated. O'Neill proposed that vv. 6:4a, 5–7, and 17b–20 have been interpolated.[28] Bultmann agrees with O'Neill with respect to v. 6:17.[29] O'Neill and Hagen are correct with respect to v. 6:19b. O'Neill may be correct with respect to v. 6:4a. The B hemistich, v. 6:4, contains twenty-seven words and the B' hemistich, v. 6:22, contains twenty-one words. That is not greatly out of balance. Verse 6:4a does not contain any matching words with v. 6:22. It does contain nine words and removing it puts the B stich in better balance, but not perfect. Rhetorical analysis cannot determine that O'Neill is incorrect in his assessment with respect to v. 6:4a, but the stich is not so far out of balance that it can clearly be identified as an interpolation. However, the chiastic structure detected by rhetorical analysis has "death" in v. 6:21, the C' hemistich, matching "death" in v. 6:5, the C hemistich. Also phrases about sin are found three times in vv. 6:6–7, the D hemistich, and three times in vv. 6:17–20, the D' hemistich even if v. 6:19b is removed. This demonstrates that O'Neill is incorrect about vv. 6:5–7 being an interpolation. If O'Neill were correct that Paul's original Rom 6 did not contain vv. 6:5–7 nor 17b–19, then Paul had a faulty chiastic structure and the interpolator saved it by inserting just the right words.

Stiches	Words in first half	Words in second half	Words in interpolation
D	Rom 6:6–9–49	Rom 6:17–20–70	Rom 6:19b—26

---

27. Hagen, "Two Glosses," 364–67.
28. O'Neill, *Romans*, 110.
29. Bultmann, "Glossen," 202.

PART I | THE UNDISPUTED LETTERS

Romans 7

Romans 7 contains only one literary unit with a parallel structure defined by an inclusio. Each stich has two hemistiches except the D stich that contains six elements. O'Neill thought that the second half of the chapter has been interpolated,[30] but the literary structure, especially the inclusio, shows that to be unlikely.

Rom 7:1–25

  A 7:1 Or are you ignorant, brothers, (for I speak to those knowing the *law*) that the *law* has authority over a *man* for *as long a time as he lives*?
    B 7:2 For the married woman is bound by law to *the husband while he lives*. But if the *husband should die, she is discharged from the law* of the husband.
    B' 7:3 So then if *while the husband lives* she be joined to another man, she will be called an adulteress. However, if the *husband should die, she is free from the law*, so that she is not an adulteress though she be joined to another man.
      C 7:4 Therefore, my brothers, you also *were put to death* to *the law through the body* of Christ so that you should be joined to another even to him who was raised from the dead that we might *bring forth fruit* to God.
      C' 7:5 For when we were in the flesh the sinful passions, which were *through the law, working in our body parts* to *bring forth fruit* to death.
        D 7:6 But now we have been discharged from the law, *having died to that wherein we were held*. So that we serve in newness of the spirit and not in oldness of the letter. 7:7 What shall we say then? Is the law sin? May it never be. However, I had not known sin, except through the law. For I had not known coveting except *the law had said you will not covet*.
        D' 7:8 But sin finding occasion wrought in me through the *commandment* all manner of coveting. For apart from the law *sin is dead*.
        D" 7:9 And I was alive apart from the law once. But when the *commandment* came sin revived *and I died*.
        D''' 7:10 And the *commandment* that was to life, this I found to be *to death*.
        D"" 7:11 For sin finding occasion through the *commandment* beguiled me and through it *put me to death*. 7:12 So that the law is holy, and the *commandment* holy, and righteous, and good.
        D""' 7:13 Then did the thing that is good become death to me? May it never be. But sin that it might be shown to be sin by *working death* to me through the thing that is good. So that through the *commandment* sin might become exceeding sinful.
          E 7:14 For we know that the law is spiritual. But I am carnal sold under sin. 7:15 For *what I accomplish* I do not understand. For what I do not desire

---

30. O'Neill, *Romans*, 267–68.

that I practice. But what I hate *that I do.* 7:16 But if what I do not desire *that I do*, I consent to the law that it is good. 7:17 So now *it is no longer I that accomplish it but sin that dwells in me.*

E' 7:18 For I know that in me, that is, in my flesh dwells no good thing. For to desire is present with me but *to accomplish the thing* that is good is not. 7:19 For the good that *I desire I do not do*, but the evil that I do not desire *that I practice.* 7:20 But if what I do not desire *that I do, it is no longer I that accomplish it*, but *sin that dwells in me.*

F 7:21 *Therefore I find the law* that to me who desires do good evil is present with me. 7:22 For I delight *in the law of God with the inner man.*
F' 7:23 *But I see a different law* in my body parts warring against *the law of my mind* and making me captive to the law of sin which is in my body parts.

A' 7:24 Wretched *man that I am! Who will rescue me out of the body of this death?* 7:25 Thanks to God through Jesus Christ our Lord. So then I myself with the mind indeed serve God's *law* but with the flesh the *law of sin.*

Rom 7:1–25 Parallel Structure with Inclusio Table

A 7:1—law . . . law . . . man . . . as long a time as he lives	A' 7:24-25—law . . . law . . . man . . . will rescue me out of the body of this death				
B 7:2—husband while he lives . . . husband should die . . . she is discharged from the law	B' 7:3—while the husband lives . . . husband should die . . . she is free from the law				
C 7:4—were put to death . . . the law through the body . . . bring forth fruit	C' 7:5—to death . . . through the law working in our body parts . . . bring forth fruit				
D 7:6-7—having died to that wherein we were held . . . the law had said you will not covet	D' 7:8—sin is dead . . . commandment	D" 7:9—and I died . . . commandment	D''' 7:10—to death . . . commandment	D'''' 7:11-12—put me to death . . . commandment . . . commandment	D''''' 7:13—working death to me . . . commandment
E 7:14-17—what I accomplish . . . that I practice . . . that I do . . . that I do . . . it is no longer I that accomplish it . . . sin that dwells in me	E' 7:18-20—to accomplish that . . . that I practice . . . that I do . . . that I do . . . it is no longer I that accomplish it . . . sin that dwells in me				
F 7:21-22—therefore I find the law . . . in the law of God with the inner man	F' 7:23—but I see a different law . . . the law of my mind				

Part I | The Undisputed Letters

Commentary

Romans 7 is another chapter with only one literary structure. This is evident because of the inclusio, the A stich. Both hemistiches of the inclusio contain the words "man" once and "law" twice. There is also the phrase "for as long a time as he lives" in the A hemistich matching "will rescue me out of the body of this death" in the A' hemistich. The inclusio signals that the literary structure encompasses the entire chapter.

Joseph Fitzmeyer proposed that v. 7:6 is an interpolation.[31] However, v. 7:6 begins the D stich and sets out the full statement about having died to the law that is summarized in the following five D elements. If v. 7:6 were removed the matching phrases about death in the D stich would only exist in five of the six elements. Fitzmeyer is incorrect. O'Neil thought that the entire second half of the chapter vv. 7:14-25 is an interpolation. Bultmann agrees with O'Neill with regard to v. 7:25b.[32] Unfortunately, neither O'Neill nor Bultmann recognized the inclusio A stich with words throughout vv. 7:24-25 matching words found in v. 7:1, especially "law" twice in both hemistiches, which renders their opinions unlikely. In addition, the E and F stiches, vv. 7:14-23, are in the typical Pauline style with numerous parallel phrases. Within the inclusio the balance of the structure is a parallel one containing two hemistiches in each of the B, C, E, and F stiches and six elements in the D stich. The literary unit has a typical Pauline symmetry with two two-element stiches before and after the six-element D stich and the inclusio.

The B stich has three matches. First, "the husband while he lives" matches "while the husband lives." Second, "husband should die" is found in both hemistiches. Third, "she is discharged from the law" matches "she is free from the law." The C stich also has three matching phrases: "were put to death" matching "to death," "the law through the body" matching "through the law working in our body parts," and finally "bring forth fruit" found in both hemistiches.

The D stich interestingly contains six elements in the center of the literary unit. The parallelisms are based on dying to sin and commandments of the law. The initial D element is wordier than the following elements using "having died to that wherein we were held" while the remaining elements use "sin is dead," "and I died," "to death," "put me to death," and "working death to me." Likewise the second parallelism in the D element is "the law had said you will not covet" while the following elements use only "commandment."

In the E stich Paul is having fun with language. In these two hemistiches which encompass seven verses he uses three separate verbs that mean "to do:" "*katergazesthai*," "*poiō*" and "*prassō*." "*Katergazesthai*" is translated herein as "to accomplish," "*poiō*" as "I do," and "*prassō*" as "I practice" in order to show Paul's usage. He has used "to do" three times in the two hemistiches, "to accomplish" four times and "to practice"

---

31. Fitzmeyer, *Romans*, 65.
32. Bultmann, "Glossen," 198-99.

only twice. The use of "*prassō*" twice is the clue that there are only two hemistiches. In addition, "sin that dwells in me" is found only once in each hemistich.

In the F stich there are two parallel phrases in each hemistich. The first is "therefore I find the law" in the F hemistich parallel to "but I see a different law" in the F' hemistich. The second is "in the law of God with the inner man" in the F hemistich and "the law of my mind" in the F' hemistich.

Romans 8

Romans 8 has an interesting six-stich chiastic structure revealing two interpolations. The structure encompasses the entire chapter, and the D stich has three parallel elements in both hemistiches. In the D hemistich the word "spirit" is used in all three sub-hemistiches, but the word "spirit" found in the D' hemistich is only in the D'A' sub-hemistich.

Rom 8:1–39

  A 8:1 There is therefore now no condemnation to *those who are in Christ Jesus*.
    B 8:2 For the law of the spirit of *life* in Christ Jesus made you free from the law of sin and of *death*.
      C 8:3 For the law being powerless in that it was weak through the flesh, *God, sending his own son in the likeness of sinful flesh* and around sin, condemned sin in the flesh.
        DA 8:4 So that the righteousness of the law might be fulfilled in us, who do not walk according to the flesh but according to the *spirit*. 8:5 For those who are according to the flesh mind the things of the flesh. But those who are according to the *spirit*, the things of the *spirit*. 8:6 For the *mind* of the flesh is death, but the *mind of the spirit*, life and peace.
        DB 8:7 Because the mind of the flesh is hostility against *God*. For it is not subject to the law of *God*, neither indeed can it be. 8:8 And those who are in the flesh cannot please *God*. 8:9a Now you are not in the flesh but in the *spirit*, if indeed the *spirit* of God dwells in you.
        DC 8:9b But if any man does not have the *spirit* of *Christ* he is not of him. 8:10 If however *Christ* is in you, indeed the body is dead because of sin but the *spirit* is life because of righteousness. 8:11 But if the *spirit* of him that raised up *Jesus* from the dead dwells in you, he that raised up *Christ Jesus* from the dead shall give life also to your mortal bodies through his *spirit* that dwells in you. 8:12 So then, *brothers*, we are debtors not to the flesh to live according to the flesh.
          E 8:13 For if you live according to the flesh, you must die. But if by the spirit you put to death the deeds of the body, you shall live. 8:14

For as many as are led by the spirit of God these are *sons of God*. 8:15 For you did not receive the spirit of *bondage* again to fear. But you received the *spirit of adoption whereby we cry*, Abba, Father. 8:16 The spirit himself bears witness with our spirit, that we are *children of God*. 8:17a And if children, then heirs, heirs of God and *joint-heirs with Christ*.

> F 8:17b If indeed we *suffer* with him, so that we may be also *glorified* with him.
>
> F' 8:18 For I reckon that the *sufferings* of this present time are not comparable with the *glory* which shall be revealed to us.

E' 8:19 For the earnest expectation of the creation awaits the revelation of the *sons of God*. 8:20 For the creation was subjected to futility, not willingly, but by reason of him who subjected it, in hope 8:21 that the creation itself also shall be delivered from the *bondage* of corruption into the freedom of the glory of the *children of God*. 8:22 For we know that the whole creation groans and pains together until now. 8:23 And not only so but ourselves also who have the *first-fruits of the spirit*, even we ourselves *groan within ourselves awaiting adoption*, the redemption of our body.

(8:24 For in hope were we saved. But hope that is seen is not hope. For who hopes for that which he sees? 8:25 But if we hope for that which we do not see, we await it with patience.)

> D'A' 8:26 And in like manner the *spirit* also helps our frailty. For we do not know how to pray as we should. But the *spirit* himself makes intercession with unutterable groans. 8:27a And he that searches the hearts knows what is the *mind of the spirit*,
>
> > D'B' 8:27b because he makes intercession for the saints according to *God*. 8:28 And we know that to those who love *God* all things work together for good to those who are called according to his purpose.
> >
> > D'C' 8:29 For those whom he foreknew he also foreordained to be conformed to the image of his *son* that he might be the *firstborn* among many *brothers*. 8:30 And whom he foreordained, them he also called. And whom he called, them he also justified. And whom he justified, them he also glorified.

C' 8:31 What then shall we say to these things? If *God* is for us, who can be against us? 8:32 He who indeed did not spare *his own son but delivered him up for all of us*, how shall he not also freely grant us all things with him?

(8:33 Who shall bring accusation against God's elect? God justifies. 8:34 Who is one condemning? It is Christ Jesus who died but rather who was raised from the dead, who is at the right hand of God, who also intercedes for us. 8:35 Who will separate us from the love of Christ? Tribulation, or anguish, or persecution, or famine, or nakedness, or peril, or sword? 8:36 As it is written, "For your sake we are killed all the day long. We were regarded as sheep for the slaughter." 8:37 But in all these things we are more than conquerors through him that loved us.)

    B' 8:38 For I am persuaded that neither *death*, nor *life*, nor angels, nor principalities, nor things present, nor things to come, nor powers,
  A' 8:39 nor height, nor depth, nor any created thing, will be able to *separate us from the love of God in Christ Jesus* our Lord.

Rom 8:1-39 Chiastic Structure

A 8:1—those who are in Christ Jesus	A' 8:39—separate us from the love of God in Christ Jesus
B 8:2—life ... death	B' 8:38—life ... death
C 8:3—God having sent his own son in the likeness of sinful flesh	C 8:31-32—God his own son but delivered him up
DA 8:4-6—spirit ... spirit ... spirit ... mind ... mind ... mind of the spirit	D'A' 8:26-27a—spirit ... spirit ... mind of the spirit
DB 8:7-9a—God ... God ... God ... God	D'B' 8:27b-28—God ... God
DC 8:9b-12—Christ ... Christ ... Jesus ... Christ Jesus ... brothers	D'C' 8:29-30—son ... firstborn ... brothers
E 8:13-17a—sons of God ... bondage ... spirit of adoption ... whereby we cry ... children of God ... joint heirs with Christ	E' 8:19-23—son of God ... bondage ... awaiting adoption ... groan within ourselves ... children of God ... first fruits of the spirit
F 8:17b—suffer ... glorified	F' 8:18—suffering ... glory

Commentary

Romans 8 is another chapter with only one literary unit. It has a chiastic structure with an atypical parallel D stich, the fourth stich of six total. A number of Paul's chiastic structures have parallel sub-stiches, usually in the center stich, such as Rom 1:1-6 and 1 Cor 11. Here in Rom 8 the A stich matches "those who are in Christ Jesus" with "separate us from the love of God in Christ Jesus" and the B stich contains "life and death" in both hemistiches. The C stich has an interesting match with "God having sent his own son in the likeness of sinful flesh" in the C hemistich matching "his own son, but delivered him up." In this case the matching concept is God sending his son and delivering up his son.

The D stich is very interesting because each hemistich has three parallel sub-stiches. In the DA sub-stich both hemistiches contain the words "spirit" and "mind of the spirit." In the DB sub-stich both hemistiches contain the word "God," but the DB sub-hemistich continues the use of "spirit" while that is missing from the D'B' sub-hemistich. The DC sub-hemistich contains "Christ," "Jesus," and "Christ Jesus" while the D'C' sub-hemistich matches that with "son" and "firstborn." Both sub-hemistiches contain the word "brothers." The DC sub-hemistich also continues the use of the word "spirit," not found in the D'C' sub-hemistich.

Interpolations

Rom 8:24–25

There appear to be two interpolations into Rom 8, vv. 8:24–25 and vv. 8:33–37. Testing the text surrounding the apparent interpolation at vv. 8:24–25 finds that the DA sub-hemistich contains forty-six words and the D'A' sub-hemistich as defined herein (vv. 8:26–27) contains forty-one words. That is an acceptable balance. The hemistich adjacent to the D'A' sub-hemistich is the E' hemistich; therefore, the E stich must be tested. The E hemistich contains sixty-five words and the E' hemistich as defined contains eighty-two words. This appears to be somewhat unbalanced and further analysis is needed.

The initial conclusion is that the E' stich cannot bear the additional wording of vv. 8:24–25 because that exacerbates the lack of balance. In fact, it suggests that the interpolation is larger than initially assumed. A comparison of the E and E' hemistiches shows that "groan within in ourselves awaiting adoption" at the end of the E' hemistich matches nicely with "spirit of adoption whereby we cry" near the beginning of the E hemistich. Both phrases discussing adoption and uttering sounds. There are several more pairs of exact matching language in both hemistiches: "sons of God," "bondage," and "children of God." Moreover, there is a probable match of "joint heirs with Christ" in the E hemistich with "first fruit of the spirit" in the E' hemistich. It is assumed that Paul intended this match based on 1 Cor 15:23 wherein Paul calls Christ "the first fruits." The large number of matching phrases in the E and E' hemistiches as defined implies that Paul intended this parallel construction despite the lack of precise balance between the hemistiches.

Stiches	Words in first half	Words in second half	Words in interpolation
E' – D'A'	8:4–6, 8:13–17a—111	8:19–27a—148	8:24–25–25

Rom 8:33–37

The apparent interpolation at vv. 8:33–37 was analyzed. This passage falls between the C' and B' hemistiches. The B hemistich contains twenty words and the B' hemistich as defined contains seventeen words, a good balance. The C hemistich contains thirty words and the C' hemistich as defined contains thirty-five words, also a good balance. Neither the C' hemistich nor the B' hemistich can accept the large amount of text in vv. 8:33–37. Also militating against accepting it as original to Paul, vv. 8:33–37 contains no language matching either the B or C hemistiches and it disrupts Paul's train of thought. Romans 8:33 imposes a new term, "God's elect" (*electōn Theou*). In the Pauline letters this term is only used in Colossians, Titus and here in v. 8:33. This assumed interpolation also introduces a new concept into this literary unit regarding Christ's intercession with God for Christians. Plus, the interpolator anticipates Paul's conclusion that nothing can "separate us from the love of God in Christ Jesus our Lord" by asking "who will separate us from the love of Christ," which is not exactly the same thing. At v. 8:36 the interpolator quotes Ps 44:22 which seems out of place in the context of Paul's argument. In any case, the relatively short B and C stiches prove beyond doubt that vv. 8:33–37 are an interpolation.

Bultmann proposed that v. 8:1 is an interpolation,[33] and François Refoule proposed that vv. 8:9–11 is an interpolation.[34] O'Neill eliminated fully half (nineteen verses) of Rom 8.[35] His exorcism destroys the chiastic structure that rhetorical analysis reveals in the literary unit. Bultmann's elimination destroys the A stich by removing the A hemistich. The A hemistich has "those who are in Christ Jesus" which matches "separate us from the love of God in Christ Jesus." Paul managed to put "in Christ Jesus" (*en Christō Iēsou*) in both hemistiches making Bultmann's proposal unlikely. O'Neill eliminates v. 8:2, which removes the matching "life and death" of the B stich. However, in this particular case he also removes v. 8:38 that contains the matching "death and life." Therefore, in this particular case he has not harmed the chiastic structure. However, his actions assume that the interpolator realized there was a chiastic structure and when he added v. 8:2 realized he needed to add v. 8:38 to keep the structure balanced. Additionally, O'Neill has assumed the interpolator was astute enough to reverse the matching phrase to make it a chiasm within the chiastic structure, as Paul does a number of times in the undisputed letters. Or else it was just an amazing coincidence. It is more reasonable to conclude that O'Neill is wrong about his putative interpolations.

O'Neill's eliminations get rid of most of the unique D stich. He eliminated vv. 8:4b–10 and vv. 8:11c–14 in the D hemistich. Only v. 8:11a–b is retained. This removes all of the matching words and phrases found in the D stich except one occurrence each

33. Bultmann, "Glossen," 199.
34. Refoule, "Romains," 219–42.
35. O'Neill, *Romans*, 268.

of "spirit," "Jesus," and "Christ Jesus." In the D' hemistich O'Neill retains only v. 8:26 which contains "spirit" twice. So technically the D stich remains viable in O'Neill's revision with a match of the word "spirit." However, once again, O'Neill's supposed redactor cleverly constructed his interpolation to match the words "spirit," "mind of the spirit," "God," "son," "firstborn," and "brothers." Not only that, the redactor designed an atypical parallel sequence within the chiastic structure that is only found four other times in the undisputed letters at Rom 1:1–6, 1 Cor 11:1–34, 2 Cor 11:20–32, and Phil 1:7–2:4. If he existed, he would have been a very clever redactor indeed.

O'Neill also proposed eliminating 8:19–20 but retains most of the E stich. Interestingly, since he also eliminated 8:14, his redactor was clever enough to match "sons of God" in v. 8:14 and 19 in order to keep the chiastic structure balanced. Finally, O'Neill removes vv. 8:33 and 36 with which rhetorical analysis agrees, but he retains vv. 8:34 and 35 which greatly imbalances the remaining C stich. Then he eliminates vv. 8:38–39 which destroys the A stich as rhetorical analysis has determined it. This has the effect of making the C stich become the A stich because it contains the first matching phrases of the structure but it is greatly imbalanced and very un-Pauline.

Stiches	Words in first half	Words in second half	Words in interpolation
C' ⊥ B'	8:2–3–50	8:31–38–126	8:33–37–74

Romans 9

Romans 9 begins a sequence of three chapters containing some unusual aspects, and a number of scholars believe that Rom 9–11 is an interpolation. The reader will immediately see that this sequence contains typical Pauline literary units. A commentary section following Rom 11 discusses the arguments for and against Rom 9–11 being an interpolation. Romans 9 has a parallel structure with the first four stiches containing three elements.

Rom 9:1–33

The literary unit of Rom 9 is a parallel structure with fifteen stiches encompassing the entire chapter.

> A 9:1 I speak the truth in *Christ*, I am not lying, my conscience bearing witness with me in the Holy Spirit 9:2 that I have great sorrow and unceasing pain in my *heart*.
> A' 9:3 For I could wish that I myself were anathema from *Christ* for my brother's sake, my kinsmen according to the *flesh*,
> A" 9:4 who are Israelites. Whose is the adoption, and the glory, and the covenants, and the lawgiving, and the service, and the promises. 9:5 Whose are the patriarchs

and from whom is *Christ* as concerning the *flesh* who is over all, God blessed for ever. Amen.

B 9:6 But it is not as though the word of God has come to nothing. For they are not all *Israel that are of Israel*.

B' 9:7a Neither, because they are *Abraham's descendant* are they all children.

B" 9:7b But in *Isaac your descendants* will be called.

  C 9:8a That is, it is not the *children of the flesh*

  C' 9:8b that are *children of God*,

  C" 9:8c but the *children of the promise* are reckoned for a descendant.

    D 9:9 For this is a word of promise at the proper time I will come and *Sarah will have a son*.

    D' 9:10 And not only that, but *Rebecca also having conceived by one* by our father Isaac.

    D" 9:11 *For those not yet being born* neither having done anything good or bad that the purpose of God according to election might stand, not of works, but of the one calling.

      E 9:12 *It was said to her, "The elder will serve the younger."*

      E' 9:13 *As it is written, "Jacob I loved, but Esau I hated."*

        F 9:14 What shall we say then? Is there unrighteousness with God? May it never be! 9:15 For *he says to Moses*, "I will have mercy on whom I have mercy, and I will have compassion on whom I have compassion."

        F' 9:16 So then it is not of the willing nor of the running but showing mercy of God. 9:17 For the *scripture says to Pharaoh*, "For this very purpose did I raise you up, that I might show in you my power, and that my name might be declared throughout the Earth."

          G 9:18a So then he has *mercy on whom he will*,

          G' 9:18b and *whom he will he hardens*.

            H 9:19 You will *say then to me*, "Why does he still *find fault*? For who resists his will?"

            H' 9:20 Nay rather, O man, who are you that contradicts God? Shall the thing formed *say to him* that formed it, *Why did you make me this way*?

              I 9:21a Or has not the potter a right over the clay, from the same lump to make *one part a vessel to honor*,

              I' 9:21b and *another to dishonor*?

                J 9:22 But what if God willing to show his wrath and to make his power known, endured with much patience *vessels of wrath fitted for destruction*.

                J' 9:23 And that he might declare the riches of his glory upon *vessels of mercy*, which he *prepared beforehand for glory*.

                  K 9:24a Even us whom he called, not only *from the Jews*,

K' 9:24b but also *from the Gentiles?*

L 9:25 Also as *he says in Hosea*, "I will call those my people *who were not my people* and her beloved, who was not beloved."

L' 9:26 And it will happen that in the place where *it was said to them*, "You are not my people. There shall they be called sons of the living God."

M 9:27 And *Isaiah cries* concerning Israel, "If the number of the children of Israel be as the sand of the sea, the *remnant will be saved.*" 9:28 For the Lord will swiftly accomplish his word upon the Earth.

M' 9:29 And as *Isaiah foretold*, "Except the *Lord of Hosts had left us descendants*, we had become like Sodom and had been made like Gomorrah."

N 9:30 What shall we say then? That the Gentiles, who did not follow after righteousness, *attained righteousness*, the *righteousness of faith.*

N' 9:31 But Israel, following a *law of righteousness*, did not attain that law.

O 9:32 Why? Because it was not by *faith*, but by works. They stumbled at the *stone of stumbling.*

O' 9:33 As it is written, "Behold, I lay in Zion a *stone of stumbling* and a rock of offence. And he that *believes* on him will not be put to shame."

Romans 9:1-33 Parallel Structure Table

A 9:1-2—Christ...heart	A' 9:3—Christ...flesh	A" 9:4-5—Christ...flesh
B 9:6—Israel that are of Israel	B' 9:7a—Abraham's descendants	B" 9:7b—in Isaac your descendants
C 9:8a—children of the flesh	C' 9:8b—children of God	C" 9:8c—children of the promise
D 9:9—Sarah will have a son	D' 9:10—Rebecca also having conceived by one	D" 9:11—those not yet born
E 9:12—it was said to her...the elder will serve the younger	E' 9:13—as it is written...Jacob I loved, but Esau I hated	
F 9:14-15—he says to Moses	F' 9:16-17—scripture says to Pharaoh	
G 9:18a—mercy on whom he will	G' 9:18b—whom he will he hardens	
H 9:19—say then to me...why does he still find fault	H' 9:20—say to him...why did you make me this way	

I 9:21a – one part a vessel to honor	I' 9:21b—another to dishonor
J 9:22—vessels of wrath fitted for destruction	J' 9:23—vessels of mercy prepared beforehand for glory
K 9:24a—from the Jews	K' 9:24b—from the Gentiles
L 9:25—He says in Hosea . . . who were not my people	L' 9:26—it was said to them . . . you are not my people
M 9:27–28—Isaiah cries . . . the remnant will be saved	M' 9:29—Isaiah foretold . . . the Lord of hosts had left us descendants
N 9:30—attained righteousness . . . righteousness of faith	N' 9:31—did not attain that law . . . law of righteousness
O 9:32—faith . . . stone of stumbling	O' 9:33—believes . . . stone of stumbling

Commentary

The literary unit of Rom 9 has a parallel structure with fifteen stiches filled with quotations from the Old Testament. The first four stiches have three elements each and the remaining eleven have only two elements. There appears to be almost an inclusio since the A element contains the word "heart" and the same word is found at v. 10:1; however, v. 10:1 does not contain the word "Christ" as the other A elements do and "heart" is a common word in Paul's letters. This is probably a coincidence and not an intended inclusio.

In the A stich the A element contains "Christ" and "heart" while both the A' and A" elements contain "Christ" and "flesh." In the B stich there is a progression from "Israel, that are of Israel" in the B element to "Abraham's descendents" in the B' element to "in Isaac your descendents" in the B" element. The B" element is a quote of Gen 21:12. Then the C stich has another progression "children of the flesh," "children of God," and "children of the promise." Finally, the last three-element progression goes through the birth process in reverse in the D stich. This is "Sarah will have a son" in the D element, "Rebecca also having conceived by one" in the D' element, and "for those not yet being born" in the D" element. The D element is a quote of Gen 18:10 and 14.

The balance of the unit has parallel stiches with only two elements or hemistiches. The E stich contains quotes of Gen 25:23 and Mal 1:3. In the F hemistich there is a quote of Exod 33:19, and in the F' hemistich there is a quote of Exod 9:16. The H' hemistich contains quotes of Isa 29:16 and 45:9. In the L stich Paul first quotes Hos 2:23 and then Hos 1:10. The M stich contains two quotes from Isaiah, first is Isa 10:22–23 followed by Isa 1:9. In the O' hemistich, which ends the unit, Paul apparently has combined two quotes from Isaiah. He has combined elements of Isa 8:14 with Isa 28:16.

In twelve of the fifteen stiches Paul has mentioned some form of communication: speaking, saying, crying, written, or word. "I speak the truth" is in the A stich.

"Word of God" is in the B stich. "Word of promise" is in the D stich. "It was said to her" and "it is written" are in the E stich. "What shall we say then," "He says to Moses," and "scripture says to Pharaoh" are all in the F stich. "Say then to me" and " the thing formed say to him" are in the H stich. "He might declare" is in the J stich. "Whom he called" is in the K stich. "He says to Hosea" and "it was said to them" are in the L stich. "Isaiah cries" and "Isaiah foretold" are in the M stich. "What will we say then" is in the N stich. Finally "as it is written" is in the O stich.

Romans 10

Romans 10 has a nine-stich dual chiastic/parallel structure that reveals an interpolation at 10:6–7. The interpolation is a corrupted quote of Deut 30:12–13. The parallel structure is defined by an inclusio.

Rom 10:1–21

Chiastic Structure

> A 10:1 Brothers, my heart's desire and *my supplication to God is for their salvation.*
>> B 10:2 For I bear them witness that they have a zeal for God, but *not according to knowledge.*
>>> C 10:3 For *being ignorant of God's righteousness* and seeking to establish their own they did not submit themselves to the righteousness of God.
>>>> D 10:4 For *Christ* is the end of the law to righteousness to everyone who *believes.*
>>>>> E 10:5 For *Moses writes* that the man who does the righteousness of the law will live in it.

(10:6 But the righteousness which is of faith says thus, "Do not say in your heart, Who shall ascend into Heaven? (that is, to bring Christ down), 10:7 or, Who shall descend into the abyss? (That is, to bring Christ up from the dead).")

>>>>>> F 10:8 But *what does it say? The word is near you, in your mouth, and in your heart.* That is, the word of faith, which *we proclaim.*
>>>>>>> G 10:9a Because if you confess with your mouth Jesus is Lord, and *believe* in your heart that God raised him from the dead,
>>>>>>>> H 10:9b you *will be saved.*
>>>>>>>>> I 10:10 For with the heart is belief to righteousness. And *with the mouth is confession to salvation.* 10:11 For the scripture says, "Whoever believes in him shall not be put to shame."

I' 10:12 For there is no distinction between Jew and Greek. For the same Lord is Lord of all, and is *riches to all who call upon him*.

H' 10:13 For, "Whoever will call on the name of the Lord *will be saved*"

G' 10:14 How then will they call on him in whom they have not *believed*? And how will they *believe* in him whom they have not heard? And how will they hear without preaching?

F' 10:15 And how *will they proclaim* unless they be sent? Even *as it is written, "How beautiful are the feet of those proclaiming good news of good things!"*

E' 10:16 But they did not all heed the good news. For *Isaiah said*, "Lord, who has believed our report?"

D' 10:17 So *faith* comes from hearing, and hearing by the word of *Christ*.

C' 10:18 But I say, "*Did they not hear?*" Truly, Their sound went out into all the Earth, And their words to the ends of the world.

B' 10:19 But I say, "*Did Israel not know?*" First Moses says, "I will provoke you to jealousy with that which is no nation. With a nation without *understanding* I will anger you."

A' 10:20 And Isaiah is very bold and says, "I was found by those who did not seek me. I became manifest to those who did not ask about me." 10:21 But as to Israel he says, "*All day long I spread out my hands to a disobedient and contradicting people.*"

Rom 10:1-21 Chiastic Structure Table

A 10:1—my supplication to God is for their salvation	A' 10:20-21—all day long I spread out my hands to a disobedient and contradicting people
B 10:2—not according to knowledge	B' 10:19—did Israel not know . . . understanding
C 10:3—being ignorant of God's righteousness	C' 10:18—did they not hear
D 10:4—Christ . . . believes	D' 10:17—Christ . . . faith
E 10:5—Moses writes	E' 10:16—Isaiah said
F 10:8—what does it say . . . the word is near you in your mouth and in your heart . . . proclaim	F' 10:14b-15—as it is written . . . how beautiful are the feet of those proclaiming good news of good things . . . they will proclaim
G 10:9a—believe	G' 10:14a—believed
H 10:9b—will be saved	H' 10:13—will be saved
I 10:10-11—with the mouth is confession to salvation	I' 10:12—riches to all who call upon him

Parallel Structure

A 10:1 Brothers, my heart's desire and my *supplication to God is for their salvation*. 10:2 For I bear them witness that they have a zeal for God but not according to knowledge.

  B 10:3a For being ignorant of *God's righteousness* and seeking to establish their own,

  B' 10:3b they did not submit themselves to the *righteousness of God*.

    C 10:4 For Christ is the end of the *law to righteousness* to everyone who believes.

    C' 10:5 For Moses writes that the man who does the *righteousness of the law* will live in it.

(10:6 But the righteousness which is of faith says thus, "Do not say in your heart, Who shall ascend into Heaven? (that is, to bring Christ down), 10:7 or, Who shall descend into the abyss? (That is, to bring Christ up from the dead).")

    D 10:8 But what does it say? The *word is near you in your mouth* and in your heart. That is, the word of faith, which we proclaim.

    D' 10:9 Because if you *confess with your mouth* Jesus is lord and believe in your heart that God raised him from the dead, you will be saved.

      E 10:10 For with the heart is *belief to righteousness*. And with the mouth is confession to salvation.

      E' 10:11 For the scripture says, "Whoever *believes in him* shall not be put to shame."

        F 10:12 For there is no distinction between Jew and Greek. For the same lord is lord of all and is riches to all who call upon him. 10:13 For, "*Whoever will call on the name of the Lord* will be saved"

        F' 10:14 How then will *they call on him* in whom they have not believed? And how will they believe in him whom they have not heard? And how will they hear without preaching?

          G 10:15 And how will they proclaim, unless they be sent? Even as it is written, "How beautiful are the feet of them *proclaiming good news of good things!*"

          G' 10:16 But they did not *all heed the good news*. For Isaiah said, "Lord, who has believed our report?"

            H 10:17 So faith comes from hearing, and *hearing by the word of Christ*.

            H' 10:18 But I say, "*Did they not hear?*" Truly, their sound went out into all the Earth and their words to the ends of the world.

              I 10:19a But I say, "*Did Israel not know?*" First Moses says, "I will provoke you to jealousy with that which is no nation.

I' 10:19b *With a nation without understanding* I will anger you."

J 10:20a And Isaiah is very bold, and says, "*I was found by those who did not seek me.*

J' 10:20b I became *manifest to those who did not ask about me.*"

A' 10:21 But as to Israel he says, "All day long I spread out my hands to a *disobedient and contradicting people.*"

Rom 10:1–21 Parallel Structure Table

A 10:1–2—supplication to God is for their salvation	A' 10:21—disobedient and contradicting people
B 10:3a—God's righteousness	B' 10:3b—righteousness of God
C 10:4—law to righteousness	C' 10:5—righteousness of the law
D 10:8—word is near you in your mouth	D' 10:9—confess with your mouth
E 10:10—belief to righteousness	E' 10:11—believes in him
F 10:12–13 whoever will call on the name of the Lord	F' 10:14 they call on him
G 10:15—proclaiming good news of good things	G' 10:16—all heed the good news
H 10:17—hearing the word of Christ	H' 10:18—did they not hear
I 10:19a—did Israel not know	I' 10:19b—a nation without understanding
J 10:20—I was found by those who did not seek me	J' 10:20b—I became manifest to those who did not ask about me.

Commentary

Chiastic Structure

In the A stich Paul writes with regard to Israel that "my supplication to God is for their salvation" in the A hemistich. Then in the A' hemistich he gives God's answer to his prayer: "All day long I spread my arms to a disobedient and contradicting people" quoting Isa 65:2. The B stich is also about Israel and matches "not according to knowledge" with "did Israel not know." Paul also quotes Isa 65:1 in the B' hemistich. The C stich matches "being ignorant of God's righteousness" with "did they not hear." The D stich matches "Christ" and "believing" with "Christ" and "faith."

The E stich matches "Moses writes" and "Isaiah says" followed by a quote of Lev 18:5 in the E hemistich and Isa 53:1 in the E' hemistich. Leviticus 18:5 is a good summary of Deut 30:15–20 and provides a segue for Paul to quote Deut 30:14 in the F hemistich. The F stich matches "we proclaim" with "will they proclaim." Similarly, it matches "what does it say" with "as it is written." Then it matches two Old Testament quotes "the word is near you, in your mouth and in your heart" from Deut 30:14 with "how beautiful are the feet of those proclaiming good news of good things" from Isa 52:7. Obviously, "words in your mouth and heart" is parallel to "proclaiming good news." These two matching quotes of about the same length are additional proof that the longer quote from Deut 30:12–13 is an interpolation in that the longer quote overbalances the stich.

The G stich matches "believe" once in the G hemistich and twice in the G' hemistich. The H stich matches "will be saved" in both hemistiches. The center I stich matches "with the mouth a confession to salvation" with "riches to all who call upon him." The match here is "confession" with "call upon him" and "salvation" with "riches" matching similar theological concepts. At Rom 10:11 Paul again quotes Isa 28:16 repeating the quote from Rom 9:33.

Parallel Structure

In the parallel structure the A stich is an inclusio identical to the A stich in the chiastic structure. The remaining ten stiches all have two hemistiches. The B stich matches "God's righteousness" with "the righteousness of God." The C stich has a similar match "the law to righteousness" and "righteousness of the law." The D stich continues matching phrases containing identical words with "word is near you in your mouth" in the D hemistich matching "confess with your mouth." The E stich of the parallel structure matches "belief to righteousness" with "believes in him" quoting Isa 28:16. The F stich has "whoever will call upon the name of the Lord" in the F hemistich and "they call on him" in the F' hemistich. The G stich matches "proclaiming good news of good things" with "all heed the good news." The H hemistich has "hearing by the word of Christ," and the H' hemistich has "did they not hear." In the I stich "did Israel not know" matches "a nation without understanding" as Paul quotes Moses obviously writing about Israel. The J stich is a match containing another quote from Isaiah "I was found by them that did not seek me" in the J hemistich matching "manifest to those who did not ask about me" in the J' hemistich.

Interpolation Rom 10:6–8

The chiastic structure of Rom 10 reveals an interpolation at vv. 10:6–7 which is a corruption of Deut 30:12–13. This is interesting because Paul quotes Deut 30:14 at v. 10:8. Paul often quotes the Old Testament especially in Romans. It would be impossible for scholars using traditional methods of detecting interpolations to detect an interpolation of an Old Testament quote. This is because Paul often quotes the Old Testament and the wording and phraseology would be expected to differ from Paul's style of writing. However, rhetorical analysis can reveal an offending Old Testament quote that Paul did not intend. Looking at the E' and F' hemistiches in the chiastic structure there are a total of forty-two words in both hemistiches. However, in the E and

F hemistiches, including the suspected interpolation, there are a total of seventy-six words, obviously too many for balanced stiches. Eliminating the interpolation reduces the E and F hemistiches to forty-three words, much more balanced. In addition, the E hemistich quotes Lev 18:5. The F hemistich as it is defined above quotes Deut 30:14. The E' hemistich quotes Isa 53:1, and the F' hemistich quotes Isa 52:7. Apparently the interpolator recognized that v. 10:8 quoted Deut 30:14, and he thought it would be clever to quote Deut 30:12–13 immediately before that, substituting "Christ" for "commandments" and "abyss" for "sea" as found in Deuteronomy.

Stiches	Words in first half	Words in second half	Words in interpolation
E – F	10:5–8 – 76	10:14b–16–42	10:6–7–33

Romans 11

Romans 11 has a parallel structure encompassing the entire chapter with a three-element stich ending the literary unit. There is an unusual interpolation at the end of the chapter.

Rom 11:1–32

A 11:1 I say then, *"Did not God reject his people?"* May it never be. For I am also an Israelite of the seed of Abraham of the tribe of Benjamin.
A' 11:2 *God did not reject his people* whom he foreknew. Or do you not know what the scripture says in Elijah? How he pleads with God against Israel.
 B 11:3 "Lord, they have killed your prophets, they have demolished your altars, *and I am left alone*, and they are seeking my life."
 B' 11:4 But what was the divine answer to him? *"I have left for myself seven thousand men* who have not bowed a knee to Baal."
  C 11:5 Thus then also at the present time there has been a *remnant according to the election of grace.* 11:6a But if it is by *grace*, it is not by works.
  C' 11:6b Otherwise *grace is not grace.* 11:7 What then? That which Israel seeks it did not obtain. *Now the elect obtained it*, but the rest were hardened.
   D 11:8 *As it has been written,* "God gave them a spirit of stupor, *eyes that do not see,* and *ears that do not hear* to this very day."
   D' 11:9 *And David says,* "Let their table be a snare and a trap and a stumbling block and a retribution to them. 11:10 Let their eyes be darkened that they may not see, and their *backs forever bent over."*
    E 11:11 I say then, "Did they not stumble that they might fall?" May it never be! *But in their transgression is salvation to the Gentiles* to provoke them to jealousy.

E' 11:12 But if their transgression is the riches of the world *and their loss the riches to the Gentiles*, how much more their fullness?

F 11:13 But *I speak to you who are Gentiles*. Inasmuch then as I am an apostle to the Gentiles, I honor my ministry.

F' 11:14 If at all *I will provoke to anger my kin* and shall save some of them.

G 11:15a For if the *rejection of them* is the *reconciliation of the world*,

G' 11:15b what will the *acceptance of them* be except *life out from the dead*?

H 11:16 And if the first fruit is sacred, so is the lump. And if the *root* is sacred, so are the *branches*. 11:17 But if some of the *branches* were broken off and you, being a wild olive were *grafted* in among them and became partaker with them of the rich *root* of the olive tree,

H' 11:18 do not boast about the *branches*. But if you boast, it is not you that supports the *root* but the *root* supports you. 11:19 You will say then, branches were broken off that I might be *grafted* in.

I 11:20 Rightly so for *their lack of faith* they were broken off, but you stand by your faith. Do not be high minded but be afraid. 11:21 For if *God* did not spare the natural branches *neither will he spare you*.

I' 11:22 Behold then the kindness and severity of *God. Toward those who fell, severity*, but toward you, *God's* kindness, if you continue in his kindness. Otherwise you also will be cut off. 11:23 And they also, if they do not continue *their lack of faith*, will be grafted in. For *God* is able to graft them in again.

J 11:24a For if you were cut out of a natural wild *olive tree* and were *grafted* contrary to nature into a cultivated *olive tree*,

J' 11:24b how much more shall these natural branches be *grafted* into their own *olive tree*?

K 11:25 For brothers, I would not want you to be ignorant of this mystery, lest you be wise in your own opinion, that a *hardness* in part has occurred to *Israel* until the *fullness of the Gentiles may arrive*.

K' 11:26 And so all *Israel* shall be saved. As it has been written, "There shall come out of Zion the Deliverer. He shall take away *ungodliness* from Jacob. 11:27 And this is my covenant to them, Then *I will take away their sins*."

L 11:28a *Regarding the gospel*, they are enemies for your sake.

L' 11:28b But *regarding the election*, they are beloved because of the patriarchs.

M 11:29 For the gifts and the calling of God are irrevocable. 11:30 For just as you in time past were *disobedient* to God, but now have obtained *mercy* by their *disobedience*.

M' 11:31 So also have these now been *disobedient*, that by the *mercy* shown to you they also may now obtain *mercy*.
M" 11:32 For God has subjected all to *disobedience*, that he might have *mercy* upon all.

(11:33 O the depth of the riches both of the wisdom and the knowledge of God! how unfathomable are his judgments, and his ways incomprehensible! 11:34 For who has known the mind of the Lord? Or who has been his counselor? 11:35 Or who has first given to him, and it shall be recompensed to him again? 11:36 For of him, and through him, and to him, are all things. To him be the glory for ever. Amen.)

Rom 11:1-32 Parallel Structure Table

A 11:1—did not God reject his people	A' 11:2—God did not reject his people
B 11:3—and I am left alone	B' 11:4—I have left for myself seven thousand men
C 11:5-6a—remnant according to the election . . . grace . . . grace	C' 11:6b-7—now the elect obtained it . . . grace . . . grace
D 11:8—as it has been written . . . eyes that do not see . . . ears that do not hear	D' 11:9-10—and David says . . . let their eyes be darkened that they may not see . . . backs forever bent over
E 11:11—but in their transgression is salvation to the Gentiles	E' 11:12—and their loss the riches to the Gentiles
F 11:13—I speak to you who are Gentiles	F' 11:14—I will provoke to anger my kin
G 11:15a—rejection of them . . . reconciliation of the world	G' 11:15b—acceptance of them . . . life out from the dead
H 11:16-17—root . . . branches . . . branches . . . grafted . . . root	H' 11:18-19—root . . . branches . . . branches . . . grafted . . . root
I 11:20-21—their lack of faith . . . God . . . neither will he spare you	I' 11:22-23—their lack of faith . . . God . . . God . . . God . . . toward those who fell severity
J 11:24a—olive tree . . . grafted . . . olive tree	J' 11:24b—grafted . . . olive tree
K 11:25—hardness . . . Israel . . . fullness of the Gentiles may arrive	K' 11:26-27—ungodliness . . . Israel . . . I will take away their sins
L 11:28a—regarding the gospel	L' 11:28b—regarding the election
M 11:29-30—disobedient . . . mercy . . . disobedience	M' 11:31—disobedient . . . mercy . . . mercy / M" 11:32—disobedience . . . mercy

Part I | The Undisputed Letters

Commentary

The A stich matches "did God not reject his people" with "God did not reject his people." The B stich matches "and I am left alone" with "I have left for myself seven thousand men." The C stich matches "a remnant according to the election" and "grace" twice in the C hemistich with "now the elect obtained it" and "grace" twice in the C' hemistich. The D stich contains three matching phrases: first, "as it has been written" matches "David says," second, "eyes that do not see" matches "let their eyes be darkened that they do not see," and third, "ears that do not hear" matches "backs forever bent over."

The E stich matches "in their transgression is salvation for the Gentiles" with "their loss riches to the Gentiles." Here is another match of "salvation" with "riches" or "treasure." The F stich matches "I speak to you who are Gentiles" with "I will provoke to anger my kin," Paul's kin being Jews. The G stich contains two matches: first, "rejection of them" in the G hemistich matches its opposite "acceptance of them," then "reconciliation of the world" in the G hemistich matches "life out from the dead" in the G' hemistich. Both hemistiches of the H stich contain "root" twice, "branches" twice, and "grafted" once. Both hemistiches of the I stich contain "God" and "their lack of faith." The I stich also matches "neither will he spare you" with "toward those who fell, severity."

Both hemistiches of the J stich contain "olive tree" and "grafted." Both hemistiches of the K stich contain "Israel." "Hardness" in the K hemistich is matched with "ungodliness" in the K' hemistich, and "fullness of the Gentiles may arrive" in the K hemistich is matched with "I will take away their sins." In the L stich "regarding the gospel" is matched with "regarding the election." The M final stich contains three elements. All three contain "disobedience" and "mercy."

Interpolation Rom 11:33–36

In Rom 11 there is a thirteen stich parallel structure in the A, A'; B, B'; C, C' format and apparently an interpolator has stuck in another Old Testament quote from Isa 40:13–14. The quote begins at v. 11:34, with the interpolator providing an introduction at v. 11:33 and a closing at 11:36. To be fair, Paul actually does quote Isa 40:13–14 at 1 Cor 2:16, but vv. 11:34–35 seems to be an interpolation. As an initial proposition, the usual rhetorical analysis is not applicable in this case because this suspected interpolation comes at the end of a parallel literary unit and not between stiches. Therefore, there cannot be an analysis of the balance of elements or hemistiches. However, other aspects can be investigated. In each of the thirteen stiches of the Rom 11 literary unit there is always a repeated significant word, but there seem to be no repeated significant words in vv. 11:33–36. In addition, the entire sequence seems to have nothing to do with the rest of the unit about Jews straying from God, Gentiles inheriting their position with God, and God accepting back the Jews who repent. The suspect passage is a disruption. The interpolator acknowledges that his addition is a disruption by ending it with "amen." This has occurred previously in the interpolation at Rom 1:20–25.

It is clear that the suspect passage vv. 11:33–36 is devoid of repeating significant words unlike the stiches in the literary unit Paul wrote. The offending passage does not fit into this literary unit and is probably an interpolation. O'Neill thought that the entire chapter 11 of Romans is an interpolation.[36]

Stiches	Words in first half	Words in second half	Words in interpolation
-	-	-	11:33–36–53

Romans 9–11 As an Interpolation

There are oddities in Rom 9–11 that have caused scholars to question whether these three chapters of Romans are in fact by Paul.[37] One apparent anomaly in Rom 9–11 is that except for vv. 9:24 and 10:12, Paul uses the word "Israel" to refer to the Jews in these three chapters while the balance of Romans refers to Israelites as "Jews." Paul does use the term "Israel" in 1 Corinthians, 2 Corinthians, Galatians, and Philippians so it is not unheard of in Pauline letters. Analyzing Paul's use of "Jews" and "Israel" more closely, one finds that in the undisputed letters Paul used "Jews" eighteen times and "Israel" twenty-one times. Basically Paul uses the term "Jews" to contrast with Greeks six times, to contrast with Gentiles seven times, to accuse of being corrupt three times, plus Paul says he "became like a Jew to gain the Jews." When Paul uses the term "Israel" it is in conjunction with an Old Testament character, Moses, Abraham, Isaiah, Elijah, David, God, or the tribe of Benjamin. He also uses it in identifying his kinsmen, the law of righteousness, or eating sacrifices of the altar. The uses of "Jews" at Rom 9:24 and 10:12 are in contrast with Gentiles and Greeks respectively. The use of "Israel" at 1 Cor 10:18 is in the context of eating sacrifices at the altar. The uses of "Israel" at 2 Cor 3:7 and 13 are connected to Moses. The use of "Israel" at 2 Cor 11:22 is in connection with Abraham. The use of "Israel at Gal 6:16 is in connection with God. Finally, the use of "Israel" at Phil 3:5 is in connection with the tribe of Benjamin. Therefore, the use of "Israel" in Rom 9–11 is not anomalous as compared to the other undisputed letters and is very munch in keeping with Paul's style.

There is an anomaly in this section concerning quotations from the Old Testament. In Paul's seven undisputed letters he quotes the Old Testament eighty-three times. Most of the time he either fails to tell the reader he is quoting the Old Testament or he introduces the quote with the generic "as it is written." However, seventeen times

---

36. O'Neill, *Romans*, 269.
37. Van Manen, "Romans (Epistle)," 4129.

out of the eighty-three Paul informs the reader that he is quoting Isaiah, Moses, David, Elijah, or Hosea. Of those seventeen attributed quotes, twelve are in Rom 9–11, four are in Rom 15 and one is in 1 Corinthians. Therefore, Romans contains ninety-four percent of all of Paul's attributed quotes from the Old Testament, and Rom 9–11 contains seventy-one percent of those. This may indicate there is a connection between Rom 9–11 and Rom 15. It so happens that there are early manuscripts of Romans that do not contain Rom 15–16 leading some scholars to opine that Rom 15–16 is also a later addition.[38] Marcion's copy of Romans did not contain chapters 15 and 16.[39] This is some evidence that Rom 9–11 was not original to Romans.

In addition, there seems to be a rather smooth transition from the end of Rom 8 to the beginning of Rom 12. Here is the text without Rom 9–11:

> 8:38 For I am persuaded, that neither death, nor life, nor angels, nor principalities, nor things present, nor things to come, nor powers, 8:39 nor height, nor depth, nor any created thing, will be able to separate us from the love of God in Christ Jesus our Lord.
>
> 12:1 I beseech you therefore, brothers, by the mercies of God, to present your bodies a living sacrifice, holy, acceptable to God, which is your reasonable worship.

Note how "neither death nor life" in 8:38 is echoed by "living sacrifice" in 12:1. Additionally, the use of "therefore" (*oun*) in 12:1 makes perfect sense.

With respect to rhetorical analysis, Rom 9–11 certainly appears Pauline. Romans 9 has a long parallel structure with fifteen stiches, Rom 10 has a dual chiastic/parallel structure, and Rom 11 also has a long parallel structure with twelve stiches. Romans 9:1 begins the section with Paul saying, "I speak the truth in Christ, I am not lying." This is not unusual of Paul. In three of the seven undisputed letters Paul says he is not lying.[40] The first three stiches in Rom 9 each have three elements and the last stich in Rom 11 has three elements. When compared to the rest of the undisputed letters these three literary units appear to be structures one would expect Paul to have written. In the comments to Rom 6 it was noted that v. 6:1 contained the same word "grace" that appeared in v. 5:21, implying that there was a connection between the Rom 5 literary unit and the Rom 6 literary unit, providing evidence that they were consecutive in the original letter. A similar construction is found at v. 12:1 where Paul has written "mercies of God" (*oiktirmōn tou Theou*). A similar phrase "he might have mercy upon all" (*pantas eleēsē*) is the last phrase of v.11:32 before the interpolation identified at vv. 11:33–36. In fact, "mercy" is a matching word defining the three-element M stich concluding Rom 11. A different word for "mercy" has been used in v. 12:1, but the phrase at the beginning of Rom 12 appears to echo the end of Rom 11. "*Oiktirmōn*"

---

38. Bruce, *Romans*.
39. Van Manen, "Romans (Epistle)," 4128.
40. Rom 9:1; 2 Cor 11:31; Gal 1:20.

is a noun and "*eleēsē*" is a verb with a different root. Paul uses both "*oiktirmōn*" and "*eleēsē*" in other undisputed letters. This would imply that Rom 9–11 is original to the letter and its original position was immediately preceding Rom 12.

As a separate unit Rom 9–11 is very symmetrical with Rom 9 having a parallel structure, Rom 10 having a dual chiastic/parallel structure, and Rom 11 having a parallel structure. The first stich in Rom 9 has three elements and the last stich in Rom 11 has three elements. The section has Pauline style literary units although it has unusual attributes in vocabulary and argument as compared to other undisputed letters as discussed. The conclusion here is that Paul wrote Rom 9–11, perhaps for another purpose, and he thought that this exposition on the salvation of Israel fit into the letter and he inserted it into Romans after Rom 8. This conclusion is similar to that of C.H. Dodd in his *Epistle of Paul to the Romans*.[41] Rhetorical analysis shows that an interpolator added vv. 10:6–8 and 11:33–36.

O'Neill, on the other hand, cuts the baby in half. He thought almost half of Rom 9 is original to Paul as is about a third of Rom 10.[42] He thought vv. 9:4–5 are an interpolation.[43] Fitzmeyer agrees with him with regard to v. 9:5.[44] From a rhetorical analysis standpoint that eliminates the third element of the parallel A stich with its matching language of "Christ" and "flesh." In rhetorical analysis the first four stiches of Rom 9 all have three elements. If O'Neill is correct, the interpolator supplied a missing third element of Paul's original A stich. O'Neill also declared that vv. 9:11–24 is an interpolation.[45] Eliminating v. 9:11 destroys Paul's regression found in the D stich from "Sarah will have a son" to "Rebecca having conceived by one" to "for those not yet being born," and it means the interpolator recognized the regression and continued it. So according to O'Neill's analysis the interpolator inserted third elements in both the A and D stiches to match Paul's original three-element B and C stiches. This seems highly unlikely.

According to O'Neill after supplying third elements to the A and D stiches, the interpolator continued Paul's parallelism inserting the E – K stiches in the Pauline style, but only used two elements in each of these stiches. O'Neill declared that the final interpolation into Rom 9 is vv. 9:28–29.[46] The problem with removing v. 9:29 is that it destroys the M stich by removing the M' hemistich and the second quote from Isaiah which provides a match for the first quote. This means that v. 9:27 is part of either the L' hemistich or the N' hemistich and whichever one it is assigned to becomes much too long and destroys the Pauline balance. The analysis of the literary unit shows that both the L and N stiches are nicely balanced as is.

41. Dodd, *Romans*.
42. O'Neill, *Romans*, 268–69.
43. O'Neill, *Romans*, 153.
44. Fitzmeyer, *Romans*, 65.
45. O'Neill, *Romans*, 155.
46. O'Neill, *Romans*, 161.

O'Neill retains vv. 10:1–6a as being original to Paul and discards the rest of Rom 10 and all of Rom 11,[47] Fitzmeyer agrees with O'Neill with respect to vv. 10:9 and 11:6,[48] and Bultmann agrees with him with respect to v. 10:19.[49] For O'Neill to be correct, however, one would have to assume that the interpolator took Paul's vv. 10:1–5, which only had the beginnings of a structure (two matching phrases), and constructed a dual chiastic/parallel literary unit for the balance of Rom 10, which is blatantly preposterous. Finally, the interpolator constructed Rom 11 as a parallel literary unit to match the Rom 9 unit so that the section as a whole has a symmetrical construction.

Romans 12–13

The two relatively short chapters of Rom 12–13 are actually one Pauline literary unit. Both chapters are series of admonitions by Paul and there is no obvious break. Apparently Bishop Langdon did not want to make this literary unit one long chapter of thirty-five verses.

Rom 12:1—13:14

A 12:1 I beseech you therefore, brothers, by the mercies of *God* to present your bodies a living sacrifice, *holy, acceptable* to *God*, which is your reasonable worship.
A' 12:2 And not be conforming to this age. But be transformed by the renewing of your mind for you to prove what is the *good and acceptable* and perfect will of *God*.
 B 12:3 For I say, through *the grace having been given to me* to everyone being among you, not to think of himself more highly than he ought to think. But to think as to be sober minded, as God has *allotted to each a measure of faith*. 12:4a For even as we have many members in one body.
 B' 12:4b And all the members have not the same function. 12:5 So we who are many are one body in Christ and individually members one of another. 12:6 However, we are having different gifts according to *the grace having been given to us*, if prophecy, prophesy *according to the proportion of your faith*.
  C 12:7a Or *ministry*, in the ministry,
  C' 12:7b or *teaching*, in the teaching,
  C" 12:7c or *encouraging*, in the encouraging.
  C'" 12:8a. *Giving*, in generosity;
  C"" 12:8b *leading*, in diligence;
  C""" 12:8c *showing mercy*, in cheerfulness.
   D 12:9a Let *love* be sincere.
   D' 12:9b *Abhorring evil.*

---

47. O'Neill, *Romans*, 168–70.
48. Fitzmeyer, *Romans*, 65.
49. Bultmann, "Glossen," 199.

D" 12:9c *Cleaving to good.*
D''' 12:10a In *brotherly love* be devoted to one another;
D'''' 12:10b in *honor* preferring one another;
D''''' 12:11a in *diligence* not slothful;
D'''''' 12:11b being *fervent* in spirit;
D''''''' 12:11c *serving* the Lord;
D'''''''' 12:12a *rejoicing* in hope;
D''''''''' 12:12b being *patient* in tribulation;
D'''''''''' 12:12c *continuing* steadfastly in prayer;
D''''''''''' 12:13a *contributing* to the needs of the saints;
D'''''''''''' 12:13b *pursuing* hospitality.
  E 12:14a *Bless* those who persecute you.
  E' 12:14b *Bless*, and do not curse.
   F 12:15a *Rejoice* with the rejoicing.
   F' 12:15b *Weep* with the weeping.
    G 12:16a *Be of the same mind* toward one another.
    G' 12:16b *Do not set your mind* on high things, but go along with the lowly.
    G" 12:16c *Do not become wise* in your own opinion.
     H 12:17a Render to *no one evil for evil.*
     H' 12:17b Plan to be *virtuous in the sight of all men.*
     H" 12:18 If possible for you *be at peace with all men.*
      I 12:19a Do not *avenge* yourselves, beloved, but give place to his wrath.
      I' 12:19b For it is written, "*Vengeance* is mine." "I will recompense," the Lord says.
       J 12:20a But if your enemy be *hungry*, feed him.
       J' 12:20b If he be *thirsty*, give him drink. For in doing this you will heap coals of fire upon his head.
        K 12:21a Do not be *overcome by evil*,
        K' 12:21b but *overcome evil* with good.
         L 13:1 Let every soul *obey* the superior *authorities*. For there is no *authority* but from *God*; and those having been *ordained* by God.
         L' 13:2 Therefore anyone *resisting* the *authority*, withstands the *ordinance* of God. And those *resisting* will receive judgment on themselves.
          M 13:3 *For rulers are not a terror* to *good* work but to *evil.* And do you desire not to fear the *authority*? Do *good* things, and you will have praise from him.

M' 13:4a *For he is a servant of God* to you for *good*. But if you do *evil* things be afraid. For he does not bear the sword in vain.

M" 13:4b *For he is a servant of God*, an avenger for wrath to anyone doing *evil*. 13:5 Therefore you need to be subject, not only because of the wrath, but also for the sake of conscience.

N 13:6 Because of this *you pay taxes also*. For they are servants of God, attending upon this very thing.

N' 13:7 *Render* to all what is due them. *Tax to whom tax is due*, revenue to whom revenue, respect to whom respect, honor to whom honor.

O 13:8 Owe no man anything, except to love one another. For *he that loves another* has *fulfilled the law*.

O' 13:9 For this, you shall not commit adultery, you shall not kill, you shall not steal, you shall not covet, and if there be any other *commandment*, it is summed up in this word, namely, *you will love your neighbor* as yourself.

O" 13:10 *Love does no evil to his neighbor*. Love therefore is the *fulfillment of the law*.

P 13:11 And this, knowing the season, that already *it is the hour for you to awaken out of sleep*. For now is salvation nearer to us than when we first believed.

P' 13:12 *The night is nearly over, and the day draws near*. We should therefore cast off the works of darkness, but we should put on the armor of light.

P" 13:13 *We should walk properly, as in the day*; not in reveling and drunkenness, not in sexual immorality and licentiousness, not in strife and jealousy.

P'" 13:14 But *put on the Lord Jesus Christ*, and do not make provision for desires of the flesh.

Rom 12:1-13:14 Parallel Structure Table

With thirteen elements in the D stich, the below table splits the D stich into two rows of seven and six elements respectively.

| A 12:1—God . . . holy, acceptable . . . God | A' 12:2—God . . . the good and acceptable |

B 12:3-4a—the grace having been given to me . . . allotted to each a measure of faith				B' 12:4b-6—the grace having been given to me . . . according to the proportion of your faith			
C 12:7a —ministry	C' 12:7b—teaching	C" 12:7c —encouraging	C''' 12:8a—giving		C'''' 12:8b —leading	C''''' 12:8c— showing mercy	
D 12:9a—love	D' 12:9b— abhorring evil	D" 12:9c— cleaving to good	D''' 12:10a —brotherly love	D'''' 12:10b — honor	D''''' 12:11a —diligence	D'''''' 12:11b— fervent	
D''''''' 12:11c —serving	D'''''''' 12:12a —rejoicing	D''''''''' 12:12b —patient	D'''''''''' 12:12c —continuing	D''''''''''' 12:13a— contributing	D'''''''''''' 12:13b -pursuing		
E 12:14a—bless				E' 12:14b—bless			
F 12:15a—rejoice				F' 12:15b—weep			
G 12:16a—be of the same mind			G' 12:16b—do not set your mind		G" 12:16c—do not become wise		
H 12:17a—no one evil for evil			H' 12:17b—virtuous in the sight of all men		H" 12:18—be at peace with all men		
I 12:19a—avenge				I' 12:19b—vengeance			
J 12:20a—hungry				J' 12:20b—thirsty			
K 12:21a—overcome by evil				K' 12:21b—overcome evil			
L 13:1—obey . . . authorities . . . authority . . . God . . . resisting				L' 13:2—ordinance . . . authority . . . God . . . resisting . . . resisting			
M 13:3—for rulers are not a terror . . . good . . . evil . . . authority . . . good			M' 13:4a—for he is a servant of God . . . good . . . evil		M" 13:4b-5—for he is a servant of God . . . evil		
N 13:6—you pay taxes				N' 13:7—Render . . . tax to whom tax is due			
O 13:8—he that loves another . . . fulfilled the law			O' 13:9—you will love your neighbor . . . commandment		O" 13:10—love does no evil to his neighbor . . . fulfillment of the law		
P 13:11—it is the hour for you to awaken out of sleep		P' 13:12—the night is nearly over and the day draws near		P" 13:13—we should walk properly as in the day		P''' 13:14—put on the Lord Jesus Christ	

Commentary

O'Neill thought that both Rom 12 and 13 were interpolated.[50] Rhetorical analysis shows that they are a single constructed literary unit very much in the Pauline style of parallelism found elsewhere in the undisputed letters. Fitzmeyer proposed v. 12:11 as an interpolation.[51] Walker concludes that vv. 13:1–7 is an interpolation.[52] Bultmann agrees with respect to v. 13:5.[53] However, the parallelisms in vv. 13:1–7 clearly continue the style and structure of the parallelisms in Rom 12 and are consistent with the balance of Rom 13.

It appears that Rom 12–13 is a single literary unit. The same parallel structure is found in both chapters, having a mix of two-element stiches and multi-element stiches. In addition, in both chapters Paul gives moral admonitions. At the beginning of Rom 13 there is no typical Pauline introduction to a literary unit such as "I beseech you brothers," "What shall we say then," or "I speak the truth." Not all Pauline literary units have an introductory phrase, but some do, and there is not one at the beginning of Rom 13. "Render" (*apodidōmi*) is used in both chapters, and is only used three other times in the undisputed letters.

There seems to be a literary connection between the beginning of Rom 12 where Paul writes "But be transformed by the renewing of your mind" and the end of Rom 13:11–14 where the P stich is about waking up and facing a new day culminating with getting dressed as he writes "but put on the Lord Jesus Christ." The end of Rom 13 brings this literary unit of admonitions to a close by reiterating the beginning. It does not meet the standard for an inclusio, but there seems to be an intended connection.

The literary unit of Rom 12–13 has a parallel structure with sixteen stiches, several of them having multiple elements. The A stich matches "holy, acceptable" with "good and acceptable" and "God" is in both hemistiches. The B stich has two matching phrases: "the grace having been given to me" matching "the grace having been given to us" and "allotted to each a measure of faith" matching "according to the proportion of your faith."

The C stich has six elements as Paul enumerates the different talents various members of the congregation may have. Then the subsequent stich has thirteen elements where Paul starts his morality admonishments in the D stich. Although Paul continues his morality lesson in the E stich, it has a different quality matching two admonishments to "bless." The F stich matches the opposites of "rejoice" with "weep." The G stich concerns the mental attitude of the congregation advising "be of the same mind," "do not set your mind on high things," and "do not be wise in yourselves."

50. O'Neill, *Romans*, 269.
51. Fitzmeyer, *Romans*, 65.
52. Walker, *Interpolations*, 121–31.
53. Bultmann, "Glossen," 200.

The H stich advises on interpersonal relations with "to no one evil for evil," "virtuous in the sight of all men," and "be at peace with all men." The I stich admonishes against vengeance with a quote from Deut 32:35 matching "avenge" with "vengeance." The J stich again matches opposites with "hungry" matching "thirsty" in quoting Prov 25:21–22. The series of short admonitions ends with the K stich matching "overcome by evil" with its opposite "overcome evil." The L stich starts at v. 13:1 and there are a number of matches. "Authority" is found in both hemistiches, twice in the L hemistich. "Ordained by God" is in the L hemistich with "ordinance of God" in the L' hemistich. "Obey" is in the L hemistich matching its opposite "resisting" in the L' hemistich. Interestingly "authority" is found twice in the L hemistich and once in the L' hemistich while "obey" is found once in the L hemistich and "resisting" is found twice in the L' hemistich.

There are three elements in the M stich and all of the elements contain the word "evil" one time. "Good" is found three times in this stich, but twice in the M element, once in the M' element and not at all in the M" element. The final matching words of this stich are "for rulers are not a terror" in the M element matching "for he is a servant of God" in both the M' and M" elements.

The N stich matches "you pay taxes" with "Render . . . tax to whom tax is due." The O stich has three elements with "for he that loves another" matching "you will love your neighbor" and "love does no evil to his neighbor." This stich contains a second set of matching phrases "fulfilled the law" in the O element, "commandment" in the O' element, and "fulfillment of the law" in the O" element.

The final stich has four elements that present a progression of waking up to a new day. The P element has "it is the hour for you to awaken out of sleep." Then the P' element has "the night is nearly over and the day draws near." Next comes the P" element with "we should walk properly as in the day." Finally in the P"' element "put on the Lord Jesus Christ."

Romans 14

Romans 14 has a unique structure. The chapter begins and ends with an inclusio marking the chapter as one large literary unit; however, there are three sub-literary units in between the elements of the inclusio: one dual chiastic/parallel, one chiastic, and one hybrid chiastic/parallel. All three literary units have "judge" and "Lord" as a matching term in two of their stiches.

Romans 14:1, 23

Romans 14:1 and 23 form the inclusio of the entire literary unit separate from the three sub-units.

14:1 Now receive him who is weak in *faith*, but not for deciding to *pass judgment*.

14:23 But he who is doubting *has been condemned* if he eats, because not of *faith*; and everything not of *faith* is sin.

The unusual aspect of having an inclusio define the chapter containing three literary sub-units dictates setting out the inclusio separately. With regard to the chapter as a whole, vv. 14:1 and 23 form an inclusio for the three literary sub-units. This is unique in the Pauline letters but is in keeping with his style of encapsulating his literary units. Romans 14:1 contains "faith" and "pass judgment" while v. 14:23 contains "faith" twice and "has been condemned." Certainly "judge" and "condemn" are related concepts, and in Greek "krino" is the root of both verbs. It is also interesting that "judge," one of the matching terms of the inclusio, is found as a matching word in one of the stiches in all three literary sub-units contained in Rom 14. The first sub-unit is also a dual chiastic/parallel structure.

Romans 14:2–6

Chiastic Structure

> A 14:2 One man believes in *eating* all things. But the weak one *eats* only vegetables. 14:3a Do not let he who *eats* ridicule he who does not *eat*.
>> B 14:3b And do not let he who does not eat *judge* he who eats. For God has welcomed him. 14:4a Who are you to be *judging* the servant of another?
>>> C 14:4b To his own *Lord* he stands or falls. Yes, he will be *upheld*.
>>> C' 14:4c For the *Lord* has power to *uphold him*.
>> B' 14:5 One man *judges* one day above other days. But another *judges* every day the same. Let each one be fully assured in his own mind.
> A' 14:6 He who regards the day, regards it to the Lord. He *eating*, *eats* to the Lord, for he gives thanks to God. And he not *eating*, does not *eat* to the Lord, and gives thanks to God.

Rom 14:2–6 Chiastic Structure Table

A 14:2–3a—eating . . . eats . . . eats . . . eat	A' 14:6—eating . . . eating . . . eats . . . eat
B 14:3b–14a—judge . . . judging	B' 14:5—judges . . . judges
C 14:4b—Lord . . . upheld	C' 14:4c—Lord . . . uphold him

Parallel Structure

  A 14:2 One man believes in *eating* all things. But the weak one *eats* only vegetables.

  A' 14:3a Do not let he who *eats* ridicule he who does not *eat*;

    B 14:3b And do not let he who does not eat *judge* he who eats. For God has welcomed him.

    B' 14:4a Who are you to be *judging* the servant of another?

      C 14:4b To his own *Lord* he stands or falls. Yes, he will be *upheld*.

      C' 14:4c For the *Lord* has power to *uphold him*.

        D 14:5a One man *judges* one day above other days.

        D' 14:5b But another *judges* every day the same. Let each one be fully assured in his own mind.

          E 14:6a He who regards the day, regards it to the Lord. He *eating, eats* to the Lord, for he gives thanks to God.

          E' 14:6b And he not *eating*, does not *eat* to the Lord, and gives thanks to God.

ROM 14:2–6 PARALLEL STRUCTURE TABLE

A 14:2—eating . . . eats	A' 14:3a—eats . . . eat
B 14:3b—judge	B' 14:4a—judging
C 14:4b—Lord . . . upheld	C' 14:4c—Lord . . . uphold him
D 14:5a—judges	D' 14:5b—judges
E 14:6a—eating, eats	E' 14:6b—eating . . . eat

Commentary

CHIASTIC STRUCTURE

This is the first chapter since Rom 2 to have more than one literary structure. The chiastic structure has only three stiches and the parallel structure has five. In the A stich of the chiastic structure each hemistich uses the verb "eat" four times. This becomes two parallel stiches, the A stich and the E stich in the parallel structure. However, in the A hemistich of both the chiastic and the parallel structures Paul uses two different Greek words for eat "*phagein*" and "*esthiei*." In the A' hemistich of the chiastic structure and E stich of the parallel structure Paul only uses "*esthiei*." The B stich of the chiastic structure and the B and D stiches of the parallel structure have the word "judge" in each hemistich, twice in each hemistich of the chiastic structure. The C stich is identical in both structures. In the C stich both hemistiches contain the word "Lord" and both hemistiches contain the word "upheld" or "uphold." Fitzmeyer proposed that v.

14:6 is an interpolation.[54] However, that would destroy the A' hemistich of the chiastic structure and the matching of the verb "to eat" four times in each hemistich.

Parallel Structure

The parallel structure has five stiches and the reader can see from this structure how Paul was able to construct his dual chiastic/parallel structures. In this particular parallel structure the matching words are the same as the matching words of the chiastic structure. There is "eating" and "eats" twice in vv. 14:2 and 3. That forms the A stich of the parallel structure, but "eating" and "eat" are also found twice in v. 14:6. That forms the E stich of the parallel structure, and it forms the A' hemistich of the chiastic structure. Then there is a similar pattern with the B and D stiches of the parallel structure using the word "judge" twice in v. 14:3b and 4a and twice in v. 14:5a and b. Then the C stich of the parallel structure is identical to the C stich of the chiastic structure. Not all of Paul's dual chiastic/parallel structures are formed this way, but this one shows the skeleton of the process he used.

Rom 14:7–12

This substructure is a short hybrid chiastic/parallel structure.
   A 14:7 For no one lives to *himself*, and no one dies to *himself*.
     B 14:8a For if we live, *we live to the Lord*.
       C 14:8b And if we die, *we die to the Lord*.
       C' 14:8c Whether we live therefore, or *die, we are the Lord's*.
         D 14:9a For to this end *Christ died and lived*,
           D' 14:9b that he might be *Lord* of both *the dead and the living*.
              E 14:10a But you, why do you *judge* your brother? Or you also, why do you condemn your brother?
                E' 14:10b For we will all stand before the *judgment seat* of God.
     B' 14:11 For it is written, "*As I live*," *says the Lord*, to me every knee shall bow, and every tongue will acknowledge God."
   A' 14:12 So then each of us will give account of *himself* to God.

Rom 14:7–12 Hybrid Structure Table

A 14:7—himself...himself	A' 14:12—himself
B 14:8a—we live to the Lord	B' 14:11—as I live says the Lord
C 14:8b—we die to the Lord	C' 14:8c—die we are the Lord's

54. Fitzmeyer, *Romans*, 65.

| D 14:9a—Christ died and lived | D' 14:9b—Lord . . . the dead and the living |
| E 14:10a—judge | E' 14:10b—judgment seat |

Commentary

In this structure the A and B stiches are chiastic in nature, but the C, D, and E stiches are parallel in nature. This is similar to the literary unit of Rom 4 that also has a two-stich inclusio. In the A stich both hemistiches contain the word "himself," twice in the A hemistich and once in the A' hemistich. The B hemistich matches the phrases "we live to the Lord" and "as I live says the Lord." In the parallel section the C hemistich has "we die to the Lord;" whereas the C' hemistich has "die we are the Lord's." This is the second time the word "Lord" has been used as a matching term in the Rom 14 literary unit. The D stich matches "Christ died and lived" with "Lord . . . the dead and the living." The E stich matches "judge" in the E element and "judgment seat" in the E' element, continuing the use of "judge" as a matching element in the sub-units.

Rom 14:13–22

This literary sub-unit is a chiastic structure exposing an interpolation.

> A 14:13a Therefore, no longer should we *judge* one another. But rather *judge* this,
> > B 14:13b that no man put a *stumbling block* or *snare before his brother*.
> > > C 14:14a I know, and am persuaded in the Lord Jesus, that *nothing is unclean of itself*
> > > > D 14:14b except to him who accounts something to be *unclean*.
> > > > D' 14:14c To him it is *unclean*.
> > > C' 14:15 For if because of food your brother is distressed, no longer are you walking in love. Do not destroy with your food him for whom *Christ* died.

(14:16 Therefore, do not let your good be spoken of as evil. 14:17 For the kingdom of God is not eating and drinking, but righteousness and peace and joy in the Holy Spirit. 14:18 For he who in these things serves Christ is well-pleasing to God, and approved by men. 14:19 So then we should pursue things that make for peace, and things for edification of one another. 14:20a Do not destroy the work of God for the sake of food.)

> > 14:20b *All things indeed are clean.*
> > B' 14:20c But, it is wrong for a man to be eating as a *stumbling block*. 14:21 It is good not to eat meat, nor to drink wine, nor *anything whereby your brother stumbles* or is led into sin or sickens.

A' 14:22 The faith that you have keep before God. Blessed is he who does not *judge* himself in what he *approves*.

Rom 14:13–22 Chiastic Structure Table

A 14:13a—judge . . . judge	A' 14:22—judge . . . approves
B 14:13b—stumbling block . . . snare before his brother	B' 14:20c—stumbling block . . . anything whereby your brother stumbles
C 14:14a—Lord Jesus . . . nothing is unclean of itself	C' 14:15, 20b – Christ . . . all things are indeed clean
D 14:14b—unclean	D' 14:14c—unclean

Commentary

The A stich contains "judge" twice in the A hemistich and once in the A' hemistich. The A' hemistich balances the second "judge" found in the A hemistich with "approves," the result of judging. Here is the third literary sub-unit in a row that "judge" has been used as a matching term. The B stich contains "stumbling block" in both hemistiches, and "snare before his brother" in the B hemistich matches "anything whereby your brother stumbles" in the B' hemistich. Then in the C stich "Lord Jesus" matches "Christ," and "nothing is unclean of itself" matches "all things are indeed clean." In the center D stich "unclean" is found in both hemistiches.

Interpolation 14:16–20a

As with Rom 12 and 13 O'Neill proposed that the entirety of Rom 14 is an interpolation.[55] As mentioned above Rom 14 has a very unusual style of literary construction, but the cleverness of encapsulating three literary sub-units with an inclusio and having "judge" and "Lord" matching words in all three literary units marks Rom 14 as Pauline.

The last structure of Rom 14 is a bit odd. It is a straightforward chiastic structure, but the stiches are not balanced even after eliminating the obvious interpolation. The A, B, and C hemistiches are much shorter than the A,' B,' and C' hemistiches. The A hemistich contains eight words while the A' contains eighteen. The B hemistich contains eight words and the B' twenty-seven. The C hemistich contains eleven words, the C' twenty-five. The D hemistich has seven words and the D' two. However, the rapid fire occurrence of parallelisms make it clear where the separate hemistiches begin and end despite their atypical lack of balance. The entire literary unit is atypical but

---

55. O'Neill, *Romans*, 269.

clearly Pauline in its cleverness and word usage. It is evident that the interpolation containing sixty words cannot be forced into the C' hemistich. Even with the atypical unbalanced nature of this structure, the text of vv. 14:16–20a must have been added by an interpolator.

Stiches	Words in first half	Words in second half	Words in interpolation
C	14:14a—11	14:15-20b—85	14:16-20a—60

Romans 15

Romans 15 is a long parallel literary structure with a combination of two and three-element stiches.

Rom 15:1-33

A 15:1 Now we who are strong ought to bear the infirmities of the weak and not *to please ourselves*.
A' 15:2 Let each one of us *please his neighbor* for that which is good, for edification.
A" 15:3a For even Christ did not *please himself*.
  B 15:3b But, as *it is written*, "The reproaches of those reproaching you fell upon me."
  B' 15:4a For whatever things *were written long ago were written* for our instruction.
    C 15:4b So that *through patience and through encouragement* of the scriptures we might have hope.
    C' 15:5a Now the God *of patience and of encouragement* grant you
      D 15:5b to be of the *same mind with one another* according to *Christ Jesus*.
      D' 15:6 So that *with one accord with one mouth* you may glorify the God and father of our Lord *Jesus Christ*.
        E 15:7 Therefore receive one another, as *Christ* also received you, to the *glory of God*.
        E' 15:8 For I say that *Christ* has become a servant of the circumcision for the *truth of God* in order to confirm the promises given to the fathers.
          F 15:9 And that the *Gentiles glorify God* for his mercy. As it is written, "Therefore I will confess you among the *Gentiles*, And *sing to your name*."
          F' 15:10 And again he says, "*Gentiles, rejoice with his people*." 15:11 And again, "*Praise the Lord, all you Gentiles*; And all the peoples praise him."
            G 15:12 And again, Isaiah says, "There will be the root of Jesse, and the one arising to rule over the Gentiles. The *Gentiles will hope on him*."
            G' 15:13a Now *may the God of hope fill you* with all joy and peace in belief,

G" 15:13b that *you may abound in hope*, in the power of the Holy Spirit.

H 15:14 But I myself also am persuaded of you, my brothers, that *you yourselves are full of goodness*, filled with all knowledge, able also to *admonish one another*.

H' 15:15 But *I write the more boldly to you* in part as reminding you because of *the grace that was given to me by God*.

I 15:16a That I should be a minister of *Christ Jesus* to the *Gentiles*, ministering the gospel of *God*.

I' 15:16b So that the offering of the *Gentiles* might be made acceptable, being sanctified in the Holy Spirit. 15:17 Therefore I have my boasting in *Christ Jesus* in things pertaining to *God*.

J 15:18 For *I will not dare to speak of anything* except what *Christ* has accomplished through me into the obedience of the Gentiles by word and deed.

J' 15:19 In the power of signs and wonders, in the power of the spirit, so that from Jerusalem, and around as far as Illyricum, *I have completed the gospel* of *Christ*.

J" 15:20 But making it *my strong desire to preach the gospel*, where *Christ* was not known, so that I might not build upon another's foundation. 15:21 But, as it is written, "Those, to whom no report of him came, will see. And those who have not heard will understand."

K 15:22 Therefore also I was hindered many times from *coming to you*.

K' 15:23 But now having no longer a place in these regions and having for many years a longing *to come to you*,

K" 15:24 whenever I go to Spain *I hope to see you* during my journey and to be resupplied there by you if first in some measure I may meet with your satisfaction.

L 15:25 But now I go to Jerusalem, *to be of service* to the saints. 15:26 For *Macedonia and Achaia were pleased to make a certain contribution* for the poor among the saints that are at Jerusalem.

L' 15:27 They *were pleased, and they are in their debt*. For if the *Gentiles* have shared their spiritual things, they owe it also *to minister* in material things.

M 15:28 When therefore I have accomplished this and have sealed to them this fruit, *I will set off via you* to Spain.

M' 15:29 And I know that, *coming to you*, I will come in the fullness of the blessing of Christ.

N 15:30 Now I beseech you, brothers, by our Lord Jesus Christ, and by the love of the spirit, that *you strive together with me* in your prayers to God for me. 15:31a That I may be delivered from those in Judea who are disbelievers,

N' 15:31b and my service which for Jerusalem may be acceptable to the saints. 15:32 So that I may come to you in joy through the will of God, *and may be rested with you.* 15:33 And the God of peace be with you all. Amen.

Rom 15:1-33 Parallel Structure Table

A 15:1—to please ourselves	A' 15:2—please his neighbor	A" 15:3a—please himself
B 15:3b—it is written	B' 15:4a—were written long ago ... were written	
C 15:4b—through patience and through encouragement	C' 15:5a—of patience and of encouragement	
D 15:5b—same mind with one another ... Christ Jesus	D' 15:6—with one accord and one mouth ... Jesus Christ	
E 15:7—Christ ... glory of God	E' 15:8—Christ ... truth of God	
F 15:9—Gentiles glorify God ... Gentiles ... sing your name	F' 15:10-11—praise the Lord all you Gentiles ... Gentiles ... rejoice with his people	
G 15:12—Gentiles will hope on him	G' 15:13a—may the God of hope fill you	G" 15:13b—you may abound in hope
H 15:14—you yourselves are full of goodness ... admonish one another	H' 15:15—the grace that was given to me ... I write the more boldly to you	
I 15:16a—Christ Jesus ... Gentiles ... God	I' 15:16b-17—Christ Jesus ... Gentiles ... God	
J 15:18—I will not dare to speak of anything ... Christ	J' 15:19—I have completed the gospel ... Christ	J" 15:20-21—my strong sense to preach the gospel ... Christ
K 15:22—coming to you	K' 15:23—to come to you	K" 15:24—I hope to see you
L 15:25-26—to be of service ... Macedonia and Achaia ... were pleased to make a certain contribution	L' 15:27—to minister ... Gentiles ... were pleased and they are in their debt	
M 15:28—I will set off via you	M' 15:29—coming to you	
N 15:30-31—you strive together with me	N' 15:32-33—and may be rested with you	

Part I | The Undisputed Letters

Commentary

This long parallel structure certainly has all the earmarks having been written by Paul and belies those scholars who have branded Rom 15–16 a later interpolation. This literary unit begins with a three element stich having "to please ourselves" in the A element match "please our neighbor" in the A' element and "please himself" in the A" element. The B stich matches "it is written" in the B hemistich with "were written long ago" and "were written" in the B' hemistich. In the B hemistich Paul quotes Ps 68:9. The C stich matches "through patience and through encouragement" in the C hemistich with "patience and encouragement" in the C' hemistich.

The D stich contains two matching phrases with "same mind with one another" parallel to "with one accord with one mouth," and secondly, "Christ Jesus" is parallel to "Jesus Christ." The E stich has "Christ" in both hemistiches, plus the E hemistich contains "the glory of God" while the E' hemistich contains "the truth of God." The F stich has "Gentiles glorify God" in the F hemistich matching "praise the Lord all the Gentiles" as Paul quotes Ps 117:1. "Gentiles" is found in both hemistiches of the F stich a second time, and Paul quotes 2 Sam 22:50 and Ps 118:49 with "sing to your name" in the F hemistich and matches that with a quote from Deut 32:43 "rejoice with his people"

There are three elements in the G stich and Paul continues his quotes of the Old Testament in the G element, this time attributing the quote to Isaiah from Isa 11:10 with "the Gentiles will hope on him." This matches "may the God of hope fill you" in the G' element and "you may abound in hope" in the G" element. The H stich matches "you yourselves are full of goodness" in the H hemistich and "the grace that was given to me" in the H' hemistich. In addition, "admonish one another" in the H hemistich matches "more boldly I have written to you." In the I stich both hemistiches contain the same three words "Christ Jesus," "God," and "Gentiles."

In the three-element J stich there are phrases in each element concerning Paul's preaching and message: "I will dare not speak of anything" in the J element, "I have completed the gospel" in the J' element, and "my strong desire to preach the gospel" in the J" element. "Christ" is found in all three elements also. The K stich also has three elements, and they deal with Paul going to visit the church at Rome. The K element has "coming to you." The K' element has "to come to you." The K" element contains "I hope to see you." The L stich matches "to be of service" in the L hemistich with "to minister" in the L' hemistich. "Macedonia and Achaia" matches "Gentiles," and "were pleased to make a certain contribution" in the L hemistich matches "were pleased and they are in their debt" in the L' hemistich.

In the M stich Paul returns to the subject of visiting the Romans with "I will set off via you" in the M hemistich matching "coming to you" in the M' hemistich. In the final N stich "you strive together with me" matches "together with you."

O'Neill eliminates vv. 15:1–13 as having been interpolated. However, if he is correct the interpolator seamlessly added his text in exactly the same style as Paul's vv. 15:14–33 deftly using a combination of two and three-element stiches. The first half of Rom 15 is so similar to the second half in literary style, both halves must have been written by the same person.

Romans 16

Romans 16 closes the letter and is mostly a series of greetings, but it was written with a chiastic structure and an interpolator has inserted greetings of his own. The final literary unit is thought by many scholars to have been interpolated because of its double benediction. John Knox thought it likely that Rom 16 was an interpolation.[56] Rhetorical analysis shows Paul was just making a typical chiastic parallelism.

Rom 16:1–23

  A 16:1a I commend to you *Phoebe our sister*,
    B 16:1b being a servant of the *church* that is at Cenchreae.
      C 16:2 So that you might receive her in the Lord appropriately of saints and you might assist her in whatever matter she may have need from you. For she also has been a *patroness* of many, and *of me myself*.
        D 16:3 Greet Prisca and Aquila my fellow-workers in *Christ Jesus*,
          E 16:4 who for my life laid down their own necks. For which I not only give thanks, but also all the *churches of the Gentiles*.
            F 16:5 And the church that is in their house. Greet Epaenetus my *beloved*, who is first-fruit of Asia of Christ. 16:6 Greet Mary, who *labored* much for you.
              G 16:7a Greet Andronicus and Junias, *my kinsmen*, and my fellow-prisoners,
                H 16:7b who are noted among the apostles, who also have been *in Christ* before me.
                  I 16:8 Greet Ampliatus my *beloved in the Lord*.
                  I' 16:9 Greet Urbanus our fellow-worker *in Christ* and Stachys my *beloved*.
                H' 16:10 Greet Apelles the approved *in Christ*. Greet those who are of the household of Aristobulus.
              G' 16:11 Greet Herodion *my kinsman*. Greet those of the household of Narcissus, being in the Lord.

---

56. Knox, "Romans," 354.

F' 16:12 Greet Tryphaena and Tryphosa, who *labor* in the Lord. Greet Persis the *beloved*, who *labored* much in the Lord. 16:13 Greet Rufus, the elect in the Lord, and mother of him and me.

(16:14 Greet Asyncritus, Phlegon, Hermes, Patrobas, Hermas, and the brothers who are with them. 16:15 Greet Philologus and Julia, Nereus and his sister, and Olympas, and all the saints that are with them.)

E' 16:16 Greet each other with a kiss. All the *churches of Christ* greet you.

(16:17 Now I beseech you, brothers, beware those who are causing the divisions and stumbling blocks, contrary to the teaching that you learned. And turn away from them. 16:18 For such as they do not serve our Lord Christ, but their own desires. And by their smooth speech and flattery they deceive the hearts of the unsuspecting. 16:19 For your obedience has reached to everyone. Therefore, I rejoice over you, but I would have you wise to that which is good, and innocent to that which is evil. 16:20a And the God of peace shall crush Satan under your feet shortly.)

D' 16:20b The grace of our Lord *Jesus Christ* be with you.
C' 16:21 Timothy *my fellow-worker* greets you; and Lucius and Jason and Sosipater, my kinsmen. 16:22 I, Tertius, who writes the letter, greet you in the Lord.
B' 16:23a Gaius my host, and of the whole *church*, greets you.
A' 16:23b Erastus the treasurer of the city greets you, and *Quartus the brother*.

Rom 16:1–23 Chiastic Structure Table

A 16:1a—Phoebe our sister	A' 16:23b—Quartus the brother
B 16:1b—church	B' 16:23a—church
C 16:2—patroness . . . of me myself	C' 16:21–22—my fellow worker
D 16:3—Christ Jesus	D' 16:20b—Jesus Christ
E 16:4—churches of the Gentiles	E' 16:16—churches of Christ
F 16:5–6—beloved . . . labored	F' 16:12–13—beloved . . . labor . . . labored
G 16:7a—my kinsmen	G' 16:11—my kinsman
H 16:7b—in Christ	H' 16:10—in Christ
I 16:8—beloved . . . in the Lord	I' 16:9—beloved . . . in Christ

Commentary

This nine-stich chiastic structure shows clearly that Rom 16 is not an interpolation. It has all the markings of a Pauline chiastic literary unit. In the A stich "Phoebe our sister" matches "Quartus the brother." Both hemistiches of the B stich contain "church." In the C stich "patroness . . . of me myself" matches "fellow worker." The D hemistich contains "Christ Jesus" whereas the D' hemistich contains "Jesus Christ," another chiasm within the chiastic structure. In the E stich "churches of the Gentiles" matches "churches of Christ." In the F stich "beloved" and "labored" are found in both hemistiches with "labor" twice in the F' hemistich. Fitzmeyer proposed that v. 16:5, the first half of the F hemistich, is an interpolation, but the use of "beloved" matching with v. 16:12 shows him to be incorrect. The G hemistich has "my kinsmen" in the G hemistich and the singular "my kinsman" in the G' hemistich. In the H stich "in Christ" is in both hemistiches. The center I stich has "beloved" in both hemistiches. In addition "in the Lord" is in the I hemistich and "in Christ" is in the I' hemistich.

The center I stich is about greeting congregants at Rome. As mentioned earlier the center stich of a chiastic structure is typically the theme of the literary unit. The greeting nature of the instant center stich is additional evidence that the admonitions found at vv. 16:17–20a are off topic and an interpolation. This passage is out of place in this literary structure.

Interpolations

Rom 16:14–15

In this structure most of the hemistiches are very short. These short hemistiches expose an interpolation at vv. 16:14–15. There seem to be too many greetings in this section that do not balance with the short E and F hemistiches. O'Neill does not identify vv. 16:14–15 as an interpolation.[57] Apparently to him it was a series of greetings. He would not have noticed how it unbalances the text in the E and F stiches..

Stiches	Words in first half	Words in second half	Words in interpolation
E—F	16:4–6–46	16:12–16 – 69	16:14–15–28

Rom 16:17–20a

The admonition at vv. 16:17–20a is reminiscent of 1 Corinthians and is out of place here at the end of Romans. At the point of writing this letter Paul had never been to Rome nor visited the church there. He would not have known about divisions and stumbling blocks among the congregation as he did in Corinth. The short D and E

---

57. Knox, "Romans," 257.

hemistiches reveal this admonition to have been interpolated. Here O'Neill and rhetorical analysis agree for the most part. He also thought v. 16b is an interpolation and remarks that "churches of Christ" is found nowhere else in the Pauline corpus.[58] However, he failed to notice the chiastic match that it makes with v. 16:4 to complete the E stich. O'Neill also has v. 16:20b as part of the interpolation, whereas rhetorical analysis shows that it is original to Paul completing the D stich with a match of v. 16:3.

Stiches	Words in first half	Words in second half	Words in interpolation
D—E	16:3-4-31	16:16-20-99	16:17-20a—85

Rom 16:24–27

The final literary structure of Romans is a short chiastic structure.

   A 16:24 The grace of our Lord *Jesus Christ* be with you all. *Amen.*
     B 16:25a Now to him who has the power to strengthen you *according to my gospel and the proclamation of Jesus Christ,*
        C 16:25b *according to the revelation of the mystery*
        C' 16:25c *having been kept secret* throughout the ages, 16:26a but *now has been revealed,*
     B' 16:26b both *by the prophetic scriptures, and according to the commandment of the eternal God,* into the obedience of faith having been made known to all the Gentiles.
   A' 16:27 Of the only wise God, through *Jesus Christ*, to whom be the glory forever and ever. *Amen.*

Rom 16:24–27 Chiastic Structure Table

A 16:24—Jesus Christ … amen	A' 16:27—Jesus Christ … Amen
B 16:25a—according to my gospel and proclamation of Jesus Christ	B' 16:26b—by the prophetic scriptures and according to the commandment of the eternal God
C 16:25b—according to the revelation of the mystery	16:25c-26a—now has been revealed … having been kept secret

---

58. Knox, "Romans," 258.

Commentary

This three-stich chiastic structure ends the letter. A number of scholars, including O'Neill, have expressed the opinion that vv. 16:25–27 are an interpolation.[59] It certainly appears as if Paul has ended the letter at v. 16:24 with a benediction, but then adds another benediction. However, rhetorical analysis shows that the apparent benediction is only the A hemistich of a chiastic structure with both hemistiches containing "Jesus Christ" and "amen." It appears that Paul wanted to end the letter with a benediction containing "Jesus Christ" and "amen," but it did not chiastically match v. 16:23 so he added another benediction so that the unit would be symmetrical. The B stich matches "according to my gospel and the proclamation of Jesus Christ" with " by the prophetic scriptures and according to the commandment of the eternal God." "My gospel" is parallel to "prophetic scriptures," and "proclamation of Jesus Christ" is parallel to "commandment of the eternal God." The center C stich matches "according to the revelation of the mystery" with "having been kept secret . . . now has been revealed." Of course it is possible that a clever interpolator knew Paul's style of creating chiastic structures and added this benediction in a chiastic format. However, it seems unlikely.

---

59. Walker, *Interpolations*, 191–99.

4

First Letter To The Corinthians

"Kephas" As an Interpolation Throughout 1 Corinthians.

ANALYSIS OF 1 CORINTHIANS as a whole determined that every mention of Kephas in 1 Corinthians is probably an interpolation. It strikes a discordant note for Paul to put Kephas on an equal footing with Apollos and himself. Paul shows animosity toward Kephas in Galatians[1] and animosity toward the chief Jerusalem apostles collectively in 2 Corinthians.[2] Paul also complains about those advocating circumcision in Philippians.[3] It is not likely that Paul and Kephas became mutually respectful colleagues.

Below rhetorical analysis exposes obvious interpolations at vv. 9:5–7a and 15:3–11 both of which mention Kephas. It is not as obvious from a rhetorical analysis perspective that the other places Kephas is mentioned in this letter, vv. 1:12, and 3:21 are in fact interpolations. Although Kephas is mentioned at v. 3:21, he is not mentioned at v. 3:4. Unbeknownst to the interpolator "Paul and Apollos" in v. 3:4 is a chiastic parallelism matching "Paul and Apollos" at v. 3:21 in the B stich of a chiastic structure. If Paul had intended to include Kephas at v. 3:21, he probably would have included him at v. 3:4. In vv. 4:9–13 Paul tells how the apostles are disrespected; however, that section only applies to Paul and Apollos being the only apostles mentioned at v. 4:6. In addition Timothy and Apollos are mentioned at vv. 16:10 and 12 respectively. Apollos has been mentioned throughout the entire letter. Timothy has been mentioned once before in 1 Cor 4. If Paul had also mentioned Kephas throughout the letter, it would seem likely that he would have mentioned him along with Timothy and Apollos at the end of the letter. It appears that the interpolator forgot to include Kephas at vv. 3:4, 4:6, and 16:12. This may be a case of "editorial fatigue" as described by Mark Goodacre[4] wherein an editor desires to change the meaning of a written text and makes changes

---

1. Gal 2:6, 9, 11–14, 5:10, 12.

2. 2 Cor 11:12–15, 12:11. It seems reasonable to assume that the chief apostles in 2 Corinthians are the pillars mentioned in Gal 2, since Gal 1:19 refers to the pillars as apostles.

3. Phil 3:2.

4. Goodacre, "Fatigue," 45–58.

in a document to accomplish that, but neglects to carefully search the entire document to change all instances of the offending language.

1 Corinthians 1

The initial chapter of 1 Corinthians contains four literary units: two chiastic and two parallel. One of the parallel structures reveals three short interpolations.

1 Cor 1:1–9

The first literary unit of 1 Corinthians is a short chiastic structure with a three-element center stich.

> A 1:1 Paul, a *called* apostle of *Christ Jesus* through the will of *God* and Sosthenes our brother,
>> B 1:2 to the church of God being in Corinth, *having been sanctified* in Christ Jesus, called saints, with all those calling on the name of *our Lord Jesus Christ* in every place theirs and ours.
>>> C 1:3 *Grace* to you and peace from God our father and *Lord Jesus Christ*.
>>>> D 1:4 I thank my God always concerning you for the *grace God having been given you in Christ Jesus*.
>>>> D' 1:5 That in everything *you were enriched in him* in all speech and all knowledge.
>>>> D" 1:6 As the testimony about *Christ was confirmed in you*.
>>> C' 1:7 So that you are not lacking in any *gift*, eagerly awaiting the revelation of our *Lord Jesus Christ*.
>> B' 1:8 Who shall also sustain you *blameless* to the end until the day of *our Lord Jesus Christ*.
> A' 1:9 *God* is faithful, through whom *you were called* into the fellowship of his son *Jesus Christ* our Lord.

1 Cor 1:1–9 Chiastic Structure Table

A 1:1—called … Christ Jesus … God	A' 1:9—you were called … Jesus Christ … God	
B 1:2—having been sanctified … our Lord Jesus Christ	B' 1:8—blameless … our Lord Jesus Christ	
C 1:3—grace … Lord Jesus Christ	C' 1:7—gift … Lord Jesus Christ	
D 1:4—grace God having been given you in Christ Jesus	D' 1:5—you were enriched in him	D" 1:6—Christ was confirmed in you

Part I | The Undisputed Letters

Commentary

This short four-stich chiastic structure introduces the first letter to the Corinthians. Interestingly, "Christ" is a matching term in every stich. The only element that uses the pronoun "him" to refer to Christ is the very center D' element that is the center element of a three-element center stich. Paul's structures were typically symmetrical. The A stich matches "called" with "you were called," "Christ Jesus" with "Jesus Christ," and "God" is in both hemistiches. In the B stich "having been sanctified" matches "blameless," and "our Lord Jesus Christ" is in both hemistiches. In the C stich "grace" (*charis*) matches "gift" (*charismati*), and both hemistiches contain "Lord Jesus Christ" again. "Grace" and "gift" have the same root in Greek. The center D stich contains an unusual three elements and the matching language does not have the usual word or phrase repetition. The D element has "grace of God having been given you in Christ Jesus." The D' element has "you were enriched in him." The D" element contains "Christ was confirmed in you." All three elements refer to Christ, all three refer to the Corinthians, and all three mention a gift bestowed on the Corinthians. Every element/hemistich in this literary unit contains a reference to Christ. Plus the D' element, the very center of the literary unit, refers to Christ as "him," the only time in this structure a pronoun is used to refer to Christ. In this literary unit Paul says the Corinthians are "sanctified" have "grace" (twice) "enriched" "confirmed in Christ," "blameless," and "called."

Forty-three years apart Johannes Weiss and Günter Zuntz proposed that v. 1:2 is an interpolation.[5] Verse 1:2 is the B hemistich, and there are two phrases therein that match phrases in v. 1:8, the B' hemistich. Removing v. 1:2 would result in unbalancing either the C stich or the A stich. Rhetorical analysis shows that those scholars were incorrect in their assessments.

1 Cor 1:10–16

This literary unit is a three-stich parallel structure with possible interpolations.

> A 1:10a Now I encourage you, *brothers*, through the name of our Lord Jesus Christ that
>
> (1:10b you all speak the same thing and)
>
> 1:10c *there be no divisions among you.*
>
> (1:10d But you be joined together in the same mind and in the same opinion.)

---

5. Weiss, *Korintherbrief,* 91–92.

A' 1:11 For it has been revealed to me concerning you, my *brothers*, by those of Chloe *that there are quarrels among you*.
    B 1:12a Now I mean this, that each of you says indeed I am of *Paul* but I of Apollos.

(1:12b but I of Kephas, but I of Christ.)

    B' 1:13a Has Christ been divided? *Paul* was not crucified for you.
        C 1:13b Or was it into the name of *Paul* that you were *baptized*?
        C' 1:14 I thank God that *I baptized* none of you, save Crispus and Gaius.
        C" 1:15 So that any man should say that you were *baptized* into *my name*.
        C'" 1:16a Now also *I baptized* the household of Stephanas.
        C"" 1:16b Beyond that I do not know whether *I baptized* any other.

1 Cor 1:10-16 Parallel Structure Table

A 1:10—brothers . . . that there be no divisions among you		A' 1:11—brothers . . . that there are quarrels among you			
B 1:12—Paul		B' 1:13a—Paul			
C 1:13b—Paul . . . baptized	C' 1:14—I baptized	C" 1:15—baptized in my name	C'" 1:16a—I baptized	C"" 1:16b—I baptized

Commentary

After removing the interpolations the A stich matches "brothers" in both hemistiches, and "there be divisions among you" in the A hemistich matches "there are quarrels among you" in the A' hemistich. "Paul" is found in both hemistiches of the B stich. The C stich has five elements with each one expressing something about Paul baptizing congregants.

Interpolations 1 Cor 1:10b, 10:d, 12b

The second literary unit of 1 Cor 1 is also short, having only three stiches, but the final C stich has five elements. It appears that there are three interpolations into this literary unit. As mentioned, rhetorical analysis is not a good tool to isolate short interpolations, but here are tentatively identified three short interpolations. As the letter exists in canonical 1 Corinthians the A hemistich is not balanced with the A' hemistich, the A hemistich containing too much text. If "you all speak the same thing and" and "but you be joined together in the same mind and in the same opinion" are removed from

v. 1:10 the A and A' hemistiches balance nicely, having eighteen and fifteen words respectively. These two phrases express the same idea, and it might be that an interpolator was anxious to encourage all early Christian into a uniform Christology. This is also expressed in a later interpolation at 1 Cor 15:11 "whether then I or they, so we preach, and so you believed." In v. 15:11 the interpolator wrote that Paul, James, Kephas, and all the apostles preached the same message, attempting to obscure the ongoing conflict between Paul and the Jerusalem apostles, James, Kephas, and John. The interpolations at vv. 1:10b and d are probably the handiwork of the same interpolator.

In the B stich, removing "but I of Kephas, but I of Christ" (*egō de Kēpha, egō de Christou*) results in the B hemistich containing fourteen words and the B' hemistich eight but two of the words in the B' hemistich both have four syllables. Since Paul and Apollos are mentioned in 1 Cor 3, 4, and 9, the probability is that they would be the only ones mentioned in 1 Cor 1, setting the tone for the entire letter.

Stiches	Words in first half	Words in second half	Words in interpolation
A	1:10–35	1:11–15	1:10b, 10d—16
B	1:12–20	1:13a—8	1:12b—6

1 Cor 1:17–24

This literary unit is a short chiastic structure with a three-element center stich.

  A 1:17a For *Christ* did not *send me* to baptize, but *to preach the gospel*,
    B 1:17b not in *wisdom of words*, else the *cross of Christ* would be *made void*. 1:18a For the *word of the cross* to those perishing is *foolishness*.
      C. 1:18b But to *those being saved* to us it is the power of *God*.
        D 1:19 For it is written, "I will destroy the *wisdom of the wise*, And the *intellect of the intellectuals* I will make void."
          E 1:20a *Where is the wise?*
          E' 1:20b *Where is the scribe?*
          E" 1:20c *Where is the debater* of this age?
        D' 1:20d Has not God made the *wisdom of the world* foolish? 1:21a Because in the wisdom of God the *world through its wisdom* did not know God.
      C' 1:21b *God* was pleased through the foolishness of the preaching *to save those who believe*.
    B' 1:22 Seeing that Jews ask for signs and Greeks seek *wisdom*. 1:23 But we *preach Christ crucified*, to Jews indeed a *stumbling block* but to Gentiles *foolishness*.
  A' 1:24 But to *those who are called*, both Jews and Greeks, *Christ*, God's power, and God's wisdom.

1 Cor 17-24 Chiastic Structure Table

A 1:17a—Christ . . . send me . . . to preach the gospel	A' 1:24—Christ . . . those who are called	
B 1:17b-18a—wisdom . . . cross of Christ . . . made void . . . word of the cross . . . foolishness	B' 1:22-23—wisdom . . . preach Christ crucified . . . stumbling block . . . foolishness	
C 1:18b—those being saved . . . God	C' 1:21b—to save those . . . God	
D 1:19—wisdom of the wise . . . intellect of the intellectual	D' 1:20d-1:21a—wisdom of the world . . . world through its wisdom	
E 1:20a—where is the wise	E' 1:20b—where is the scribe	E" 1:20c—where is the debater

Commentary

The third literary unit in 1 Cor 1 has a chiastic structure with a three-element center stich, the same pattern as the first literary unit in 1 Cor 1. In the A stich Paul has used opposite concepts to express the same idea with "send me . . . to preach the gospel" matching "those who are called." In this case "send" and "called" mean the same thing although they are opposites. "Christ" is also in both hemistiches. In the B stich "wisdom" is in both hemistiches. "Words . . . cross of Christ" and "word of the cross" in the B hemistich match "preach Christ crucified" in the B' hemistich. The third B stich match has "made void" matching "stumbling block," and the final match has "foolishness" in both hemistiches. In the C stich "those being saved" matches "to save those" and "God" is found in both hemistiches. In the D stich Paul quoted Isa 29:14 with "wisdom of the wise" in the D hemistich matching "wisdom of the world" in the D' hemistich and "intellect of the intellectuals" matching "world through its wisdom." The center E stich has three elements, all parallel questions: "where is the wise" "where is the scribe" and "where is the debater." The first three literary units of 1 Corinthians are a symmetrical sequence, chiastic/parallel/chiastic, with both chiastic structures having atypical three-element center stiches.

1 Cor 1:25-31

The final literary unit of 1 Cor 1 is a short parallel structure with four stiches.

   A 1:25a Because the *foolishness of God is wiser than men.*
     B 1:25b And the *weakness of God is stronger than men.*
        C 1:26 For consider your calling, brothers, that not many wise according to the flesh, not many mighty, *not many noble.*

A' 1:27a But God has chosen the *foolish things of the world that he might shame the wise*.

  B' 1:27b And God has chosen the *weak things of the world that he might shame the strong*.

    C' 1:28a And God has chosen the *ignoble of the world*, and those who are despised

      D 1:28b and the things that are not, that he might annul the things that are. 1:29 That no flesh should *boast before God*. 1:30a But out of him you are in Christ Jesus,

      D' 1:30b who was made wisdom to us from God, righteousness and sanctification, and redemption. 1:31 So that, as it is written, "He that boasts, let him *boast in the Lord.*"

1 Cor 1:25-31 Parallel Structure Table

A 1:25a—foolishness of God is wiser than men	A' 1:27a—foolish thing of the world that he might shame the wise
B 1:25b-26a—weakness of God is stronger than men	B' 1:27b—weak things of the world that he might shame the strong
C 1:26b—not many noble	C' 1:28a—ignoble of the world
D 1:28b-30a—boast before God	D' 1:30b-31—boast in the Lord

Commentary

The fourth and final literary unit of 1 Cor 1 has an atypical parallel structure with four stiches. The structure is A, B, C; A', B', C'; D, D'. The A stich matches "the foolishness of God is wiser than men" with "the foolishness of the world that he might shame the wise." The B stich matches "the weakness of God is stronger than men" with "the weakness of the world that he might shame the strong." The C stich matches "not many noble" with "the ignoble of the world." The D stich contains a quote of Jer 9:24 in the D' hemistich, with "boast before God" in the D hemistich matching "boast in the Lord" in the D' hemistich.

1 Corinthians 2

First Corinthians 2 contains the first long chiastic structure in the letter that encompasses the entire chapter. The stiches in this structure are not balanced very well, but the first half of the structure as a whole balances nicely with the second half of the structure as a whole.

1 Cor 2:1–16

A 2:1 And I, having come to you, brothers, did not come with excellent speech or wisdom, proclaiming to you the testimony of God. 2:2 For *I determined not to know* anything among you save Jesus *Christ* and him crucified.

  B 2:3 And I was with you in weakness and in fear and in much trembling. 2:4 And my speech and my preaching were not in persuasive words of wisdom but in *demonstration of the spirit* and of power.

    C 2:5 So that your faith should not stand in the *wisdom of men* but in the *power of God*.

      D 2:6a But *we speak wisdom* among those who are mature.

        E 2:6b But a *wisdom not of this age* nor of the rulers of this age who are coming to naught.

          F 2:7 But we speak *God's wisdom in a mystery* that has been hidden,

            G *that God foreordained* before the ages for our glory,

              H 2:8 which *none of the rulers of this age has understood*. For had they understood it, they would not have crucified the Lord of glory.

              H' 2:9 But as it is written, "*That which eye has not seen, and ear has not heard, and has not entered into the heart of man*, God has prepared for those who love him."

            G' 2:10 For to us *God has revealed through the spirit*. For the spirit searches all things even the depths of God.

          F' 2:11 For who among men knows the things of a man if not the spirit of the man which is in him? So also *the things of God no one knows* except the spirit of God.

        E' 2:12 But we received, *not the spirit of the world*, but the spirit that is from God, that we may know the things that were granted to us by God.

      D' 2:13 *Which we also speak*, not in words that man's *wisdom* teaches, but those that the spirit teaches combining spiritual things with spiritual words.

    C' 2:14a Now the *natural man* does not accept the things of the *spirit of God* for they are foolishness to him.

  B' 2:14b And he cannot know them because *they are spiritually discerned*. 2:15 But he that is spiritual judges all things, and he himself is judged by no one.

A' 2:16 For *who has known* the mind of the Lord? Who will instruct him? But we have the mind of *Christ*.

Part I | The Undisputed Letters

1 Cor 2:1–16 Chiastic Structure Table

A 2:1–2—I determined not to know … Christ	A' 2:16—who has known … Christ
B 2:3–4—demonstration of the spirit	B' 2:14b–15—they are spiritually discerned
C 2:5—wisdom of men … power of God	C' 2:14a—natural man … spirit of God
D 2:6a—we speak wisdom	D' 2:13—which we also speak … wisdom
E 2:6b—wisdom not of this age	E' 2:12—not the spirit of the world
F 2:7a—God's wisdom in a mystery	F' 2:11—the things of God no one knows
G 2:7b—that God foreordained	G' 2:10—God has revealed through the spirit
H 2:8—none of the rulers of this age has understood	H' 2:9—that which eye has not seen and ear has not heard and has not entered the heart of man

Commentary

As noted in chapter 2 Walker is of the opinion that vv. 2:6–16 are an interpolation. Rhetorical analysis does not agree for the reasons stated therein. The A and B hemistiches of this chiastic literary unit encompass vv. 2:1–4. That is fifty-four words. The A' and B' hemistiches of the unit encompass 1 Cor 2:14b–16 that has only thirty-one words. These stiches do not have the typical Pauline balance. Rhetorical analysis suggests that vv. 2:2–3 may be an interpolation. Removing these verses reduces the A and B hemistiches to thirty-seven words, much more balanced. However, v. 2:2 contains the matching language of the A hemistich "I determined not to know" matching "who has known" in v. 2:16, the A' hemistich. In addition, both vv. 2:2 and 2:16 contain "Christ." Further, the additional text in the A and B hemistiches in the first half of the structure, balance with extra text in the G' – D' hemistiches in the second half of the structure. Overall, there are one hundred thirty-three words in the first half of the structure and one hundred fifty-four words in the second half. This is only a fifteen percent difference. It appears that this structure is only balanced by halves and not by stiches as is the usual Pauline structure. No definite interpolation can be discerned.

Paul quotes Isa 40:13–14 in the A' hemistich. The B stich matches "demonstration of the spirit" with "they are spiritually discerned." In both halves of the C stich the foolishness of man is contrasted with the might of God by matching of "wisdom of men" with "natural man," and matching "power of God" with "spirit of God." In the D stich "we speak wisdom" in the D hemistich matches "which we also speak … wisdom" in the D' hemistich. The E stich matches "wisdom not of this age" with "not the spirit of the world." The F stich matches "God's wisdom in a mystery" with "the things of God no one knows." The G stich matches "that God foreordained" with "God has revealed through the spirit." In the H stich the H hemistich contains "none of the rulers of this age had understood" and is parallel to a misquote of Isa 64:4 and/or Isa 52:15 "what the eye has not seen and the ear has not heard and has not entered into the heart of man."

1 Corinthians 3

Three interpolations in 1 Cor 3 are exposed by the long dual chiastic/parallel structure that encompasses the entire chapter. The interpolator added Kephas to v. 3:22 but neglected to add him into v. 3:4.

1 Cor 3:1–23

Chiastic Structure

>A 3:1 And I, brothers, could not speak to you as to spiritual, but as to carnal, as to *babes in Christ*.

(3:2 I fed you with milk, not with meat. For you were not yet able, but not even now are you able. 3:3 For you are still carnal. Since there is jealousy and strife among you, are you not carnal, and do you not walk after the manner of men?)

>>B 3:4 For when one says, *I am of Paul, and another I am of Apollos*, are you not men?
>>>C 3:5 What then is Apollos, and what is Paul? Ministers through whom you believed, and each as the Lord gave to him. 3:6 *I planted, Apollos watered*, but God gave the increase.
>>>>D 3:7 Therefore *neither the one planting, nor the one watering is anything*. But God that gives the increase.
>>>>>E 3:8 Now *he who plants and he who waters are one*, but *each will receive his own reward according to his own labor.*
>>>>>E' 3:9 For we are God's fellow-workers. You are God's husbandry, God's building. 3:10 According to the grace of God which was given to me as a wise master builder, *I laid a foundation; and another builds on it*. But let each one take heed how he builds on it.
>>>>D' 3:11 For *no one can lay another foundation than that which is laid*, which is Jesus Christ.
>>>C' 3:12 But if any man builds on the foundation gold, silver, costly stones, wood, hay, straw, 3:13a *each one's work will become manifest*.

(3:13b For the day shall disclose it, because it is revealed in fire. And the fire itself shall prove of what sort the work of each is. 3:14 If any man's work shall remain that he built, he shall receive a reward. 3:15 If any man's work shall be burned, he shall suffer loss. But he himself shall be saved, but only through fire. 3:16 Do you not know that you are a temple of God, and the spirit of God dwells in you? 3:17 If any man destroys the temple of God, God shall destroy him. For the temple of God is holy, and such are you. 3:18 Let no man deceive himself. If any man thinks that he is wise among you in this world, let him become a fool, that he may become wise. 3:19 For the wisdom of this world is foolishness with God. For it is written, "He that takes the wise in their craftiness." 3:20 And again, "The Lord knows the reasoning of the wise that they are futile.")

B' 3:21 Therefore let no one boast in *men*. For all things are yours. 3:22a Whether *Paul or Apollos*,

(3:22b or Kephas or the world, or life or death,)

3:22c or things present or things to come; all are yours.
A' 3:23 *Now you are Christ's*; and Christ is God's.

1 Cor 3:1–23 Chiastic Structure Table

A 3:1—babes in Christ	A' 3:23—now you are Christ's
B 3:4—I am of Paul and another I am of Apollos . . . men	B' 3:21–22a, c—Paul or Apollos . . . men
C 3:5–6—I planted Apollos watered	C' 3:12–13a—each one's work will become manifest
D 3:7—neither the one planting or the one watering is anything	D' 3:11—no one can lay another foundation than that which is laid
E 3:8—he who plants and he who waters are one, . . . each shall receive his own reward according to his own labor	E' 3:9–10—I laid a foundation; and another builds on it. . . . each one take heed how he builds on it

Parallel Structure

A 3:1 And I, brothers, could not speak to you as to spiritual, but as to carnal, as to *babes in Christ*.

(3:2 I fed you with milk, not with meat. For you were not yet able, but not even now are you able. 3:3 For you are still carnal. Since there is jealousy and strife among you, are you not carnal, and do you not walk after the manner of men?)

A' 3:4 For when one says, I am of Paul and another I am of Apollos, *are you not men?*
  B 3:5 *What then is Apollos, and what is Paul?* Ministers through whom you believed, and each as the *Lord gave to him.*
  B' 3:6 *I planted, Apollos watered,* but *God gave the increase.*
  B" 3:7 Therefore neither *the one planting, nor the one watering is anything.* But *God that gives the increase.*
    C 3:8 *Now he who plants and he who waters are one,* but *each will receive his own reward according to his own labor.*
    C' 3:9 For we are God's fellow-workers. You are God's husbandry, God's building. 3:10 According to the grace of God which was given to me as a wise master builder, *I laid a foundation, and another builds on it.* But let *each one take heed how he builds on it.*
      D 3:11 For *no one can lay another foundation* than that which is laid, which is Jesus Christ.
      D' 3:12 But if *any man builds on the foundation* gold, silver, costly stones, wood, hay, straw, 3:13a each one's work will become manifest.

(3:13b For the day shall disclose it, because it is revealed in fire. And the fire itself shall prove of what sort the work of each is. 3:14 If any man's work shall remain that he built, he shall receive a reward. 3:15 If any man's work shall be burned, he shall suffer loss. But he himself shall be saved, but only through fire. 3:16 Do you not know that you are a temple of God, and the spirit of God dwells in you? 3:17 If any man destroys the temple of God, God shall destroy him. For the temple of God is holy, and such are you. 3:18 Let no man deceive himself. If any man thinks that he is wise among you in this world, let him become a fool, that he may become wise. 3:19 For the wisdom of this world is foolishness with God. For it is written, "He that takes the wise in their craftiness." 3:20 And again, "The lord knows the reasoning of the wise that they are futile.")

  E 3:21 Therefore let no one boast in men. For *all things are yours.* 3:22a Whether Paul or Apollos,

(3:22b or Kephas or the world, or life or death,)

  E' 3:22c or *things present or things to come, all are yours.* 3:23 Now you are Christ's; and Christ is God's.

1 Cor 3:1–23 Parallel Structure Table

A 3:1—babes in Christ		A' 3:4—are you not men
B 3:5—what then is Apollos and what is Paul . . . Lord gave to him	B' 3:6—I planted, Apollos watered . . . God gave the increase	B" 3:7—the one planting nor the one watering is anything . . . God gives the increase
C 3:8—now he who plants and he who waters are one . . . each will receive his own reward according to his own labor		C' 3:9–10—I laid a foundation and another builds on it . . . each one take heed how he builds on it
D 3:11—no one can lay another foundation		D' 3:12—any man builds on the foundation
E 3:21–22a—all things are yours		E' 3:22a–23—things present or things to come, all are yours

Commentary

Chiastic Structure

The A stich of the chiastic structure matches "babes in Christ" with "now you are Christ's." Obviously a baby of Christ belongs to Christ. The B stich of the chiastic structure has "Paul and Apollos" in both hemistiches, but not "Kephas" who only shows up in the B' hemistich and is probably an interpolation as discussed in the introduction to 1 Corinthians. "Men" is found in both hemistiches of the B stich. The C stich of the chiastic structure matches "I planted, Apollos watered" with "each one's work will become manifest." The C hemistich relates the work of Paul and Apollos and the C' hemistich says that God knows who did what work. The D stich of the chiastic structure matches "neither the one planting or the one watering is anything" and "no one can lay a foundation than that which is laid." Clearly Paul is writing about his laying the foundation of Christ in the D hemistich and mixing his metaphors of planting and building. The center E stich of the chiastic structure matches "he who plants and he who waters are one" with "I laid a foundation and another builds on it," repeating the match of the D stich. Then there is a second match in the E stich of "each will receive his own reward according to his labor" matching "each one take heed how he builds upon it" with matching cautionary statements for the Corinthians.

Parallel Structure

The A stich of the parallel structure matches "babes in Christ" at v.3:1 with "are you not men" at v. 3:4 with the first interpolation of vv. 3:2–3 coming in between. The B stich contains three elements with all three referring to Paul and Apollos and all three referring to God's grace. In the C stich of the parallel structure Paul mixes his metaphors by matching his planting and watering metaphor with a building metaphor. In the D stich both hemistiches mention a foundation with laying it in the D hemistich and building on it in the D' hemistich. The second interpolation at vv. 3:13b–20 contains a number of parallel words and phrases in Paul's style such that only the chiastic structure exposes this interpolation. The E stich matches "all things are yours" with "all are yours.

Interpolations

The chiastic structure reveals three interpolations. The parallel structure only reveals the first interpolation. The proposed third interpolation into this chapter at v. 3:22, "or Kephas or the world or life or death" as explained above, is as much the result of a conclusion that every mention of Kephas in 1 Corinthians is an interpolation in addition to the result of rhetorical analysis. While rhetorical analysis is not a good tool to detect short interpolations, no type of analysis is up to that task because the sample is not usually large enough to compare word choice, theology, or phraseology. However, rhetorical analysis can give a hint as to whether a parallel/matching word or phrase is missing. In the B stich "Paul and Apollos" are found in both hemistiches (vv. 3:4, 21). If Paul had written "Kephas" in v. 3:22, it is very likely that he would have written it at v. 3:4 as a chiastic match. Apparently there were divisions in the Corinthian congregation with regard to some preferring Paul and some preferring Apollos. If Kephas had been preaching in Corinth, no doubt some would have preferred him and Paul would have included him in v. 3:4 as the interpolator did at v. 1:12.

In Paul's chiastic structures he usually matches the same number of persons mentioned in one hemistich with the number mentioned in the other hemistich if the matching language includes the persons. For example, in Rom 16:1 "Phoebe our sister" matches "Quartus the brother" at v.16:23, no other names are mentioned. Again in Gal 1:18 "went up to Jerusalem, Kephas, and James" matches "went up to Jerusalem, Barnabas, and Titus" at Gal 2:1, no other names are mentioned. Also in Gal 2:3 "Titus and circumcised" matches "Barnabas and circumcised" at Gal 2:9, no other names are mentioned. With regard to mentioning Kephas in 1 Cor 3, it is also likely Paul would have mentioned Kephas at v. 3:5 for the sake of completeness. The fact that "Kephas" is not found at v. 3:4 or 5 puts in serious doubt that "Kephas" was at v. 1:12 in Paul's original autograph. It is clear that v. 3:4 is specifically referring back to v. 1:12. As mentioned above this looks like a case of editorial fatigue by the interpolator.

It appears that Paul trapped the interpolator with his planting metaphor at vv. 3:6–9. While the interpolator could reasonably add Kephas to vv. 1:12 and 3:22, he could not add Kephas to the planting or building metaphors without doing serious damage to the message. The interpolator decided to leave well enough alone. Certainly if Paul had originally included Kephas at v. 1:12, he would have included him at v. 3:4 and expanded the metaphor.

Part I | The Undisputed Letters

Granting that the eight words mentioned above should be removed from the B' hemistich of the chiastic structure (v. 3:22), the A and B hemistiches of the chiastic structure contain sixty words while the A' and B' hemistiches only contain twenty-five, a serious imbalance. First Corinthians 3:2–3 is the best candidate for interpolation since it has a large number of words without a matching word or phrase at the end of the literary unit. Although it relates to v. 3:1, it goes a bit overboard in its belittling of the Corinthians. In addition, it contradicts 1 Cor 1:4–7. Removing vv. 3:2–3 reduces the word count in the A and B hemistiches to thirty words. That provides a nice typical Pauline balance in the hemistiches.

With regard to the second interpolation into this unit, the B and C hemistiches of the chiastic structure contain forty-one words while the B' and C' hemistiches contain one hundred and forty-six words. Removal of vv. 13b–20 reduces the B' and C' hemistiches to forty-two words, a perfect balance. In addition, the interpolation seems to be seriously off the topic of Paul and Apollos preaching the same message. The interpolation introduces images of hell fire and purgatory that are not found in other undisputed letters.

1 Cor 3:2–3

Stiches	Words in first half	Words in second half	Words in interpolation
A—B	3:1–4–60	3:21–23–25	3:2–3–30

1 Cor 3:13b–20

Stiches	Words in first half	Words in second half	Words in interpolation
B—C	3:4–6–41	3:12–22a—146	3:13b–20–104

1 Cor 3:22b

Stiches	Words in first half	Words in second half	Words in interpolation
B	3:4–15	3:21–22–27	3:22b—8

1 Corinthians 4

First Corinthians 4 has three parallel structures; however, there are clear demarcations between the structures because the middle structure is set off with an inclusio. Paul clearly delineated the limits of his literary units in the undisputed letters.

1 Cor 4:1-8

The first literary unit of 1 Cor 4 is a parallel structure containing five stiches. It also contains another mention of Apollos and not Kephas.

  A 4:1 So let a man regard us as servants of Christ, and *stewards* of the mysteries of God.
  A' 4:2 In this case, moreover, it is required in *stewards*, that a man be found faithful.
    B 4:3a But with me it is the smallest matter that *I should be examined by you* or by man's court.
    B' 4:3b But *I do not examine myself.* 4:4 For I know nothing against myself. Yet am I not hereby justified. But he that judges me is the Lord.
      C 4:5 Therefore judge nothing before its time until the Lord come who will both bring to light the hidden things of darkness and *reveal the motives of the hearts*. And then each one shall have his praise from God.
      C' 4:6 Now these things, brothers, *I have transfigured myself and Apollos* for your sakes so that in us you might not learn beyond what has been written. That no one of you be puffed up one against the other. 4:7a For what makes you different?
        D 4:7b What do you have now that *you did not receive*?
        D' 4:7c And if *you did receive* it,
        D" 4:7d why do you boast as if *you had not received* it?
          E 4:8a Already you are satiated, already you are rich, without us you *reigned*.
          E' 4:8b And I wish that you did indeed *reign*.
          E" 4:8c So that we also might *reign* with you.

1 Cor 4:1-8 Parallel Structure Table

A 4:1—stewards		A' 4:2—stewards		
B 4:3a—I should be examined by you		B' 4:3b-4—I do not examine myself		
C 4:5—reveal motives of the heart		C' 4:6-7a—I have transfigured myself and Apollos		
D 4:7b—you did not receive	D' 4:7c—you did receive		D" 4:7d—you had not received	
E 4:8a—reigned		E' 4:8b—reign		E" 4:8c—reign

Part I | The Undisputed Letters

Commentary

The A stich matches "stewards" in both hemistiches. In the B stich "I should be examined by you" matches "I do not examine myself." The C stich matches "reveal the motives of the hearts" with "I have transfigured myself and Apollos." The parallel here is one of inner qualities being revealed, "motives of the heart" and "transfiguration." Here again Paul uses Apollos as a colleague apostle and fails to mention Kephas. It would seem that if Paul and Apollos are stewards of God's mysteries as stated in v. 4:1, Kephas should also be mentioned if Paul had mentioned him at vv. 1:12 and 3:22. In the D stich all three elements contain "you . . . receive." The three elements of the E stich all contain "reign."

John Strugnell proposed that the words "not beyond what has been written" (*to mē hyper ha gegraptai*) found at v. 4:6c is an interpolation.[6] Since the proposed interpolation contains so few words and there are no matching words or phrases within those five words, rhetorical analysis cannot definitely refute his proposal. However, vv. 4:6–7a is the C' hemistich, and as rhetorical analysis has defined it the C and C' hemistiches both contain thirty-three Greek words, perfectly balanced. Removing those five words would make the stich slightly imbalanced, but not to a great extent. It is possible that Strugnell is correct.

1 Cor 4:9–13

The center literary unit of 1 Cor 4 is a parallel structure with an inclusio, clearly marking the beginning and ending of each of these three units.

> A 4:9 For I think God has proclaimed us apostles last as *condemned to death*. For we have become a *spectacle to the world* both to angels and to men.
> > B 4:10a We are *fools* for Christ's sake, but you are *wise* in Christ.
> > > C 4:10b We are *weak*, but you are *strong*.
> > > > D 4:10c You are *honored*, but we are *despised*.
> > B' 4:11a Even to the present hour we both *hunger*, and *thirst*,
> > > C' 4:11b and are *naked*, and are *mistreated*,
> > > > D' 4:11c and are *homeless*. 4:12a And we *grow weary working* these hands.
> > B" 4:12b Being *reviled*, we *bless*.
> > > C" 4:12c Being *persecuted*, we *endure*.
> > > > D" 4:13a Being *slandered*, we *encourage*.
> A' 4:13b As *the scum of the Earth*, we have become the *refuse of all things* until now.

---

6. Strugnell, "1 Cor 4:6," 543–58.

1 Cor 4:9-13 Parallel Structure Table

A 4:9—condemned to death . . . spectacle to the world	A' 4:13b—refuse of all things . . . scum of the Earth	
B 4:10a—fools .. wise	B' 4:11a—hunger . . . thirst	B" 4:12b—reviled . . . bless
C 4:10b—weak . . . strong	C' 4:11b—naked . . . mistreated	C" 4:12c—persecuted . . . endure
D 4:10c—honored . . . despised	D' 4:11c—homeless . . . grow weary working	D" 4:13a—slandered . . . encourage

Commentary

In this literary unit the A stich is an inclusio beginning and ending the unit. All of the parallelisms in this literary unit are of abstract concepts. There is only one exact matching word found in the A stich with "*kosmō*" matching "*kosmou*" (world, Earth, or universe). The grammatical construction is also parallel. The A stich has "condemned to death" in the A hemistich matching "refuse of all things" in the A' hemistich, and "spectacle to the world" in the A hemistich matching "the scum of the Earth" in the A' hemistich. The B, C, and D stiches all have 3 elements containing opposites. The balance of the literary unit could be viewed either as B, C, D; B,' C,' D;' B," C," D" as shown here, or B, B,' B;" C, C,' C;" D, D,' D."

Here again Paul is presumably writing about all apostles as stated in v. 4:9 but the nearest antecedent reference to apostles is v. 4:6 which includes only Paul and Apollos, not Kephas. Since the wording of this literary unit is uncomplimentary to the apostles, perhaps the interpolator, who was apparently attempting to promote Kephas as Paul's colleague, did not want to include him in the deprecatory language.

1 Cor 4:14-21

The third literary unit in this series is a parallel structure with only two three-element stiches. It is clear that this literary unit is not connected to the prior parallel unit because the prior unit is defined by an inclusio. Once again Paul insures that his literary units have a definite beginning and ending.

> A 4:14 I do not write these things to shame you, but to admonish you as *my beloved children*. 4:15a For though you might have ten thousand guardians in *Christ* yet not many fathers.
> A' 4:15b For in *Christ Jesus* through the gospel *I have begotten you*. 4:16 I implore you therefore, become imitators of me.

A" 4:17a To this end I have sent Timothy to you, who is *my beloved* and faithful *child* in the Lord, who will remind you of my ways in *Christ Jesus,*

B 4:17b as I teach everywhere in every church. 4:18 But as to my not *coming to you* some have become puffed up.

B' 4:19 But *I will come to you shortly* if the Lord wills. And I will know, not the word of them that are puffed up, but the power.

B" 4:20 For the kingdom of God is not in word but in power. 4:21 Which would you rather? Shall *I come to you* with a rod or in love and a spirit of gentleness?

1 Cor 4:14–21 Parallel Structure Table

| A 4:14–15a—my beloved children . . . Christ | A' 4:15b–16—I have begotten you . . . Christ Jesus | A" 4:17a—my beloved . . . child . . . Christ Jesus |
| B 4:17b–18—coming to you | B' 4:19—I will come to you shortly | B" 4:20—I come to you |

Commentary

Each element of the three element A stich refers to children: "my beloved children" in the A element, "I have begotten you" in the A' element, and "my beloved . . . child" in the A" element. All three elements also contain "Christ." The B stich also contains three elements all referring to Paul's coming to visit the Corinthians: "coming to you" in the B element, "I will come to you shortly" in the B' element, and "I come to you" in the B" element.

Johannes Weiss proposed that v. 4:17 is an interpolation.[7] However, v. 4:17a is the A" element and contains "my beloved . . . child" perfectly matching the language of the A and A' elements. Canonical 1 Cor 4:14–21 is symmetrical with a three-element A stich and a 3-element B stich. Removing v. 4:17 would destroy Paul's symmetry.

1 Corinthians 5

First Corinthians 5 is a dual chiastic/parallel structure encompassing the entire chapter. The chiastic structure has very few exact word or phrase matches, but the parallel structure does have typical Pauline repetition.

---

7. Weiss, *Korinthebrief*, xli.

1 Cor 5:1–13

Chiastic Structure

A 5:1 It is actually reported that *there is sexual immorality among you*, and such sexual immorality as is not even among the Gentiles. That one has taken his father's wife.

> B 5:2 And you are puffed up rather than mourn that he who has done this deed *might be taken away from among you.*
>
>> C 5:3 For I truly being absent in body but present in spirit *have already judged him who did this thing* as though I were present.
>>
>>> D 5:4 In the name of our Lord Jesus *you being gathered together* and my spirit, with the power of our Lord Jesus
>>>
>>>> E 5:5 *to deliver such a one to Satan* for the destruction of the flesh that the spirit may be saved in the day of the Lord Jesus.
>>>>
>>>>> F 5:6 Your boasting is not good. Do you not know that a little leaven *leavens the entire lump?* 5:7a *Clean out the old leaven,* that you may be a new lump, as you are *unleavened.*
>>>>>
>>>>>> G 5:7b And *our Passover lamb has been sacrificed,* Christ.
>>>>>>
>>>>>> G' 5:8a Therefore *let us keep the feast,*
>>>>>
>>>>> F' 5:8b *not with old leaven,* not with the *leaven of malice and wickedness,* but with the *unleavened* of sincerity and truth.
>>>>
>>>> E' 5:9 I wrote to you in my letter *not to associate with the sexually immoral.*
>>>
>>> D' 5:10 Not the sexually immoral of this world, or with the covetous and thieves, or with idolaters, for then must *you must depart from the world.*
>>
>> C' 5:11 Now I wrote to you not to associate with *anyone that is named a brother if he be sexually immoral,* or covetous, or an idolater, or a reviler, or a drunkard, or a thief. Do not even eat with such a one.
>
> B' 5:12 For what have I to do with judging them that are outside? *Do you not judge those who are inside?*

A' 5:13 But those outside God judges. *Expel the wicked man from among yourselves.*

1 Cor 5:1–13 Chiastic Structure Table

A 5:1—there is sexual immorality among you	A' 5:13—expel the wicked man from among yourselves
B 5:2—might be taken away from you	B' 5:12—do you not judge those who are inside
C 5:3—have already judged him who did this thing	C' 5:11—anyone that is named a brother if he be sexually immoral
D 5:4—you being gathered together	D' 5:10—you must depart from the world

E 5:5—to deliver such a one to Satan	E' 5:9—not to associate with the sexually immoral
F 5:6–7a—leavens the entire lump ... clean out the old leaven ... unleavened	F' 5:8b—leaven of malice and wickedness ... not with the old leaven ... unleavened
G 5:7b—our Passover lamb has been sacrificed	G' 5:8a—let us keep the feast

Parallel Structure

A 5:1a It is actually reported that there is *sexual immorality among you,*
A' 5:1b and *such sexual immorality as is not even among the Gentiles.* That one has taken his father's wife.
  B 5:2 And you are puffed up, rather than mourn that *he who has done this deed* might be taken away from among you.
  B' 5:3 For I truly being absent in body but present in spirit, have already judged *him who did this thing* as though I were present.
    C 5:4 In the name of *our Lord Jesus* you being gathered together *and my spirit* with the power of *our Lord Jesus*
    C' 5:5 to deliver such a one to Satan for the destruction of the flesh that *the spirit may be saved* in the day of *the Lord Jesus.*
      D 5:6 Your boasting is not good. Do you not know that a little *leaven leavens the entire lump?*
      D' 5:7a Clean out the old *leaven, that you may be a new lump,* as you are unleavened.
        E 5:7b And our *Passover lamb has been sacrificed,* Christ.
        E' 5:8a Therefore *let us keep the feast,*
          F 5:8b not with old leaven, *not with the leaven of malice and wickedness,*
          F' 5:8c but with the *unleavened of sincerity and truth.*
            G 5:9 I wrote to you in my letter not to associate with the *sexually immoral.* 5:10 Not the *sexually immoral* of this world, or with the *covetous and thieves, or with idolaters,* for then must you must depart from the world.
            G' 5:11 Now I wrote to you not to associate with anyone that is named a brother if he be *sexually immoral, or covetous, or an idolater, or a reviler, or a drunkard, or a thief.* Do not even eat with such a one.
              H 5:12 For what have I to do with judging them that are outside? *Do you not judge those who are inside?*
              H' 5:13 *But those outside God judges.* Expel the wicked man from among yourselves.

1 Cor 5:1–13 Parallel Structure Table

A 5:1a—Sexual immorality among you	A' 5:1b—such sexual immorality as is not even among the Gentiles
B 5:2—he who has done this deed	B' 5:3—him who did this thing
C 5:4—our Lord Jesus … and my spirit … our Lord Jesus	C' 5:5—the Lord Jesus … the spirit may be saved
D 5:6—leaven leavens the entire lump	D' 5:7a—leaven that you may be a new lump
E 5:7b—Passover lamb has been sacrificed	E 5:8a—let us keep the feast
F 5:8b—not with the leaven of malice and wickedness	F' 5:8c – unleavened of sincerity and truth
G 5:9–10—sexually immoral … sexually immoral … covetous and thieves or with idolaters	G' 5:11—sexually immoral … covetous or an idolater or a revile or a drunkard or a thief
H 5:12—Do you not judge those who are inside	H' 5:13—but those on the outside God judges

Commentary

Chiastic Structure

This is a six-stich chiastic structure and all of the stiches except in the F stich have either parallel or opposite abstract concepts. The F stich matches "leavened" and "unleavened." The A stich matches "there is sexual immorality among you" with "expel the wicked man from among yourselves" as Paul institutes excommunication into church discipline. The B stich matches "might be taken away from you" with "do you not judge those who are inside." This is not an obvious match but the B hemistich is the result of Paul's judgment, while the B' hemistich has a rhetorical question about judgment. The C stich matches "have already judged him who did this thing" with "anyone that is named a brother if be sexually immoral." Both hemistiches refer to the crime and the perpetrator.

The D stich matches opposite concepts with "you being gathered together" and "you must depart from the world." The E stich matches "to deliver such a one to Satan" with "not to associate with the sexually immoral," both hemistiches referring to the perpetrator of the offense. In the F stich there are matches with exact words. "Clean out the old leaven" in the F hemistich matches "not with old leaven" in the F' hemistich, and "unleavened" is in both stiches. In addition "leavens the entire lump" in the F hemistich matches "leaven of malice and wickedness" in the F' hemistich. In the center G stich "our Passover lamb has been sacrificed" matches "let us keep the feast."

PARALLEL STRUCTURE

The parallel structure of 1 Cor 5 contains eight stiches and the E stich is identical to the chiastic structure's center G stich. Whereas the matching parallelisms that make up the chiastic structure were mostly parallel or opposite abstract concepts, the matching parallelisms in the parallel structure are mostly exact words or phrases. The A stich matches "sexual immorality among you" in the A hemistich with "such sexual immorality as is not even among the Gentiles" in the A' hemistich. The B stich matches "he who has done this deed" in the B hemistich with "him who did this thing" in the B' hemistich. The C stich contains two matching phrases. "Our Lord Jesus" is found twice in the C hemistich and "the Lord Jesus" is found once in the C' hemistich. The C hemistich also contains "and my spirit" matching "the spirit may be saved" in the C' hemistich. The D stich has matches of "leaven" and "lump" as "leaven leavens the entire lump" in the D hemistich matches "leaven that you may be a new lump" in the D' hemistich.

As mentioned, the E stich of the parallel structure is identical to the G stich of the chiastic structure as "Passover lamb has been sacrificed" matches "let us keep the feast." The F stich resumes discussion of leaven matching opposites "not with the leaven of malice and wickedness" in the F hemistich matching "unleavened of sincerity and truth" in the F' hemistich. The G stich resumes discussion of sexual immorality with "sexually immoral" being found twice in the G hemistich and once in the G' hemistich. In addition, both hemistiches contain "covetous," "thief" and "idolater." The final H stich matches "do you not judge those who are inside" in the H hemistich with "but those outside God judges" in the H' hemistich.

1 Corinthians 6

First Corinthians 6 contains two dual chiastic/parallel structures with a one-stich transitional parallel structure between them. The transitional unit is related to both chiastic units.

1 Cor 6:1–7a

This literary unit has a short dual chiastic/parallel structure, both structures containing five stiches. The parallel structure is defined by an inclusio. Typically dual chiastic/parallel structures are relatively long, most encompassing entire chapters. This structure is the shortest of the thirteen.

Chiastic Structure

    A 6:1a Having a *matter against another,*

    B 6:1b do you dare *to go to court before the unrighteous* and *not before the saints*?
        C 6:2a Or do you not know that the *saints will judge the world*?
            D 6:2b And if *the world is to be judged by you*, are you unworthy of the smallest cases?
                E 6:3a Do you not know that *we will judge angels*?
                E' 6:3b How much more *things of this life*?
            D' 6:4 If then *you have to judge things of this life*, would you set those who are not respected in the church to judge?
        C' 6:5 I say this to shame you. Thus is there no one among you *wise enough who will be able to decide between his brothers*?
    B' 6:6 But brother *goes to court against brother* and this *before unbelievers*!
A' 6:7a Indeed, already it is altogether a failure for you that you have *lawsuits against one another*.

1 Cor 6:1–7a Chiastic Structure Table

A 6:1a—matter against another	A' 6:7—lawsuits against one another
B 6:1b—to go to court before the unrighteous ... before the saints	B' 6:6—goes to court against brother ... before unbelievers
C 6:2a—saints shall judge the world	C' 6:5—wise enough who will be able to decide between his brothers
D 6:2b—the world is to be judged by you	D' 6:4—you have to judge things of this life
E 6:3a—we will judge angels	E' 6:3b—things of this life

Parallel Structure

A 6:1a Having a *matter against another*,
    B 6:1b do you dare *to go to court* before the unrighteous and not *before the saints*?
    B' 6:2a Or do you not know that the *saints will judge the world*?
        C 6:2b And if the *world is to be judged by you*, are you unworthy of the smallest cases?
        C' 6:3a Do you not know that *we will judge angels*?
      D 6:3b How much more *things of this life*?
      D' 6:4 If then you have to judge *things of this life*, would you set those who are not respected in the church to judge?
        E 6:5 I say this to shame you. Thus is there no one among you wise enough *who will be able to decide between his brothers*?
        E' 6:6 But *brother goes to court against brother*, and this before unbelievers!

A' 6:7a Indeed, already it is altogether a failure for you that you have *lawsuits against one another.*

1 Cor 6:1–7a Parallel Structure Table

A 6:1a—matter against another	A' 6:7—lawsuits against one another
B 6:1b—to go to court … before the saints	B' 6:2a—saints will judge the world
C 6:2b—world is to be judged by you	C' 6:3a—we will judge angels
D 6:3b—things of this life	D' 6:4—things of this life
E 6:5—who will be able to decide between his brothers	E' 6:6—brother goes to court against brother

Commentary

Chiastic Structure

In the A stich "matter against another" matches "lawsuits against one another." The B stich matches a pair of opposites with "to go to court before the unrighteous" matching "goes to court against brother" and "before the saints" matches "before unbelievers." In the C stich "saints shall judge the world" matches "wise enough who will be able to decide between his brothers," both phrases being about making judicial decisions. In the D stich "the world is to be judged by you" matches "you have to judge the things of this life." In the center E stich there is a match of opposites: "we will judge the angels" matches "things of this life."

Parallel Structure

The parallel structure of 1 Cor 6:1–7a is defined by an inclusio A stich that is identical to the A stich of the chiastic structure. The B stich matches two phrases about the saints involved in legal actions. The C stich matches two phrases about Christians judging the world and judging the angels. The D stich in the parallel structure matches two identical phrases "things of this life." The E stich matches phrases concerning brothers being involved in legal actions.

1 Cor 6:7b–8

This is one of the shortest literary units in the undisputed letters of Paul, a transitional unit containing one parallel stich.

A 6:7b Why not rather *suffer wrong*? why not rather be *defrauded*?

A' 6:8 But you yourselves *do wrong*, and *defraud*, and do these things to brothers.

1 Cor 6:7b–8 Parallel Structure

| A 6:7b—suffer wrong . . . defrauded | A' 6:8—do wrong . . . defraud |

Commentary

This literary unit is an unusual transitional literary unit with only one stich wherein the A hemistich is related thematically to the previous chiastic unit by asking a rhetorical question to end the previous unit. The A' hemistich is related to the next chiastic unit by anticipating the admonitions Paul is about to give. However, the hemistiches are related to each other with both containing the words "wrong" and "defraud." Here one can see the clumsy versification because the versifier did not appreciate the literary units constructed by Paul.

1 Cor 6:9–19

This is the second short dual chiastic/parallel structure in 1 Cor 6.

Chiastic Structure

A 6:9a *Or do you not know that* the unrighteous will not inherit the kingdom of God?
  B 6:9b Do not be deceived. Neither the *sexually immoral, nor idolaters, nor adulterers, nor effeminate, nor homosexuals,* 6:10 *nor thieves, nor covetous ones, nor drunkards, nor verbal abusers, nor swindlers* shall inherit the kingdom of God.
    C 6:11 And such were some of you. But you were washed, but you were sanctified, but you were justified in the name of the *Lord Jesus Christ, and in the spirit* of our God.
      D 6:12 All things are lawful for me, but *not all things are profitable*. All things are lawful for me, but I will not be mastered by anything.
        E 6:13 Food for the belly and the belly for food. But God shall destroy both it and them. But the *body* is not for *sexual immorality* but for the *Lord*, and the *Lord* for the *body*.
          F 6:14a And God both *raised the Lord,*
          F' 6:14b and *will raise us up* by his power.

E' 6:15 Do you not know that your *bodies* are members of *Christ*? Shall I then take away the members of *Christ*, and make them members of a *harlot*? May it never be!

D' 6:16 Or do you not know that *he who is joined to a harlot* is one body? For the two, it says, shall become one flesh.

C' 6:17 But he that is joined to the *Lord is one spirit*.

B' 6:18 Flee *sexual immorality*. *Every sin* that a man does is outside the body; but he that commits *sexual immorality sins* against his own body.

A' 6:19 *Or do you not know that* your body is a temple of the Holy Spirit which is in you, which you have from *God*, and you are not your own? 6:20 For you were bought with a price. Therefore glorify *God* in your body.

1 Cor 6:9–19 Chiastic Structure Table

A 6:9a—or do you not know that … God	A' 6:19-20—or do you not know that … God … God
B 6:9b-10—sexually immoral, nor idolaters, nor adulterers, nor effeminate, nor homosexuals, nor thieves, nor covetous ones, nor drunkards, nor verbal abusers, nor swindlers	B' 6:18—sexual immorality … every sin … sexual immorality … sins
C 6:11—Lord Jesus Christ and in the spirit	C' 6:17—Lord is one spirit
D 6:12—not all things are profitable	D' 6:16—he that is joined to a harlot
E 6:13—body … sexual immorality … Lord … Lord … body	E' 6:15—bodies … harlot … Christ … Christ
F 6:14a—raised the Lord	F' 6:14b—will raise us up

Parallel Structure

A 6:9 Or do you not know that the unrighteous will not *inherit the kingdom of God*? Do not be deceived. Neither the sexually immoral, nor idolaters, nor adulterers, nor effeminate, nor homosexuals,

A' 6:10 nor thieves, nor covetous ones, nor drunkards, nor verbal abusers, nor swindlers, shall *inherit the kingdom of God*.

B 6:11a And such were some of you. *But you were washed*,

B' 6:11b *but you were sanctified*,

B" 6:11c *but you were justified* in the name of the Lord Jesus Christ, and in the spirit of our God.

C 6:12a *All things are lawful for me*, but not all things are profitable.

C' 6:12b *All things are lawful for me*, but I will not be mastered by anything.

D 6:13a Food for the belly, and the *belly for food*. But God shall destroy both it and them.

D' 6:13b But the *body is not for sexual immorality*, but for the Lord; and the Lord for the body.

  E 6:14a And God both *raised the Lord*,

  E' 6:14b and will *raise us up* by his power.

    F 6:15a Do you not know that your bodies are *members of Christ*?

    F' 6:15b Shall I then take away the *members of Christ*,

      G 6:15c and make them *members of a harlot*? May it never be!.

      G' 6:16 Or do you not know that he who is *joined to a harlot* is one body? For the two, it says, shall become one flesh.

        H 6:17 But he that is joined to the Lord is one spirit. 6:18a Flee *sexual immorality*.

        H' 6:18b Every sin that a man does is outside the body, but he that commits *sexual immorality* sins against his own body.

          I' 6:19a Or do you not know that *your body* is a temple of the Holy Spirit which is in you, which you have from *God*,

          I' 6:19b and you are not your own? 6:20 For you were bought with a price. Therefore glorify *God* in *your body*.

1 Cor 6:9–19 Parallel Structure Table

A 6:9—inherit the kingdom of God		A' 6:10—inherit the kingdom of God
B 6:11a—but you were washed	B' 6:11b—but you were sanctified	B" 6:11c—but you were justified
C 6:12a—all things are lawful for me		C' 6:12b—all things are lawful for me
D 6:13a—belly for food		D' 6:13b—body is not for sexual immorality
E 6:14a—raised the Lord		E' 6:14b—raise us up
F 6:15a—members of Christ		F' 6:15b—members of Christ
G 6:15c—members of a harlot		G' 6:16—joined to a harlot
H 6:17–18a—sexual immorality		H' 6:18b—sexual immorality
I 6:19a—your body … God		I' 6:19b–20—your body … God

Commentary

Udo Schnelle proposed that v. 6:14 is an interpolation.[8] It must be admitted that v. 6:14 seems to be slightly off topic and does not exactly fit into the context of this

---

8. Schnelle, "1 Kor 6:14," 217–19.

literary unit. It appears to foreshadow Paul's argument about resurrection in 1 Cor 15. However, it does fit in with Paul's mentioning twice inheriting the kingdom of God in vv. 6:9–10. It also fits as a contrast to the destruction by God mentioned in v. 6:13. In addition, the beginning and the ending of this literary unit refer to soteriological matters. It fits with Paul's penchant for symmetry to have the center of the unit refer to soteriological matters also. If v. 6:14 were removed, the unit would still make sense. However, from a rhetorical analysis viewpoint it exactly fits, forming both the center F stich of the chiastic structure and the E stich of the parallel structure. If a redactor added v. 6:14, he must have been very perceptive with regard to Paul's literary structures or he was incredibly fortunate to add a verse with a parallelism that happened to fit both the chiastic and parallel structures.

Chiastic Structure

Both hemistiches in the A stich contain "Or do you not know that" and "God." Both hemistiches of the B stich on the other hand contain "sexual immorality" plus a long string of specifically named moral shortcomings in Paul's view, "idolaters, nor adulterers, nor effeminate, nor homosexuals, nor thieves, nor coveters, nor drunkards nor verbal abusers nor swindlers" matching "every sin." The C stich matches "Lord Jesus Christ and in the spirit" with "Lord is one spirit." The D stich matches a concept with an example. "Not all things are profitable" in the D hemistich matches "he that is joined to a harlot" in the D' hemistich. The E hemistich contains "body" twice and "Lord" once while the E' hemistich has "bodies" once and "Christ" twice. In addition "sexual immorality" (*porneia*) matches "harlot" (*pornē*). The F center stich matches "raised the Lord" and "will raise us up."

Parallel Structure

In the parallel structure the matches are mostly identical phrases found in both hemistiches. The B stich of this structure contains three elements, and the E stich is identical to the center F stich of the chiastic structure. Both hemistiches of the A stich contain "inherit the kingdom of God." The three elements of the B stich matches three benefits the Corinthians received by becoming Christians: "you were washed," "you were sanctified," and "you were justified." The C stich has "all things are lawful for me" repeated twice. The D stich analogizes "belly for food" with "body (not) for sexual immorality." The E stich is identical to the F stich of the chiastic structure. The F stich of the parallel structure has "members of Christ" repeated twice. Then the G stich matches "members of a harlot" with "joined to a harlot." The H stich has "sexual immorality" in both hemistiches. The final I stich has "your body" and "God" in both hemistiches in a chiastic format (your body, God, God, your body).

1 Corinthians 7

First Corinthians 7 contains six literary units. This is the most units found in any chapter of the undisputed letters. The first three units are: a parallel structure with an inclusio, a one verse chiastic transitional unit, and second parallel structure with an inclusio. This sequence is very reminiscent of the sequence in 1 Cor 6. Then the final literary unit in 1 Cor 7 is a unique chiastic structure with every stich containing parallel sub-stiches.

1 Cor 7:1–8

The first unit in this sequence is a parallel structure with an inclusio.

  A 7:1 Now concerning the things about which you wrote. *It is good for a man not to touch a woman.*
    B 7:2a But because of sexual immorality *let each man have his own wife,*
    B' 7:2b and *let each woman have her own husband.*
      C 7:3a *Let the husband fulfill his duty to the wife.*
      C' 7:3b Likewise *also the wife to the husband.*
        D 7:4a *The wife does not have authority over her own body, but the husband.*
        D' 7:4b Likewise also *the husband does not have authority over his own body, but the wife.*
          E 7:5a *Do not deprive one another* except it be by consent for a time that you may *devote yourselves to prayer.*
          E' 7:5b And *you may be together again* so that *Satan may not tempt you* because of your lack of restraint.
            F 7:6a But this I say *by way of concession,*
            F' 7:6b not *by way of command.*
              G 7:7a Now I wish that *all men were even as I am.*
              G' 7:7b But *each has his own gift* from God.
                H 7:7c Indeed *one has this,*
                H' 7:7d but *one has that.*
  A' 7:8 But I say to the unmarried and to widows, *it is good for them if they should remain even as I do.*

1 Cor 7:1–8 Parallel Structure Table

A 7:1—it is good for a man not to touch a woman	A' 7:8—it is good for them if they should remain even as I do

B 7:2a—let each man have his own wife	B' 7:2b—let each woman have her own husband
C 7:3a—let the husband fulfill his duty to the wife	C' 7:3b—also the wife to the husband
D 7:4a—the wife does not have authority over her own body but the husband	D' 7:4b—the husband does not have authority over his own body but the wife
E 7:5a—do not deprive one another . . . devote yourselves to prayer	E' 7:5b—you may be together again . . . Satan may not tempt you
F 7:6a—by way of concession	F' 7:6b—by way of command
G 7:7a—all men were even as I am	G' 7:7b—each has his own gift
H 7:7c—one has this	H' 7:7d—one has that

Commentary

The A stich is an inclusio with "it is good for a man not to touch a woman" matching "it is good for them if they should remain even as I do." These two statements, of course, mean the same thing. All of the matching language in this literary structure consists of abstract concepts with either the same or the opposite meaning. There is no real matching of exact words or phrases. The parallel stiches begin with the B stich with "let each man have his own wife" matching "let each woman have her own husband." The C stich matches "let the husband fulfill his duty to the wife" and "also the wife to the husband." The D stich matches "the wife does not have authority over her own body, but the husband" with "the husband does not have authority over his own body, but the wife."

The E stich has two matching phrases in each hemistich that are similar in concept. "Do not deprive one another" matches "you may be together again," and "devote yourselves to prayer" matches "Satan may not tempt you." The F stich matches "by way of concession" with "by way of command." The G stich matches "all men were even as I am" with "each has his own gift." Presumably Paul means he is celibate. This becomes important in identifying an interpolation at 1 Cor 9:5. Finishing the parallel stiches is the H stich matching "one has this" with "one has that."

1 Cor 7:9

The second literary unit in this sequence is a short transitional chiastic unit encompassing only one verse.

   A 7:9a But if they *do not have self control,*
     B 7:9b *let them marry.*
     B' 7:9c For it is *better to marry* than

A' 7:9d *to burn with passion.*

1 Cor 7:9 Chiastic Structure Table

| A 7:9a—do not have self control | A' 7:9d—than to burn with passion |
| B 7:9b—let them marry | B' 7:9c—better to marry |

Commentary

This unit is another transitional unit similar to the one at 1 Cor 6:7b–8. However, here it has a chiastic structure. The A stich refers to the previous literary unit with "not have self control" and "to burn with passion." The B stich refers to the next literary unit with "marry" in both hemistiches.

1 Cor 7:10–17

The third literary unit of 1 Cor 7 is another parallel structure with an inclusio.

  A 7:10a Now to the married *I command*, not I, but the *Lord*,
    B 7:10b *a wife is not to depart from her husband.* 7:11a But if she departs, let her remain unmarried,
    B' 7:11b or be reconciled to her husband. And *a husband may not send away his wife*.
      C 7:12 Now to the rest I say, I, not the Lord. *If any brother has an unbelieving wife* and she consents to dwell with him, *let him not send her away.*
      C' 7:13 And *if any woman has an unbelieving husband* and he consents to dwell with her, *let her not send her husband away.*
        D 7:14a For *the unbelieving husband is made holy in the wife.*
        D' 7:14b And *the unbelieving wife is made holy in the brother.*
        D" 7:14c Before *your children were unclean, but now are they holy.*
          E 7:15a *If, however, the unbeliever departs, let him depart.* The brother or the sister is not under bondage
          E' 7:15b in such cases. *But God has called you in peace.*
            F 7:16a For *how do you know, wife, whether you will save your husband?*
            F' 7:16b Or *how do you know, husband, whether you will save your wife?*
A' 7:17 Only as the *Lord* has bestowed to each, as God has called, so let him walk. And so *I prescribe* in all the churches.

PART I | THE UNDISPUTED LETTERS

1 Cor 7:10-17 Parallel Structure Table

A 7:10a—I command . . . Lord	A' 7:17—I prescribe . . . Lord
B 7:10b-11a—wife is not to depart from her husband	B' 7:11b—husband may not send away his wife
C 7:12—if any brother has an unbelieving wife . . . let him not send her away	C' 7:13—if any woman has an unbelieving husband . . . let her not send her husband away
D 7:14a—the unbelieving husband is made holy in the wife	D' 7:14b—the unbelieving wife is made holy in the brother	D" 7:14c—your children were unclean but now they are holy
E 7:15a—if however the believer departs let him depart	E' 7:15b—but God has called you in peace
F 7:16a—for how do you know, wife, whether you will save your husband	F' 7:16b—how do you know, husband, whether you will save your wife

Commentary

This is another parallel structure with an inclusio. In 1 Cor 6 is found the pattern: dual chiastic/parallel – transitional – dual chiastic/parallel, and in 1 Cor 7 there is the pattern: parallel w/inclusio – transitional – parallel w/inclusio. The dual chiastic/parallel structures have a parallel transition, and the parallel structures have a chiastic transition. This large pattern of six consecutive literary units is evidence that in Paul's original letter to the Corinthians chapter seven probably followed chapter six. This literary unit has a Pauline symmetry: the A stich is an inclusio, the B and C stiches are parallel with two elements, the D stich is parallel with three elements, and the E and F stiches are again parallel with two stiches. In other words this literary unit has a 1, 2, 3, 2, 1 symmetry.

In this literary unit the A stich matches "I command" with "I prescribe" and "Lord" is in both hemistiches. In Paul's letters "Lord" is an ambiguous term. Sometimes it means "Jesus" and sometimes it means "God." Here "Lord" means "God" which is made clear in v. 7:17. Before analyzing this literary unit, it was thought likely that "not I, but the Lord" found at v. 7:10 was an interpolation added by a latter day redactor making reference to the gospels wherein Jesus gives a pronouncement on divorce.[9] Surprisingly, it was discovered that the clumsy wording is probably original to Paul allowing him to match "I command" and "Lord" in an inclusio. In this case "Lord" is referring to God and not Jesus.

In the B stich "wife is not to depart from her husband" matches "husband may not send away his wife." The C stich has two matching phrases. The first is "if any brother has an unbelieving wife" matching "if any woman has an unbelieving husband." The

---

9. Matt 19:3-9, Mark 10:2-12, Luke 16:18.

second C stich match is "let him not send her away" parallel to "let her not send her husband away." The D stich has three elements with husbands, wives, and children being holy or sanctified: "the unbelieving husband is made holy in the wife" in the D element, "the unbelieving wife is made holy in the husband" in the D' element, and "your children were unclean, but now they are holy" in the D" element. The E stich matches "If however the unbeliever departs, let him depart" with "but God has called you in peace." The E hemistich advocates a peaceful separation, and the E' hemistich says that God wants peace. The F stich matches two almost exact phrases "for how do you know, wife, if you will save your husband" and "how do you know, husband, if you will save your wife."

1 Cor 7:18–19

This is a short transitional parallel structure based on "circumcision."

A 7:18a Was any one *called circumcised?*
 B 7:18b He *should not be uncircumcised.*
A' 7:18c Was anyone *called in uncircumcision?*
 B' 7:18d He *should not be circumcised.*
  C 7:19a *Circumcision is nothing,*
  C' 7:19b and *uncircumcision is nothing* but keeping commandments of God.

1 Cor 7:18–19 Parallel Structure Table

A 7:18a—called circumcised	A' 7:18c—called in uncircumcision
B 7:18b—he should not be uncircumcised	B' 7:18d—he should not be circumcised
C 7:19a—circumcision is nothing	C' 7:19c—uncircumcision is nothing

Commentary

This structure is reminiscent of the structure at Rom 2:25–29 also based on "circumcision." In this transitional literary structure all the matching phrases contain either "circumcision" or "uncircumcision." "Circumcision" (*peritetmēmenos, peritemnesthō, peritomē*) is found three times, and "uncircumcision" (*epispasthō, akrobystia*) is found three times. "*Epispathō*" is a verb and "*akrobystia*" is a noun. One could also diagram this structure as A, B, B,' A,' A," B" based on the words "circumcision" and "uncircumcision."

Part I | The Undisputed Letters

1 Cor 7:20–24

This short literary unit has a chiastic structure with a preponderance of matching exact words and phrases.

> A 7:20 *Let each one remain* in that calling *wherein he was called.*
> > B 7:21a Were you called as a *slave*? Do not care about it.
> > > C 7:21b But if *you can become free*, rather take advantage.
> > > > D 7:22a For he that was *called* in the *Lord being a slave* is the Lord's *freed* man.
> > > > D' 7:22b Likewise he that was *called* being *free* is Christ's slave.
> > > C' 7:23a *You were bought with a price.*
> > B' 7:23b Do not become *slaves* of men.
> A' 7:24 Brothers, *let each one remain wherein he was called* with God.

1 Cor 7:20–24 Chiastic Structure Table

A 7:20—let each one remain ... wherein he was called	A' 7:24—let each one remain ... wherein he was called
B 7:21a—slave	B' 7:23b—slaves
C 7:21b—you can become free	C' 7:23a—you were bought with a price
D 7:22a—called ... Lord being a slave ... Lord's freed	D' 7:22b—called ... Christ's slave ... free

Comments on this structure were previously set out in chapter 1 as an example of a chiastic structure and explanation of the principles in recognizing a chiastic structure. It will not be repeated here.

1 Cor 7:25–40

The final literary unit in 1 Cor 7 is an extremely complicated chiastic structure that goes to an unprecedented third level of parallelism.

> A 7:25 Now concerning virgins I have no commandment of the Lord. But *I give my judgment, as one who has obtained mercy of the Lord* to be trustworthy.
> > B 7:26 I think therefore *this is good* by reason of the present distress, *that it is good* for a man *to remain in the same manner.*
> > > C 7:27 *Are you bound to a wife? Do not seek a divorce. Have you been freed from a wife? Do not seek a wife.*
> > > > D 7:28 However, *if also you marry, you have not sinned. And if a virgin marry, she did not sin.* Yet such shall have concerns of the world and I would spare you.

E 7:29a *But this I say*, brothers,
  EA 7:29b *the time is shortened*,
    EAA 7:29c that soon both those *having wives* may be as though *having none*;
    EAA' 7:30a and *those weeping*, as *not weeping*;
    EAA'' 7:30b and *those rejoicing*, as *not rejoicing*;
    EAA''' 7:30c and *those buying*, as *not possessing*;
    EAA'''' 7:31a and *those using* the world, as *not using it* to the full.
  EB 7:31b For *the present form of this world is passing away*.
  FA 7:32 But I would have you to be free from cares. *The unmarried man cares for the things of the Lord*, how he may please the Lord.
    FB 7:33a *But he who is married cares for the things of the world*.
      FC 7:33b *How he may please his wife*,
  F'A' 7:34a and is divided. Also *the unmarried woman and the virgin care for the things of the Lord*, that she may be holy both in body and in spirit.
    F'B' 7:34b *But she who is married cares for the things of the world*.
      F'C' 7:34c *How she may please her husband*.
E' 7:35a *But this I say* for your own benefit, not that I may cast a snare upon you,
  E'A' 7:35b but for *that which is seemly*, and that you may attend to the Lord without distraction. 7:36a But if any man supposes he is *behaving unseemly* toward his fiancé if she be mature
    E'B' 7:36b and *so it ought to be, let him do what he will*. He does not sin. Let them marry. 7:37 But he that stands strong in his heart, *having no necessity*, but *has will power* to watch over his fiancé shall do well.
D' 7:38 So then both *the one marrying his fiancé does well*, and *the one not marrying her will do better*.
C' 7:39 *A wife is bound* for so long a time as *her husband may live*. But if *the husband be dead*, she is *free to be married to whom she will* only in the Lord.
B' 7:40a But she is *more blessed* if she *stay as she is*
A' 7:40b *according to my judgment*. And I think that *I also have the spirit of God*.

1 Cor 7:25-40 Chiastic Structure Table

A 7:25—I give my judgment ... As one who has obtained mercy of the Lord	A' 7:40b—according to my judgment ... I also have the spirit of God
B 7:26—this is good ... that this is good ... to remain in the same manner	B' 7:40a—more blessed ... stay as she is

C 7:27—Are you bound to a wife? Do not seek a divorce. Have you been freed from a wife? Do not seek a wife		C' 7:39—a wife is bound . . . her husband may live . . . the husband be dead . . . free to be married to whom she will		
D 7:28—if you also marry you have not sinned . . . if a virgin marry she did not sin		D' 7:38—the one marrying his fiancé does well . . . the one not marrying her will do better		
E 7:29a—but this I say		E' 7:35a—but this I say		
EA 7:29b—the time is shortened	EB 7:31b—the present form of this world is passing away	E'A' 7:35b-36—that which is seemly . . . behaving unseemly	E'B' 7:36b-37—so it ought to be . . . let him do what he will . . . having no necessity . . . has will power	
EAA 7:29c—having . . . wives having none	EAA' 7:30a—those weeping . . . not weeping	EAA" 7:30c—those rejoicing . . . not rejoicing	EAA''' 7:30e—those buying . . . not possessing	EAA"" 7:31a—those using . . . not using
FA 7:32—the unmarried man cares for the things of the Lord		F'A' 7:34a—the unmarried woman and the virgin care for the things of the Lord		
FB 7:33a—but he who is married cares for things of the world		F'B' 7:34b—but she who is married cares for things of the world		
FC 7:33b—how he may please his wife		F'C' 7:34c—how she may please her husband		

Commentary

This may be the most complicated literary unit in the entire Pauline corpus. It has a chiastic structure, but most hemistiches contain parallelisms within themselves. It is not unheard of to have paralleled hemistiches in a chiastic center stich. An example of this is the center stich of 1 Cor 11. In addition, such structures are found in the Gospel of Mark.[10] However, it is odd that there are not the same number of parallel elements in the two halves of the chiastic structure. The E stich is especially complex and the first half of the E stich does not match the second half. Further, in the E stich there is a sub-sub-parallel structure, the only instance in the Pauline corpus. The E hemistich has six paralleled elements and an inclusio in the first half of the chiastic structure, while the E' hemistich in the second half of the structure contains two paralleled elements that seem to match the inclusio but not the parallel sub-structure within the inclusio. The center F stich has the same number of paralleled elements in each hemistich with an A, B, C; A,' B,' C' format the same as the center stich of 1 Cor 11.

---

10. Mark 8:5–7, 10:23–26, 37–40.

The A stich matches "I give my judgment" in the A hemistich, with "according to my judgment" in the A' hemistich. The second A stich match is "as one who has received mercy from the Lord" matching "I also have the spirit of God." The B stich matches "this is good" and "that it is good" in the B hemistich with "more blessed" in the B' hemistich. The second B stich match is "to remain in the same manner" matching "stay as she is." The C stich matches "are you bound to a wife" with "a wife is bound." The C hemistich states the rule for husbands in opposing situations: "are you bound to a wife? Do not seek to be freed," and "are you freed from a wife? Do not seek a wife." Then the C' hemistich states the rule for wives "her husband may live," "the husband be dead," "free to be married to whom she will."

The D stich matches "marry" twice with "marrying" twice, and "virgin" (*parthenos*) with "fiancé" (*parthenon*). The D stich matches "if also you marry, you have not sinned" in the D hemistich with "the one not marrying her will do better" in the D' hemistich. The second D stich match is "and if a virgin marry, she did not sin" with "the one marrying his fiancé does well." The E stich is the most unusual of this unusual literary unit. The only chiastic repetition match in these two long hemistiches is "but this I say" in both hemistiches. Then there is a parallel part of the E hemistich set off by an inclusio, the EA and EB elements, with "the time is shortened" matching " for the present form of this world is passing away." The EB element explains the EA element. The E'A' and E'B' match the EA and EB elements in form, but they are not parallel in repetition of words or phrases or abstract concepts. This is unique in the undisputed letters. The E'A' element has "that which is seemly" and "behaving unseemly," while these are parallel with each other, neither of which have anything to do with time being shortened or the present age passing away. The E'B' element is similar in that it has two parallel statements "so it ought to be," "having no necessity," and "let him do what he will," and "has will power."

Within the EA, EB inclusio there is a parallel sub-sub-structure advising the Corinthians of what is to happen when Christ comes to Earth from Heaven. The EAA element has "having wives" and "having none." The EAA' element has "those weeping" and "not weeping." The EAA'' element has "those rejoicing" and "not rejoicing." The EAA''' element has "those buying" and "not possessing." The EAA'''' element has "those using the world" and "not using it to the full." O'Neill proposed that vv. 7:29–31 are an interpolation.[11] Rhetorical analysis can sympathize with O'Neill's proposal because of the unusual construction of vv. 7:29–31. However, the EA-EB sub-structure appears to be very Pauline and "But this I say" at v. 7:29a matches "But this I say" at v. 7:35a. It can be viewed as chiastic or as a parallel structure with an inclusio. It is not likely that O'Neill is correct in this proposal.

All parallel elements of the center F stich match exact phrases except that the first is about men and the second is about women. The FA, F'A' elements have "the unmarried man cares for things of the Lord" matching "the unmarried woman and

---

11. O'Neill, "Glosses and Interpolations," 381–83.

the virgin care for things of the Lord." The FB, F'B' elements have " but he who is married cares for things of the world" matching "but she who is married cares for things of the world." The FC, F'C' elements have "how he should please his wife" matching "how she should please her husband."

1 Corinthians 8

This chapter of 1 Corinthians is entirely interpolated. Paul did not write this chapter. There are parallelisms in this chapter but there is no regularity and no symmetry to them. It appears that the interpolator tried to imitate Paul's style by repeating words and phrases, but did not have a grasp of Paul's use of chiasm and parallelism in symmetrical patterns.

1 Cor 8:1–13

>(A 8:1 Now concerning *things sacrificed to idols*.
>   B We *know* that we all have *knowledge. Knowledge* puffs up, but love builds up.
>   B' 8:2 If any one thinks that he *knows* anything, he does not yet *know* as much as he needs to *know*.
>   C 8:3 But if any *one loves God*,
>   B" he is *known* by Him.
> A' 8:4 Therefore concerning the *eating of things sacrificed to idols*,
>   B'" we *know* that an idol is nothing
>   C' in the world, and that there is no *God but one*. 8:5a And even if indeed there are things that are called gods, whether in Heaven or on Earth;
>   C" 8:5b as there are many gods, and many lords. 8:6 But to us there is *one God*, the father,
>   D *from whom are all things,* and we to him;
>   E and one Lord, Jesus *Christ*,
>   D' *through whom are all things,* and we through him.
>   B"" 8:7 But that *knowledge* is not in all men.
> A" But some, until now being accustomed to the idol, *eat as a thing sacrificed to an idol*;
>   F and their *weak conscience* is defiled. 8:8 But food will not commend us to God. We neither fall short if we do not eat; nor are we better off if we eat.
>   G 8:9 But be careful unless your liberty becomes a *stumbling block to the weak*.
>   B""" 8:10 For if one sees you, who has *knowledge*, reclining at dinner in an idol's temple,
>   F' if he is *weak will not his conscience* be built up

A''' to *eat things sacrificed to idols?*
　B''''' 8:11 For through your *knowledge* he that is weak perishes,
　　E' the brother for whom *Christ* died.
　　　F'' 8:12 Thus, sinning against the brothers, and wounding their *weak conscience,*
　　E'' you sin against *Christ.*
　　　G' 8:13 Therefore, if food causes my *brother to stumble,* I will not eat flesh for evermore,
　　　G'' so that I do not cause my *brother to be ensnared.*)

Commentary

First Corinthians 8 has been put into parentheses to indicate that the entire chapter has been interpolated. The chapter contains six repeated phrases making it superficially appearing to be written by Paul. It could deceive casual readers and even scholars who failed to recognize that Paul's parallelisms are in regular and symmetrical patterns. However, the pattern of the repeated phrases is unlike any other literary unit in Paul's undisputed letters. It does bear a resemblance to Ephesians in the almost random nature of its repeated phrases.[12] This literary unit also seems to have two introductory phrases at vv. 8:1 and 4 when the writer repeats "concerning" (*peri*). The theology in 1 Cor 8 conflicts with the theology of vv. 10:19–33. In 1 Cor 8 the writer says that idols are nothing. In 1 Cor 10:20–21 Paul says idols are demons. In 1 Cor 8 the writer says it is best not to eat things sacrificed to idols for the sake of others. In vv. 10:19–33 Paul says one cannot partake of the table of the Lord and the table of demons. That is, one cannot be a Christian if he joins in feasts at temples to other gods. First Corinthians 10:19–33 definitely has the characteristics of a Pauline literary unit[13] while 1 Cor 8 does not. First Corinthians 8 is an interpolated literary unit.

1 Corinthians 9

1 Cor 9:1–27

This literary unit has a parallel structure encompassing the entire chapter and containing the most stiches of any literary unit in all of the undisputed letters. This structure reveals another interpolation about Kephas.

　A 9:1 Am I not free? *Am I not an apostle?* Have I not seen Jesus our Lord? Are *you not my work in the Lord?*

---

12. See chapter 13 below.
13. See section on 1 Cor 10:19–33 below.

A' 9:2 If to others *I am not an apostle*, yet at least I am to you; for the seal of *my apostleship you are in the Lord.*
   B 9:3 My defense to those who investigate me is this. 9:4 Have we no right *to eat and to drink?*

(9:5 Have we no right to take around a believing wife, even as the rest of the apostles, and the brothers of the Lord, and Kephas? 9:6 Or is it only Barnabas and I, who do not have a right to refrain from working? 9:7a What soldier ever serves at his own expense?)

  B' 9:7b Who plants a vineyard, and does not *eat* the fruit from it? Or who shepherds a flock, and does not *drink* the milk of the flock?
    C 9:8 I do not speak these things after the manner of men. *Does not the law also say the same?*
    C' 9:9a For *it is written in the law of Moses,*
      D 9:9b "You shall not *muzzle the ox* when he treads out the grain."
      D' 9:9c Does God *care for the oxen?*
        E 9:10a Or did he surely *say it for our sake?*
        E' 9:10b It was *written for our sake.*
          F 9:10c Because *he who plows ought to plow in hope,*
          F' 9:10d and *he who threshes, in hope to partake.*
            G 9:11a *If we sowed* among you *spiritual things,*
            G' 9:11b is it a great matter *if we will reap earthly things?*
              H 9:12a If others *share this privilege* with you, should not we yet more?
              H' 9:12b But we did not *use this privilege.* Instead we endure all things, so that we may give no hindrance to the gospel of Christ.
                I 9:13a Do you not know that those who work with holy things *eat the things of the temple.*
                I' 9:13b Those attending the altar *partake of the altar?*
                  J 9:14a Thus also the Lord prescribed that those *proclaiming the gospel*
                J' 9:14b should *live from the gospel.*
                    K 9:15a But I have used none of these. Neither do I write these things so that *it may be done for me.*
                    K' 9:15b For *it would be good for me* rather to die, than that any man should make my glorifying void.
                      L 9:16a For *if I preach the gospel,* I have nothing to boast about. For necessity is laid upon me.
                      L' 9:16b For woe is to me, *if I do not preach the gospel.*
                        M 9:17a For *if I do this of my own will,* I have a reward.

M' 9:17b But *if not of my own will*, I have a stewardship entrusted to me.

N 9:18a What then is my reward? That, *in preaching the gospel gratuitously*,

N' 9:18b I establish the gospel, so as not to fully *use my privilege in the gospel*.

O 9:19a For though *I was free from all*,

O' 9:19b *I became a slave to all*, that I might gain more.

P 9:20a And to the Jews *I became like a Jew*,

P' 9:20b that *I might gain Jews*.

Q 9:20c To those who are under the law, as if under the law, not *being myself under the law*,

Q' 9:20d that I might gain *those who are under the law*.

R 9:21a To those *who are outside the law*, as if *outside the law*,

R' 9:21b not being *outside the law* of God, but under law to Christ, that I might gain those *who are outside the law*.

S 9:22a To the weak *I became weak*,

S' 9:22b that *I might gain the weak*.

T 9:22c I have become *all things to all men*,

T' 9:22d that I might *by all means* save some.

U 9:23a And *I do all things for the gospel's sake*,

U' 9:23b so that *I might become a co-participant in it*.

V 9:24a Do you not know that all indeed run in a race, but *only one receives the prize*?

V' 9:24b Therefore run, so that *you might receive it*. 9:25a And everyone competing exercises self-control in all things.

W 9:25b *Indeed, they might receive a perishable crown*;

W' 9:25c *however, we an imperishable one*.

X 9:26a *So therefore I run, not uncertainly*.

X' 9:26b *So I fight, not beating the air.*

Y 9:27a But I batter my body, and *bring it into slavery.*

Y' 9:27b Unless, having preached to others, *I should be rejected.*

1 Cor 9:1-27 Parallel Structure Table

A 9:1—am I not an apostle . . . you my work in the Lord	A' 9:2—I am not an apostle . . . my apostleship you are in the Lord
B 9:3-4—to eat and to drink	B' 9:7b—eat and drink
C 9:8—does not the law also say the same	C' 9:9a—it is written in the law of Moses
D 9:9b—muzzle the ox	D' 9:9c—care for the oxen
E 9:10a—say it for our sake	E' 9:10b—written for our sake
F 9:10c—he who plows ought to plow in hope	F' 9:10d—he who threshes in hope to partake
G 9:11a—if we sowed . . . spiritual things	G' 9:11b—if we reap earthly things
H 9:12a—share this privilege	H' 9:12b—use this privilege
I 9:13a—eat the things of the temple	I' 9:13b—partake of the altar
J 9:14a—proclaiming the gospel	J' 9:14b—live from the gospel
K 9:15a—it may be done for me	K' 9:15b—it would be good for me
L 9:16a—if I preach the gospel	L' 9:16b—if I do not preach the gospel
M 9:17a—if I do this of my own will	M' 9:17b—if not of my own will
N 9:18a—in preaching the gospel gratuitously	N' 9:18b—use my privilege in the gospel
O 9:19a—I was free from all	O' 9:19b—I became a slave to all
P 9:20a—I became like a Jew	P' 9:20b—I might gain Jews
Q 9:20c—being myself under the law	Q' 9:20d—those who are under the law
R 9:21a—who are outside the law . . . outside the law	R' 9:21b—who are outside the law . . . outside the law
S 9:22a—I became weak	S' 9:22b—I might gain the weak
T 9:22c—all things to all men	T' 9:22d—by all means
U 9:23a—I do all things for the gospel's sake	U' 9:23b—I might become a co-participant in it
V 9:24a—only one receives the prize	V' 9:24b-25a—you might receive it
W 9:25b—indeed they might receive a perishable crown	W' 9:25c—however we an imperishable one
X 9:26a—therefore I run not uncertainly	X' 9:26b—so I fight not beating the air

| Y 9:27a—bring it into slavery | Y' 9:27b—I should be rejected |

Commentary

The balance of the stiches in this long literary unit is in a very consistent A, A'; B, B'; C, C' structure with the vast majority of the matches being exact words and phrases. The A stich contains two matches in each hemistich. The first is "Am I not an apostle" matching "I am not an apostle." The second is "you my work in the Lord" matching "my apostleship you are in the Lord" with only two words in between. The B stich matches "to eat and to drink" with "eat . . . drink" with nine words in between, not counting the interpolated passage, vv. 9:5–7a. The C stich matches "does not the law also say the same" with "it is written in the law of Moses" with no words in between. The D stich matches "muzzle the ox" with "care for the oxen" with only two words in between. The E stich matches "say it for our sake" with "written for our sake" with no words in between.

The F stich matches "he who plows ought to plow in hope" with "he who threshes in hope to partake" with no words in between. The G stich matches "if we sowed among you spiritual things" with "if we will reap from you earthly things" with no words in between. The H stich matches "if others share this privilege" with "we did not take advantage of the privilege" with four words in between. The I stich matches "eat the things of the temple" with "partake of the altar" with four words in between. The J stich matches "proclaiming the gospel" with "live from the gospel" with no words in between. The K stich matches "it may be done for me" with "it is good for me" with no words in between.

The L stich matches "if I preach the gospel" with "if I do not preach the gospel" with twelve words in between. The M stich matches "if I do this of my own will" with "if not of my own will" with two words in between. The N stich matches "in preaching the gospel gratuitously" with " use my privilege in the gospel" with six words in between. The O stich matches "I was free from all" matches its opposite "I became a slave to all" with no words in between. The P stich matches "I became like a Jew" with "I might gain Jews" with one word in between. The Q stich matches "being myself under the law" with "those who are under the law" with one word in between.

The R stich repeats "outside the law" (*anomos*) four times, two in each hemistich, with two words in between. The S stich matches "I became weak" with "I might gain the weak" with one word in between. The T stich matches "all things to all men" with "by all means" with one word in between. The U stich matches "I do all things for the sake of the gospel" with "I might become a fellow partaker with it" with one word in between. The V stich matches "only one receives the prize" with "you might receive it." The W stich matches "indeed, they might receive a perishable crown" with "however, we an imperishable one." The X stich matches "so therefore I run not uncertainly" with "so I fight not beating the air." The Y stich matches "bring it into slavery" with "I should be rejected."

Interpolation 1 Cor 9:5–7a

With twenty-five stiches this literary unit is the longest in Paul's undisputed letters. Having twenty-five stiches within only twenty-four and a half verses means that there are at least fifty matching phrases. However, the A and R stiches actually have two matching phrases in each hemistich. The result is that there is comparatively very little text outside of the matching phrases. Such a rapid repetition of repeated words, phrases, and concepts allows the easy identification of an interpolation at vv. 9:5–7a. Coming in between the B hemistich and the B' hemistich, this passage has thirty-four words without a repeated word or phrase. In all of the other twenty-four stiches the stich with the next most words in between matching phrases of two hemistiches is in the L hemistich with only twelve.

Predictably, this interpolated passage contains the name of Kephas, confirming the previous conclusion that every mention of Kephas in 1 Corinthians is the result of an interpolation. It also contains the only mention of Barnabas in 1 Corinthians. If this had been written by Paul one would expect him to have mentioned Apollos as he had in 1 Cor 1, 3, and 4. Analyzing this suspected interpolated phrase in the traditional manner shows at least two anomalies. One, Paul mentions that he is not allowed to "take around a believing wife." However, in the previous chapter (1 Cor 7 assuming 1 Cor 8 is an interpolation) Paul has used his celibacy as an admirable example in vv. 7:7–8. If Paul is an unmarried celibate, it seems highly unlikely that he would complain that he was not allowed to take around a believing wife. Two, v. 9:4 says Paul is not allowed to eat and drink, but his defense to that prohibition is not stated until vv. 9:7b–8, with the suspected interpolated phrase intervening. In addition to the interpolated passage being out of place in this rapid-fire literary unit, his argument would have more force if the defense came immediately after the charge.

Stiches	Words in first half	Words in second half	Words in interpolation
B	9:3-4—15	9:7b—21	9:5-7a—34

1 Corinthians 10

1 Cor 10:1–18

This literary unit is a chiastic structure with a three-element center stich

> A 10:1 For I do not want you to be ignorant, brothers, that *our fathers* were all under the cloud, and all passed through the sea.

B 10:2 And were all baptized into Moses in the cloud and in the sea. 10:3 And all *ate* the same *spiritual food*;

  C 10:4 And all *drank* the same *spiritual drink*. For *they were drinking* from a spiritual rock that was with them. But the rock was *Christ*.

   D 10:5 However, God was not well pleased with most of them. *For they were laid low in the wilderness.*

    E 10:6 Now these things have become examples to us, that we should not be *desirers of evil things* as they also desired.

     F 10:7 Neither should you be idolaters as were some of them. *As it is written* "The people sat down to eat and drink, and rose up to play."

      G 10:8 *Neither should we be sexually immoral, as some of them were sexually immoral.* And in one day *twenty-three thousand fell.*

      G' 10:9 *Neither should we test the Christ, as some of them tested,* and were *destroyed by serpents.*

      G" 10:10 *Neither should you grumble, as some of them grumbled,* and *perished by the destroyer.*

     F' 10:11 Now these things happened to them as examples. And *they were written* for our admonition to whom the ends of the ages has arrived. 10:12 Therefore let him who thinks he stands take heed lest he fall.

    E' 10:13 No *temptation* has taken you but what a man can bear. But God is faithful, who will not allow you *to be tempted* beyond what you are able. But with the *temptation* will provide also the escape that you may be able to endure it.

   D' 10:14 Therefore, my beloved, *flee from idolatry*. 10:15 I speak as to wise ones. Judge for yourselves what I say.

  C' 10:16a The *cup* of blessing that we bless, is it not a *communion of the blood of Christ*?

 B' 10:16b The *bread* which we break, is it not a *communion of the body of Christ*? 10:17 Seeing that we, who are many, are one *loaf*, one body, for we all partake of the one *loaf*.

A' 10:18 Behold *Israel according to the flesh*. Are not they who eat the sacrifices in communion with the altar?

1 Cor 10:1-18 Chiastic Structure Table

A 10:1—our fathers	A' 10:18—Israel according to the flesh
B 10:2-3—ate ... spiritual food	10:16b-17—communion of the body of Christ ... bread ... loaf ... loaf
C 10:4—drank ... spiritual drink ... they were drinking ... Christ	C' 10:16a—communion of the blood of Christ ... cup

D 10:5—for they were laid low in the wilderness	D' 10:14—flee from idolatry	
E 10:6—desirers of evil things	E' 10:13—temptation . . . temptation . . . to be tempted	
F 10:7—as it is written	F' 10:11–12—they were written	
G 10:8—Neither should we be sexually immoral, as some of them were sexually immoral . . . twenty-three thousand fell	G' 10:9—Neither should we test the Christ as some of them tested . . . destroyed by serpents	G" 10:10—Neither should you grumble as some of them grumble . . . perished by the destroyer

Commentary

This chiastic structure has a center stich with three elements. The matching language in this structure is also more matching abstract concepts than exact words and phrases. Walker thinks that vv. 10:1–22 is an interpolation.[14] He notes unusual language and midrashic style not found elsewhere in Paul. His main argument seems to be that 10:19–22 conflicts with the theology of 1 Cor 8. Lamar Cope agreed with Walker.[15] Rhetorical analysis shows Walker and Cope have picked the wrong horse. It is 1 Cor 8 that is the interpolation, not vv. 10:19–22. This is discussed in the following section on the literary unit 1 Cor 10:19–33.

In the A stich "our fathers" matches "Israel according to the flesh." It is clear that Paul is writing about the Israelites in the A hemistich because he relates events reported in Exodus; therefore, "Israel according to the flesh" is an appropriate match for "our fathers," Paul being Jewish. The B stich has two matching phrases in each hemistich. The principal match is "spiritual food" with "communion in the body of Christ." Clearly communion in the body of Christ is spiritual food. The second match is "ate" with "bread" or "loaf" three times. The C stich is similar to the B stich in that it matches "spiritual drink" with "communion of the blood of Christ" with "drink" parallel to the "food" of the B stich. Also in the C stich "drank" and "they were drinking" match "cup," another parallel with the B stich. "Christ" is also in both hemistiches. The matching language in the D stich is not very obvious. It seems that Paul intended a match between "they were laid low in the wilderness" and "flee from idolatry. The phrase "laid low in the wilderness" is a reference to Num 16 wherein Moses puts down a rebellion of some of the Levites who questioned his leadership. According to Num 16:31 God opened the ground and swallowed up the rebels. It is assumed Paul intended the match mentioned in the sense that God will punish those who practice idolatry. The E stich matches "desirers of evil things" with "temptation" twice and "to be tempted." The F stich matches " just as it is written" with "they were written." The

14. Walker, *Interpolations*, 232–36.
15. Cope, "First Corinthians 8–10," 114–23.

center G stich has three elements matching three sins with three punishments for committing those sins. The three sins are "neither should we be sexually immoral as some of them were sexually immoral," "Neither should we test the Christ as some of them tested," and "neither should you grumble as some of them grumbled." The three punishments are "twenty-three thousand fell," "destroyed by serpents," and "perished by the destroyer." This is the third chiastic structure found in 1 Corinthians with a three-element center stich.

1 Cor 10:19–33

This literary unit has a parallel structure, each stich having two hemistiches.

  A 10:19a What do I mean then? That *a thing sacrificed to an idol is anything*,
  A' 10:19b or that *an idol is anything*?
    B 10:20a But that which the Gentiles *sacrifice is to demons*, and they do not sacrifice to God.
    B' 10:20b But I do not want you to become a *communicant with demons*.
      C 10:21a You cannot drink the *cup of the Lord*
      C' 10:21b and the *cup of demons*.
        D 10:21c You cannot partake of the *table of the Lord*
        D' 10:21d and of the *table of demons*.
          E 10:22a Or *do we provoke the Lord to jealousy*?
          E' 10:22b Are *we stronger than he*?
            F 10:23a *All things are lawful, but not all things are profitable*.
            F' 10:23b *All things are lawful, but not all things edify*.
              G 10:24 Let no man seek his own but his neighbor's. 10:25 *Whatsoever is sold in the market, eat, asking no question for conscience sake*.
              G' 10:26 For the Earth is the Lord's, and the fullness thereof. 10:27 If one of those who does not believe invites you, and you wish to go, *whatsoever is set before you, eat, asking no question for conscience sake*.
                H 10:28 But if any one say to you, "This has been offered to an idol," do not eat for his sake that showed it *and for conscience sake*.
                H' 10:29 Conscience, I say, not your own, but the other's. For why is my freedom *judged by another's conscience*?
                  I 10:30a If I *partake with thankfulness*,
                  I' 10:30b why am I denounced for that *for which I give thanks*?
                    J 10:31 Whether therefore you eat, or drink, or whatever you do, *do all to the glory of God*.
                    J' 10:32 Give no occasions of stumbling, either to Jews, or to Greeks, or *to the church of God*.

K 10:33a As I also please everyone in all things, *not seeking my own profit,*

K' 10:33b but that of the many *so they may be saved.*

1 Cor 10:19-33 Parallel Structure Table

A 10:19a—a thing sacrificed to an idol is anything	A' 10:19b—an idol is anything
B 10:20a—sacrifice to demons	B' 10:20b—communicant with demons
C 10:21a—cup of the Lord	C' 10:21b—cup of demons
D 10:21c—table of the Lord	D' 10:21d—table of demons
E 10:22a—do we provoke the Lord to jealousy	E' 10:22b—stronger than he
F 10:23a—all things are lawful, but not all things are profitable	F' 10:23b—all things are lawful, but not all things edify
G 10:24-25—whatsoever is sold in the market eat asking no questions for conscience sake	G' 10:26-27 - whatsoever is set before you eat asking no questions for conscience sake
H 10:28—and for conscience sake	H' 10:29—judged by another's conscience
I 10:30a—partake with thankfulness	I' 10:30b—for which I give thanks
J 10:31—do all to the glory of God	J' 10:32—to the church of God
K 10:33a—not seeking my own profit	K' 10:33b—so they may be saved

Commentary

The second literary unit in 1 Cor 10 is a parallel structure with mostly repeated phrases uniting the stiches. This structure covers eating food sacrificed to idols, the same subject dealt with in 1 Cor 8. Rhetorical analysis determined 1 Cor 8 is an interpolation. Since this structure is typically Pauline, 1 Cor 10 seems to be the genuine advice Paul gave to the Corinthians about eating food sacrificed to idols. As noted in the previous section Walker and Cope do not appreciate the Pauline structure of 1 Cor 10 and the lack of it in 1 Cor 8. In the A stich "a thing sacrificed to an idol is anything" matches "an idol is anything" although the A hemistich uses a verb (*eidōlothyton*) about idols and the A' hemistich uses the noun "idol" (*eidōlon*). The B stich matches "sacrifice to demons" with "a communicant with demons." The C stich matches "the cup of the Lord" with "the cup of demons." The D stich matches "the table of the Lord" with "the table of demons." The E stich matches "do we provoke the Lord to jealousy" with "we stronger than he." The words are not parallel in the E hemistiches but Paul is asking two questions about Christians' relationship with God. The F stich matches "all things are lawful but not all things are profitable" with "all things are lawful but not all things edify." The G stich contains the exact phrase "asking no questions for conscience sake" in both hemistiches. Both are introduced by parallel phrases "whatsoever is sold in the market, eat" and "whatsoever is set before you, eat." The H stich matches "and for conscience sake" with "judged by another's conscience." The I stich matches "partake with thankfulness" with "for which I give thanks." The J stich matches "do all for the glory of God" with "to the church of God." The final K stich matches "not seeking my own profit" with "so they may be saved." The parallel here is that both hemistiches concerning Paul's self sacrifice.

Interpolation

As stated Walker and Cope think that 1 Cor 10:1–22 is an interpolation, but rhetorical analysis shows that vv. 1–18 have a chiastic structure very much in the Pauline style and vv. 19–33 have a parallel structure very much in the Pauline style. Walker would have us believe: 1) that an interpolator appreciated that 1 Cor 9 was a long parallel structure containing the most stiches of any literary structure in the undisputed letters, 2) that originally the long parallel structure continued for ten more verses, 1 Cor 10:23–33, 3) that the interpolator decided to structure his interpolation in a chiastic structure starting at 1 Cor 10:1, 4) that he continued the chiastic structure through v. 10:18, and 5) that he then switched his chiastic structure to a parallel structure at v. 10:19 to fit in with the remainder of the parallel structure that runs from v. 10:23–33. The reader can see how failure to appreciate Paul's literary structures can lead to erroneous conclusions about interpolations.

1 Corinthians 11

1 Cor 11:1–34

This long dual chiastic/parallel structure encompassing the entire chapter reveals a long interpolation.

Chiastic Structure

> A 11:1 Be imitators of me even as I also am of Christ. 11:2a Now *I commend you* that you remember me in all things.
>   B 11:2b And hold fast the teachings as I delivered them to you.

(11:3 But I would have you know, that the head of every man is Christ. And the head of the woman is the man. And the head of Christ is God. 11:4 Every man praying or prophesying, having his head covered, dishonors his head. 11:5 But every woman praying or prophesying with her head unveiled dishonors her head. For it is one and the same thing as if she were shaven. 11:6 For if a woman is not veiled, let her also be shorn. But if it is a shame to a woman to be shorn or shaven, let her be veiled. 11:7 For a man indeed ought not to have his head veiled forasmuch as he is the image and glory of God. But the woman is the glory of the man. 11:8 For the man is not of the woman, but the woman of the man. 11:9 For neither was the man created for the woman, but the woman for the man. 11:10 For this cause ought the woman to have authority on her head because of the angels. 11:11 Nevertheless, neither is the woman without the man nor the man without the woman in the Lord. 11:12 For as the woman is of the man, so is the man also by the woman. But all things are of God. 11:13 Judge in yourselves. Is it seemly that a woman pray to God unveiled? 11:14 Does not even nature itself teach you that if a man has long hair, it is a dishonor to him? 11:15 But if a woman has long hair, it is a glory to her. For her hair is given her for a covering. 11:16 But if any man seems to be contentious, we have no such custom, neither the churches of God.)

  B 11:17 But in giving you this commandment, I do not commend you, because you do not *come together* for the better but for the worse. 11:18 For first of all, when *you come together in the church*, I hear that divisions exist among you, and I partly believe it.

    C 11:19 For there must also be factions among you, so that *those who are approved* should become evident among you.

      D 11:20 Therefore when you assemble together it is not *to eat the Lord's supper*. 11:21 For in your eating each *one takes before the other* his own supper; and *this one is hungry*, and *that one is drunk*.

        E 11:22a For do you not have houses in which *to eat and to drink*? Or do you despise the church of God, and you are shaming those that have nothing?

          F 11:22b What shall I say to you? Shall I commend you? *In this I do not commend you.*

            G 11:23a For I received from the Lord that which also I delivered to you. That the Lord Jesus in the night in which *he was delivered up*

              HA 11:23b took *bread*. 11:24a And when he had given thanks, he broke it,

                HB 11:24b *and said, "This is my body*, which is for you.

                HC 11:24c *Do this in remembrance of me.*"

              H'A' 11:25a Likewise after supper also the *cup*,

                H'B' 11:25b *saying, "This cup is the new covenant in my blood.* As often as you drink it,

                H'C' 11:25c *do this in remembrance of me.*"

            G' 11:26 For as often as you eat this bread, and drink the cup, you proclaim the *Lord's death* until he should come.

F' 11:27 Therefore whoever will eat the bread or drink the cup of the Lord in an unworthy manner will be *guilty of the body and the blood of the Lord*.

E' 11:28 But let a man prove himself, and so let him *eat of the bread and drink of the cup*.

D' 11:29 For he that *eats and drinks, eats and drinks judgment* to himself, if he does not discern the body. 11:30 For this cause many among *you are weak* and *sickly*, and many *sleep*. 11:31 But if we were judging ourselves, we would not be condemned.

C' 11:32 But being judged by the Lord we are trained so that *we may not be condemned* with the world.

B' 11:33 Therefore, my brothers, *when you come together to eat* wait one for another. 11:34a If any man is hungry, let him eat at home. So that your *coming together* not be for judgment.

A' 11:34b And the *rest I will set in order* when ever I come.

1 Cor 11:1–34 Chiastic Structure Table

A 11:1–2a—I commend you	A' 11:34b—I will set in order
B 11:17–18—you . . . come together . . . you come together in the church	B' 11:33–34a—you come together to eat . . . your coming together
C 11:19—those who are approved	C' 11:32—we may not be condemned
D 11:20–21—eat the Lord's Supper . . . one takes before other . . . this one is hungry . . . that one is drunk	D' 11:29–31—eats and drinks . . . eats and drinks judgment . . . you are weak . . . sickly
E 11:22a—to eat and to drink	E' 11:28—eat of the bread and drink of the cup
F 11:22b—in this I do not commend you	F' 11:27—guilty of the body and the blood of the Lord
G 11:23a—he was delivered up	G' 11:26—the Lord's death
HA 11:23b–24a—bread	H'A' 11:25a—cup
HB 11:24b—said this is my body	H'B' 11:25b—saying this cup is the new covenant in my blood
HC 11:24c—do this in remembrance of me	H'C' 11:25c—do this in remembrance of me

Part I | The Undisputed Letters

Parallel Structure

A 11:1 Be imitators of me even as I also am of Christ. 11:2 Now *I commend you* that you remember me in all things. And hold fast the teachings as I delivered them to you.

(11:3 But I would have you know, that the head of every man is Christ. And the head of the woman is the man. And the head of Christ is God. 11:4 Every man praying or prophesying, having his head covered, dishonors his head. 11:5 But every woman praying or prophesying with her head unveiled dishonors her head. For it is one and the same thing as if she were shaven. 11:6 For if a woman is not veiled, let her also be shorn. But if it is a shame to a woman to be shorn or shaven, let her be veiled. 11:7 For a man indeed ought not to have his head veiled, forasmuch as he is the image and glory of God. But the woman is the glory of the man. 11:8 For the man is not of the woman, but the woman of the man. 11:9 For neither was the man created for the woman, but the woman for the man. 11:10 For this cause ought the woman to have authority on her head because of the angels. 11:11 Nevertheless, neither is the woman without the man nor the man without the woman in the Lord. 11:12 For as the woman is of the man, so is the man also by the woman. But all things are of God. 11:13 Judge in yourselves. Is it seemly that a woman pray to God unveiled? 11:14 Does not even nature itself teach you, that, if a man has long hair, it is a dishonor to him? 11:15 But if a woman has long hair, it is a glory to her. For her hair is given her for a covering. 11:16 But if any man seems to be contentious, we have no such custom, neither the churches of God.)

A' 11:17a But in giving you this commandment *I do not commend you*,
   B 11:17b because *you do not come together* for the better but for the worse.
   B' 11:18a For first of all, when *you come together* in the church
      C 11:18b I hear that *divisions exist among you*, and I partly believe it.
      C' 11:19 For *there must also be factions among you*, so that those who are approved should become evident among you.
         D 11:20 Therefore when you assemble together *it is not to eat* the lord's supper.
         D' 11:21a For *in your eating* each one takes before other his own supper.
           E 11:21b And *this one is hungry, and that one is drunk*.
           E' 11:22a For do you not have houses in which *to eat and to drink*? Or do you despise the church of God, and you are shaming those that have nothing?
              F 11:22b What shall I say to you? *shall I commend you*?
              F' 11:22c In this *I do not commend you*.
                 G 11:23a For I received from the Lord that which also *I delivered to you*,
                 G' 11:23b that the Lord Jesus in the night in which *he was delivered up*

HA 11:23c took *bread*. 11:24a And when he had given thanks he broke it,
> HB 11:24b *and said, "This is my body,* which is for you.
>> HC 11:24c *Do this in remembrance of me."*
> H'A' 11:25a Likewise after supper also the *cup*,
>> H'B' 11:25b *saying, "This cup is the new covenant in my blood.* As often as you drink it,
>>> H'C' 11:25c *do this in remembrance of me."*

I 11:26 For as often as *you eat this bread, and drink the cup,* you proclaim the lord's death until he should come.

I' 11:27 Therefore whoever shall *eat the bread or drink the cup* of the lord in an unworthy manner, shall be guilty of the body and the blood of the lord.

I" 11:28 But let a man prove himself, and so let him *eat of the bread, and drink of the cup.*

J 11:29 For he that eats and drinks, eats and drinks *judgment to himself,* if he does not discern the body.

J' 11:30 For this cause many among you are weak and sickly, and many sleep. 11:31 But if we were *judging ourselves,* we would not be condemned.

J" 11:32 But being *judged by the Lord,* we are trained, so that we may not be condemned with the world.

K' 11:33 Therefore, my brothers, *when you come together* to eat, wait one for another.

K' 11:34 If any man is hungry, let him eat at home, so that *your coming together* not be for judgment. And the rest I will set in order when ever I come.

Parallel Structure Table 1 Cor 11:1–34

A 11:1–2a—I commend you	A' 11:2b–17a—I do not commend you
B 11:17b—you come together	B' 11:18a—you come together
C 11:18b—divisions exist among you	C' 11:19—there must also be factions among you
D 11:20—it is not to eat	D' 11:21a—in your eating
E 11:21b—this one is hungry and that one is drunk	E' 11:22a—to eat and to drink
F 11:22b—shall I commend you	F' 11:22b—I do not commend you
G 11:23a—I delivered to you	G' 11:23b—he was delivered up

HA 11:23c-24a—bread	H'A' 11:25a—cup	
HB 11:24b—said this is my body	H'B' 11:25b—saying this cup is the new covenant in my blood	
HC 11:24c—do this in temperance of me	H'C' 11:25c—do this in remembrance of me	
I 11:26—eat this bread and drink the cup	I' 11:27—eat the bread or drink the cup	I" 11:28—eat of the bread and drink of the cup
J 11:29—judgment to himself	J' 11:30-31—judging ourselves	J" 11:32—judged by the Lord
K 11:33—when you come together	K' 11:34—your coming together	

Commentary

CHIASTIC STRUCTURE

In the chiastic structure the A stich matches "I commend you" with "the rest I will set in order" with both being actions by Paul, one in the present and one in the future. The B hemistich has two phrases "come together" and "you come together in the church" matching two phrases, "coming together" and "when you come together to eat" in the B' hemistich with the eating taking place in the church. The C stich matches "those who are approved" with "we may not be condemned," stating the same concept in the positive and the negative. In the D stich "eat the Lord's Supper" in the D hemistich matches "eats and drinks, eats and drinks judgment" in the D' hemistich. Then also in the D hemistich there are three actions disapproved by Paul, "one takes before another," "this one is hungry," "that one is drunk." Matching these in the D' hemistich are three poor characteristics of the Corinthians "you are weak," "sickly," and "sleep." The E stich matches "to eat and to drink" with "eat of the bread and drink of the cup." In the F' hemistich Paul gives an admonition "guilty of the body and the blood of the Lord" while earlier in the F hemistich Paul gives the result "in this I do not commend you." The G stich refers to Christ's passion with "he was delivered up" in the G hemistich matching "the Lord's death" in the G' hemistich. The H center stich is parallel in an A, B, C, A,' B,' C' format as Paul describes Jesus's actions with first the bread and then the cup at the Last Supper. This is the same center stich format as the F stich of the chiastic structure at 1 Cor 7:25-40.

PARALLEL STRUCTURE

In the parallel structure the A hemistich is identical to the A hemistich in the chiastic structure "I commend you," but the A' hemistich in the parallel structure comes after the interpolation at vv. 3-16 and is "I do not commend you" exposing the interpolation. The B stich is another pair of opposites "you do not come together" and "you come together." The C hemistich is two phrases that mean the same thing "divisions exist among you" and "there must also be factions among you." Both hemistiches of the D stich and the E stich are concerned with eating. The F hemistich asks the question "shall I commend you," and the F' hemistich answers it "I do not commend you." The G stich matches "I delivered to you" in the G hemistich with "he was delivered up" in the G' hemistich writing about Jesus. The same verb "*paradidōmi*" is used in both. Then the H stich in the parallel structure is identical with the center H stich of the chiastic structure concerning the actions of Christ at the Last Supper. The I stich has three elements all concerning eating bread and drinking the cup. The J stich also contains three elements and all three concern judging. The final K stich has both hemistiches referring to the Corinthians coming together.

Interpolation 1 Cor 11:3–16

The interpolation was explained in detail in chapter 2 in the example of how rhetorical analysis can expose interpolations.

Stich	Words in first half	Words in second half	Interpolation words
A	11:1–2a—12	11:2b–17a—135	113

Jean Magne proposed that vv. 11:23–26, the recitation of Jesus at the Last Supper, are an interpolation.[16] That segment appears to be very Pauline in construction, and as pointed out the same format as found in 1 Cor 7:25–40. Within it is the parallel H stich of both the chiastic structure and the parallel structure. Also included is Paul's clever word play parallelism of "delivered" in the G stich of the parallel structure. This segment is clearly original to Paul and was probably used by Mark in his Gospel to construct his pericope about the Last Supper.[17]

1 Corinthians 12

The literary unit of 1 Cor 12 is a chiastic structure encompassing the entire chapter with an unusually long C stich.

1 Cor 12:1–31

A 12:1 Now *concerning the spiritual*, brothers, *I do not want you to be ignorant.*

---

16. Magne, "Les paroles sur la coupe," 485–90.
17. Smith, *Matthew*, 208–210.

B 12:2 You know that when you were Gentiles you were led astray to those *mute* idols. 12:3 Therefore I declare to you that no one *speaking* in the spirit of God *says* Jesus is accursed. And no one is able *to say* Jesus is Lord except in the Holy Spirit.

  C 12:4 Now there are diversities of *gifts* but the same spirit. 12:5 And there are diversities of services and the same *Lord*. 12:6 And there are diversities of workings but the same *God* who works all things in everyone. 12:7 But to each one is *given* the manifestation of the spirit for the common profit. 12:8 For to one is *given* through the spirit a word of wisdom; and to another a word of knowledge, according to the same spirit, 12:9 to another faith, in the same spirit, but to another *gifts of healings*, in the one spirit. 12:10 and to another workings of *miracles*, and to another *prophecy*. and to another discernings of spirits, to another *kinds of tongues*, and to another the interpretation of tongues. 12:11 But all these work the one and the same spirit, dividing to each one severally even as he will.

    D 12:12 For just as the *body is one*, and has many members, and all the *members of the body* being many are *one body*. So also is Christ. 12:13 For in one spirit were we all baptized into *one body*, whether Jews or Greeks, whether slave or free. And were all made to drink of one spirit.

      E 12:14 For the body is not one member but many. 12:15a If the *foot* shall say

        F 12:15b because I am not the *hand*

          G 12:15c I am not of the *body*. It is not thereby not of the *body*.

            H 12:16a And if the *ear* shall say

              I 12:16b because I am not the *eye* I am not of the *body*. It is not thereby not of the *body*.

              I' 12:17a If the whole *body* were an *eye*,

            H' 12:17b where is the *hearing*? If the whole is *hearing*, where is the smelling?

          G' 12:18 But now has God set the members each one of them in the *body* as he desired. 12:19 And if they were all one member, where would be the *body*? 12:20 But now they are many members but one *body*.

        F' 12:21a And the eye cannot say to the *hand*, I have no need of you.

      E' 12:21b Or again the head to the *feet* I have no need of you.

    D' 12:22 But much more those *members of the body* which seem to be weaker are essential.

  C' 12:23 And those of the body which we think to be less honorable upon these we bestow more abundant honor. And our indecent have more abundant decorum. 12:24 Whereas our decent parts have no need. But *God* united the body together, *having given* more abundant honor to the deficient parts. 12:25 So that there should be no division in the body. But the members should have the same concern one for another. 12:26 And if one member suffers, all the members suffer together. If a member is honored, all the members rejoice together. 12:27 Now you are the body of *Christ* and sharing members thereof. 12:28 And *God* has set some in the church, first apostles, second *prophets*, third teachers, then *miracles*, then *gifts of healings*, helping, administration, *kinds of tongues*.

B' 12:29 Are all apostles? Are all prophets? Are all teachers? Are all miracles? 12:30 Have all gifts of healings? Do all *speak* with tongues? Do all interpret?

A' 12:31 But earnestly desire *the greater gifts*. And moreover the *most excellent way I show to you*.

1 Cor 12:1–31 Chiastic Structure Table

A 12:1—concerning the spiritual . . . I do not want you to be ignorant	A' 12:31—greater gifts . . . most excellent way I show to you.
B 12:2-3—mute . . . speaking . . . says . . . to say	B' 12:29-30—speak
C 12:4-11—gifts . . . Lord . . . God . . . given . . . given . . . gifts of healing . . . miracles . . . prophecy . . . kinds of tongues	C' 12:23-28—Christ . . . God . . . God . . . having given . . . gifts of healing . . . miracles . . . prophets . . . kinds of tongues
D 12:12-13—body is one . . . members of the body . . . one body . . . one body	D' 12:22—members of the body
E 12:14-15a—foot	E' 12:21b—feet
F 12:15b—hand	F' 12:21a—hand
G 12:15c—body	G' 12:18-20—body . . . body . . . body
H 12:16a—ear	H' 12:17b—hearing . . . hearing
I 12:16b—eye . . . body . . . body	I' 12:17a—eye . . . body

Commentary

This chiastic structure encompasses all of 1 Cor 12. The A stich matches first, "now concerning the spiritual" with "the greater gifts" and second, "I do not want you to be ignorant" with "the most excellent way I show to you." The matches here are that the greater gifts are spiritual and that Paul's instruction will eliminate the Corinthians' ignorance. The B stich has "mute" "speaking" "says," and "to say" in the B hemistich matching "speak" in the B' hemistich. After the matching of similar words and phrases in the A and B stiches, the rest of the structure matches exact words for the most part. The C stich is unusually long with the C hemistich containing one hundred five words and the C' hemistich containing one hundred one words, and amazing balance for such a long a stich. The identical words found in both hemistiches are "God," "gifts of healing," "kinds of tongues," and "miracles." Similar words found in the stich are "Lord" and "Christ;" "prophesy" and "prophet;" "given" and "having given."

In the D stich both hemistiches contain "members of the body" and the D hemistich also contains "the body is one" and "one body" twice. The E stich matches "foot" and "feet." The F stich has "hand" in both hemistiches. The G hemistich contains "body" twice while the G' hemistich has it three times. The H stich matches "ear" with "hearing" twice. The I center stich has "eye" and "body" in both hemistiches.

1 Corinthians 13

First Corinthians 13 has a parallel structure encompassing the entire chapter that overlaps into the first verse of 1 Cor 14.

1 Cor 13:1–14:1a

   AA 13:1a *If I speak with the tongues of men and of angels*
     AB 13:1b *but have not love,*
        AC 13:1c *I am become sounding brass, or a clanging cymbal.*
   A'A' 13:2a *And if I have prophecy, and know all mysteries and all knowledge, and if I have all faith, so as to remove mountains,*
     A' B' 13:2b *but have not love,*
        A' C' 13:2c *I am nothing.*
   A"A" 13:3a *And if I bestow all my goods to feed, and if I give my body to be burned,*
     A" B" 13:3b *but have not love,*
        A"C" 13:3c *it profits me nothing.*
     B 13:4a *Love suffers long, is kind;*
     B' 13:4b *love does not envy;*
     B" 13:4c *love does not vaunt itself,*
        C 13:4d *is not puffed up,*
        C' 13:5a *does not behave itself unseemly,*
        C" 13:5b *does not desire things for itself,*
        C'" 13:5c *is not provoked,*
        C"" 13:5d *does not keep account of wrongs;*
        C""' 13:6a *does not rejoice in unrighteousness,*
           D 13:6b *but rejoices with the truth;*
           D' 13:7a *bears all things,*
           D" 13:7b *believes all things,*
           D"' 13:7c *hopes all things,*
           D"" 13:7d *endures all things.*
           D""' 13:8a *Love never fails.*
               E 13:8b *But if there be prophecies, they will be done away.*
               E' 13:8c *If there be tongues, they will cease.*
               E" 13:8d *If there be knowledge, it will be done away.*

F 13:9a For *we know in part*,
F' 13:9b and *we prophesy in part*.
F" 13:10 But when that which is perfect is come *that which is in part* shall be done away.
    G 13:11a When I was a child *I spoke as a child*,
    G' 13:11b *I felt as a child*,
    G" 13:11c *I thought as a child*. Now that I am become a man I have put away childish things.
        H 13:12a For *now we see in a mirror* darkly;
        H' 13:12b but *then face to face*.
            I 13:12c *Now I know in part*,
            I' 13:12d but *then I will know fully* even as also I was fully known.
                J 13:13a But now there are faith, hope, *love*, these three things.
                J' 13:13b But the greatest of these is *love*.
                J" 14:1a Earnestly pursue *love*.

1 Cor 13:1–14:1a Parallel Structure Table

AA 13:1a—if I speak with tongues of men and of angels		A'A' 13:2a—and if I have prophecy and know all mysteries and all knowledge and if I have all faith so as to remove mountains		A"A" 13:3a—and if I bestow all my goods to feed and if I give my body to be burned	
AB 13:1b—but have not love		A'B' 13:2b—but have not love		A"B" 13:3b—but have not love	
AC 13:1c—I am become sounding brass or clanging cymbal		A'C' 13:2c—I am nothing		A"C" 13:3c—it profits me nothing	
B 13:4—love suffers long		B' 13:4b—love does not envy		B" 13:4c—love does not vaunt itself	
C 13:4d—not puffed up	C' 13:5a—not behave itself unseemly	C" 13:5b—not desire things for itself	C'" 13:5c—not provoked	C"" 13:5d—not keep account of wrongs	C""' 13:6a—not rejoice in unrighteousness
D 13:6b—rejoices in the truth	D' 13:7a—bears all things	D" 13:7b—believes all things	D'" 13:7c—hopes all things	D"" 13:7d—endures all things	D""' 13:8a—love never fails

E 13:8b—if there be prophecies they will be done away	E' 13:8c—if there be tongues they will cease	E" 13:8d—if there be knowledge it will be done away
F 13:9a—know in part	F' 13:9b—prophesy in part	F" 13:10—that which is in part
G 13:11a—I spoke as a child	G' 13:11b—I felt as a child	G" 13:11c—I thought as a child
H 13:12a—now we see in a mirror	H' 13:12b—face to face	
I 13:12c—now I know in part	I' 13:12d—I will know fully	
J 13:13a—love	J' 13:13b—love	J" 14:1a—love

Commentary

This chapter of 1 Corinthians is Paul's popular poem to love. It is commonly read at weddings. Walker believes it is an interpolation. In fact, his proposed interpolation runs from 12:31b—14:1a.[18] It does seem as if a poem to love is out of place in First Corinthians. However, the parallel structure I have set out above is in keeping with Pauline literary structures. It does have an unusual A stich in the AA, AB, AC; A'A,' A'B,' A'C'; A"A," A"B," A"C" format but then follows that with straight forward multi-element stiches. It has an erotic rhythm to it, and one could believe that it was a poem to "*eros*" instead of "*agape*." It begins with an uncertain format as I mentioned, containing relatively long elements. It then settles down with multi-element parallel stiches. The B stich has three elements. The C and D stiches, getting longer, have five elements. Then the E, F, and G stiches have three elements as the ideas come faster. Finally the H and I stiches have only two elements as the poem rapidly approaches the end. The J stich contains three elements including 14:1a, but the climax is "and the greatest of these is love." The third J element "earnestly pursue love" is a dénouement. The J stich could be viewed as a concluding element of an inclusio with the AB sub-stich containing the word "love" three times and the J stich also containing "love" three times. No wonder it is a popular bible text to be read at Christian weddings.

Perhaps it was an already existing poem and Paul adapted it, changing "eros" to "agape." Rhetorical analysis shows that 1 Cor 13 it is original to 1 Corinthians, but it is out of order. Chapter 14 of 1 Corinthians (minus v. 14:1a) should follow chapter 12. Then 1 Cor 13 should follow 1 Cor 14. It has been noted that there are other places where the beginning of a literary unit echoes the end of the previous literary unit. Here v. 14:1b contains "now earnestly desire spiritual gifts" echoing 12:31 "now earnestly desire the greater gifts." "Greater gifts" at 12:31 is a chiastic match for "concerning the spiritual" at 12:1. Therefore, it is clear that Walker is incorrect to judge 12:31 b and 14:1a to have been interpolated. This is the same sort of transition rhetorical analysis noted from Rom 4 to Rom 5, from Rom 5 to Rom 6, and from

18. Walker, *Interpolations*, 147–165.

Rom 11 to Rom 12. Also 1 Cor 12 ends with Paul writing about prophecy and speaking in tongues at vv. 12:28–30. First Corinthians 14 begins with Paul writing how prophecy is better than speaking in tongues. Ignoring the interpolations into 1 Cor 14, the entire chapter is about prophecy and speaking in tongues. Then 1 Cor 14 ends with comments about prophecy and speaking in tongues. It also contains the word "earnestly desire" (*zēloute*) again. Then 1 Cor 13 originally followed with its beginning "if I speak with the tongues of men and of angels" followed quickly with "and if I have prophecy." Once again this shows the transition from v. 14:39 to 13:1, more evidence that the original order was 1 Cor 12, 1 Cor 14, 1 Cor. 13. The themes of speaking in tongues and prophecy are repeated in the middle of 1 Cor 13 at v. 13:8.

This three-chapter section of 1 Cor concerns the spiritual as stated by Paul at v. 12:1. Paul's message is the following: Everybody has different spiritual gifts, but the separate gifts make for a unified congregation. Prophecy is superior to speaking in tongues, but speaking in tongues is acceptable. Prophecy and speaking in tongues are admirable spiritual gifts, but one should earnestly pursue love. Love enhances spiritual gifts and can be developed even by those who have not been granted spiritual gifts.

1 Corinthians 14

Chapter 14 of 1 Corinthians is out of order. It should precede 1 Cor 13 as noted above. It has one literary unit that has a chiastic structure with the fourth three-element center stich of a chiastic structure found in 1 Corinthians. Two interpolations are revealed.

1 Cor 14:1b–40

A 14:1b Now *earnestly desire* the spiritual, but rather that you may *prophesy*. 14:2a For he that *speaks in a tongue* does not speak to men, but to God.
  B 14:2b *For no one understands*, but in the spirit he speaks mysteries.
    C 14:3 But the one *prophesying* speaks edification, and exhortation, and consolation to men. 14:4 He that speaks in a tongue edifies himself, but the one *prophesying* edifies the church.
      D 14:5a Now I wish you all could speak in tongues, but rather that *you should prophesy*.
        E 14:5b Now greater is he that prophesies than the one *speaking in tongues*, unless he interpret so that the church may receive edifying. 14:6a But now, brothers, if I come to you *speaking in tongues*,
          F 14:6b what will I *profit you*, unless I speak to you either by way of *revelation, or of knowledge, or of prophesying, or of teaching*?
            G 14:7 Even things without life, giving a voice, whether pipe or harp, if they do not give a distinction in the sounds, how shall it be known

what is piped or harped? 14:8 For if the trumpet gives an uncertain voice, who shall prepare himself for war? 14:9 So also you, *unless you utter by the tongue intelligible speech*, how shall it be known what is spoken? For you will be speaking into the air.

 H 14:10 There are, it may be, so many kinds of *languages* in the world, and *none is without meaning*.

  I 14:11 If then I do not know the meaning of the language, *I will be to him who speaks a foreigner, and he who speaks will be a foreigner to me.*

   J 14:12 So you also, since you are zealous of spiritual, seek that you may abound to the *edification of the church*.

    K 14:13 Therefore let him *who speaks in a tongue* pray that he may interpret.

     L 14:14 For if *I pray in a tongue, my spirit prays*, but my understanding is unfruitful.

      M 14:15a What is it then? *I will pray with the spirit, and I will pray with understanding also.*

      M' 14:15b *I will sing with the spirit,* and *I will sing with understanding also.*

      M" 14:16 Otherwise *if you bless with the spirit*, how shall he that fills the place of the unlearned say the Amen at your giving of thanks, seeing *he does not know what you say*?

     L' 14:17 For you truly *give thanks* well, but the other is not edified.

    K' 14:18 I thank God, *I speak in tongues* more than all of you.

   J' 14:19 However *in the church* I had rather speak five words with my understanding that I might instruct others also than ten thousand words in a tongue.

(14:20 Brothers, do not be children in mind. But in malice be babes, in mind be men.)

  I' 14:21 In the law it is written, "*By men of strange tongues and by the lips of strangers I will speak to this people. And not even then will they hear me, says the Lord.*"

  H' 14:22 Therefore *tongues are for a sign*, not to them that believe, but to the unbelieving. But prophesying, not to the unbelieving, but to them that believe.

 G' 14:23 If therefore the whole church be assembled together and *all speak in tongues,* and there come in men unlearned or unbelieving, will they not say that you are mad? 14:24 But if all prophesy, and there come in one unbelieving or unlearned, he is reproved by all, he is judged by all. 14:25 The secrets of his heart are made manifest. And so he will fall down on his face and worship God, declaring that God is among you indeed.

F' 14:26 What is it then, brothers? When you come together, each one *has a psalm, has a teaching, has a revelation, has a tongue, has an interpretation*. Let all things be done to *edify*.

E' 14:27 If *anyone speaks in a tongue*, by two, or at the most three, and in turn, and let one interpret. 14:28 But if there be no interpreter, let him keep silence in the church, and let him *speak* to himself and to God. 14:29 And let the prophets *speak* by two or three and let the others discern.

D' 14:30 But if a revelation be made to another sitting by, let the first keep silence. 14:31 *For you all can prophesy* one by one that all may learn and all may be exhorted.

(14:32 And the spirits of the prophets are subject to the prophets. 14:33 For God is not confusion, but of peace. As in all the churches of the saints, 14:34 let the women keep silence in the churches. For it is not permitted for them to speak; but let them be in subjection, as also says the law. 14:35 And if they would learn anything, let them ask their own husbands at home. For it is shameful for a woman to speak in the church. 14:36 Was it from you that the word of God went forth? Or did it come to you only?)

C' 14:37 If anyone thinks himself to be a *prophet* or spiritual, let him acknowledge the things that I write to you that they are the commandment of the Lord.

B' 14:38 *But if anyone does not know*, let him be ignored.

A' 14:39 Therefore, my brothers, *earnestly desire* to *prophesy* and do not forbid *to speak with tongues*. 14:40 But let all things be done properly and in order.

1 Cor 14:1b-40 Chiastic Structure Table

A 14:1b-2a—earnestly desire . . . prophesy . . . speaks in a tongue	A' 14:39-40—earnestly desire . . . prophesy . . . to speak with tongues
B 14:2b—for no one understands	B' 14:38—but if anyone does not know
C 14:3-4—prophesying . . . prophesying	C' 14:37—prophet
D 14:5a—you should prophesy	D' 14:30-31—for you all can prophesy
E 14:5b-6a—speaking in tongues	E' 14:27-29—anyone speaks in a tongue . . . speak . . . speak

F 14:6b—profit you . . . revelation or of knowledge or of prophesying or of teaching	F' 14:26—to edify . . . has a psalm has a teaching has a revelation has a tongue has an interpretation
G 14:7-9—unless you utter by the tongue of intelligible speech	G' 14:23-25—all speak in tongues
H 14:10—language . . . none is without meaning	H' 14:22—tongues are for a sign
I 14:11—I will be to him who speaks a foreigner and he who speaks will be a foreigner to me	I' 14:21—by men of strange tongues and by the lips of strangers I will speak to this people
J 14:12—edification of the church	J' 14:19—in the church . . . I might instruct
K 14:13—who speaks in a tongue	K' 14:18—I speak in tongues
L 14:14—I pray	L' 14:17—give thanks
M 14:15a—I will pray with the spirit . . . I will pray with understanding also	M' 14:15b—I will sing with the spirit . . . I will sing with understanding also M" 14:16—if you bless with the spirit . . . he does not know what you say

Commentary

This literary unit begins at v. 14:1b because v. 14:1a is part of the literary unit encompassing 1 Cor 13. This would have been clear to Bishop Langdon when he was dividing 1 Corinthians into chapters if a redactor had not put 1 Cor 13 out of order long before Langdon was analyzing it.

The A stich has "earnestly desire," "prophesy," and "speak in tongues" in both hemistiches. "For no one understands" in the B hemistich matches "but if one does not know" in the B' hemistich. In the C hemistich there is "prophesying" twice matching "prophet" in the C' hemistich. The D stich has "you should prophesy" matching "For you all can prophesy." The E hemistich has "speaking in tongues" twice while the E' hemistich has "anyone speaks in a tongue" and "speaks" twice.

The F stich matches lists of beneficial conduct in both hemistiches. The F hemistich has "revelation, or of knowledge, or of prophecy, or of teaching" matching "has a psalm, has a teaching, has a revelation, has a tongue, has an interpretation." There is also a matching of the benefit with the F hemistich containing "profit you" and the F' hemistich containing "to edify." The G stich contains a great deal of text in both hemistiches but only one matching phrase. "Unless you utter intelligible speech by the tongue" in the G hemistich matches "all speak in tongues." In addition, Paul's meaning matches since if everyone were speaking in tongues it would not be intelligible.

The H stich matches a concept instead of exact words or phrases. In the H hemistich there is "language . . . none without meaning" and in the H' hemistich there is "tongues are for a sign." In the I stich a long phrase "I will be to him who speaks a foreigner and he will be a foreigner to me" in the I hemistich matches a quote of Isa 28:11–12 "by men of strange tongues and by the lips of strangers I will speak to this people." "Foreigner" is in the I hemistich twice and "stranger" is in the I' hemistich twice. In the J hemistich there is "edification of the church." and in the J' hemistich there is "the church . . . I might instruct." The K hemistich contains "who speaks in a tongue" and the K' hemistich contains "I speak in tongues." The L stich has "I pray" matching "give thanks." The center M stich has three elements each with two parts. This is the fourth chiastic structure in 1 Corinthians that contains a three-element center stich. Part one of the M element is "I will pray with the spirit" matching "I will sing with the spirit" in the M' element and "if you bless with the spirit" in the M" element. Part two of the matching phrases is "I will pray with understanding also" in the M element, "I will sing with understanding also" in the M' element, and the M" element expresses the opposite "he does not know what you say."

Interpolations

1 Cor 14:20

The chiastic structure of this unit exposes two interpolations: one at 14:20 and the other at 14:32–36. The J' and I' hemistiches at 14:19–21 contain fifty-six words. On the other hand, the I and J hemistiches at 14:11–12 contain only thirty-three words. This is unbalanced implying that a redactor has added text to vv. 19–21. First Corinthians 14:20 in the center of the J', I' hemistiches contains fifteen words and does not contain any words or phrases that are parallel to words or phrases in the I or J hemistiches. In addition, it is off topic. The entire chapter is about prophecy and speaking in tongues. Advice to be adult in your thinking is out of place. This must be the text that has been added to the sequence.

Stiches	Words in first half	Words in second half	Words in interpolation
J" – I'	14:11–12–33	14:19–21–56	14:20–15

1 Cor 14:30–37

The second interpolation is included in the D' and C' hemistiches at vv. 14:30–37. That entire sequence contains one hundred three words while the C and D hemistiches at vv. 14:3–5a contain only thirty words – an extreme unbalance. The word count in vv. 14:32–36 is sixty-nine. Removing that passage reduces the D' and C' hemistiches to thirty-four words, now nicely balanced. Once again, the presumed interpolated passage has nothing to do with prophecy or speaking in tongues. Walker proposed that

vv. 14:33b–36 have been interpolated.[19] Rhetorical analysis agrees, but would add vv. 14:32–33a.

Stiches	Words in first half	Words in second half	Words in interpolation
D' – C'	14:3–5a—33	14:30–37–103	14:32–36–69

1 Corinthians 15

1 Cor 15:1–15

This literary unit has a chiastic structure revealing a long interpolation.

> A 15:1 Now I make known to you brothers *the gospel that I proclaimed to you*, that also you received, wherein also you stand.
>> B 15:2a By which also you are saved, if you hold fast the word which *I proclaimed to you*,
>>> C 15:2b unless *you have believed in vain*.

(15:3 For I delivered to you first of all that which also I received. That Christ died for our sins according to the scriptures. 15:4 And that he was buried. And that he has been raised on the third day according to the scriptures. 15:5 And that he appeared to Kephas, then to the twelve. 15:6 Then he appeared to above five hundred brothers at once, of whom the greater part remain until now, but some are fallen asleep. 15:7 Then he appeared to James then to all the apostles. 15:8 And last of all, as to the untimely born, he appeared to me also. 15:9 For I am the least of the apostles, that am not meet to be called an apostle, because I persecuted the church of God. 15:10 But by the grace of God I am what I am. And his grace which was bestowed upon me was not found vain. But I labored more abundantly than they all. Yet not I, but the grace of God which was with me. 15:11 Whether then I or they so we preach, and so you believed.)

> D 15:12a Now if Christ is *preached*
>> E 15:12b that *he has been raised from the dead*,
>>> F 15:12c how say some among you that there is no *resurrection of the dead*?
>>> F' 15:13a But if there is no *resurrection of the dead*,
>> E' 15:13b neither has *Christ been raised*. 15:14a And if Christ has not been raised,
> D' 15:14b then is our *preaching* is in vain.

---

19. Walker, *Interpolations*, 147–65.

C' 15:14c *Your belief is also in vain.*

B' 15:15a But also *we are found false witnesses* of God

A' 15:15b because *we witnessed of God that he raised up Christ* whom he did not raise up. If so, the dead are not raised.

1 Cor 15:1–15 Chiastic Structure Table

A 15:1—the gospel that I proclaimed to you	A' 15:15b—we witnessed of God that he raised up Christ
B 15:2a—I proclaimed to you	B' 15:15a—we are found false witnesses
C 15:2b—you have believed in vain	C' 15:14c—your belief is also in vain
D 15:12a—preached	D' 15:14b—preaching
E 15:12b—he has been raised from the dead	E' 15:13b–14a—has Christ been raised
F 15:12c—resurrection of the dead	F' 15:13a—resurrection of the dead

Commentary

The A stich matches "the gospel that I proclaimed to you" with "we witnessed of God that he raised up Christ." In this stich the A' hemistich explains the gospel that Paul says he proclaimed in the A hemistich. The B stich matches "I proclaimed to you" with "we are found false witnesses." This is a match of opposites as Paul argues that his teaching is false if Christ was not resurrected from the dead. The C stich matches "you have believed in vain" with "your belief is also in vain." Paul has used two different words for which the best English translation in this context is "in vain": "*eikē*" and "*kenē*." He has also matched the noun "*pistis*" with the verb "*episteusate*," both having the same root.

The D stich matches "preached" with "preaching." The E hemistich has "he has been raised from the dead" while the E' hemistich has "Christ has been raised." The F center stich sets out the topic of the literary unit and has "resurrection of the dead" in both hemistiches. The entire chapter of 1 Cor 15 appears to be Paul's argument against some in Corinth who deny resurrection of the dead.

Interpolation 1 Cor 15:3–11

This first literary unit of 1 Cor 15 has unusually short stiches. This makes it easier for the rhetorical analyst to detect an interpolation. There appears to be one at vv. 15:3–11. Walker agrees[20] with Robert M. Price that this is an interpolation.[21] Look-

---

20. Walker, *Interpolations*, 147–65.
21. Price, "1 Corinthians 15:3–11," 60–99.

ing at the stiches that contain the assumed interpolation, the C' and D' hemistiches have a total of nine words. The C and D hemistiches are enormous containing nine entire verses. Removing vv. 15:3–11 from the unit reduces the C and D stiches to nine words, a perfect balance.

Once the interpolation has been disentangled from the original literary unit, it can be discerned that vv. 3–11 are wildly off Paul's intended topic which is resurrection of the dead. The center F stich shows that Paul is addressing whether Christians will be resurrected. The report of various persons having seen the risen Christ is not part of Paul's argument. He is addressing Christians who already believe that God raised Christ from the dead. The question he is dealing with here is whether Christians will be resurrected from the dead as Christ was. He addressed the crucifixion of Christ in 1 Cor 1. Here near the end of the letter he is addressing the resurrection part of his gospel. Verses 3–11 confuse the argument Paul is making. This interpolation also mentions "Kephas" and is further evidence that the other mentions of Kephas in 1 Corinthians are probably also interpolations.

This literary unit is structured to set up the argument Paul is about to make in the next literary unit. At vv. 15:16–19 he follows the subject unit by outlining the dire results if Christ has not been raised from the dead, and then at vv. 15:20–26 Paul makes his concluding argument, ending with "the last enemy abolished, death." The text at 15:3–11 distracts from Paul's argument. Also the self-deprecating language at vv. 15:8–9 contradicts 2 Cor 12:11 where Paul says he is in no way inferior to other apostles.

Stiches	Words in first half	Words in second half	Words in interpolation
C—D	15:2b–12a—139	15:14b–c—9	15:3–11–130

1 Cor 15:16–30

This literary unit has a parallel structure with an inclusio revealing two short interpolations.

> A 15:16a For *if the dead are not raised,*
>   B 15:16b *neither has Christ been raised.*
>   B' 15:17a And if *Christ has not been raised,*
>   C 15:17b *your faith is vain. You are still in your sins.* 15:18 Then they also who have fallen asleep in *Christ* have perished.
>   C' 15:19 If we have only hoped in *Christ* in this life, *we are the most pitiable of all men.*

D 15:20 But now *Christ has been raised from the dead*, the first fruits of them that are asleep.

D' 15:21 For since by man came death, by *man also the resurrection of the dead*. 15:22a For as in Adam all die.

D" 15:22b So also *in Christ will all be made alive*. 15:23 But each in his own order. Christ the first fruits. Then they that are Christ's at his coming.

 E 15:24 Then the end, when he shall *deliver up the kingdom to God*, even the father. When he shall have *abolished all rule and all authority and power*.

 E' 15:25 For *he must reign* until he has put all his enemies under his feet. 15:26 The last *enemy to be abolished is death*.

  F 15:27a For "*He put all things in subjection under his feet.*"
  F' 15:27b But when he says, "*All things are put in subjection*,"
  F" 15:27c it is evident that he is excepted who did *subject all things to him*.
  F''' 15:28a And when *all things have been subjected to him*,
  F'''' 15:28b then the *son will also himself be subjected to him*
  F''''' 15:28c who did *subject all things to him*, that God may be all in all.

(15:29a Else what shall they do that are baptized for the dead?)

A' 15:29b *If the dead are not raised* at all,

(15:29c why then are they baptized for them?)

15:30 Why then are we in danger every hour?

1 Cor 15:16–30 Parallel Structure Table

A 15:16a—if the dead are not raised			A' 15:29b, 30—if the dead are not raised		
B 15:16b—neither has Christ been raised			B' 15:17a—Christ has not been raised		
C 15:17b–18—your faith is in vain you are still in your sins … Christ			C' 15:19—we are the most pitiable of men … Christ		
D 15:20—Christ has been raised from the dead		D' 15:21–22a—man also the resurrection of the dead		D" 15:22b–23—in Christ will all be made alive	
E 15:24—deliver up the kingdom to God … abolished all rule and all authority and power			E' 15:25–26—he must reign … enemy to be abolished is death		
F 15:27a—all things in subjection under his feet	F' 15:27b—All things are put in subjection	F" 15:27c—subject all things to him	F''' 15:28a—all things have been subjected to him	F'''' 15:28b—son will also himself be subjected to him	F''''' 15:28c—subject all things to him

Commentary

The A stich is an inclusio having the identical words "if the dead are not raised" in both hemistiches. The B stich has two hemistiches, the first "neither has Christ been raised" and the second "if Christ has not been raised." The C stich also has two hemistiches. The C hemistich has "your faith is in vain you are still in your sins" matching "we are the most pitiable of all men." "Christ" is also in both hemistiches. The D stich has three elements "Christ has been raised from the dead" in the D element, and "man also resurrection of the dead" in the D' element. Here "man" is referring to Christ. In the D" element is "in Christ will all be made alive." In this stich Paul has used three different words to mean "raised from the dead," "*egēgertai*," "*anastasis*," and "*zōopoiēthēsontai*." The E stich only contains two hemistiches each with two parts. The E hemistich has "deliver up the kingdom to God" matching "he must reign" in the E' hemistich. Then "abolished all rule and all authority and all power" in the E hemistich matches "enemy to be abolished is death." The F stich contains five elements all containing the verb "to be subject to" each in a different form.

Interpolation 1 Cor 15:29a, c

O'Neill proposed that vv. 15:21–22 are an interpolation.[22] O'Neill would destroy the D stich in this parallel structure by eliminating the D' and D" elements. These two verses seem to be essential to Paul's argument that he makes throughout 1 Cor 15. Rhetorical analysis does not agree with O'Neill.

This parallel literary structure with an inclusio reveals two short interpolations, both about baptism of the dead. The F stich ends with the fifth element repeating "subject to all things." Then comes the A' hemistich at 15:29 that contains "if the dead are not raised" that matches the exact words of the A hemistich at 15:16, making it an inclusio of this parallel structure. However, the A hemistich only contains five words. Verses 29 and 30 together contain twenty-four words, extremely unbalanced. Removing both phrases about baptism of the dead reduces the A' hemistich to eleven words and retains the parallelism. After removing the interpolation the A' hemistich reads "if the dead are not raised at all, why then are we in danger every hour?" Paul is asking a rhetorical question about the wisdom of putting himself in harm's way if there is no resurrection of the dead. As with most interpolations, the phrases about baptism of the dead are off topic.

Stiches	Words in first half	Words in second half	Words in interpolation
A	15:16–9	15:29–30–24	15:29a, c—13

22. O'Neill, *Glosses*, 384–85.

1 Cor 15:31–58

The final literary unit of 1 Cor 15 completes Paul's essay on resurrection of the dead. It has a chiastic structure with a parallel center stich.

  A 15:31 I die every day as surely as the boasting in you, *brothers*, which I have in *Christ Jesus our Lord*.
    B 15:32 If after the manner of men I fought with beasts at Ephesus, what does it profit me? If the *dead* are not raised let us eat and drink for tomorrow we *die*.
      C 15:33 Be not deceived. *Evil* companionships *corrupt good morals*. 15:34 Awake to soberness righteously, and do not *sin*. For some have no knowledge of God. I speak to move you to shame.
        D 15:35 But some one will say, "*How are the dead raised? And with what manner of body do they come?*" 15:36 You foolish one, that which you yourself sows is not quickened except it die.
          E 15:37 And that which you sow you do not sow the *body* that will be but a bare grain. It may perhaps be wheat, or of some other kind. 15:38 But God gives it a *body* even as it pleased him, and to each seed a *body* of its own. 15:39 All *flesh* is not the same *flesh*. But there is one of men, and another *flesh* of beasts, and another *flesh* of birds, and another of fishes.
            F 15:40 There are also *heavenly bodies, and terrestrial bodies*. But the glory of the *heavenly* is one, and that of the *terrestrial* is another. 15:41 There is one glory of the *sun*, and another glory of the *moon*, and another glory of the *stars*. For one *star* differs from another *star* in glory.
              GA 15:42 So also is the resurrection of the dead. It is sown in *corruption*. It is raised in *incorruption*.
                GB 15:43a It is sown in *dishonor*; it is raised in *glory*.
                  GC 15:43b It is sown in weakness; it is raised in power. 15:44a It is sown a *natural* body; it is raised a *spiritual* body.
              G'A' 15:44b If there is a *natural* body, there is also a *spiritual*. 15:45a So also it is written,
                G'B' 15:45b "The first man Adam became a *living soul*." The last Adam a *life-giving spirit*.
                  G'C' 15:46 However, it is not first which is *spiritual*, but that which is *natural*, then that which is *spiritual*.
            F' 15:47 The first man is of the *Earth, earthy*. The second man is of *Heaven*. 15:48 As is the *earthy* such are they also that are *earthy*. And as is the *heavenly* such are they also that are *heavenly*. 15:49 And as we have borne the image of the *earthy* we shall also bear the image of the *heavenly*.
          E' 15:50 Now this I say, brothers, that *flesh and blood* cannot inherit the kingdom of God. Neither does corruption inherit incorruption.

Part I | The Undisputed Letters

D' 15:51 Behold, I tell you a mystery. We all will not sleep, but we will all be changed 15:52 in a moment, in the twinkling of an eye, at the last trumpet. For the trumpet will sound, and the *dead will be raised* incorruptible, and *we will be changed.*

C' 15:53 For this *corruptible must put on incorruption*, and this mortal must put on *immortality*. 15:54a But when this *corruptible will have put on incorruption*,

B' 15:54b and this mortal shall have put on immortality, then will come to pass the saying that is written, "*Death is swallowed up in victory.* 15:55 O *death*, where is thy victory? O *death*, where is thy sting?" 15:56 The sting of *death* is sin; and the power of sin is the law."

A' 15:57 But thanks be to God, who gives us the victory through *our Lord Jesus Christ.* 15:58 Therefore, my beloved *brothers*, be steadfast, unmovable, always abounding in the work of the Lord. Forasmuch as you know that your labor is not vain in the Lord.

1 Cor 15:31-58 Chiastic Structure Table

A 15:31—brothers ... Christ Jesus our Lord	A' 15:57-58—brothers ... our Lord Jesus Christ
B 15:32—dead ... die	B' 15:54b-56—death ... death ... death ... death
C 15:33-34—evil ... corrupt good morals ... sin	C' 15:53—corruptible must put on incorruption ... corruptible will have put on incorruption ... immorality
D 15:35-36—how are the dead raised ... with what manner of body do they come	D' 15:51—dead will be raised ... we will be changed
E 15:37-39—body ... body ... body ... flesh ... flesh ... flesh ... flesh	E' 15:50—flesh and blood
F 15:40-41—heavenly bodies ... terrestrial bodies ... heavenly ... terrestrial ... sun ... moon ... stars ... star ... star	F' 15:47-49—Earth ... earthy ... Heaven ... earthy ... earthy ... heavenly ... heavenly ... earthy ... heavenly
GA 15:42—corruption ... incorruption	G'A' 15:44b-45a—natural ... spiritual
GB 15:43a—dishonor ... glory	G'B' 15:45b—living soul ... life giving spirit
GC 15:43b-44a—natural ... spiritual	G'C' 15:46 – spiritual ... natural ... spiritual

Commentary

Paul begins this literary structure echoing the end of the previous structure. That structure ended with "every hour," and this structure begins "every day. This is the same pattern of the beginning of a literary unit echoing the end of the previous literary unit that has been noted earlier. In this chiastic structure the A stich contains "brothers" in both hemistiches. For the other match Paul forms a chiasm with "Christ Jesus our Lord" (*Christō Iēsou tō kyriō hēmōn*) matching "our Lord Jesus Christ" (*tou kyriō hēmōn Iēsou Christō*). In the B stich Paul is very clever quoting Isa 22:13 in the B hemistich and quoting Isa 25:8 combining it with a quote from Hos 13:14 in the B' hemistich. Also all three quotes are about death. The B hemistich has "dead" and "die" while the B' hemistich has "death" four times. Dennis R. MacDonald proposed that vv. 15:31–32 are an interpolation.[23] His emendation destroys the first half of both the A and B stiches. MacDonald would have us believe that an interpolator noticed that Paul had a defective chiastic structure that ran from 15:33–58, but the concluding hemistich was grossly out of balance containing an extra five verses (15:54b–58). Therefore, the interpolator repaired Paul's chiastic structure adding the chiasm of v. 15:31, and a matching quote from Isaiah at v. 15:32. Rhetorical analysis shows that MacDonald's conjecture is off the mark.

In the C stich "corrupt good morals" in the C hemistich matches "corruptible must put on incorruption" in the C' hemistich twice. The D stich has two parts in each hemistich. The first part "how are the dead raised" in the D hemistich matches "the dead will be raised" in the D' hemistich. With the second part "what manner of body do they come" in the D hemistich matches "we will be changed" in the D' hemistich. The D' hemistich answers the questions posed in the D hemistich. The E hemistich contains "body" three times and "flesh" four times while the E' hemistich contains "flesh and blood," but only once. The F stich concerns celestial matters in both hemistiches. The F hemistich contains "heavenly bodies and terrestrial bodies" and "sun," "moon," and "star." The F' hemistich contains "Earth" and "earthy" five times and "Heaven" four times. The G stich has three parallel sub-stiches. This is the third chiastic structure in 1 Corinthians that contains a parallel center stich with three elements. In the G hemistich there are three parallels of sowing and raising in Paul's agricultural metaphor. In the G' hemistich there are three parallels of natural and spiritual. In v. 15:45 Paul quotes Gen 2:7 that Adam became a living soul. Paul has quoted the Old Testament at the beginning, middle, and end of this literary structure.

M. Widmann proposed that vv. 15:44b–48 are an interpolation.[24] Eliminating those verses would destroy the paralleled center G stich and the F stich and would eliminate Paul's middle quotation of the Old Testament. Rhetorical analysis shows that Widmann is incorrect and his proposed interpolation was original to Paul.

Friedrich Wilhelm Horn proposed that v. 15:56 is an interpolation.[25] It is true that the B' hemistich that includes v. 15:56 is out of balance with the B hemistich. The B hemistich has only twenty words while the B' hemistich contains forty. Eliminating v. 15:56 with its fourteen words would bring it more into balance. However, one of

23. MacDonald, "1 Cor 15:31–32," 265–76.
24. Widmann, "1 Kor 2:6–16," 47–48.
25. Horn, "1 Korinther 15:56," 88–105.

the instances of "death" (*thanatou*) is found in v. 15:56. That may be a coincidence since there are three other instances of "death" in the B' hemistich. Rhetorical analysis cannot demonstrate that Horn's proposed interpolation is incorrect. It is a possibility.

1 Corinthians 16

The final chapter of 1 Corinthians has a literary unit with a parallel structure encompassing the entire chapter. All stiches in the structure contain two hemistiches, except for a four-element G stich.

1 Cor 16:1–24

> A 16:1 Now concerning the *collection* for the saints, as I gave order to the churches of Galatia, so also you must do.
> A' 16:2 On the first day of the week let each one of you put aside what he has saved as he has prospered so that no *collections* be made when I arrive.
>> B 16:3 And when I arrive whomever you will approve *I will send them with letters* to carry your bounty to Jerusalem.
>> B' 16:4 And if it be meet for me to go also *they will go with me*.
>>> C 16:5 But *I will come to you* when I have passed through Macedonia. For I pass through Macedonia.
>>> C' 16:6 But it may be that *I will stay with you* or even winter so that you may set me forward on my journey where ever I go.
>>>> D 16:7 For I do not wish to see you now by the way. For *I hope to tarry a while with you* if the Lord permit.
>>>> D' 16:8 But *I will tarry at Ephesus* until Pentecost. 16:9 For a great door and effectual is opened to me and there are many adversaries.
>>>>> E 16:10 Now if Timothy come, *see that he be with you without fear*. For he works the work of the Lord as I also do.
>>>>> E' 16:11 *Therefore no one should despise him*. But set him forward on his journey in peace that he may come to me. For I expect him with the brothers.
>>>>>> F 16:12a But as touching Apollos, the brother, *I greatly encouraged him to come to you* with the brothers.
>>>>>> F' 16:12b And it was not all his will to come now. *But he will come when he will have opportunity*.
>>>>>>> GA 16:13 Watch, stand fast in the faith, acquit yourselves like men, be strong. 16:14 Let all that you do be done in love.
>>>>>>> GB 16:15a Now I beseech you, brothers, (you know the house of *Stephanas*,
>>>>>>>> GC 16:15b that it is the first fruits of *Achaia*,

First Letter To The Corinthians

GD 16:15c and that *they have devoted themselves to minister* to the saints),

G'A' 16:16 that you also be in subjection to such, and to *every one who helps in the work and labors.*

G'B' 16:17a And I rejoice at the coming of *Stephanas*

G'C' 16:17b and Fortunatus and *Achaicus.*

G'D' 16:17c For *that which you lacked they supplied.*

H 16:18 For they refreshed my spirit and yours. Acknowledge therefore those who are such. 16:19 The churches of Asia *greet* you. Aquila and Prisca *greet* you much in the Lord, with the church that is in their house.

H' 16:20 All the brothers *greet* you. *Greet* one another with a holy kiss.

I 16:21 The salutation of me Paul with mine own hand. 16:22 If *anyone does not love the Lord*, let him be anathema. Maranatha.

I' 16:23 The grace of the Lord Jesus Christ be with you. 16:24 *My love be with you all in Christ Jesus*. Amen.

1 Cor 16:1–24 Parallel Structure Table

A 16:1—collection	A 16:2—collections
B 16:3—I will send them with letters	B' 16:4—they will go with me
C 16:5—I will come to you	C' 16:6—I will stay with you
D 16:7 I hope to tarry awhile with you	D' 16:8-9 I will tarry at Ephesus
E 16:10—see that he be with you without fear	E' 16:11—therefore no one should despise him
F 16:12a—I greatly encouraged him to come to you	F' 16:12b—but he will come when he will have opportunity
GA 16:13-14—let all that you do be done in love	G'A' 16:16—every one who helps in the work and labor
GB 16:15a—Stephanas	G'B' 16:17a—Stephanas
GC 16:15b—Achaia	G'C' 16:17b—Achaicus
GD 16:15c—they have devoted themselves to minister	G'D' 16:17c—that which you lacked they supplied
H 16:18-19—greet . . . greet	H' 16:20—greet . . . greet
I 16:21—anyone does not love the Lord	I' 16:23-24—my love be with you all in Christ Jesus

PART I | THE UNDISPUTED LETTERS

Commentary

The last chapter of 1 Corinthians is a typical Pauline parallel structure containing two hemistiches in each stich. However, the G stich switches from and A, A,' B, B,' C, C,' format to an A, B, C, A,' B,' C,' format. Both hemistiches of the A stich contain the word "collection." The B hemistich has "I will send them with letters" matching "they will go with me" in the B' hemistich. The C hemistich has "I will come to you" matching "I will stay with you" in the C' hemistich. The D hemistich has "I hope to tarry with you a while" matching "I will tarry at Ephesus" in the D' hemistich. The E stich is about Paul's disciple Timothy and "see that he be with you without fear" in the first hemistich matches "therefore no one should despise him" in the E' hemistich. The F stich is about Apollos, and once again Kephas is not mentioned in this context. The F hemistich contains "I greatly encouraged him to come to you" matching "but he will come to you when he has the opportunity."

The G stich has four parts. The first part has "let all you do be done in love" matching "everyone who helps in work and labors." The second part matches "Stephanas." The third part matches "Achaia." The fourth part has "they have devoted themselves to minister" matching "that which you lacked they supplied." Of course supplying is part of ministerial duties. The H stich has "greet" twice in both hemistiches. The final I stich has "anyone does not love the Lord" matching "my love be with you in Christ Jesus."

5

SECOND LETTER TO THE CORINTHIANS

2 Corinthians 1

THE FIRST LITERARY UNIT of 2 Corinthians has a parallel structure with an inclusio. The unit encompasses the entire chapter and reveals a possible interpolation.

2 Cor 1–21

> A 1:1 Paul, an apostle of *Christ Jesus* through the will of *God*, and Timothy, brother, to the church of *God* being at *Corinth* with all the saints being in the entire Achaia.
> > B 1:2 Grace to you and peace from *God* our *father* and the *Lord Jesus Christ*.
> > B' 1:3 Blessed be the *God* and *father* of our *Lord Jesus Christ*, the *father* of mercies and *God* of all encouragement,
> > > C 1:4 who *encourages* us in all our *affliction*, that we may be able to *encourage* those who are in any *affliction*, through the *encouragement* with which we ourselves are *encouraged* by God.
> > > C' 1:5 For as the *sufferings* of Christ over flow into us even so the *encouragement* to us also overflows through Christ. 1:6 If however we are constricted, it is for your *encouragement* and salvation. If we are *encouraged*, it is for your *encouragement*, working in the endurance of the same *sufferings* that we also suffer.
> > > C" 1:7 And our hope for you is certain. Knowing that as you are partners of the *sufferings* so also are you of the *encouragement*. 1:8a For we would not have you ignorant, brothers, concerning our *affliction* having happened in Asia.
> > > > D 1:8b That we were greatly weighed down beyond our power so that *we despaired even of life.*
> > > > D' 1:9 But we ourselves had the *sentence of death within ourselves* so that we should not trust in ourselves but in God who raises the dead.
> > > > D" 1:10 Who *delivered us from a great death* and will deliver us. In whom we have hope that he will also still deliver us.

Part I | The Undisputed Letters

    E 1:11a By your joining in *prayers on our behalf* thanks may be *given by many* persons

    E' 1:11b for the *grace bestowed on our behalf by many*.

        F 1:12a For our boasting is this, the testimony of our conscience, that in the holiness and *sincerity of God*,

        F' 1:12b not in fleshly wisdom but in the *grace of God*, we conducted ourselves in the world, and more abundantly toward you.

            G 1:13a For we write no other things to *you* than what you read or *even acknowledge*.

            G' 1:13b And I hope *you will acknowledge* to the end.

            G" 1:14 As also *you did acknowledge* us in part that we are boasting about you even as you also are ours in the day of our Lord Jesus.

                H 1:15 And in this confidence I was planning previously *to come to you*, so that you might have a second benefit.

                H' 1:16 And through you to pass into Macedonia, and again from Macedonia *to come to you*, and from you to be set forward to Judea.

                    I 1:17 Therefore thus planning did I show fickleness? Or the things that I determine do I determine according to the flesh that with me there should be *yes yes and no no*?

                    I' 1:18 But as God is faithful our word toward you is not *yes and no*.

                    I" 1:19 For the son of God, Jesus Christ, who was preached among you by us, by me and Silvanus and Timothy, was not *yes and no* but in him is yes.

                        J 1:20a For how many so ever be the *promises of God*, in him is the yes.

                        J' 1:20b Therefore also through him is the Amen, to the *glory of God* through us.

A' 1:21 Now he that establishes us with you in *Christ* and anointed us is *God*.

(1:22 He who also attested us, and provided the security of the spirit in our hearts.)

1:23 But I call God for a witness upon my soul that to spare you I have not yet come to *Corinth*.

(1:24 Not that we have lordship over your faith but are helpers of your joy. For in faith you stand firm.)

2 Cor 1:1–24 Parallel Structure Table

A 1:1—Christ Jesus . . . God . . . God . . Corinth	A' 1:21-23—Christ . . . God . . . God . . . Corinth	
B 1:2—God . . . father . . . Lord Jesus Christ	B' 1:3—God . . . father . . . Lord Jesus Christ . . . father . . . God	
C 1:4—encourages . . . affliction . . . encourage . . . affliction . . . encouragement . . . encourage	C' 1:5-6—encouragement . . . sufferings . . . encouragement . . . sufferings . . . encouragement. . . encouraged	C" 1:7-8a—encouragement . . . sufferings . . . affliction
D 1:8b—we despaired even of life	D' 1:9—sentence of death within ourselves	D" 1:10—delivered us from a great death
E 1:11a—prayers on our behalf . . . given by many	E' 1:11b—grace bestowed on our behalf by many	
F 1:12a—sincerity of God	F' 1:12b—grace of God	
G 1:13a—you . . . even acknowledge	G' 1:13b—you will acknowledge	G" 1:14—you did acknowledge
H 1:15—to come to you	H' 1:16—to come to you	
I 1:17—yes yes and no no	I' 1:18—yes and no	I" 1:19—yes and no
J 1:20a—promises of God	J' 1:20b—glory of God	

Commentary

Both hemistiches of the A stich contain "God" twice and "Corinth." The A hemistich contains "Christ Jesus" while the A' hemistich contains only "Christ." Both hemistiches of the B stich contain "God," "father," and "Lord Jesus Christ," but the B' hemistich is a chiasm "God, father, Lord Jesus Christ, father, God." The C stich has an interesting structure. It contains three elements. The C and C' elements both contain the word "encourage" four times in various forms. The C element contains the word "affliction" twice while the C' element contains "sufferings" twice as a matching term. The C" element is a combination of the C and C' elements. It contains "sufferings," "encouragement," and "affliction" each once in that order. The D stich also contains three elements, but not of matching words or phrases. This stich has matching concepts. In the D element is "we despaired even of life." The D' element has a matching concept "sentence of death within ourselves." The D" element has "delivered us from a great death." All three concepts contain the third person plural and all three deal with death.

In the E stich the E hemistich has "prayers on our behalf . . . given by many" matching "grace bestowed on our behalf by many" in the E' hemistich. The F stich matches "sincerity of God" with "grace of God." The G stich contains three elements: "you . . . even acknowledge" in the G element, "you will acknowledge" in the G' element, and "you did acknowledge" in the G" element. Both hemistiches of the H stich contain "to come to you." The I stich has three elements: "yes, yes and no, no" in the I element and "yes and no" in both the I' and I" elements. The J stich matches "promises of God" with "glory of God."

Interpolation 2 Cor 1:22, 24

This literary unit encompasses the entirety of 2 Cor 1 and is defined by an inclusio. The A and A' hemistiches do not have the usual Pauline balance. The A hemistich contains twenty-nine words and the A' hemistich contains fifty-nine words. This imbalance leads the rhetorical analysis investigator to suspect an interpolation. Verses 1:22 and 24 appear not to be compatible with vv. 1:21 and 23 and do not contain any matching words. Interestingly, vv. 1:22 and 24 contain thirty words and if they are removed, the A' hemistich is reduced to twenty-nine words, perfectly matching the A hemistich. In addition, v.1:22 contains the word *"arrabōn"* (security or earnest payment) which is only used one other time in Paul's undisputed letters at 2 Cor 5:5, that rhetorical analysis also reveals as an interpolation. Another attribute implying that v.1:24 may be an interpolation is that v. 1:23 and v. 2:1 both mention Paul's visiting the Corinthians. This is a familiar technique in Paul's letters wherein he unites consecutive literary units by repeating a phrase in the last hemistich of one literary unit and in the first stich of the following literary unit. The inclusion of v.1:24 weakens that unity.

Stiches	Words in first half	Words in second half	Words in interpolation
A	1:1–29	1:21–24–59	1:22, 24–30

2 Corinthians 2

The second chapter of 2 Corinthians is a unique progressive parallel structure encompassing the entire chapter. It does not have a typical parallel structure, but it does have a deliberate structure progressing from "sorrow" and "joy" to "forgiveness" and then to "Christ" and "God" and finally to the "fragrance" of eternal life. However, the structure fittingly ends with "Christ."

2 Cor 2:1–17

> A 2:1 For I determined this for myself that I would not come again to you in *sorrow*.
> B 2:2 For if I make you sorry, who then is he that makes me *glad* but he that is made sorry by me?

A' 2:3a And I wrote this very thing lest when I came I should have *sorrow* from them of whom
  B' 2:3b I ought to *rejoice*. Trusting in you all
  B" 2:3c that my *joy* is yours.
    C 2:4a For out of much *affliction*
     C' 2:4b and *anguish* of heart
      C" 2:4c I wrote to you with *many tears*. Not that you should be made sorry,
  B''' 2:4d but that you might know the abundant *love* that I have for you.
A" 2:5a But if anyone has caused *sorrow*,
A''' 2:5b he has caused *sorrow* not to me, but in part (that I might not put it too severely) to you all.
    C''' 2:6 Sufficient to such a one is this *punishment* which was from the majority.
     D 2:7a So that to the contrary you should rather *forgive* him and encourage him,
    C'''' 2:7b lest perhaps such a one should be *destroyed*
A'''' 2:7c by more abundant *sorrow*.
  B'''' 2:8 Therefore I encourage you to confirm your *love* toward him.
    D' 2:9 For indeed I wrote also that I might test you whether you are obedient in all things. 2:10a But whomever you *forgive* anything
    D" 2:10b I also *forgive*.
    D''' 2:10c For what I also have *forgiven*,
    D'''' 2:10d if I have *forgiven* anything,
     E 2:10e it is for your sakes in the presence of *Christ*. 2:11 So that we should not be outwitted by Satan. For we are not ignorant of his schemes.
     E' 2:12 Now having come to Troas for the gospel of *Christ*, and a door was opened to me in the Lord. 2:13 I had no rest in my spirit, because I did not find Titus my brother. But taking my leave of them I went to Macedonia.
      F 2:14a But thanks be to *God*,
     E" 2:14b who always leads us in triumph in *Christ*
       G 2:14c and the *fragrance* of his knowledge is made manifest through us in every place.
        G' 2:15a For we are a *sweet perfume*
     E''' 2:15b of *Christ*
      F' 2:15c to *God* in those who are saved and in those who perish.
       G" 2:16a To the one a *fragrance* from death to death.
       G''' 2:16b To the other a *fragrance* from life to life. And who is sufficient for these things?
      F" 2:17a For we are not as the many selling the word of *God* for profit.
      F''' 2:17b But in sincerity but from *God*,
      F'''' 2:17c in the sight of *God*,
     E'''' 2:17d we speak in *Christ*.

Part I | The Undisputed Letters

2 Cor 2:1-17 Progressive Parallel Structure Table

A 2:1—sorrow	A' 2:3a—sorrow	A" 2:5a—sorrow	A'" 2:5b—sorrow	A"" 2:7c—sorrow
B 2:2—glad	B' 2:3b—rejoice	B" 2:3c—joy	B'" 2:4d—love	B"" 2:8—love
C 2:4a—affliction	C' 2:4b—anguish	C" 2:4c—many tears	C'" 2:6—punishment	C"" 2:7b—destroyed
D 2:7a—forgive	D' 2:9-10a—forgive	D" 2:10b—forgive	D'" 2:10c—forgive	D"" 2:10d—forgive
E 2:10e-11—Christ	E' 2:12-13—Christ	E" 2:14b—Christ	E'" 2:15b—Christ	E"" 2:17d—Christ
F 2:14a—God	F' 2:15c—God	F" 2:17a—God	F'" 2:17b—God	F"" 2:17c—God
G 2:14c—fragrance	G' 2:15a—sweet perfume	G" 2:16a—fragrance	G'" 2:16b—fragrance	

This literary unit has a unique progressive parallel structure wherein there are five repetitions of each element for seven stiches. In the first half of the unit, the A stich, "sorrow" blends into the B stich "glad," "rejoice," "joy," "love" which blends into the C stich, "affliction," "anguish," "many tears," "punishment," and "destroyed." The C stich does not use the same word twice. These all blend into the D stich "forgive" occurring at the center of the structure. The second half of the structure contains the E stich "Christ" which blends into the F stich "God" which blends into the G stich, "fragrance," and "sweet perfume."

The center D stich only repeats "forgive" four times in Greek but the second "forgive" in v. 2:10 is understood. In addition, there are only four occurrences of the G stich "fragrance." It is not clear whether this was intentional by Paul, he lost count, or a sloppy scribe inadvertently removed one occurrence. By Greek word count, the second word of v. 2:10 is the center of the unit. After the first occurrence of "forgive" at v.2:7 there are the last elements of the A, B, and C stiches. The E stich begins immediately after the center D stich ends. Romans 4 has a literary structure somewhat similar to 2 Cor 2, except that Rom 4 ends with a two-element inclusio. First Thessalonians 3 is also somewhat similar to 2 Cor 2, containing only one stich with three elements, each element having the same five repeated words or phrases.

2 Corinthians 3

The third chapter of 2 Corinthians is a single parallel-chiastic-parallel hybrid structure that encompasses the entire chapter. This structure is similar to Gal 3 in having a parallel-chiastic-parallel structure, with the initial parallel structure being one element longer than the final parallel structure.

2 Cor 3:1–18

A 3:1 Are we beginning again to commend ourselves? Or do we need as do some *letters* of commendation to you or from you?

A' 3:2 You are our *letter* inscribed in our hearts being known and read by all.

A" 3:3a Revealing that you are a *letter* of Christ ministered by us,

  B 3:3b inscribed not with ink but with the *spirit of the living God*, not on tables of stone but on tables of human hearts.

    C 3:4 And such confidence we have through *Christ* toward *God*. 3:5 Not that we are sufficient of ourselves to conclude anything as from ourselves. But our sufficiency is from *God*,

      D 3:6 who also made us sufficient as ministers of a *new covenant not of writing but of the spirit*. For writing kills but the spirit gives life.

        E 3:7 But if the ministry of death having been engraved on stones was made with glory such that the *children of Israel could not look intently upon the face of Moses* because of the glory of his face which is fading.

          F 3:8 How could it be that the ministry of the spirit will not be in *glory*? 3:9 For if the ministry of condemnation has *glory*, much more does the ministry of righteousness excel in *glory*.

          F' 3:10 For that which has been made glorious has not been made glorious in this respect, because of the *glory* that surpasses. 3:11 For if that which is fading was with *glory*, much more is that which remains in *glory*.

        E' 3:12 Having therefore such a hope, we use great boldness, 3:13 and not as *Moses, putting a veil over his face that the children of Israel not look intently* on the end of that fading away.

      D' 3:14a But their minds were hardened. For until this present day at the *reading of the old covenant* the same veil remains not uncovered,

    C' 3:14b which in *Christ* has been abolished. 3:15 But to this day whenever Moses is read a veil lies upon their heart. 3:16 But whenever it reverts to the *Lord* the veil is removed.

  B' 3:17 Now the *Lord is the spirit*. And where the *spirit of the Lord* is there is freedom.

        G 3:18a But we all with unveiled face beholding the *glory* of the *Lord* as in a mirror

        G' 3:18b are transfigured into the same image from *glory* to *glory*, just as from the *Lord* the spirit.

Part I | The Undisputed Letters

2 Cor 3:1–18 Hybrid Chiastic/Parallel Structure Table

A 3:1—letter	A' 3:2—letter	A" 3:3a—letter
B 3:3b—spirit of the living God		B' 3:17—Lord is the spirit . . . spirit of the Lord
C 3:4-5—Christ . . . God . . . God		C' 3:14b-16—Christ . . . Lord
D 3:6—new covenant not of writing		D' 3:14a—reading of the old covenant
E 3:7—children of Israel could not look intently upon the face of Moses		E' 3:12-13—Moses putting a veil over his face that the children of Israel could not look intently
F 3:8-9—glory . . . glory . . . glory		F' 3:10-11—glory . . . glory . . .
G 3:18a—glory . . . Lord		G' 3:18b—glory . . . glory . . . Lord

Commentary

The literary unit of 2 Cor 3 is unusual in that it is an overall structure with three substructures: a short three-element parallel structure followed by a five-stich chiastic structure and then a final two-element parallel structure. There is a similar structure of Gal 3:1–17 that is analyzed in the following chapter. The initial A stich sub-structure has three parallel elements containing the word "letter." The final G stich sub-structure appears to have only two elements because there are only two occurrences of "Lord" although there are three occurrences of "glory." The main sub-structure is a five-stich chiastic structure. The B hemistich contains "spirit of . . . God" matching "spirit of the Lord" and "Lord . . . the spirit" in the B' hemistich. In this context "Lord" is a reference to God and not Jesus. In the C hemistich is "Christ" and "God" matching "Christ" and "Lord" in the C' hemistich. Again in this context "Lord" means "God." The D stich matches a pair of opposites with "new covenant, not of writing" matching "reading of the old covenant"

    The E stich matches "the children of Israel could not look intently into the face of Moses" in the E hemistich with "Moses putting a veil over his face that the children of Israel not look intently." The chiastic center F stich contains "glory" three times in each hemistich. Using "glory" three times is repeated in the final sub-structure and confirms that both sub-structures are part of the same overall structure.

2 Corinthians 4

Chapter 4 of 2 Corinthians is a single chiastic structure. The structure reveals an interpolation and a verse out of order. Perhaps the out of order verse was a scribal mistake. Rhetorical analysis reveals other verses out of order in 2 Cor 6, and Gal 3. The out of order verses are marked with an asterisk (*).

2 Cor 4:1–18

A 4:1 Because of this, having this ministry, as we received mercy *we do not lose heart*.

B 4:2 But we have renounced the *hidden things* of disgrace not walking in craftiness nor falsifying the word of God. But by *revealing the truth* commending ourselves to every man's conscience before God. 4:3 And even *if our gospel is concealed*, it is *concealed* to those perishing.

C 4:4 The god of this age has blinded the minds of the unbelieving so that the light of the gospel of the *glory of Christ*, who is the image of God, should not beam upon them.

D 4:5 For we do not proclaim ourselves but *Christ Jesus Lord* and ourselves as your servants for the sake of *Jesus*. 4:6 For God, having said light shall shine out of darkness, who shone in our hearts to give the light of the knowledge of the glory of God in the face of *Jesus Christ*.

(4:7 But we have this treasure in earthen vessels, that the exceeding greatness of the power may be of God, and not from ourselves. 4:8 Being hard pressed on every side, but not crushed. Being perplexed, but not despairing. 4:9 Being persecuted, but not forsaken. Being struck down, but not destroyed.)

E 4:10 Always carrying around in our body the *death of Jesus so that also the life of Jesus may be revealed in our body*.

E' 4:11 For we the living are always delivered to *death for the sake of Jesus so that also the life of Jesus may be revealed in our mortal flesh*. 4:12 So then death works in us but life in you.

D' 4:13 But having the same spirit of faith according to that which is written I believed and therefore I spoke. We also believe and therefore we also speak. 4:14 Knowing that he who raised up the *Lord Jesus* shall also raise us up with *Jesus* and will present us with you.

C' 4:15 For all things are for your sakes that the grace being multiplied through many the thanksgiving may increase to the *glory of God*.

*B' 4:17 For our presently bearable affliction is producing for us more exceedingly an eternal weight of glory. 4:18 While we do not look at the *things that are seen* but at the *things that are not seen*. For the *things that are seen* are temporal. But the *things that are not seen* are eternal.

*A' 4:16 Therefore *we do not lose heart*. But though our outward man is decaying yet our inward is being renewed day by day.

2 Cor 4:1-18 Chiastic Structure Table

A 4:1—we do not lose heart	A' *4:16—we do not lose heart
B 4:2-3—hidden things . . . revealing the truth . . . if our gospel is concealed . . . concealed	B' *4:17-18—things that are not seen . . . things that are seen . . . things that are seen . . . things that are not seen
C 4:4—glory of Christ	C' 4:15—glory of God
D 4:5-6—Christ Jesus Lord . . . Jesus . . . Jesus Christ	D' 4:13-14—Lord Jesus . . . Jesus
E 4:10—death of Jesus so that also the life of Jesus may be revealed in our body	E' 4:11-12—death for the sake of Jesus so that also the life of Jesus may be revealed in our mortal flesh

Commentary

The A stich in this literary unit reveals a verse out of order. The chiastic structure of 2 Cor 4 is clear having five stiches, all of which have matching phrases except the A stich. Therefore, it becomes obvious that v. 4:16 is out of order, and Paul intended it to be the close of the literary unit. Both vv. 4:1 and 16 contain the phrase "we do not lose heart." Perhaps a scribe's eye skipped down as he was copying the sentence, and wrote v.4:16 after writing v. 4:15, inadvertently skipping vv. 4:17 and 18. Then he noticed his mistake, and instead of starting over, he followed v. 4:16 with vv. 4:17 and 18 and thought it still made sense. Through the centuries his error was preserved. It was noted above that there appear to be other verses out of order in 2 Cor 6. There is also an out of order verse in Gal 3. The B stich does not have any exact matching phrases in both hemistiches, but they both deal with seeing and not seeing. The B hemistich contains "hidden things," "revealing the truth," "if our gospel is concealed," and "concealed" a second time. In the B' hemistich is found "things that are seen" twice and "things that are not seen" twice. The C hemistich contains "the glory of Christ," and the C' hemistich contains "the glory of God."

The D hemistich contains "Christ Jesus Lord," "Jesus," and "Jesus Christ" while the D' hemistich contains "the Lord Jesus" and "Jesus." In the D stich at v. 4:13 Paul quotes Ps 115:1 (Septuagint). The center E stich matches "the death of Jesus so that also the life of Jesus is revealed in our body" with "to death for the sake of Jesus so that the life of Jesus may be revealed in our mortal flesh." All of these exact word and phrase matches of the C, D, and E stiches and the concept matches of the B stich and the fifty other chiastic structures in the undisputed letters are a clear indication that the A' stich, v. 4:16, is out of order. It also makes more sense as the concluding verse of the structure.

Interpolation 2 Cor 4:7–9

There is an interpolation between the D hemistich and the E hemistich. As found in canonical 2 Cor 4 there are ninety-nine words in vv. 4:5–10 that encompass the D and E hemistiches. However, in the E' and D' hemistiches, vv. 4:13–15, there are only fifty-five words, definitely imbalanced. If vv. 4:7–9 are removed, the D and E stiches are reduced to sixty-one words, a more acceptable balance. There are parallelisms in the proposed interpolation, especially in vv. 4:8–9, but they do not fit into the chiastic structure of the literary unit. The E stich, vv. 4:10–12, is clearly the center stich having almost the exact same phrase repeated. The interpolation seems to be based on 1 Cor 4:9–13. In addition the sense of vv. 4:7–9 is not in keeping with the rest of 2 Cor 4 with its theme of shining light that continued from 2 Cor 3.

Stiches	Words in first half	Words in second half	Words in interpolation
D—E	4:5–10–99	4:13–15–55	4:7–9–38

2 Corinthians 5

Chapter 5 of 2 Corinthians is another parallel structure that encompasses the entire chapter. The structure has nine stiches with each stich containing two hemistiches.

2 Cor 5:1–21

A 5:1 For we know that if the earthly house of our tent be dissolved, *we have a building from God* a *house* not made with hands eternal in the *heavens.*
A' 5:2 And indeed in this we groan longing to be clothed upon with our *dwelling that is from Heaven.*

  B 5:3 If indeed also *being clothed we will not be found naked.* 5:4a For indeed we that are in this tent do groan being burdened.
  B' 5:4b Because *we wish not to be unclothed but to be clothed* so that the mortal may be swallowed up by life.

    C 5:5 Now he that has prepared us for this very thing is God, who gave to us the security of the spirit. 5:6 Therefore *always being confidant* and knowing that *being at home in the body we are absent from the Lord.*
    C' 5:7 For we walk by faith not by sight. 5:8 *Now we are confidant* and are pleased rather *to be absent out of the body and to be at home with the Lord.* 5:9 Therefore also whether at home or absent we are zealous to be acceptable to him.

      D 5:10 For *we must all be revealed before the judgment seat of Christ.* That each one may bear the things done in the body according to what he did whether good or evil.

D' 5:11 Knowing therefore the fear of the Lord we persuade men *but we are revealed to God*. And I hope that we have been revealed also in your consciences.

E 5:12a We are not again commending ourselves to you but giving you occasion of *boasting on our behalf*.

E' 5:12b So that you might have an answer to those that *boast in appearance* and not in heart. 5:13 For if we are mad, it is to God. If we are of sound mind, it is to you.

F 5:14 For the love of Christ compels us, having concluded this, *that one died for all* therefore all died.

F' 5:15 And *he died for all*. So that those living should no longer live for themselves but for him who died for them and was raised.

G 5:16 Therefore we now know no one according to the flesh. Even though *we have known Christ according to the flesh* but now we no longer know him thus.

G' 5:17 Therefore *if any one is in Christ, he is a new creation*. The old things have passed away. Behold, the new has come into being.

H 5:18 But all things are of *God, who reconciled us to himself through Christ* and gave us the ministry of *reconciliation*.

H' 5:19 Such that *God was in Christ reconciling the world to himself*, not reckoning to them their trespasses and having established for us the word of *reconciliation*.

I 5:20 Therefore we are ambassadors for Christ as though God were inviting through us. We implore for Christ. *Be reconciled to God*.

I' 5:21 He who knew no sin made sin for us so that we might *become the righteousness of God* in him.

2 Cor 5:1-21 Parallel Structure Table

A 5:1—we have a building from God ... house ... heavens	A' 5:2—our dwelling that is from Heaven
B 5:3-4a—being clothed we will not be found naked	B' 5:4b—we wish not to be unclothed but to be clothed
C 5:5-6—always being confidant ... being at home in the body we are absent from the Lord	C' 5:7-9—now we are confident ... to be absent out of the body and to be at home with the Lord
D 5:10—we must all be revealed before the judgment seat of Christ	D' 5:11—but we are revealed to God
E 5:12a—boasting on our behalf	E' 5:12b-13—boast in appearance
F 5:14—that one died for all	F' 5:15—he died for all

G 5:16—we have known Christ according to the flesh	G' 5:17—if anyone is in Christ he is a new creation
H 5:18—God who reconciled us to himself through Christ . . . reconciliation	H' 5:19—God was in Christ reconciling the world to himself . . . reconciliation
I 5:20—be reconciled to God	I' 5:21—become the righteousness of God

Commentary

This is a parallel structure containing nine stiches. Each stich has two hemistiches. The A hemistich contains "we have a building from God, a house . . . in the heavens" matching "our dwelling that is from Heaven" in the A' hemistich. The B hemistich has "being clothed . . . not found naked" matching "we wish not to be unclothed but to be clothed" in the B' hemistich. The C hemistich contains "always being confidant" matching "now we are confidant" in the C' hemistich. Also "being at home in the body we are absent from the Lord" in the C hemistich matches its opposite "to be absent out of the body and to be at home with the Lord" in the C' hemistich. The D stich matches "we must all be revealed before the judgment seat of Christ" with "we are revealed to God."

The E hemistich contains "boasting on our behalf," and the E' hemistich contains "boast in appearance." The F hemistich has "one died for all," matching "he died for all" in the F' hemistich. The G hemistich contains "we have known Christ according to the flesh," matching "if anyone is in Christ he is a new creation." The H hemistich contains "God who reconciled us to himself through Christ," while the H' hemistich contains "God was in Christ reconciling the world to himself." In addition, both hemistiches contain "reconciling, reconciliation" again. The final I stich matches "be reconciled to God" with "righteousness of God."

2 Corinthians 6

The structure of 2 Cor 6 is a parallel structure with an inclusio that defines the structure. Once again the structure encompasses the entire chapter and it reveals two verses that are out of order. This may be the work of the same scribe that got the verse out of order in 2 Cor 4. Several stiches in this structure contain multiple elements. The D stich has ten consecutive parallels as Paul expounds on his hardships to the Corinthians. The out of order verses are marked with an asterisk (*).

2 Cor 6:1–18

A 6:1 Now working together we also implore that *you do not receive the grace of God in vain*.
  B 6:2a For he says, "At an *acceptable time* I heard you. And in a day of salvation I rescued you."
  B' 6:2b Look! Now is the *acceptable time*.
  B" 6:2c Look! Now is the *day of salvation*.
    C 6:3 In no way placing a stumbling block so that *our ministry* may not be blamed.
    C' 6:4a But in everything we are commending *ourselves as ministers* of God,
      D 6:4b in great *endurance*,
      D' 6:4c in *afflictions*,
      D" 6:4d in *hardships*,
      D''' 6:4e in *distresses*,
      D'''' 6:5a in *floggings*,
      D''''' 6:5b in *imprisonments*,
      D'''''' 6:5c in *riots*,
      D''''''' 6:5d in *toils*,
      D'''''''' 6:5e in *sleepless nights*,
      D''''''''' 6:5f in *hunger*,
        E 6:6a in *purity*,
        E' 6:6b in *knowledge*,
        E" 6:6c in *patience*,
        E''' 6:6d in *goodness*,
        E'''' 6:6e in the *Holy Spirit*,
        E''''' 6:6f in *genuine love*,
          F 6:7a in the *word of truth*,
          F' 6:7b in the *power of God*,
          F" 6:7c by the *weapons of righteousness on the right hand and on the left*,
          G 6:8a through *glory and dishonor*,
          G' 6:8b by *defamation and praise*,
          G" 6:8c as *imposters and true*,
          G''' 6:9a as being *unknown and being well known*,
          G'''' 6:9b as *dying, and look, we live*.
          G''''' 6:9c As being *chastened and not being killed*.
          G'''''' 6:10a As being *sorrowful, but always rejoicing*.
          G''''''' 6:10b As *poor but enriching many*.
          G'''''''' 6:10c As having *nothing and possessing all things*.
            H 6:11a Our *mouth is open* to you, Corinthians,
            H' 6:11b our *heart is expanded*.

Second Letter To The Corinthians

H" *6:13 Now as a just reward (I speak as to children), *be expanded* also.

   *I 6:12a You are not *restrained* by us.

   *I' 6:12b But you are *restrained* in your affections.

     J 6:14a Do not be *joined with unbelievers*.

     J' 6:14b For what *fellowship have righteousness and iniquity*?

     J" 6:14c Or what *communion has light with darkness*?

     J'" 6:15a And what *harmony has Christ with Belial*?

     J"" 6:15b Or what *portion has a believer with an unbeliever*?

       K 6:16a And what agreement has a *temple of God* with idols?

       K' 6:16b For we are the *temple of the living God*.

         L 6:16c *As God said*, "I will dwell in them, and walk among them. And I will be their God, and they will be my people.

         *L' 6:18 And I will be to you a father, And you will be sons and daughters to me, *says the Lord Almighty*."

         *L" 6:17a "Therefore come out from among them, and separate yourselves," *says the Lord*.

*A' 6:17b And touch no unclean thing. And *I will receive you*.

2 Cor 6:1-18 Parallel Structure Table

With ten elements in the D stich and nine elements in the G stich, the heretofore organization of the structure table with one row per stich is inadequate to represent the parallelisms of this literary unit. The below table will use two rows of five elements to present the D stich and one row of five elements plus one row of four elements to represent the G stich.

A 6:1—you do not receive the grace of God		A' 6:17b—I will receive you		
B 6:2a—acceptable time		B' 6:2b—acceptable time		B" 6:2c—day of salvation
C 6:3—our ministry		C' 6:4a—ourselves as ministers		
D 6:4b—endurance	D' 6:4c—afflictions	D" 6:4d—hardships	D'" 6:4e—distresses	D"" 6:5a—floggings
D""" 6:5b—imprisonments	D"""" 6:5c—riots	D""""" 6:5d—toils	D"""""" 6:5e—sleepless nights	D""""""" 6:5f—hunger
E 6:6a—purity	E' 6:6b—knowledge	E" 6:6c—patience	E'" 6:6d—goodness	E"" 6:6e—Holy Spirit	E""" 6:6f—genuine love

F 6:7a—word of truth		F 6:7b—power of God			F 6:7c—weapons of righteousness on the right hand and on the left	
G 6:8a—glory and dishonor	G' 6:8b—defamation and praise	G" 6:8c—imposters and true	G'" 6:9a—being unknown and being well known		G"" 6:9b—dying and look we live	
G""' 6:9c—chastened and not being killed	G"""' 6:10a—being sorrowful but always rejoicing		G""""' 6:10b—poor but enriching many		G"""""' 6:10c—having nothing and possessing all things	
H 6:11a—mouth is opened		H' 6:11b—heart is expanded			H" *6:13a—be expanded	
I *6:12a—restrained			I' *6:12b—restrained			
J 6:14a—joined with unbelievers	J' 6:14b—fellowship have righteousness and iniquity	J" 6:14c—communion has light with darkness	J'" 6:15a—harmony has Christ with Belial		J"" 6:15b—portion has a believer with an unbeliever	
K 6:16a—temple of God		K' 6:16b—temple of the living God				
L 6:16c—As God said		L' *6:18—says the Lord Almighty			L" *6:17a—says the Lord	

Commentary

This parallel structure is defined by the inclusio of the A stich. "You do not receive the grace of God in vain" in the A hemistich matches "and I will receive you" in the A' hemistich. The defined parallel structure assumes that vv. 6:17 and 18 are out of order and v. 6:17 should follow v. 6:18. This puts v. 6:17b in position be the closing hemistich of the inclusio, a typical Pauline construction. In the stich preceding the A' hemistich vv. 6:16, 17, 18 are all quotes of Old Testament scripture. Verse 6:16 is a quote of Lev 26:12. Verse 6:18 is a quote of Jer 38:9 (Septuagint), and v. 6:17 is a quote of Isa 52:11. The final words of v. 6:17, "I will receive you" do not appear to be a quote from the Old Testament. Paul added them to form the inclusio with v. 6:1. In addition, the use of "therefore" at the beginning of v. 6:17 implies that v. 6:17 is the last sentence in the literary unit. In this unit Paul also quotes Isa 49:8 at v. 6:2. The D stich contains ten elements which is an unusual amount. The G stich contains nine elements.

Walker states that vv. 6:14–7:1 are an interpolation.[1] Walker anticipated the rhetorical analysis technique noting that there is a "perfect chiasmus" if vv. 6:14–7:1 are removed. However, his chiasmus is not one of repeated phrases but of intended meaning of the phrases. In Walker's chiasmus he has the A stich being v. 6:11 "Our mouth is open to you, Corinthians, our heart is expanded" matching v. 7:3 "I say it not to condemn: for I have said before, that you are in our hearts to die together and live together." Admittedly "heart" is a matching word, but Walker ignores that and proposes a matching concept of "assurance of affection." Then he sees the B stich as a matching concept of "disclaimer of responsibility for alienation" with v. 6:12 "You are not restrained by us. But you are restrained in your affections" matching v. 7:2b "We wronged no one. We corrupted no one. We took advantage of no one." This putative stich has no matching words or phrases, and the B hemistich has the Corinthians as the subject, while the B' stich has Paul as the subject. Walker's C stich has v. 6:13, "Now as a just reward (I speak as to children), be expanded also" matching v. 7:2a "make room for us." Walker interprets the C stich as meaning "appeal for affection."

It appears that canonical 2 Corinthians may have vv. 6:12 and 13 reversed. If this is correct, it destroys Walker's chiasmus. Although v. 6:13 makes sense following v. 6:12, it is more typical of Paul to have three consecutive parallels in the H stich "mouth is open," "is expanded," "be expanded" followed by two consecutive parallels in the I stich "restrained" and "restrained." Also v. 6:17 that Walker says is an interpolation is the second half of an inclusio A stich having "you do not receive the grace of God" matching "I will receive you." This assessment means that vv. 6:17 and 18 have also been reversed. Some ancient scribe must have been having a bad day.

2 Corinthians 7

Chapter 7 of 2 Corinthians is a single chiastic structure having nine stiches.

2 Cor 7:1–16

> A 7:1 Having therefore these promises, beloved, we should *cleanse ourselves from all defilement of flesh and spirit* perfecting holiness in the fear of God.
>   B 7:2 *Make room for us.* We wronged no one. We corrupted no one. We took advantage of no one.
>   C 7:3 *I say it not to condemn.* For *I have said before* that you are in our hearts to die together and live together.
>   D 7:4 Great is my frankness toward you. Great is my boasting about you. *I am filled with encouragement.* I overflow with *joy* in all our affliction.

---

1. Walker, *Interpolations*, 199–209.

E 7:5 For even when we had come into Macedonia our flesh had no relief, but *we were afflicted* from the outside, controversy on the inside, fears.

  F 7:6 But he that encourages the lowly, God, encouraged us by the coming of Titus. 7:7 And not by his coming only, but also by the encouragement with which he was encouraged as to you, while he told us your *strong affection, your sorrow, your zeal* for me. So that I rejoiced even more.

    G 7:8 For though *I have grieved you with my letter*, I do not regret it. Though I did regret it for I see that the letter grieved you if even for an hour.

      H 7:9a Now I rejoice, not that you were grieved, but that *you were grieved to repentance*.

        I 7:9b For *you were grieved according to God* that you might be injured by us in nothing.

        I' 7:10a For *grief according to God*

      H' 7:10b produces *repentance to salvation*, without regret. But the grief of the world produces death.

    G' 7:11a Look, this very same thing that *you were grieved according to God*.

  F' 7:11b What diligence it produced in you, but reasoned defense, but indignation, but fear, but *strong affection, but zeal, but vindication*! In everything you proved yourselves to be innocent in the matter.

  E' 7:12 So although I wrote to you, I did not write for the sake of him who did the wrong, nor for the sake of him that *suffered the wrong*, but that your enthusiasm for us might be revealed in the sight of God.

D' 7:13 On account of this *we have been encouraged*. And in our encouragement we have rejoiced all the more with the *joy* of Titus, because his spirit has been refreshed by all of you.

C' 7:14 For if in anything *I have boasted to him about you*, I was not put to shame. But as we have spoken all things to you in truth, so our boasting also which I made to Titus became the truth.

B' 7:15 And his affection is more abundantly toward you, remembering the obedience of all of you how with fear and trembling *you welcomed him*.

A' 7:16 I rejoice that *in everything I am confident in you*.

2 Cor 7:1-16 Chiastic Structure Table

A 7:1—Cleanse ourselves from all defilement of flesh and spirit	A' 7:16—in everything I am confident in you
B 7:2—make room for us	B' 7:15—you welcomed him

C 7:3—I say it not to condemn ... I have said	C' 7:14—I have boasted to him about you ... we have spoken
D 7:4—I am filled with encouragement ... joy	D' 7:13—we have been encouraged ... joy
E 7:5—we were afflicted	E' 7:12—suffered the wrong
F 7:6-7—strong affection your sorrow your zeal	F' 7:11b—strong affection but zeal but vindication
G 7:8—I have grieved you with my letter ... the letter grieved you	G' 7:11a—that you were grieved according to God
H 7:9a—you were grieved to repentance	H' 7:10b—repentance to salvation
I 7:9b—you were grieved according to God	I' 7:10a—grief according to God

Commentary

Walker proposes that v. 7:1 as an interpolation,[2] but v. 7:1 appears to be the A hemistich in a chiastic structure matching v. 7:16. The A stich has "cleanse ourselves from all defilement of flesh and spirit" matching "in everything I am confident in you." The only matching word is "all/everything" (*pantos*), but the literary unit begins with an admonition and ends with a complement for doing everything correctly. In addition there are eight additional matches in chiastic order, solidifying the proposed A stich. The B stich has "make room for us" in the B hemistich matching "you welcomed him" in the B' hemistich, with welcoming expressed in both hemistiches. The C stich matches "I say it not to condemn" and "I have said" in the C hemistich with "I have boasted to him about you" and "we have spoken" in the C' hemistich.

The D hemistich contains "I am filled with encouragement" matching "we have been encouraged" in the D' hemistich. Both hemistiches also contain "joy." The E stich matches "we were afflicted" in the E hemistich with "suffered the wrong" in the E' hemistich. The F stich matches "strong affection, your sorrow, your zeal" with "strong affection, but zeal, but vindication." The G stich has "I have grieved you with my letter" and "the letter grieved you" in the G hemistich matching "you were grieved according to God" in the G' hemistich. The H stich matches "you were grieved to repentance" with "repentance to salvation." The center I stich contains "you were grieved according to God" matching "grief according to God."

2 Corinthians 8

Chapter 8 of 2 Corinthians has a hybrid chiastic/parallel structure with an inclusio encompassing the entire chapter. The A stich is an inclusio. The B and C stiches, the

2. Walker, *Interpolations*, 199–209.

D and E stiches, the I and J stiches, the M and N stiches, the O and P stiches, and the Q and R stiches are chiastic while the others are parallel. All stiches have two hemistiches.

2 Cor 8:1–24

  A 8:1 Now, brothers, we make known to you the grace of God that having been given in the *churches* of Macedonia.
    B 8:2 That in much proof of affliction the abundance of their joy and their deep poverty abounded into the *riches of their generosity*.
      C 8:3a For *according to their ability*,
      C' 8:3b I testify, and *beyond their ability*
    B' 8:3c *they voluntarily gave*.
        D 8:4 Asking us with *much encouragement for the grace* and the fellowship in ministering to the saints.
          E 8:5a And not only as we had hoped, but first they *gave themselves to the Lord*,
          E' 8:5b and *to us through the will of God*.
        D' 8:6 Insomuch that *we encouraged Titus* that as he had begun so he might also complete in you *this grace* also.
          F 8:7 But as you excel in everything, faith, and speech, and knowledge, and *all enthusiasm, and in the love from us to you*, that you should abound in this grace also.
          F' 8:8 I do not speak by way of commandment, but as proving *through the enthusiasm* of others the sincerity *and of your love*.
            G 8:9a For you know the grace of our Lord Jesus Christ, that, for your sakes *he became poor even though he was rich*.
            G' 8:9b So that *through his poverty you might become rich*.
              H 8:10 And I give a judgment in this. For this is profitable for you, *not only to act but also to will. You made a beginning* a year ago.
              H' 8:11 But now complete *the acting also. So that just as there was the readiness to will* so also *to complete with your ability*. 8:12 For if the readiness is present, it is acceptable according as one has, not according as he has not.
                I 8:13 For that others may be relieved and you distressed, but in *fairness*.
                  J 8:14a At the present time *your abundance is for those in need*.
                  J' 8:14b So that *their abundance also may be for your need*.
                I' 8:14c So that there may be *fairness*.
                    K 8:15a As it is written, "He that *gathered much had nothing over*.

K' 8:15b And he that *gathered little had no lack.*"

L 8:16 But thanks be to God, who puts the same *enthusiasm for you* into the heart of Titus.

L' 8:17 For he accepted indeed our appeal. But being *very enthusiastic he went forth to you* of his own accord.

M 8:18a Now *we have sent together with him*

N 8:18b the brother *whose praise in the gospel is through all the churches.*

N' 8:19a And not only so, but *who also having been chosen by the churches*

M' 8:19b *to travel with us* in this grace, which is administered by us to the glory of the Lord, and our readiness.

O 8:20a Avoiding this, that *any one should find fault with us* in this generosity

P 8:20b which is *administered by us.*

P' 8:21a For *we take care to do* what is right.

O' 8:21b Not only in the sight of the Lord, but also *in the sight of men.*

Q 8:22a Now we have sent with them *our brother,*

R 8:22b whom we have often proved *enthusiastic* in many things.

R' 8:22c But now much more *enthusiastic* by reason of his great confidence in you.

Q' 8:23 As regards Titus, my partner and fellow-worker as to you, as to *our brothers,* apostles of the churches to the glory of Christ.

A' 8:24 Therefore show to them your love and our boasting about you in the face of the *churches.*

2 Cor 8:1–24 Chiastic Structure Table

A 8:1—churches	A' 8:24—churches
B 8:2—riches of their generosity	B' 8:2b—they voluntarily gave
C 8:3a— according to their ability	C' 8:3b—beyond their ability
D 8:4—much encouragement for the grace	D' 8:6—we encouraged Titus ... this grace
E 8:5a—gave themselves to the Lord	E' 8:5b—to us through the will of God
F 8:7—all enthusiasm ... and in the love from us to you	F' 8:8—through the enthusiasm ... and of your love
G 8:9a—he became poor even though he was rich	G' 8:9b—through his poverty you might become rich

H 8:10—not only to act but also to will . . . you made a beginning	H' 8:11–12—the acting also so that just as there was the readiness to will . . . to complete with your ability
I 8:13—fairness	I' 8:14c—fairness
J 8:14a—your abundance is for those in need	J' 8:14b—their abundance also may be for your need
K 8:15a—gathered much had nothing over	K' 8:15b—gathered little had no lack
L 8:16—enthusiasm for you	L' 8:17—very enthusiastic he went forth to you
M 8:18a—we have sent together with him	M' 8:19b—to travel with us
N 8:18b—whose praise in the gospel is through all the churches	N' 8:19a—who also having been chosen by the churches
O 8:20a—any one should find fault with us	O' 8:21b—in the sight of men
P 8:20b—administered by us	P' 8:21a—we take care to do
Q 8:22a—our brother	Q' 8:23—our brothers
R 8:22b—enthusiastic	R' 8:22c—enthusiastic

Commentary

This literary unit has a hybrid structure defined by an inclusio. This is one of the longest structures in Paul's undisputed letters, containing eighteen stiches. While five stiches are strictly parallel, twelve stiches are in a chiastic sub-structure (A, B, B,' A'), and one is the inclusio. The inclusio, the A stich, has "churches" in both hemistiches, clearly delineating the beginning and ending of this literary unit. Next is a chiastic sub-structure involving the B and C stiches in a B, C, C,' B' format. The B hemistich contains "riches of their generosity" and the B' hemistich contains "they voluntarily gave." In the B' hemistich the "gave" is understood. The C stich has "their ability" in both hemistiches. This is followed by another chiastic sub-structure with a D, E, E,' D' format. The D hemistich has "much encouragement for the grace," and the D' hemistich has "we encouraged Titus . . . this grace." The E hemistich has "gave themselves to the Lord" and the E' hemistich has "to us through the will of God." At this juncture the sub-structures change to strictly parallel. The F stich has "all enthusiasm" matching "through the enthusiasm" and "and in the love from us to you" matching "and your love." The G parallel stich has "he became poor even though he was rich" matching "through his poverty you might become rich." The parallel sub-structure continues in the H stich with "not only to act but also to will" matching "the acting also, so that just as there was the readiness to will." There is a second set of matching opposite phrases in the H stich with "you made a beginning" with "to complete with your ability."

At the I and J stiches a chiastic sub-structure intervenes with the I stich having "fairness" in both hemistiches. The J stich matches "your abundance for those in need" with "their abundance may be for your need." A parallel sub-structure resumes at the K stich with "gathered much had nothing over" matching "gathered little had no lack" as Paul quotes Exod 6:18. The L stich continues with "enthusiasm for you" matching "very enthusiastic he went forth to you." From this point to the end of the structure and second half of the inclusio the sub-structures are all chiastic. The M, N, N,' M' sub-structure has "we have sent together with him" matching "to travel with us" in the M stich. The N stich matches "whose praise in the gospel is through all the churches" with "having been chosen by the churches." The O, P, P,' O' chiastic sub-structure matches "any one should find fault with us" with "in the sight of men" in the O stich. The P stich matches "administered by us" with "we are taking great care to do." The last chiastic sub-structure is the Q, R, R,' Q' sub-structure matching "our brother" in the Q hemistich with "our brothers" in the Q' hemistich. The R stich has "enthusiastic" in both hemistiches.

2 Corinthians 9

Chapter 9 of 2 Corinthians is the first chapter of the letter that contains more than one literary unit. The first unit is five verses long in an A, B, C, D, A,' B,' C,' D,' parallel format. The second unit is also parallel but in the A, A,' B, B' format.

2 Cor 9:1–5

A 9:1 Now concerning the ministering to the saints, it is superfluous for me to write to you. 9:2a For I know your readiness, of which *I boast about you*
  B 9:2b to *Macedonians*,
    C 9:2c that *Achaia has been prepared* for a year past. And your zeal has stirred up very many.
      D 9:3a But I have sent the *brothers*
A' 9:3b that *our boasting about you* may not be false in this respect. That, as I have been saying, you may be prepared.
  B' 9:4a Lest perhaps, if any *Macedonians* come with me
    C' 9:4b and *find you unprepared*, we, that we may say not you, should be put to shame in this assurance.
      D' 9:5 I thought it necessary therefore to encourage the *brothers*, that they should complete beforehand your previously promised blessing that the same might be ready as a matter of blessing, and not of extortion.

2 Cor 9:1–5 Parallel Structure Table

A 9:1–92a—I boast about you	A' 9:3b—our boasting about you

B 9:2b—Macedonians	B' 9:4a—Macedonians
C 9:2c—Achaia has been prepared	C' 9:4 b—find you unprepared
D 9:3a—brothers	D' 9:5—brothers

Commentary

This literary unit has a different kind of parallel structure from the typical Pauline parallel units. This has an A, B, C, D, A,' B,' C,' D' structure. The A stich matches "I boast about you" with "our boasting about you." The B stich has "Macedonians" in both hemistiches. The C stich matches "Achaia has been prepared" with "find you unprepared." The final D stich has "brothers" in both stiches.

2 Cor 9:6–15

This literary unit has a five-stich parallel structure with a typical A, A,' B, B,' C, C' Pauline format.

  A 9:6a But this: *he who sows sparingly will also reap sparingly.*
  A' 9:6b And *he who sows bountifully will also reap bountifully.*
    B 9:7 Each one does according as he purposes his heart not from regret or of necessity. For *God loves a cheerful giver.*
    B' 9:8 Now *God is able to make all grace abound to you.* That having always all sufficiency in everything you may excel to every good work.
      C 9:9 As it is written, "He has scattered abroad, he has given to the poor. His righteousness abides for ever." 9:10a And he that *supplies seed to the sower and bread* for food,
      C' 9:10b will *supply* and multiply your *seed for sowing* and increase the *fruits* of your righteousness,
        D 9:11 in every way enriching you to all generosity, which produces *through us thanksgiving to God.* 9:12a For the *ministry of this service* not only is completely filling up the
        D' 9:12b needs of the saints but also is overflowing *through many thanksgivings to God,* 9:13a through the proof by *this ministry* they glorify God for the submission of your confession to the gospel of Christ,
          E 9:13b and the *generosity of the contribution to them and to all.*
          E' 9:14 And their supplication is for you, a longing for you by reason of the exceeding grace of God upon you. 9:15 Thanks to God for *his unspeakable gift.*

2 Cor 9:6-15 Parallel Structure Table

A 9:6a—he who sows sparingly will also reap sparingly	A' 9:6b—he who sows bountifully will also reap bountifully
B 9:7—God loves a cheerful giver	B' 9:8—God is able to make all grace abound to you
C 9:9-10a—supplies seed to the sower and bread	C' 9:10b—supply . . . seed for sowing . . . fruits
D 9:11-12a—through us thanksgiving to God . . . ministration of this service	D' 9:12b-13a—through many thanksgivings to God . . . this ministration
E 9:13b—generosity of the contribution to them and to all	E' 9:14-15—his unspeakable gift

Commentary

For the second half of 2 Cor 9 Paul returns to a typical A, A,' B, B,' C, C' parallel structure. The reader can discern the beginning and endings of the literary units by the shift in the pattern of the parallelisms. The A stich is a Pauline aphorism and matches "he who sows sparingly shall also reap sparingly" with "he who sows bountifully shall also reap bountifully." The B stich matches "God loves a cheerful giver" with "God is able to make all grace abound to you." The C stich begins with Paul quoting Ps 111:9 (Septuagint) then matches "supplies seed to the sower and bread" with "supply . . . seed for sowing . . . fruits." The D stich contains two matching phrases "through us thanksgiving to God" in the D hemistich with "through many thanksgivings to God" in the D' hemistich. Then "ministration of this service" in the D hemistich matches "this ministration." The final E stich matches "generosity of the contribution to them and to all" with "his unspeakable gift."

2 Corinthians 10

The tenth chapter of 2 Corinthians is the second one in the letter to have more than one literary unit. Interestingly, they are both unusual. The first unit has a dual chiastic/parallel structure, and the second unit has a hybrid chiastic/parallel structure.

2 Cor 10:1-11

This first literary unit of 2 Cor 10 has a dual chiastic/parallel structure containing eight stiches.

Chiastic Structure

A 10:1a I, Paul, myself encourage you by the meekness and gentleness of Christ, *who as to appearance indeed am humble among you,*
  B 10:1b *but being absent am bold toward you.*
    C 10:2a Now I implore you that *I may not be bold when present* with the
      D 10:2b confidence with which *I consider to be daring* against some who consider us as if we walked according to the flesh.
        E 10:3 For though we walk in the flesh, we do not wage war according to the flesh. 10:4a For *the weapons of our warfare are not of the flesh,*
          F 10:4b but powerful before God to the *demolition of fortresses,* 10:5 demolishing arguments, and every barrier that is erected against the knowledge of God, and subduing every thought to the obedience of Christ.
            G 10:6 And being ready to punish all disobedience, when *your submission may be complete.*
              H 10:7a You look at things as they appear to be. If any man persuades himself that *he is of Christ,*
              H' 10:7b let him again consider this, that just as *he is of Christ,* so also are we. 10:8a For though I should boast more about our authority
            G' 10:8b that the Lord has given for *building you up,* and not for demolishing you, I will not be put to shame
          F' 10:9 so that I might not appear to *terrify you by my letters.*
        E' 10:10a For they say *his letters*
      D' 10:10b indeed *are weighty and strong,*
    C' 10:10c but his *bodily presence is weak* and his speech can be ignored.
  B' 10:11a Let such a one consider this. That what *we are in word by letters when absent,*
A' 10:11b such *we are also in action when present.*

2 Cor 10:1–11 Chiastic Structure Table

A 10:1a—who as to appearance indeed am humble among you	A' 10:11b—we are also in action when present
B 10:1b—but being absent am bold toward you	B' 10:11a—we are in word by letters when absent
C 10:2a—I may not be bold when present	C' 10:10c—bodily presence is weak
D 10:2b—I consider to be daring	D' 10:10b—we are weighty and strong
E 10:3–4a—the weapons of our warfare are not of the flesh	E' 10:10a—letters

F 10:4b–5—demolition of fortresses demolishing arguments and every barrier that is erected against the knowledge of God and subduing every thought to the obedience of Christ	F' 10:9—terrify you by my letters
G 10:6—your submission may be complete	G' 10:8b—building you up
H 10:7a—he is of Christ	H' 10:7b–8a—he is of Christ

Parallel Structure

   A 10:1a I, Paul, myself encourage you by the *meekness and gentleness* of Christ,
   A' 10:1b who as to appearance indeed am *humble among you,*
     B 10:1c but being absent am *bold toward you.*
     B' 10:2a Now I implore you that I may not *be bold when present* with the
        C 10:2b confidence with which I consider to be daring against some who consider us as if we *walked according to the flesh.*
      C' 10:3a For though we *walk in the flesh,*
         D 10:3b we do not *wage war according to the flesh.*
         D' 10:4a For the weapons of our *warfare are not of the flesh,*
           E 10:4b but powerful before God to the *demolition of fortresses,*
           E' 10:5a *demolishing arguments,* and every barrier that is erected against the knowledge of God,
              F 10:5b and *subduing every thought* to the *obedience of Christ.*
              F' 10:6 And being ready to *punish all disobedience,* when your *submission may be complete.*
                 G 10:7a You look at things as they appear to be. If any man persuades himself that *he is of Christ,*
                 G' 10:7b let him again consider this. That just as *he is of Christ* so also are we.
                    H 10:8a For though I should boast more about our authority that the Lord has given for *building you up,*
                    H' 10:8b and *not for demolishing you,* I will not be put to shame.
                       I 10:9 So that I might not appear to terrify you by *my letters.*
                       I' 10:10a For *his letters* they say
                          J 10:10b indeed are *weighty and strong,*
                          J' 10:10c but his bodily *presence is weak and his speech can be ignored.*
                             K 10:11a Let such a one consider this. That what we are in word *by letters when absent,*
                             K' 10:11b such we are also *in action when present.*

Part I | The Undisputed Letters

2 Cor 10:1–11 Parallel Structure Table

A 10:1a—meekness and gentleness	A' 10:1b—humble among you
B 10:1c—bold toward you	B' 10:2a—be bold when present
C 10:2b—walked according to the flesh	C' 10:3a—we walk in the flesh
D 10:3b—wage war according to the flesh	D' 10:4a—warfare are not of the flesh
E 10:4b—demolition of fortresses	E' 10:5a—demolishing arguments
F 10:5b—subduing every thought . . . obedience of Christ	F' 10:6—submission may be complete . . . punish all disobedience
G 10:7a—he is of Christ	G' 10:7b—he is of Christ
H 10:8a—building you up	H' 10:8b—not for demolishing you
I 10:9—my letters	I' 10:10a—his letters
J 10:10b—weighty and strong	J' 10:10c—presence is weak and his speech can be ignored
K 10:11a—letters when absent	K' 10:11b—in action when present

Commentary

Chiastic Structure

The chiastic structure of this literary unit does not have the typical Pauline balance. The D', E', and F' hemistiches are all shorter than one would expect given the length of the D, E, and F hemistiches. Nevertheless, there does not appear to be an interpolation into this structure. The parallel structure is balanced, and it was deemed that Paul unbalanced the chiastic structure to accommodate the parallel structure. The A hemistich has "as to appearance am humble among you" matching "we are also in action when present" in the A' hemistich, both expressing Paul's attitude when in Corinth. The B hemistich has "but being absent am bold toward you" matching "we are in word by letters when absent" in the B' hemistich. The C stich matches "I may not be bold when present" with "bodily presence is weak," expressing the same idea first negatively then positively. The D hemistich has "I consider to be daring" matching "are weighty and strong" in the D' hemistich.

The E stich is interesting with "the weapons of our warfare are not of the flesh" matching the one word "letters," meaning "the pen is mightier than the sword." The F stich is similar to the E stich in that a very long phrase matches a short phrase. The F hemistich has "demolition of fortresses, demolishing arguments and every barrier that is erected against the knowledge of God and subduing every thought to the obedience of Christ" matching "terrify you by my letters." The G stich matches opposite concepts with "your submission may be complete" matching "building you up." The center H stich has "he is of Christ" matching "he is of Christ."

Parallel Structure

In the parallel structure the G stich is identical to the center H stich of the chiastic structure with "he is of Christ" in both hemistiches. All stiches in the parallel structure contain two hemistiches. The A stich matches "meekness and gentleness" with "humble among you." Both hemistiches of the B stich contain the word "bold." The C and D stiches both make two statements about "flesh." The E hemistich has "demolition of fortresses" while the E' hemistich contains "demolishing arguments." In the F stich both hemistiches contain two phrases, one about "subduing" or "submission" and the other having opposing statements about "obedience" and "disobedience." The H stich matches a concept stated in the positive and the negative with "building you up" in the H hemistich matching "not for demolishing you" in the H' hemistich. Both hemistiches in the I stich are about Paul's letters, and the J stich matches opposites with "weighty and strong" matching "presence is weak and his speech can be ignored." The final K stich has more opposites with "letters when absent" matching "in action when present."

2 Cor 10:12–18

This is a literary unit with a hybrid chiastic/parallel structure. There is a chiastic beginning and ending enclosing a parallel center.

  A 10:12a For *we dare not number or commend ourselves* with those who
    B 10:12b *commend themselves*. But they are measuring themselves by themselves and comparing themselves with themselves. They do not understand.
      C 10:13a But *we will not boast beyond measure*,
        D 10:13b but *according to the measure of the province*
          E 10:13c that God assigned to us as *a measure*, to reach even to you.
            F 10:14 For we are not overextending ourselves as though we did not reach to you. For we came even as far as you in the *gospel of Christ*.
      C' 10:15a *Not boasting beyond measure* in another's labors. But having hope that as your faith grows we shall be magnified in you
        D' 10:15b *according to our province*
          E' 1015c to *abundance*.
            F' 10:16 So as to *preach the gospel* to the parts beyond you, not to boast in another's province in things ready to boast about. 10:17 But he that boasts, let him boast in the *Lord*.
    B' 10:18a For he who *commends himself* is not approved,
  A' 10:18b but *whom the Lord commends*.

2 Cor 10:12–18 Hybrid Chiastic/Parallel Structure Table

A 10:12a—we dare not number or commend ourselves	A' 10:18b—whom the Lord commends
B 10:12b—commend themselves	B' 10:18a—commends himself
C 10:13a—we will not boast beyond measure	C' 10:15a—not boasting beyond measure
D 10:13b—according to the measure of the province	D' 10:15b—according to our province
E 10:13c—a measure	E' 10:15c—abundance
F 10:14—gospel of Christ	F' 10:16–17—preach the gospel ... Lord

Commentary

This is an interesting literary unit that is similar to the literary unit at Rom 14:7–12 in that it has an A, B, B,' A' chiastic beginning and ending but parallel center stiches. The A hemistich has "we dare not number or commend ourselves" matching "whom the Lord commends" in the A' hemistich. Then in the B stich "commend themselves" matches "commends himself." It is interesting that the A and B stiches are also parallel to each other.

The balance of the unit has a C, D, E, F, C,' D,' E,' F' parallel structure. The C hemistich has "we will not boast beyond measure" matching "not boast beyond measure" in the C' hemistich. The D stich has "according to the measure of the province" in the first half and "according to our province" in the second half. The E stich matches "a measure" with "abundance." The F hemistich has "gospel of Christ" while the F' hemistich has "preach the gospel . . . Lord." "Measure" is used five times in the unit although two of those are "without measure" or "beyond measure" (*ametra*).

2 Corinthians 11

As with 2 Cor 10, 2 Cor 11 contains two literary units the first of which is a dual chiastic/parallel structure with eight stiches. The parallel structure of the dual chiastic/parallel structure is defined by an inclusio with the A stich being identical to the A stich of the chiastic structure.

2 Cor 11:1–19

Chiastic Structure

> A 11:1 I wish that you *were bearing with me* in a little *foolishness*. But indeed you do bear with me.

B 11:2 For I am jealous as to you with a godly jealousy. For *I have given you in marriage* to one husband, a pure virgin to present to *Christ*.

 C 11:3 But I fear, lest by any means as the *serpent deceived Eve in his craftiness your minds might be corrupted* from the simplicity and the purity in *Christ*.

  D 11:4 For if *he who is coming proclaims another Jesus* whom we did not proclaim or you receive a different spirit, which you did not receive, or a different gospel, which you did not accept, you are bearing it well.

   E 11:5 For I conclude that *I am inferior in nothing* to the *most chief apostles*.

    F 11:6 But though I am unpolished in speech, yet *I am not in knowledge*. But in every way we have revealed this to you in all things.

     G 11:7 Or did I commit a sin in humbling myself so that you might be exalted because *I gratuitously proclaimed to you the gospel of God*?

      H 11:8 *I robbed other churches*, having received support for the ministry to you. 11:9a And when I was present with you and was in need *I did not burden anyone*.

      H' 11:9b For *the brothers coming from Macedonia fully supplied my need*. And in everything *I kept from being a burden to you*, and so will I keep.

     G' 11:10 The *truth of Christ is in me* so that this boasting of mine will not be obstructed in the regions of Achaia.

    F' 11:11 Why? Because I do not love you? God knows I do. 11:12a But what I do that I will do, so that *I might cut off the opportunity*

   E' 11:12b from *those who desire an opportunity*. That in what they are boasting, they might be found *as we are*.

  D' 11:13 For such as *these are false apostles*, deceitful workers, *disguising themselves as apostles of Christ*.

 C' 11:14 And no wonder, for even *Satan disguises himself* as an *angel of light*. 11:15 It is no great thing therefore if his *ministers also disguise themselves* as ministers of righteousness, whose end shall be according to their works.

B' 11:16 I say again no one should think I am a fool. But if so, *receive me* as a fool, that I also may boast a little. 11:17a What I am saying I am not saying according to the *Lord*,

A' 11:17b but in *foolishness*, in this confidence of boasting. 11:18 Since many boast according to the flesh I will boast also. 11:19 For being wise *you bear fools gladly*.

2 COR 11:1–19 CHIASTIC STRUCTURE TABLE

A 11:1—bearing with me ... foolishness ... bear with me	A' 11:17b–19—you bear fools gladly ... foolishness

B 11:2—I have given you in marriage . . . Christ	B' 11:16–17a—receive me . . . Lord
C 11:3—serpent deceived Eve in his craftiness . . . your minds might be corrupted . . . Christ	C' 11:14–15—Satan disguises himself . . . ministers also disguise themselves . . . angel of light
D 11:4—he who is coming . . . proclaims another Jesus	D' 11:13—these are false apostles . . . disguising themselves as apostles of Christ
E 11:5—I am inferior in nothing . . . most chief apostles	E' 11:12b—as we are . . . those who desire an opportunity
F 11:6—I am not in knowledge	F' 11:11–12a—I might cut off the opportunity
G 11:7—I gratuitously proclaimed to you the gospel of Christ	G' 11:10—the truth of Christ is in me
H 11:8–9a—I robbed other churches . . . I did not burden anyone	H' 11:9b—the brothers coming from Macedonia fully supplied my need . . . I kept from being a burden to you

Parallel Structure

   A 11:1 I wish that you were *bearing with me* in a little *foolishness*. But indeed you do *bear with me*.
    B 11:2 For I am jealous as to you with a godly jealousy. For I have betrothed you to one husband, a *pure virgin to present to Christ*.
    B' 11:3 But I fear lest by any means as the serpent deceived Eve in his craftiness, your minds might be corrupted from the *simplicity and the purity in Christ*.
     C 11:4a For if he who is coming *proclaims another Jesus whom we did not proclaim*,
     C' 114:4b or you *receive a different spirit, which you did not receive*,
     C" 11:4c or a *different gospel, which you did not accept*, you are bearing it well.
      D 11:5 For I conclude that *I am inferior in nothing* to the most chief apostles.
      D' 11:6 But though I am unpolished in speech yet *I am not in knowledge*. But in every way we have revealed this to you in all things.
       E 11:7 Or did *I commit a sin in humbling myself* so that *you might be exalted* because I gratuitously proclaimed to you the gospel of God?
       E' 11:8 *I robbed other churches*, having received support for the ministry to you. 11:9a And when I was present with you and was in need *I did not burden anyone*.
        F 11:9b For the brothers *coming from Macedonia* fully supplied my need. And in everything I kept from being a burden to you, and so will I keep.
        F' 11:10 The truth of Christ is in me so that this boasting of mine will not be obstructed *in the regions of Achaia*.

G 11:11 Why? Because I do not love you? God knows I do. 11:12a But what I do that I will do, so that *I might cut off the opportunity*

G' 11:12b from *those who desire an opportunity*. That in what they are boasting they might be found as we are.

H 11:13 For such as these are *false apostles*, deceitful workers, *disguising themselves* as *apostles of Christ*.

H' 11:14 And no wonder, for even *Satan disguises himself* as an *angel of light*.

H" 11:15 It is no great thing therefore if his *ministers also disguise themselves* as *ministers of righteousness*, whose end shall be according to their works.

I 11:16a *I say again*, no one should think *I am a fool*.

I' 11:16b But if so, *receive me as a fool*, that I also may boast a little. 11:17a What *I am saying*, I am not saying according to the Lord,

J 11:17b but in foolishness, in this *confidence of boasting*.

J' 11:18 Since many *boast according to the flesh*, I will boast also.

A' 11:19 For being wise *you bear fools* gladly.

2 Cor 11:1–19 Parallel Structure Table

A 11:1—bearing with me … foolishness … bear with me	A' 11:19—you bear fools	
B 11:2—pure virgin to present to Christ	B' 11:3—simplicity and the purity of Christ	
C 11:1a—proclaims another Jesus whom we did not proclaim	C' 11:4b—receive a different spirit which you did not receive	C" 11:4c—different gospel which you did not accept
D 11:5—I am inferior in nothing	D' 11:6—I am not in knowledge	
E 11:7—I commit a sin in humbling myself … you might be exalted	E' 11:8–9—I robbed other churches … I did not burden anyone	
F 11:9b—coming from Macedonia	F' 11:10—in the regions of Achaia	
G 11:11–12a—I might cut off the opportunity	G' 11:12b—those who desire an opportunity	
H 11:13—false apostles … disguise themselves … apostles of Christ	H' 11:14—Satan disguises himself … angel of light	H" 11:15—ministers also disguise themselves … ministers of righteousness
I 11:16a—I say again … I am a fool	I' 11:16b–17a—I am saying … receive me as a fool	
J 11:17b—confidence of boasting	J' 11:18—boast according to the flesh	

Part I | The Undisputed Letters

Commentary

Chiastic Structure

The A hemistich has "bearing with me" and "bear with me" matching "you bear with fools" in the A' hemistich. Both hemistiches contain "foolishness." The B stich has a match of opposites with "I have given you in marriage" in the B hemistich matching "receive me" in the B' hemistich, matching giving and receiving. Then "Christ" matches "Lord." The C stich is interesting with Paul matching the serpent in the garden of Eden with Satan. The C hemistich has "serpent deceived Eve in his craftiness" matching "Satan disguises himself." Then "your minds might be corrupted" matches "ministers disguise themselves," and "Christ" matches "angel of light." The D stich is a diatribe against Paul's opponents with "he who is coming" in the D hemistich matches "these are false apostles" in the D' hemistich. Also "proclaims another Jesus" matches "disguising themselves as apostles of Christ." In the E stich "I am inferior in nothing" matches "as we are" meaning "as good as we are." Also in the E stich "most chief apostles matches "those who desire an opportunity."

In the F stich Paul seems to be engaged in word play while continuing his diatribe against his opponents. The F hemistich has "I am not in knowledge" meaning Paul is not unskilled in knowledge. This matches with "I might cut off the opportunity" in the F' hemistich. This is word play about circumcision being preached by Paul's opponents, Paul implying that since they like circumcision, he might cut off their entire members. The G hemistich has "I gratuitously proclaimed to you the gospel of God" matching "the truth of Christ is in me" in the G' hemistich. The center H stich has "I robbed other churches" matching "the brothers coming from Macedonia fully supplied my need." The second matching pair in the H stich is "I did not burden anyone" in the H hemistich and "I kept from being a burden to you."

Parallel Structure

The parallel structure is defined by an inclusio A stich that is close to, but not exactly the same as, the A stich of the chiastic structure. The B stich discusses "purity" and "Christ" in both hemistiches. The C stich contains three elements duplicating the three-element pattern of the H stich. The C stich is the third from the beginning and the H stich is the third from the ending. The three elements of the C stich have "proclaims another Jesus whom we did not proclaim," parallel to "receive a different spirit which you did not receive," also parallel to "different gospel which you did not accept." The D stich has Paul bragging on himself in both hemistiches with "I am inferior in nothing" matching "I am not in knowledge." The E stich matches two phrases with "I commit a sin in humbling myself" in the E hemistich matching "I robbed other churches" in the E' hemistich with "sin" and "robbery" being associated concepts. Second, "you might be exalted" in the E hemistich matches "I did not burden anyone" in the E' hemistich, both being benefits Paul conferred upon the Corinthians. The F stich mentions areas of Greece in both hemistiches. The G stich has Paul's word play about circumcision and castration of his opponents with a play on "cut off" and "opportunity." The three-element H stich has false apostles disguising themselves, Satan disguising himself, and ministers disguising themselves in the separate elements. Both hemistiches of the I stich have Paul saying something about a fool. The final J stich has both hemistiches discussing "boasting."

2 Cor 11:20–33

The second literary unit in 1 Cor 11 has a chiastic structure with eight stiches.

> A 11:20 For you bear it if anyone enslaves you, if he devours you, *if anyone takes hold of you* captive, if anyone exalts himself, if he strikes you on the face.
>
> B 11:21 *I speak dishonorably* as though *we have been weak*. But wherein *anyone might be bold (I speak in foolishness), I am bold also*. 11:22 Are they Hebrews? So am I. Are they Israelites? So am I. Are they descendants of Abraham? So am I. 11:23a Are they ministers of *Christ? (I speak as if insane.)* I more.
>
>   C 11:23b In *labors more abundantly*, in *prisons more abundantly*, in *beatings above measure*, in *deaths frequently*.
>
>   D 11:24 *From the Jews five times I received forty lashes save one.*
>
>   E 11:25 Three times was I beaten with rods. Once was I stoned. *Three times I was shipwrecked*. I have been in the deep a night and a day.
>
>   F 11:26a Traveling often in *perils of rivers*,
>
>   G 11:26b in *perils of robbers*,
>
>   H 11:26c in *perils from my countrymen*,
>
>   H' 11:26d in *perils from the Gentiles*,
>
>   G' 11:26e in *perils in the city*,
>
>   F' 11:26f in *perils in the wilderness*,
>
>   E' 11:26g in *perils in the sea*,
>
>   D' 11:26h in *perils among false brothers*.
>
>   C' 11:27 In *labor and toil*, in *sleepless nights* often, in *hunger and thirst*, in *fastings* often, in *cold and nakedness*. 11:28 Besides those external things, there is pressure upon me daily, *anxiety for all the churches*.
>
> B' 11:29 *Who is weak*, and *I am not weak*? who is led into sin, and I do not burn inside? 11:30 If it is necessary *that I boast, I will boast* about the things that *concern my weakness*. 11:31 The God and father of the *Lord Jesus* he who is blessed for ever knows that *I am not lying*.
>
> A' 11:32 In Damascus the governor under Aretas the king guarded the city of the Damascenes *in order to seize me*. 11:33 And I was let down in a basket through a window in the wall and escaped his hands.

Part I | The Undisputed Letters

2 Cor 11:20-33 Chiastic Structure Table

A 11:20b—if anyone takes hold of you	A' 11:32-33—in order to seize me
B 11:21-23a—I speak dishonorably . . . we have been weak . . . anyone might be bold . . . I speak in foolishness . . . I am bold also . . . Christ . . . I speak as if insane	B' 11:29-30—that I boast . . . who is weak . . . I am not weak . . . I will boast . . . concern my weakness . . . Lord Jesus . . . I am not lying
C 11:23b—labors more abundantly . . . prisons more abundantly . . . beating above measure . . . deaths frequently	C' 11:27-28—labor and toil . . . sleepless nights . . . hunger and thirst . . . fastings . . . cold and nakedness . . . anxiety for all the churches
D 11:24—from the Jews five times I received forty lashes	D' 11:26h—perils among false brothers
E 11:25—three times I was shipwrecked I have been in the deep night and day	E' 11:26g—perils in the sea
F 11:26a—perils of rivers	F' 11:26f—perils in the wilderness
G 11:26b—perils of robbery	G' 11:26e—perils in the city
H 11:26c—perils from my countrymen	H' 11:26d—perils from Gentiles

Commentary

The A stich has a curious match with "if anyone takes hold of you" in the A hemistich matching "in order to seize me" in the A' stich. The B stich has two concepts of speaking and inner fortitude weaving in and out of both hemistiches. The B hemistich has "I speak dishonorably," "I speak in foolishness" and "I speak as if insane" while the B' hemistich has "that I boast," "I will boast," and "I am not lying." With regard to inner fortitude the B hemistich has "we have been weak," "anyone might be bold," and "I am bold also," matching "who is weak," "I am not weak," and "concern my weakness." Also in the B stich "Christ" matches "Lord Jesus."

Beginning with the C hemistich through the C' hemistich Paul lists all the tribulations he has suffered for his faith and in his attempts to bring Christianity to the Gentiles. The C hemistich has four tribulations while the C' hemistich contains six with "labor" being common to both sets of tribulations. The D stich matches "Jews" with "false brothers" continuing Paul's diatribe against his opponents. The E stich matches "shipwrecked" and "the deep" with "perils of the sea." The F stich matches "perils of rivers" with "perils of the wilderness." The E stich matches "perils of robbery" with "perils of the city." The center H stich matches "perils from my countrymen" meaning Jews, with "perils from Gentiles."

Second Letter To The Corinthians

2 Corinthians 12

A parallel structure encompasses the entire chapter 12 of 2 Corinthians. This literary unit has an introductory verse that is not part of the literary unit. This is a rather long unit containing twelve stiches all of which contain two hemistiches.

2 Cor 12:1–21

12:1 It is necessary that I boast, though it is not expedient. Indeed I will come to visions and revelations of the Lord.

> A 12:2 *I know a man in Christ fourteen years ago whether in the body, I do not know, or whether out of the body, I do not know. God knows. Such a one was caught up to the third Heaven.*
> A' 12:3 And *I know such a man, whether in the body, or out of the body, I do not know. God knows.* 12:4 *So that he was caught up into Paradise,* and heard unspeakable words, that are not lawful for a man to utter.
>> B 12:5 About such a one *I will boast.* But about myself *I will not boast* except in weaknesses.
>> B' 12:6 For if *I should desire to boast, I will not be a fool.* For I will speak the truth. But I refrain unless anyone should conclude I am more than what he sees in me or hears from me.
>>> C 12:7a And because of the exceeding greatness of the revelations *that I should not become arrogant,*
>>> C' 12:7b there was given to me a thorn in my flesh, a messenger of Satan to buffet me, *that I should not become arrogant.*
>>>> D 12:8 Concerning this *I begged the Lord three times* that it might depart from me. 12:9a And he has said to me, "My grace is sufficient for you. For power *is perfected in weakness."*
>>>> D' 12:9b Most gladly therefore *I will rather boast in my weaknesses.* So that *the power of Christ may rest upon me.* 12:10a Therefore I take pleasure in weaknesses, in insults, in hardships,
>>>>> E 12:10b in persecutions, in difficulties, for Christ's sake. *For when I might be weak, then am I strong.*
>>>>> E' 12:11a *I am become a fool.* You compelled me. For *I ought to have been commended by you.*
>>>>>> F 12:11b For *in no way was I inferior to the very chief apostles* though I am nothing.
>>>>>> F' 12:12 *Truly the signs of an apostle were performed among you* in all patience by signs and wonders and miracles.

G 12:13a For in what is it that you were inferior concerning the rest of the churches except that *I myself did not burden you*?

G' 12:13b Forgive me this wrong. 12:14a Look, this is the third time I am ready to come to you, and *I will not burden you*.

   H 12:14b For *I seek not yours, but you*. For the children ought not to store up for the parents, but the parents for the children.

   H' 12:15 And I will most gladly spend and be spent for your souls. If *I love you more abundantly*, am I loved less?

     I 12:16 But be it so, I did not myself burden you. But being crafty *I caught you with trickery*.

     I' 12:17 *Did I take advantage of you* by any one of them whom I have sent to you?

        J 12:18 I urged Titus, and I sent the *brother* with him. Did Titus take any advantage of you? *Did we not walk in the same spirit*? In the same steps?

        J' 12:19 Do you think all this time that we are excusing ourselves to you. *Before God, we speak in Christ*. But all things, *beloved*, are for your edification.

           K 12:20a For I fear unless perhaps when I come *I may find you not such as I desire*.

           K' 12:20b And *I should be found by you not as you desire*.

              L 12:20c Perhaps *quarreling, jealousy, anger, factions, slander, gossip, conceit, disorder*. 12:21a Unless again when I come my God should humble me before you.

              L' 12:21b And I should mourn for many of them that have previously sinned and did not repent of the *uncleanness and sexual immorality and lasciviousness which they committed*.

2 Cor 12:2-21 Parallel Structure Table

A 12:2—I know a man in Christ, fourteen years ago, whether in the body, I do not know, or whether out of the body, I do not know; God knows. Such a one was caught up to the third Heaven	A' 12:3—I know such a man, whether in the body, or out of the body, I do not know. God knows. 12:4 so That he was caught up into Paradise
B 12:5—I will boast . . . I will not boast	B' 12:6—I should desire to boast . . . I will not be a fool
C 12:7a—that I should not become arrogant	C' 12:7b—that I should not become arrogant

D 12:8–9a—I begged the Lord three times... power is perfected in weakness	D' 12:9b–10a—I will rather boast in my weakness... the power of Christ may rest upon me
E 12:10b—for when I might be weak... then I am strong	E' 12:11a—I ought to have been commended by you... I am become a fool
F 12:11b—in no way was I inferior to the very chief apostles	F' 12:12—truly the signs of an apostle were performed among you
G 12:13a—I myself did not burden you	G' 12:13b–14a—I will not burden you
H 12:14b—I seek not yours but you	H' 12:15—I love you more abundantly
I 12:16—I caught you with trickery	I' 12:17—did I take advantage of you
J 12:18—brother... did we not walk in the same spirit	J' 12:19—beloved... before God we speak in Christ
K 12:20a—I may find you not such as I desire	K' 12:20b—I should be found by you not as you desire
L 12:20c–21a—quarreling, jealousy, anger, factions, slander, gossip, conceit, disorder	L' 12:21b—uncleanness and sexual immorality and lasciviousness which they committed

Commentary

This literary unit encompasses the entirety of 2 Cor 12. This unit has the only instance in the undisputed letters of an introductory verse that is not part of the structure of the unit. Verse 12:1 does not seem to be a part of the unit, having no parallel with the A stich or with the L stich. It does echo "boast" (*kauchasthai*) found in v. 11:30 and suggests that 2 Cor 12 followed 2 Cor 11 in Paul's original letter. This pattern has been noted in both Romans and 1 Corinthians. Both halves of the A stich are almost identically worded about Paul's trip to the third level of Heaven so that the parallel is obvious. The B hemistich contains "I will boast" matching "I should desire to boast" in the B' hemistich. The second match in this stich is "I will not boast" matching "I will not be a fool." The C stich has identical phrases in both hemistiches "that I should not become arrogant."

The D stich has two matching phrases in each hemistich. The first is "I begged the Lord three times" matching "the power of Christ may rest upon me." The second is "power is perfected in weakness" matching "I will boast in my weakness." The E hemistich has "when I might be weak, then I am strong" matching "I have become a fool... I ought to have been commended by you" in the E' hemistich. The F stich has "in no way was I inferior to the most chief apostles" matching "truly the signs of an apostle were performed among you." The G hemistich has "I myself did not burden you," and the G' hemistich has "I will not burden you."

The H hemistich contains "I seek not yours but you" while the H' hemistich contains "I love you more abundantly." The I stich matches "I caught you with trickery" with "did I take advantage of you." The J stich matches "brother" with "beloved" and "did we not walk in the same spirit" with "before God we speak in Christ." The K hemistich has " I may find you not such as I desire," and the K' hemistich has "I might be found by you not as you desire." The final L stich matches sets of enumerated sins with "quarreling, jealousy, anger, factions, slander, gossip, conceit, disorder" matching "uncleanliness and sexual immorality and lasciviousness that they have practiced."

2 Corinthians 13

The final literary unit in 2 Corinthians has a parallel structure encompassing the entire chapter with the first and last stiches both containing three elements.

2 Cor 13:1–14

A 13:1 This is the *third time I am coming to you*. In the mouth of two or three witnesses shall every matter be established.
A' 13:2a I have said beforehand and I say beforehand, as when I *was present the second time*, and now being absent,
A" 13:2b to those who have sinned before and to all the rest that *if I come again*, I will not spare anyone.

  B 13:3 Since you seek a proof of Christ that speaks in me, *who as to you is not weak, but is powerful* among you.
  B' 13:4a For he was *crucified through weakness yet he lives through God's power*.
  B" 13:4b For we also are *weak in him but we will live with him through God's power* toward you.

    C 13:5a *Examine yourselves*, whether you are in the faith.
    C' 13:5b *Test yourselves*. Or do you not recognize yourselves,

      D 13:5c that Jesus Christ is in you unless *you are failures*.
      D' 13:6 But I hope that you will know that *we are not failures*.

        E 13:7a Now we pray to God that you do no evil. Not that *we may appear approved*,
        E' 13:7b but that you may do that which is good, though *we may appear unapproved*.

          F 13:8 For we can do nothing against the truth but for the truth. 13:9 For we rejoice when *we are weak but you are strong*. This we also pray for your perfection.
          F' 13:10 Because of this, being absent, I write these things. So that I may not when present deal severely with you, according to the authority that the Lord has given me for *building up, and not for tearing down*.

            G 13:11a Finally, brothers, rejoice. Be perfected, be encouraged, be of the same mind, *be at peace*.

> G' 13:11b And the *God of love and peace* will be with you.
>> H 13:12 *Greet* one another with a holy kiss.
>>> H' 13:13 All the saints *greet* you.
>>>> I 13:14a *The grace of the Lord Jesus Christ,*
>>>> I' 13:14b and *the love of God,*
>>>> I" 13:14c and the *communion of the Holy Spirit,* be with all of you.

2 Cor 13:1–14 Parallel Structure Table

A 13:1—third time I am coming to you	A' 13:2a—was present the second time	A" 13:2b—if I come again
B 13:3—who as to you is not weak but is powerful	B' 13:4a—crucified through weakness yet he lives through Gods power	B" 13:4b—weak in him but we will live with him through God's power
C 13:5a—examine yourselves	C' 13:5b—test yourselves	
D 13:5c—you are failures	D' 13:6—we are not failures	
E 13:7a—we may appear approved	E' 13:7b—we may appear unapproved	
F 13:8–9—we are weak but you are strong	F' 13:10—building up and not for tearing down	
G 13:11a—be at peace	G' 13:11b—God of love and peace	
H 13:12—greet	H' 13:13—greet	
I 13:14a—the grace of the Lord Jesus Christ	I' 13:14b—the love of God	I" 13:14c—the communion of the Holy Spirit

Commentary

As with the previous literary unit this one has a parallel structure. It may be that Paul intended 2 Cor 12 and 13 to be one unit. However, since the A stich of 2 Cor 13 contains three elements and the final I stich also contains three elements, while all of the stiches in 2 Cor 12 contain only two elements, it was judged that they are separate literary units. In addition, the subject changes dramatically at v. 13:1. The three elements of the A stich show a reverse chronological progression with "third time I am coming to you" in the A element, "being present the second time" in the A' element and "If I come to you again" in the A" element. The B stich also has three elements, all three being about weakness and power. The first has "who as to you is not weak but is powerful." The B' element has "crucified through weakness he lives through God's power." The B" element has "weak in him but we will live with him through God's power."

The C stich begins the two-element format with the C hemistich containing "examine yourselves" (*heautous peirazete*), and the C' hemistich containing "test yourselves" (*heautous dokimazete*), Paul using two different words that mean "examine" and "test." The D hemistich has "you are failures," and the D' hemistich has "we are not failures." The E stich matches opposites, "we may appear approved" with "we may appear unapproved." The F stich matches "we are weak but you are strong" with "building up and not for tearing down." The G stich matches "be at peace" with "the God of love and peace." The H stich has "greet" in both hemistiches. The final I stich is the benediction having three elements: "the grace of the Lord Jesus Christ," "the love of God," and "the communion of the Holy Spirit."

6

Letter To The Galatians

Galatians 1

Gal 1:1–17

THE FIRST LITERARY UNIT of Galatians is a parallel structure with the initial stich and the final stich both containing three elements.

> A 1:1 Paul, an apostle not from men nor through man but through *Jesus Christ* and *God the father*, the one raising him from the dead,
> A' 1:2 and all the brothers that are with me, to the churches of Galatia. 1:3 Grace to you and peace from *God our father* and the *Lord Jesus Christ*
> A" 1:4 who gave *himself* for our sins, so that he might deliver us out of this presently evil age according to the will of *our God and father* 1:5 to whom be the glory for ever and ever. Amen.
>> B 1:6 I am astonished that you are so quickly deserting from the one who called you in the grace of *Christ* to a *different gospel*.
>> B' 1:7 Which is not *another one* only some who trouble you and would *pervert the gospel* of *Christ*.
>>> C 1:8 But even if we or an angel from Heaven should *preach a gospel to you other than the one that we preached to you let him be accursed*.
>>> C' 1:9 As we have said before so I now say again if anyone *preaches to you any gospel other than what you received let him be accursed*.
>>>> D 1:10 For am I now seeking the approval of *men*, or of God? Or am I striving to please *men*? If I were pleasing *men*, I would not in any way be a servant of *Christ*.
>>>> D' 1:11 For I make known to you, *brothers* regarding the gospel which was preached by me that it is not according to *man*. 1:12 For neither did I receive it from *man* nor was I taught it but through revelation of *Jesus Christ*.

E 1:13 For you have heard of my former way of life in *Judaism*. That beyond measure *I persecuted* the church of God and was *destroying* it.

E' 1:14 And *I advanced* in *Judaism* beyond many of my contemporaries among my countrymen being more *exceedingly zealous* for the traditions of my fathers.

    F 1:15 And when it pleased God who selected me from my mother's womb and *called me through his grace*

    F' 1:16 to reveal his son in me that *I might preach him among the Gentiles*, I did not immediately consult with flesh and blood.

        G 1:17a Nor did *I go up to Jerusalem* to those who were apostles before me.

        G' 1:17b But *I went away into Arabia*.

        G" 1:17c And again *I returned to Damascus*.

Gal 1:1-17 Parallel Structure Table

A 1:1—Jesus Christ . . . God the father	A' 1:2-3—Lord Jesus Christ . . . God our father	A" 1:4-5—himself . . . our God and father
B 1:6—Christ . . . different gospel	B' 1:7—Christ . . . another one . . . pervert the gospel	
C 1:8—preach a gospel to you . . . let him be accursed	C' 1:9—preaches to you any gospel . . . let him be accursed	
D 1:10—men . . . men . . . men . . . Christ	D' 1:11-12—man . . . man . . . brothers . . . Jesus Christ	
E 1:13—my former way of life in Judaism . . . I persecuted . . . destroying	E' 1:14—I advanced in Judaism . . . exceedingly zealous	
F 1:15—called me	F' 1:16—I might preach him	
G 1:17a—I go up to Jerusalem	G' 1:17b—I went away into Arabia	G" 1:17c—I returned to Damascus

Commentary

This first literary unit of Galatians has a parallel structure with each stich having two elements except for the initial A stich and the final G stich, both of which have three. J. C. O'Neil describes many interpolations and glosses in his book *The Recovery of Paul's Letter to the Galatians*.[1] This work will not comment on O'Neil's many very short glosses he proposes for Galatians. Comments will be restricted to longer interpolations proposed by O'Neil that can be confirmed or denied by rhetorical analysis. However,

---

1. O'Neill, *Galatians*.

the first one that arises happens to be a single word. O'Neil proposes to eliminate "another one" (*allo*) in v. 1:7.[2] He does not realize that there is a parallel B stich and "another one" in v. 1:7 matches "different gospel" (*heteron euangelion*) in v. 1:6. "Pervert the gospel" (*metastrepsai to euangelion*) in v. 1:7 also matches "different gospel." The B stich also has "Christ" in both hemistiches. In this first literary unit O'Neil also proposes that vv. 1:13–14 are an interpolation. It so happens that those verses define the E stich in the parallel structure. It is possible that O'Neill is correct, but if so, the interpolator must have been attuned to Paul's structural style and included the parallel language in each stich: "Judaism," "I persecuted" parallel to "I advanced," and "destroying it" parallel to "exceedingly zealous." That does not seem likely.

The three A elements have "Jesus Christ," Lord Jesus Christ," and "himself" meaning "Christ" as the first match. The second match in the A stich is either "God our father" or "God the father" found in all three elements. The C hemistich has "should preach a gospel to you other than the one that we preached, let him be accursed" matching "preaches a gospel other than what you received let him be accursed" in the C' stich. The D hemistich has "men" three times and "Christ," while the D' hemistich has "man" twice, "brothers" once, and "Jesus Christ." The F stich matches "called me through his grace" with "I might preach him among the Gentiles." This is a match because the calling was to preach. As mentioned, the final G stich contains three elements "I go up to Jerusalem," "I went away into Arabia," and "I returned to Damascus." Once again Paul's literary unit is symetrical beginning and ending with three element stiches and five two element stiches in between.

Gal 1:18–2:1

This second literary unit of Gal 1 is a short chiastic structure that carries into the first verse of Gal 2.

> A 1:18 *Then after three years I went up to Jerusalem* to visit *Kephas*, and stayed with him fifteen days. 1:19 But I saw none of the apostles except *James*, the Brother of the Lord.
> B 1:20 Look, before *God*, the things that *I write to you I do not lie.*
> C 1:21 Then I went into the *regions of Syria and Kilikia.*
> C' 1:22 But my face was unknown to the *churches of Judea* that are in Christ.
> B' 1:23 But *they only heard* that he who once persecuted us now is *preaching the faith* that he once destroyed. 1:24 And they glorified *God* in me.
> A' 2:1 *Then after fourteen years I went up again to Jerusalem* with *Barnabas*, also taking *Titus* with me.

---

2. O'Neill, *Galatians*, 22.

Part I | The Undisputed Letters

Gal 1:18-2:1 Chiastic Structure Table

A 1:18-19—then after three years I went up to Jerusalem ... Kephas ... James	A' 2:1—Then after fourteen years I went up again to Jerusalem ... Barnabas ... Titus
B 1:20—God ... I write to you ... I do not lie	B' 1:23-24—God ... they only heard ... preaching the faith
C 1:21—regions of Syria and Kilikia	C' 1:22—churches of Judea

Commentary

This literary unit contains a rare mistake by Bishop Langdon, in that he did not recognize that v. 2:1 is part of the literary unit that began at v. 1:18. Galatians 2 should start one verse later. O'Neill proposed that 1:22-24 is an interpolation.[3] Such surgery would obviously gut the entire second half of this short chiastic literary unit. If vv. 22-24 were eliminated, rhetorical analysis of the remaining section would require that vv. 20-21 also be eliminated. Then vv. 1:18, 19; 2:1 would form the final stich in the previous literary unit, except that it would be extremely awkward to have "then after three years" followed so closely by "then after fourteen years." In addition, O'Neill's proposal requires an extremely clever interpolator to match "churches of Judea" with "regions of Syria and Kilikia" to form a C stich. Further the interpolator would have added "they only heard" to match "I write to you," "preaching the faith" to match "I do not lie," and "God" to match "God" to form the B stich. O'Neill's proposed interpolation is unlikely under a rhetorical analysis.

Galatians 2

Gal 2:2-10

> A 2:2a Now I went up pursuant to a revelation and *I laid before them the gospel that I preach* among the Gentiles.
>
> (2:2b but privately to those who were esteemed unless I might be running or had run in vain.)
>
>> B 2:3 But not even *Titus* a Greek who was with me was compelled to be *circumcised*
>> C 2:4 as a result of the *false brothers* surreptitiously brought in, who came in secretly to plot against our *freedom* which we have in Christ Jesus so that we will be enslaved.

---

3. O'Neill, *Galatians*, 24-26.

> D 2:5 Not even for an hour did we yield in subjection to them so that the truth of the *gospel might continue with you.*
>> E 2:6a But from those who were *esteemed* to be something (whatsoever formerly they were it makes *no difference to me.*
>> E' 2:6b God does not accept man's person.) for the *esteemed contributed nothing to me.*
> D' 2:7a But to the contrary, when they saw that I had been entrusted with the *gospel of the uncircumcision,*

(2:7b even as Peter with that of the circumcision.)

2:8a For he worked

(2:8b in Peter for the apostleship of the circumcision also worked)

> 2:8c in me for the Gentiles.
> C' 2:9a And when they perceived the *grace* that was given to me, *James and Kephas and John*, they who were *esteemed pillars*,
> B' 2:9b gave to me and *Barnabas* the right hands of fellowship. That we should go to the Gentiles and they to the *circumcised.*

A' 2:10 They only wanted that we should remember the poor, the *very thing I was eager to do.*

Gal 2:2-10 Chiastic Structure Table

A 2:2a—I laid before them the gospel that I preach	A' 2:10—very thing I was eager to do
B 2:3—Titus . . . circumcised	B' 2:9b—Barnabas . . . circumcised
C 2:4—false brothers . . . freedom	C' 2:9a—grace . . . James and Kephas and John . . . esteemed pillars
D 2:5—gospel might continue with you	D' 2:7a—gospel of the uncircumcision
E 2:6—esteemed . . . no difference to me	E' 2:6b—esteemed . . . contributed nothing to me

Commentary

In the A stich "I laid before them the gospel that I preach" matches "the very thing I was eager to do." The Jerusalem apostles were Paul's opponents and Paul claims he was eager to explain his gospel to them hoping they would see the merit in it. In the C stich "freedom" matches "grace," and "false brothers" in the C hemistich matches "James and Kephas and John" and "esteemed pillars" in the C' hemistich. Both hemistiches of the Ɖ stich contain "gospel" with "might continue with you" in the D hemistich matching "of the uncircumcision" the Galatians obviously being uncircumcised. This is a foreshadowing of Gal 5 where Paul tells the Galatians not to be circumcised. The center E stich contains "esteemed" in both hemistiches and matches "no difference to me" with "contributed nothing to me."

Interpolations

GAL 2:2B

The A and B hemistiches contain thirty-six words including the proposed interpolation, while the A' and B' hemistiches contain only twenty-seven words. This is somewhat out of balance. If the proposed interpolation of v. 2:2b is removed, the A and B hemistiches are reduced to twenty-four words, a much better balance. O'Neill does not include this passage as an interpolation, but he does propose that "Titus" has been interpolated.[4] Since "Titus" in the B hemistich is an obvious match with "Barnabas" in the B' hemistich, O'Neill is clearly wrong. Both hemistiches also contain "circumcised."

If v. 2:2b is removed, the letter still makes sense. In fact, it makes more sense and does not contradict Gal 1:16–17, or 2 Cor 11:5 and 12:11 as does canonical Gal 2:2b. It makes no sense for Paul to get a revelation from God about Christ and then ask other apostles if his revelation was accurate. A revelation from God would trump advice from men.

Stiches	Words in first half	Words in second half	Words in interpolation
A—B	2:2-3-36	2:9b-10-27	2:2b—12

GAL 2:7B, 8B

The second interpolation comes within the D' and C' hemistiches. The first clue that there has been an interpolation here is that supposedly in these two verses Paul calls Kephas "Peter," certainly a red flag. Those hemistiches contain forty-three words including the proposed interpolation. On the other hand the C and D hemistiches contain only thirty-four words. Taking out the interpolation reduces the D' and C' hemistiches to thirty-two words, a good balance. This agrees well with O'Neill. He would eliminate "even as Peter with that of the circumcision" from 2:7, but only

---

4. O'Neill, *Galatians*, 30.

"Peter" from 2:8.[5] It would seem normal for Paul to write in v. 2:8 "for he worked in me to the Gentiles" describing the reason that the pillars realized he had been entrusted with the apostleship to the uncircumcised. Keeping those six words in v. 2:8 makes the hemistiches balance.

Stiches	Words in first half	Words in second half	Words in interpolation
D—C	2:4-5—34	2:7-9a—43	2:7b, 8b—11

Gal 2:11-21

A parallel structure containing eight stiches. The first three and the last three stiches contain two hemistiches while the middle two stiches contain three elements. Paul's literary unit is symetrical again.

A 2:11 But when Kephas came to Antioch I resisted him to his face because *he stood condemned.*
A' 2:12a For before certain ones came from James he ate with the Gentiles, but when they came *he drew back and separated himself,*
  B 2:12b fearing *those of the circumcised.*
  B' 2:13a And the *rest of the Jews* likewise acted hypocritically with him.
    C 2:13b Insomuch that even Barnabas was *carried away with their hypocrisy.*
    C' 2:14a But when I saw that they *did not walk uprightly* according to the truth of the gospel,
      D 2:14b I said to Kephas before all, "If you, being a *Jew,* live as a *Gentile*
      D' 2:14c and not as a *Jew* lives, why do you compel the *Gentiles* to live as the Jews do?"
      D" 2:15 We are *Jews* by birth, and not *Gentile* sinners.
        E 2:16a But knowing that a man is *not justified by the works of the law but through faith* in Jesus Christ.
        E' 2:16b We believed in Christ Jesus that we might be *justified by faith in Christ and not by the works of the law.*
        E" 2:16c Because *by the works of the law no flesh will be justified.*
          F 2:17 But if seeking to be justified in Christ *we ourselves also were found sinners,* is Christ a minister of sin? May it never be!
          F' 2:18 For if I build up again those things which I destroyed, *I prove myself a transgressor.*
            G 2:19 For through the law *I died to the law, that I might live to God.*

---

5. O'Neill *Galatians,* 36. Others agree that Gal 2:7-8 is an interpolation, Barnikol, "Galatians 2:7-8,"; Walker, *Interpolations,* 243.

G' 2:20a *I have been crucified* with Christ. It is no longer I that live, *but Christ living in me.*

H 2:20b And that life which I now live in the flesh I live in faith, which is in the *son of God*, who loved me and *gave himself up for me.*

H' 2:21 I do not make void the grace of God. For if justification is through the law, then *Christ died for nothing.*

Gal 2:11–21 Parallel Structure Table

A 2:11—he stood condemned	A' 2:12a—he drew back and separated himself	
B 2:12b—those of the circumcised	B' 2:13a—rest of the Jews	
C 2:13b—was carried away with their hypocrisy	C' 2:14a—did not walk uprightly	
D 2:14b—Jew . . . Gentiles	D' 2:14c—Jews . . . Gentiles	D" 2:15—Jews . . . Gentile
E 2:16a—not justified by the works of the law but through faith	E' 2:16b—justified by faith and not by works of the law	E" 2:16c—by works of the law no flesh will be justified
F 2:17—we ourselves also were found sinners	F' 2:18—I prove myself a transgressor	
G 2:19—I died to the law . . . that I might live to God	G' 2:20a—I have been crucified . . . but Christ living in me	
H 2:20b—the son of God . . . gave himself up for me	H' 2:21—Christ died for nothing	

Commentary

This is a parallel structure with eight stiches. The D and E stiches contain three elements with the rest containing two. There are three stiches with two hemistiches, then two stiches with three elements each, and finally three stiches with two hemistiches. The structure is once again symmetrical as is typical with Paul. Only the D stich has matching exact words with all three elements containing "Jews" and "Gentiles." Interestingly O'Neill would omit "like a Gentile and not" as found in v. 2:14.[6] Of course, that would destroy the match of "Gentiles" in the first element. O'Neill is incorrect in this case. All of the other stiches match phrases that are not exact but have a similar meaning. In the A stich Paul matches "he stood condemned" with "he drew back and separated himself," explaining how Kephas condemned himself. The B hemistich has "those of the circumcised" matching "rest of the Jews." The C stich matches "was

---

6. O'Neill, *Galatians*, 39–42.

carried away with their hypocrisy" with "did not walk uprightly," phrases having the same meaning. The E stich also has three elements all contrasting the law with faith. The first element has "not justified by works of the law but through faith." The second element has "justified by faith in Christ and not by works of the law." The third E" element has "by works of the law no flesh will be justified."

O'Neil proposed that v. 2:17 is an interpolation.[7] Such a conclusion would destroy the F stich. If 2:17 is an interpolation, then 2:18 is also an interpolation, because that would unbalance either the G stich or the E stich. In addition if vv. 2:17–18 is an interpolation that means that the interpolator discerned the parallel structure and created his interpolation containing parallel phrases while realizing that the phrases should not be exact. Rhetorical analysis shows that 2:17 is original to Paul contrary to O'Neill. The G stich has two matching phrases in each hemistich. The G hemistich has "I died to the law" matching "I have been crucified" in the G' stich. The second match is "that I might live to God" in the G hemistich and "but Christ living in me" in the G' stich. The final H stich matches "the son of God . . . gave himself up for me" with "Christ died for nothing."

Galatians 3

Galatians 3 has parallel-chiastic-parallel structure similar to 2 Cor 3. As also found at 2 Cor 3 the first parallel sub-structure contains one more stich than the second parallel sub-structure. This structure reveals an out of order verse. In addition, the first structure in Gal 3 is a dual chiastic/parallel structure. Both the chiastic and the parallel structures reveal that vv. 3:15 and 16 have been reversed. That is, v. 16 originally preceded v. 15.

Gal 3:1–17

Parallel-Chiastic-Parallel Structure

  A 3:1a Oh *Foolish Galatians*, who did bewitch you
    B 3:1b according to whose eyes Jesus Christ was long ago written as having been *crucified*?
      C 3:2a This only would I ask of you. *Did you receive the spirit*
        D 3:2b by the *works of the law*,
          E 3:2c or by the *hearing of faith*?
  A' 3:3 Are *you so foolish*? Having begun in the spirit are you now perfected in the flesh?
    B' 3:4 Did you *suffer* so many things in vain? If indeed it be in vain.

---

7. O'Neill, *Galatians*, 42–44.

    C' 3:5a He therefore that *supplies to you the spirit* and works miracles among you,
        D' 3:5b is it by the *works of the law*
           E' 3:5c or by the *hearing of faith*?

A 3:6 Even as *Abraham* believed *God*, and it was reckoned to him for righteousness. 3:7 Know therefore that they that are of faith are *sons of Abraham*.
    B 3:8 And the scripture foreseeing that *God* would justify the *Gentiles* by *faith* foretold the gospel to *Abraham*, "In you all the nations will be blessed." 3:9 So then those that are of *faith* are *blessed* together with the faithful *Abraham*.
        C 3:10 For as many as there are of the works of the *law they are under a curse. For it is written*, "Cursed is every one who does not continue to do all things that are written in the book of the law."
           D 3:11 Now that no man is justified by the *law* before God is evident because the righteous *will live* by *faith*.
           D' 3:12 Moreover the *law* is not of *faith*. But he that does them *will live* in them.
        C' 3:13 Christ redeemed us from the *curse of the law*, having become a *curse for us. For it is written*, "Cursed is every one that hangs on a tree."
    B' 3:14 So that on the *Gentiles* might come the *blessing of Abraham* in *Christ Jesus*. So that we might receive the *promise* of the spirit through *faith*.
*A' 3:16 Now to *Abraham* were the promises spoken and to his *seed*. And to *seeds* he does not speak as to many but as to one. And to your *seed* who is *Christ*.

*A 3:15a Brothers, *speaking* in the manner of men,
    *B 3:15b even with man if there is a *confirmed covenant*,
        *C 3:15c no one can make it *void*,
           *D 3:15d or *add to it*.
A' 3:17a Now this *I say*,
    B' 3:17b a *covenant confirmed* by God,
        C' 3:17c the law coming four hundred and thirty years later, does not *annul* it
           D' 3:17d so as to make the promise of *no effect*.

Gal 3:1–17 Complex Parallel-Chiastic-Parallel Structure Table

A 3:1a—Foolish Galatians	A' 3:3—you so foolish
B 3:1b—crucified	B' 3:4—suffer
C 3:2a—you receive the spirit	C' 3:5a—supplies to you the spirit
D 3:2b—works of the law	D' 3:5b—works of the law

E 3:2c—by the hearing of faith	E' 3:5c—by the hearing of faith
A 3:6-7—Abraham...God...sons... Abraham	A' *3:16—Abraham...Christ...seed... seeds...seed
B 3:8-9—God...Gentiles...faith...Abraham...in you all nations will be blessed...faith...blessed...Abraham	B' 3:14—Christ Jesus...Gentiles...faith...Abraham...promise...blessing
C 3:10—law they are under a curse...for it is written cursed is everyone...law	C' 3:13—curse of the law...for it is written cursed is everyone...curse for us
D 3:11—law...will live...faith	D' 3:12—law...will live...faith
A *3:15a—speaking	A' 3:17a—I say
B *3:15b—confirmed covenant	B' 3:17b—covenant confirmed
C *3:15c—void	C' 3:17c—annul
D *3:15d—add to it	D' 3:17d—no effect

Parallel Structure of Gal 3:6-16

A 3:6 Even as *Abraham* believed *God* and it was reckoned unto him for righteousness. 3:7 Know therefore that they that are of *faith* are sons of *Abraham*.

A' 3:8 And the scripture, foreseeing that *God* would justify the Gentiles by *faith*, foretold the gospel to *Abraham*, "In you all the nations will be blessed." 3:9 So then those that are of *faith* are blessed together with the *faithful Abraham*.

  B 3:10a For as many as there are of the *works of the law* they are under a curse.

  B' 3:10b For it is written, "Cursed is every one who does not continue to do all things that are written in the *book of the law*."

  B" 3:11 Now that no man is *justified by the law* before God is evident because the righteous shall live by faith.

    C 3:12 Moreover the law is not of faith. But he that does them shall live in them. 3:13a Christ redeemed us from the *curse of the law*, having become a *curse for us*.

    C' 3:13b For it is written, "*Cursed is every one* that hangs on a tree."

      D 3:14 So that on the Gentiles might come the blessing of *Abraham* in *Christ Jesus*. So that we might receive the *promise* of the spirit through faith.

      *D' 3:16 Now to *Abraham* were the *promises* spoken, and to his seed. And to seeds he does not speak as to many, but as to one. And to your seed who is *Christ*.

Part I | The Undisputed Letters

Gal 3:6–3:16 Parallel Structure Table

A 3:6–7—Abraham … God … faith … Abraham	A' 3:8–9—Abraham … God … faith … Abraham … faith … faithful	
B 3:10a—works of the law	B' 3:10b—book of the law	B 3:11—justified by the law
C 3:12–13a—curse of the law … curse for us	C' 3:13b—cursed is everyone	
D 3:14—Abraham … Christ Jesus … promise	D' 3:16—Abraham … Christ … promises	

Commentary

Parallel-Chiastic-Parallel Structure

Galatians 3:1–17 is a unified literary construction with a complex structure. The rhetorical analysis of vv. 3:1–17 shows that there is a parallel sub-structure followed by a chiastic sub-structure and finally another parallel sub-structure. However, that analysis applies only if 3:15 and 16 are reversed. The initial parallel structure has an A, B, C, D, E, A,' B,' C,' D,' E' format with vv. 3:1–2 being parallel with vv. 3:3–5. There are five words or phrases found in the exact same order in the parallel structure. "Foolish Galatians," "crucified," "you receive the spirit," "works of the law," and "by the hearing of faith" in vv. 3:1–2 match "are you so foolish," "suffer," "supplies to you the spirit," "works of the law," and "by the hearing of faith" found in vv. 3:3–5. O'Neil proposed that 3:3 is an interpolation.[8] Eliminating that verse would destroy the match of "are you so foolish" with "O foolish Galatians." O'Neill is over zealous with his interpolations once again.

As with the introductory parallel structure, the concluding parallel structure has an A, B, C, D, A,' B,' C,' D' format with four words or phrases in the exact same order, if it is assumed that vv. 3:15 was originally designed to fall between vv. 3:16 and 17 so that v. 3:15 is parallel to v. 3:17. "Speaking," " confirmed covenant," "void," and "add to it" in 3:15 match in order "I say," "covenant confirmed," "annul," and "of no effect" found in 3:17. "Add to it" and "of no effect" have an opposite meaning and they further explain "void" and "annul" respectively.

Examining the chiastic part of the structure, the A stich matches "Abraham" (twice), "God," and "sons" in vv. 3:6–7 with "Abraham," "Christ" and "seed" (three times) in v. 3:16, with "sons" and "seed" both meaning descendants. Once again, this match only works if v. 3:16 originally preceded v. 3:15. In the B stich "God" matches "Christ Jesus," "Gentiles" is in both hemistiches, "faith" is in the B hemistich twice and

---

8. O'Neill, *Galatians*, 47–48.

the B' hemistich once, "Abraham" is in the B hemistich twice and the B' hemistich once, and "are blessed" in the B hemistich matches "blessing" in the B' hemistich. "In you all nations will be blessed" in the B hemistich matches "promise" in the B' hemistich. In the C stich "law" (twice), "curse," "for it is written," and "everyone is cursed" in the C hemistich match "law," "curse" (twice), "for it is written" and "everyone is cursed" found in the C' hemistich. "Law" is found twice in the first hemistich and "curse" is found twice in the second hemistich. This appears to be a subtle message by Paul quoting Deut 21:23 and 27:26 emphasizing that the law is a curse. In the center D stich both hemistiches contain "law," "shall live" and "faith." The chiastic matches of vv. 3:6–7 with v. 3:16 and the parallel matches of v. 3:15 with v. 3:17 are clear evidence that vv. 3:15 and 3:16 have been transposed since they were originally composed.

There is another literary construction tying vv. 3:1–17 together and providing additional evidence that in the original composition v. 3:16 preceded v. 3:15. Paul has used a form of rhetorical repetition in this section of his letter to the Galatians. In creating this construction Paul uses a particular significant word in the first parallel sub-structure and then he repeats that word in the beginning of the following chiastic sub-structure. This results in an interweaving of the sub-structures and demonstrates that it is a unified literary unit.

Beginning with the junction between the first parallel sub-structure and the chiastic sub-structure, the word "faith" (*pisteōs*) is found in both the last hemistich of the parallel sub-structure and the first hemistich of the chiastic sub-structure. Proceeding to the junction between the chiastic sub-structure and the concluding parallel sub-structure, the A' hemistich of the chiastic sub-structure and A hemistich of the concluding parallel sub-structure both contain the word "speak" (*lego*).

Parallel Structure of Gal 3:6–16

The center sub-structure also has a parallel structure. "Abraham," God, and "faith" are both found in A and A' hemistiches of the parallel sub-structure. Then the B stich of the parallel sub-structure contains three elements all of which contain a phrase about the law "works of the law," "book of the law," and "justified by the law." Next, the C stich contains "curse" in both hemistiches. "Curse of the law" and "curse for us" is in the C hemistich and "cursed is everyone" is in the C' hemistich. Then the D and D' hemistiches contain several common words, "Abraham," "Christ," and "promise." The D hemistich of the center parallel sub-structure also shows that v. 3:16 properly precedes v. 3:15. However, v. 3:14, the D hemistich, does not have any common significant words with 3:15. This is additional evidence that 3:16 should precede 3:15.

"Faith," "Abraham," "written," "law," "Christ," "promise," and "speak" are all key words to Paul's thesis in this section of the letter. Paul managed to construct this section such that key words were repeated in successive hemistiches. The fact that there are no words common to vv. 3:14 and 3:15, other than the definite article "the," that

vv. 3:14 and 3:16 share the words "Abraham," "God," and "promise," and that all other consecutive hemistiches contain at least one common significant word provides proof beyond a reasonable doubt that someone early in the line of transmission of Paul's Letter to the Galatians transposed vv. 3:15 and 16.

The final proof is found in reading this entire literary unit. It makes more sense with v. 3:15 placed after v. 3:16. Beginning at v. 3:6 Paul tells the Galatians about God's promise to Abraham because of Abraham's faith. Then Paul shows why faith is better than works of the law. He then returns to the subject of Abraham and God's promise, finishing that subsection with v. 3:16 immediately following v. 3:14, both containing the word "promise." Then at v. 3:15 Paul changes the subject to covenants with the introductory phrase, "Brothers, speaking in the manner of men." However, the transition is not jarringly abrupt since at v. 3:16 he told about God speaking to Abraham and his seed to end the chiastic structure. Therefore, when Paul writes "speaking in the manner of men" he is still writing about speaking.

O'Neill would do some major surgery to vv. 3:15 and 16. He proposed eliminating every thing after "manner of men" in v. 3:15.[9] Then he proposed eliminating the second and third sentences of v. 3:16.[10] His suggestion for v. 3:15 destroys the parallels with v. 3:17 and the mirror image parallel structure of vv. 3:1–5. O'Neill's elimination of the second and third sentences of v. 3:16 probably stem from his failure to recognize that vv. 3:15 and 16 have been reversed. As stated above, v. 3:16 makes more sense following v. 3:15 than preceding it.

Gal 3:18–29

The second literary structure in Gal 3 is a parallel structure with an inclusio revealing an interpolation.

> A 3:18 For if the *law* is an inheritance it is not a promise. But God granted it to *Abraham* by *promise*.
> A' 3:19a Why then is there the *law*? It was added because of transgressions until the seed to whom the *promise* has been made came.
>
> (3:19b ordained through angels by the hand of a mediator. 3:20 Moreover a mediator is not anyone; but it is God.)
>
> B 3:21a Is the *law then contrary to the promises of God*? May it never be.
> B' 3:21b For if there had been *a law given which could impart life*, truly righteousness would have emerged from the law.

---

9. O'Neill. *Galatians*, 49–50.
10. O'Neill, *Galatians*, 50–51.

  C 3:22 But the scriptures *imprisoned all things under sin* so that the promise of *faith* in Jesus Christ might be *given to those* who believe.

  C' 3:23 But before *faith* came we were protected in ward under the law, *imprisoned from the faith to be revealed*.

   D 3:24 So that the law is become our tutor to bring us to Christ that we might be *justified by faith*.

   D' 3:25 But *now faith that is come*; we are no longer under a tutor.

    E 3:26 For you are all sons of God through *faith in Christ Jesus*.

    E' 3:27 For as many of you as were *baptized into Christ* did put on Christ.

     F 3:28a There can be neither *Jew nor Greek*.

     F' 3:28b There can be neither *slave nor free*.

     F" 3:28c Neither is there *male and female*.

      G 3:28d For you all are one man in *Christ Jesus*.

      G' 3:29a And if you are *Christ's*,

A" 3:29b then you are *Abraham's* seed, heirs according to *promise*.

Gal 3:18-29 Parallel Structure Table

A 3:18—law … Abraham … promise	A' 3:19—law … promise	A" 3:29b—Abraham … promise
B 3:21a—law then contrary to the promises of God	B' 3:21b—a law given which could impart life	
C 3:22—imprisoned all things under sin … faith … given to those	C' 3:23—imprisoned from the faith … faith … to be revealed	
D 3:24—justified by faith	D' 3:25—now faith has come	
E 3:26—faith in Christ Jesus	E' 3:27—baptized into Christ	
F 3:28a—Jew nor Greek	F' 3:28b—slave nor free	F" 3:28c—male and female
G 3:28d—Christ Jesus	G' 3:29a—Christ's	

Commentary

This literary unit has a parallel structure defined by an inclusio. However, the inclusio is somewhat different from most others in the Pauline corpus. The A stich contains three elements with the A" element being the final element of the structure. The A" element contains "Abraham" and "promise" matching those same words in the A element. The A and A' elements also both contain "law," but the A' element does not contain "Abraham." The B stich matches "law contrary to the promises of God" with "a law given which could impart life." The C stich has three parallel phrases in each hemistich. The first is "imprisoned all things under sin" in the C hemistich matching "imprisoned from the faith." The second is "faith" contained in both hemistiches. The third matching phrase is "given to those" matching "to be revealed."

The D stich matches "justified by faith" with "now that faith has come." The E hemistich has "faith in Christ Jesus" matching "baptized into Christ." The F stich has three parallel elements "Jew nor Greek," "slave nor free," and "male and female." The last stich before the closing inclusio is the G stich having "Christ" in both hemistiches.

Interpolation Gal 3:19b–20

There is an interpolation between the A and B stiches. The A element, v. 3:18, contains seventeen words. The A' element including the interpolation, vv. 3:19–20, contains thirty-two words, obviously unbalanced. The B hemistich cannot absorb these extra words since the B hemistich, v. 3:21a, contains ten words, and the B' hemistich, v. 3:21b, contains fourteen words. Elimination of the interpolation reduces the A' hemistich to fifteen words, balancing the first two elements of the A stich. O'Neill proposed the same interpolation.[11] O'Neill would also eliminate vv. 3:23–25.[12] This is obviously incorrect from a rhetorical analysis viewpoint since v. 3:23 is the C' hemistich, having three matching phrases with the C hemistich as pointed out above. If O'Neill were correct about this interpolation, then Paul included no match for the C hemistich, the interpolator supplied one, and added his own D stich, quite unlikely. O'Neil also eliminates v. 3:28, the entire F stich.[13] While this is possible under rhetorical analysis, it requires the interpolator to have recognized that this literary unit has a parallel structure and fit it in.

Stich	Words in first half	Words in second half	Words in interpolation
A	3:18–17	3:19–20–32	3:19b–20–17

Galatians 4

Galatians 4 is another dual chiastic/parallel structure containing eleven stiches encompassing the entire chapter.

---

11. O'Neill, *Galatians*, 51–52.
12. O'Neill, *Galatians*, 53–54.
13. O'Neill, *Galatians*, 55–56.

Gal 4:1–31

Chiastic Structure

A 4:1 But I say that so long as the *heir is a child* he differs nothing from a *slave* though he is Lord of all. 4:2 But is under guardians and stewards until *the day appointed of the father.*

  B 4:3 So we also when we were *children* were *held in slavery* under the rudiments of the world.

    C 4:4 But when the fullness of the time came God sent forth his son, *created from a woman, created under the law,*

      D 4:5 that he might redeem those who were under the law that *we might receive the adoption of sons.*

        E 4:6 And because you are *sons* God sent forth the spirit of his *son* into our hearts *crying*, "Abba, Father."

          F 4:7 So that you are no longer a *slave* but a *son*, and if a *son* then an *heir through God.* 4:8 However, at that time not knowing God you were *enslaved* to them that by nature are no gods.

            G 4:9 But now that you have come to know God or rather to be known by God, how can you *return to the weak and destitute principles to which you desire to be enslaved once again*? 4:10 You observe days, and months, and seasons, and years.

              H 4:11 *I am afraid for you.* Lest by any means I have bestowed labor upon you in vain.

                I 4:12 I implore you, *brothers, become as I am.* For *I also am become as you are.* You did me no wrong.

                  J 4:13 But you know that because of an infirmity of the flesh *I preached the gospel to you* the first time.

                    K 4:14 And that which was a temptation to you in my flesh you did not despise nor reject. But you *received me as an angel of God,* even as Christ Jesus.

                    K' 4:15 Where then is that gratulation of yourselves? For I bear you witness that if possible, *you would have plucked out your eyes and given them to me.*

                  J' 4:16 So then am I become your enemy by *telling you the truth*?

                I' 4:17 They zealously pursue you not in a good way but to separate you from me. They desire that *you might pursue them.* 4:18 But it is good to be zealous about good things at all times and not only when I am present with you. 4:19 *My children*, of whom I am again in travail until *Christ be formed in you,*

              H' 4:20 but I could wish to be present with you now, and to change my tone. For *I am perplexed about you.*

G' 4:21 Tell me, *you who desire to be under the law, do you not hear the law?* 4:22 For it is written that Abraham had two sons, one by the slave girl and one by the free. 4:23 However, indeed the one by the slave girl was born after the flesh. But the one of the free is born through the promise.

F' 4:24 These things contain an allegory. For these women are two covenants. One is from mount Sinai *begetting children* into *slavery* which is Hagar. 4:25 Now this Hagar is mount Sinai in Arabia and answers to the Jerusalem that now is. For she is in *slavery* with *her children*. 4:26 But the Jerusalem that is above is *free which is our mother*.

E' 4:27 For it is written, "Rejoice, you barren who cannot bear. *Break forth and shout* you who do not travail. For more are the *children* of the desolate than of her that has a *husband.*"

D' 4:28 Now *you*, brothers, *are children of promise* as Isaac was.

C' 4:29 But as then he that was *born according to the flesh* persecuted him that was *according to the spirit*. So also it is now.

B' 4:30 Nevertheless what does scripture say? Cast out the *slave girl* and her *son*. For the *son* of the *slave girl* will not inherit with the *son* of the free.

A' 4:31 Therefore, brothers, we are not *children* of the *slave* girl, but of the *free*.

Gal 4:1-31 Chiastic Structure Table

A 4:1-2—heir is a child ... slave ... the day appointed of the father	A' 4:31—children ... slave girl ... free
B 4:3—children ... held in slavery	B' 4:30—son ... slave girl ... son ... son ... slave girl
C 4:4 - created from a woman created under the law	C' 4:29—born according to the flesh ... according to the spirit
D 4:5—we might receive the adoption of sons	D' 4:28—you ... are children of the promise
E 4:6—sons ... son ... crying Abba, Father	E' 4:27—children ... husband ... break forth and shout
F 4:7-8—slave ... son ... son ... heir through God ... enslaved	F' 4:24-26—slavery ... begetting children ... her children ... free which is our mother ... slavery
G 4:9-10—return to the weak and destitute principles to which you desire to be enslaved once again	G' 4:21-23—you who desire to be under the law do you not hear the law
H 4:11—I am afraid for you	H' 4:20—I am perplexed about you
I 4:12—brother ... become as I am ... I also am become as you are	I' 4:17-19—my children ... Christ be formed in you ... you might pursue them

J 4:13—I preached the gospel to you	J' 4:16—telling you the truth
K 4:14—received me as an angel of God	K' 4:15—you would have plucked out your eyes and given them to me

Parallel Structure

A 4:1 But I say that so long as the *heir is a child* he differs nothing from a *slave* though he is lord of all. 4:2 But is under guardians and stewards until the day appointed of the father.

A' 4:3 So we also when *we were children* were held in *slavery* under the rudiments of the world.

  B 4:4 But when the fullness of the time came God sent forth his *son, created from a woman*, created under the law,

  B' 4:5 that he might redeem those who were under the law that we might *receive the adoption of sons.*

    C 4:6 And because you are *sons* God sent forth the spirit of his *son* into our hearts crying, "*Abba, Father."*

    C' 4:7 So that you are no longer a slave but a *son*. And if a *son*, then an heir through *God*. 4:8 However, at that time, not knowing *God*, you were enslaved to them that by nature are no gods.

      D 4:9a But now that you have come to know God or rather to be known by God, how can you return to the *weak and destitute principles*

      D' 4:9b to which you desire to be enslaved once again? 4:10 *You observe days, and months, and seasons, and years.*

        E 4:11 I am afraid for you. Lest by any means *I have bestowed labor upon you* in vain. I 4:12a I implore you, brothers, become as I am.

        E' 4:12b For I also am become as you are. You did me no wrong. 4:13 But you know that because of an infirmity of the flesh *I preached the gospel to you* the first time.

          F 4:14 And that which was a temptation to you in my flesh you did not despise nor reject. But *you received me as an angel of God*, even as Christ Jesus.

          F' 4:15 Where then is that gratulation of yourselves? For I bear you witness that if possible *you would have plucked out your eyes and given them to me.*

            G 4:16 So then am I become your enemy by telling you the truth? 4:17a *They zealously pursue you* not in a good way but to separate you from me.

G' 4:17b *They desire that you might pursue them.* 4:18 But it is good to be zealous about good things at all times and not only when I am present with you.

H 4:19 *My children, of whom I am again in travail* until Christ be formed in you,

H' 4:20 but I could wish to be present with you now and to change my tone. For *I am perplexed about you.*

I 4:21 Tell me, you who desire to be under the law, do you not hear the law? 4:22 For it is written that Abraham had two sons, *one by the slave girl and one by the free.*

I' 4:23 However, indeed the *one by the slave girl was born after the flesh, but the one of the free is born through the promise.*

J 4:24 These things contain an allegory. For these women are two covenants, *one from mount Sinai, begetting children into slavery which is Hagar.*

J' 4:25 Now this Hagar is mount Sinai in Arabia and answers to the Jerusalem that now is. For she is in *slavery with her children.* 4:26 But the Jerusalem that is above is free which is our mother.

K 4:27a For it is written, "*Rejoice, you barren who cannot bear. Break forth and shout, you who do not travail.*

K' 4:27b For *more are the children of the desolate* than of her that has a husband."

L 4:28 Now you, brothers, are *children of promise as Isaac was.*

L' 4:29 But as then he that was born according to the flesh persecuted *him that was according to the spirit.* So also it is now.

M 4:30 Nevertheless what does scripture say? Cast out the slave girl and her son. For the *son of the slave girl* shall not inherit with the *son of the free.*

M' 4:31 Therefore, brothers, we are not *children of the slave girl, but of the free.*

Gal 4:1-31 Parallel Structure Table

A 4:1-2—heir is a child ... slave	A' 4:3—we were children ... slavery
B 4:4—son created through a woman	B' 4:5—receive the adoption of sons
C 4:6—sons ... God ... son ... Abba, Father	C' 4:7-8—son ... God ... son ... God
D 4:9a—weak and destitute principles	D' 4:9b-10—you observe days and months and years

E 4:11–12a—I have bestowed labor upon you	E' 4:12b–13—I preached the gospel to you
F 4:14—you received me as an angel of God	F' 4:15—you would have plucked out your eyes and given them to me
G 4:16–17a—they zealously pursue you	G' 4:17b–18—they desire that you might pursue them
H 4:19—my children of whom I am again in travail	H' 4:20—I am perplexed about you
I 4:21–22—one by the slave girl and one by the free	I' 4:23—one by the slave girl was born after the flesh, but the one of the free is born through the promise
J 4:24—one from Mount Sinai . . . begetting children into slavery . . . which is Hagar	J' 4:25–26—is Mount Sinai . . . slavery with her children . . . now this is Hagar
K 4:27a—rejoice you barren who cannot bear	K' 4:27b—more are the children of the desolate
L 4:28—Isaac was . . . children of the promise	L 4:29—him that was . . . according to the spirit
M 4:30—son of the slave girl . . . son of the free	M 4:31—children of the slave girl . . . but of the free

Commentary

CHIASTIC STRUCTURE

This literary unit encompassing the entirety of Gal 4 has a chiastic structure. The F, G, and I stiches are relatively unbalanced, but that appears to be original. In each case the apparent excess text is in the second half of the structure. In the F' and I' hemistiches there are matching phrases throughout the entire text implying that the entire hemistich is original. The G' hemistich does not have matching words or phrases in vv. 4:22 or 23 but the text in the F stich makes reference to those verses authenticating them as being original.

O'Neil proposed radical surgery on Gal 4. He would eliminate vv. 4:1–3, 8–10, 17, 19b, 24b–27, and 30.[14] That, of course, would destroy the chiastic structure. The resulting Gal 4 does contain some apparent parallel stiches, but there are several long passages of text with no matching language, definitely un-Pauline. O'Neill's proposal assumes that the original form of Gal 4 had a very un-Pauline structure and then a very clever interpolator stuck in text that converted the un-Pauline structure into a Pauline chiastic structure. This is extremely improbable.

In the A stich "heir is a child" matches "children," "slave" matches "slave girl," and "day appointed of the father" matches "free." The last pair is matching because "day

---

14. O'Neill, *Galatians*, 56–64.

appointed of the father" is the day his child becomes free of his guardian. The B stich matches "children" with "son" three times and "held in slavery" with "slave girl" twice. In the B' stich Paul quotes Gen 21:10. The C hemistich has "created from a woman" matching "born according to the flesh" and "created under the law" matching "according to the spirit" with "born" being understood in the C' stich. The D stich matches "we might receive the adoption of sons" with "you . . . are children of the promise." The E hemistich has "sons" and "son" matching "children" in the E' hemistich. The E hemistich has "crying" matching "break forth and shout" in the E' hemistich. Finally the E hemistich has "Abba, Father" matching "husband" in the E' hemistich. The E' hemistich is a quote of Isa 54:1.

The F hemistich contains "slave" and "enslaved" matching "slavery" twice in the F' hemistich. "Son" is also found twice in the F hemistich matching "begetting children" and "her children" in the F' hemistich. The third match in the F stich is "heir through God" matching "free which is our mother." The G stich has "return to the weak and destitute principles, to which you desire to be enslaved once again" matching "you who desire to be under the law, do you not hear the law." The H stich matches "I am afraid for you" with "I am perplexed by you."

In the I stich "brothers" matches "my children," "become as I am" matches "Christ be formed in you," and "I also am become as you are" matches "you might pursue them." The J stich matches "I preached the gospel to you" with "telling you the truth." The center K stich matches "received me as an angel of God" with "you would have plucked out your eyes and given them to me."

PARALLEL STRUCTURE

In the parallel structure all stiches have two hemistiches, and the F stich of the parallel structure is identical to the center K stich of the chiastic structure. Both hemistiches of the A stich discuss "children" and "slavery." The B stich matches "son, created from a woman" with "receive the adoption of sons," comparing the creation of Jesus with the adoption of Christians. Both hemistiches of the C stich discuss "sons" and "God" ("Abba, Father"). The D stich matches "weak and destitute principles" in the D hemistich with "you observe days, and months, and seasons, and years" in the D' hemistich explaining what the destitute principles are. The E stich matches "I have bestowed labor upon you" with "I preached the gospel to you" explaining what Paul's labor entailed. The G stich discusses pursuit in both hemistiches. The H stich has two statements of Paul's concern about the Galatians. Both hemistiches of the I stich discuss Abraham's sons of the slave girl and the free woman. The J stich has "Hagar," "Mount Sinai," and "slavery" in both hemistiches. The K stich has a match of "rejoice you barren who cannot bear" in the K hemistich matching a similar concept "more are the children of the desolate" in the K' hemistich. The L stich matches two phrases with "Isaac was" in the L hemistich matching "him that was" in the L' stich meaning Isaac.

The second matching phrases are "children of the promise" in the L stich matching "according to the spirit" in the L' stich. Both hemistiches of the M stich discuss the children of the slave girl and the free woman.

Galatians 5

Galatians 5 contains two chiastic structures, both thirteen verses long.

Gal 5:1-13

The first literary unit of Gal 5 is a chiastic structure of the first half of the chapter containing four stiches.

> A 5:1 For *freedom* did Christ *set us free*. Stand fast therefore and *do not be entangled again in a yoke of slavery*.
>> B 5:2 Behold, I, Paul, say to you that if you *receive circumcision, Christ will profit you nothing*. 5:3 Now I testify again to every man who *receives circumcision* that he is a debtor to do the whole law. 5:4a *You are severed* from Christ.
>>> C 5:4b *Whoever would be justified by the law* you are fallen away from grace. 5:5 For *we through the spirit by faith* wait for the hope of righteousness.
>>>> D 5:6 For in *Christ Jesus* neither circumcision avails anything nor uncircumcision, but *faith working through love*.
>>>> D' 5:7 You were running well. Who hindered you that *you should not obey the truth*? 5:8 This persuasion came not of *he who calls you*.
>>> C' 5:9 *A little leaven leavens the whole lump*. 5:10 I have confidence toward you in the Lord that you will be none otherwise minded. But *he who troubles you will bear his judgment*, whosoever he be.
>> B' 5:11 But brothers, if I still preach *circumcision* why am I still persecuted? Then the *stumbling block of the cross* has been done away with. 5:12 I wish that those who unsettle you would *castrate themselves*.
> A' 5:13 For you, brothers, were called for *freedom*. Only *do not use your freedom for an occasion to the flesh* but through love be servants one to another.

Gal 5:1-13 Chiastic Structure Table

A 5:1—freedom . . . set us free . . . do not be entangled again in a yoke of slavery	A' 5:13—freedom . . . do not use your freedom for an occasion to the flesh
B 5:2-4a—receive circumcision . . . Christ will profit you nothing . . . receives circumcision . . . you are severed	B' 5:11-12—circumcision . . . stumbling block of the cross . . . castrate themselves

| C 5:4b–5—whoever would be justified by the law . . . we through the spirit by faith | C' 5:9–10—he who troubles you will bear his judgment . . . a little leaven leavens the whole lump |
| D 5:6—Christ Jesus . . . faith working through love | D' 5:7–8—he who calls you . . . you should not obey the truth |

Commentary

This short chiastic structure contains only four stiches. The A hemistich contains "freedom" and "set us free" matching "freedom" twice in the A' hemistich. The A hemistich also has "do not be entangled again in a yoke of slavery" matching "do not use your freedom for an occasion to the flesh" in the A' stich which phrase also contains the second "freedom." O'Neill proposed eliminating the A' stich, v. 5:13,[15] which would leave no matching hemistich for v. 5:1, the A hemistich. In fact, O'Neill proposed that 5:13–6:10 be eliminated as a large interpolation.[16]

The B hemistich has "receive circumcision" twice matching "circumcision" in the B' hemistich. The B hemistich also has "Christ will profit you nothing" matching "stumbling block of the cross" in the B' hemistich. Paul seems to be making a joke in the B hemistich, v. 5:4, writing "you are severed from Christ" in referring to circumcision. Then he confirms the joke by matching it with "castrate themselves" in the B' hemistich, v. 5:12. In the C stich "whoever would be justified by the law" matches "he who troubles you will bear his judgment." Also in the C stich "we through the spirit by faith" matches "a little leaven leavens the whole lump" with the leaven metaphor symbolizing the spirit moving through the congregation. The center D stich has "Christ Jesus" matching "he who calls you" and "faith working through love" matching its opposite "you should not obey the truth." "He who calls you" in the D' stich actually refers to Paul, but in Gal 1:15–16 Paul said God called him and revealed Christ in him. So that it is Christ in Paul that calls the Galatians.

Gal 5:14–26

This unit is another chiastic structure encompassing the second half of the chapter.

> A 5:14 For the whole law is fulfilled in one word, in this. *You will love your neighbor as yourself.* 5:15 But if you bite and devour one another, take heed that you are not consumed by one another.
>
> B 5:16a But I say *walk by the spirit,*

---

15. O'Neill, *Galatians*, 65–70.
16. O'Neill, *Galatians*, 65–70.

C 5:16b and you shall not fulfill the *lust* of the *flesh*. 5:17 For the *flesh lusts* against the *spirit*, and the *spirit* against the *flesh*. For these are contrary to each other. That you may not do the things that you want.
  D 5:18 But if you are led by the spirit, *you are not under the law.*
    E 5:19 Now the *works of the flesh* are manifest, which are these: *fornication, uncleanness, lasciviousness,* 5:20 *idolatry, sorcery, enmities, strife, jealousies, wraths, factions, divisions, parties,* 5:21 *a envy, drunkenness, reveling, and such like.*
      F 5:21b That I warn you about, even as *I did warn you before.*
      F' 5:21c That they who practice such things *will not inherit the kingdom of God.*
    E' 5:22 But the *fruit of the spirit is love, joy, peace, longsuffering, kindness, goodness, faithfulness,* 5:23 *a meekness, self-control.*
  D' 5:23b *Against such there is no law.*
C' 5:24 And those who are of *Christ Jesus* have crucified the *flesh* along with the passions and the *lusts* thereof.
 B' 5:25 If we live by the spirit, let us also *walk by the spirit.*
A' 5:26 *Let us not become boastful, provoking one another, envying one another.*

Gal 5:14-26 Chiastic Structure Table

A 5:14-15—you will love your neighbor as yourself	A' 5:26—let us not become boastful provoking one another envying one another
B 5:16a—walk by the spirit	B' 5:25—walk by the spirit
C 5:16b-17—lust … flesh … flesh … lusts … spirit … spirit … flesh	C' 5:24—lusts … flesh … Christ Jesus
D 5:18—you are not under the law	D' 5:23b—against such there is no law
E 5:19-21a—works of the flesh … fornication, uncleanness, lasciviousness, idolatry, sorcery, enmities, strife, jealousies, wraths, factions, divisions, parties, envy, drunkenness, reveling, and such like	E' 5:22-23a—fruit of the spirit is love, joy, peace, longsuffering, kindness, goodness, faithfulness, meekness, self-control
F 5:21b—I did warn you before	F' 5:21c—not inherit the kingdom of God

Commentary

As stated above O'Neill proposed that this entire literary structure is an interpolation; however, it has all the markings of a Pauline chiastic structure, making it unlikely that O'Neill is correct. The A hemistich contains the golden rule "you will love your neighbor as yourself," and in the A' hemistich it is stated in the negative "let us not become boastful, provoking one another, envying one another." The B stich has "walk by the spirit," using two different words for "walk" (*stoichōmen, peripateite*). The C hemistich has "lust," "flesh," and "spirit" twice each, but the C' hemistich has "lust" and "flesh" once and "Christ Jesus" matching "spirit." The D stich matches "you are not under the law" with "against such there is no law." The E stich is a match of opposites with a list of immoral behaviors matching a list of moral behaviors. The center F stich is a bit out of the ordinary with "I did warn you before" in the F hemistich matching "will not inherit the kingdom of God" in the F' hemistich. Obviously, the F' match is the warning referred to in the F hemistich.

Galatians 6

The last chapter of Galatians has a chiastic structure encompassing the entire chapter and revealing two interpolations.

Gal 6:1–18

> A 6:1 Brothers, even if a man be overtaken in any trespass, you who are *spiritual* restore him in a *spirit* of gentleness, looking to yourself unless you also are tempted.
> B 6:2 *Bear one another's burdens and so fulfill the law of Christ.*

(6:3 For if a man thinks himself to be something when he is nothing, he deceives himself. 6:4 But let each man prove his own work, and then shall he have his glorying in regard of himself alone and not of his neighbor. 6:5 For each man shall bear his own burden. 6:6 But let him that is taught in the word communicate to him that teaches in all good things. 6:7 Do not be deceived. God is not mocked. For whatever a man sows, that will he also reap. 6:8 For he that sows to his own flesh will reap corruption of the flesh. But he that sows to the spirit will reap eternal life of the spirit. 6:9 And let us not be weary in well-doing. For in due season we will reap, if we do not faint.)

> C 6:10 So then as we have opportunity *let us work* that which is *good toward all* and especially toward those who are of the *household of the faith*.

(6:11 See with what large letters I write to you with my own hand.)

> D 6:12 As many as desire to make a fair show in the *flesh*, they compel you to be *circumcised* only so they may not be persecuted for the *cross of Christ*. 6:13a For not even they who receive *circumcision* do themselves keep the law.
> D' 6:13b But they desire to have you *circumcised* so that they may boast in your *flesh*. 6:14 But far be it from me to boast save in the *cross of our Lord*

Jesus Christ, through which the world has been crucified to me, and I to the world. 6:15 For neither is *circumcision* anything, nor uncircumcision, but a new creature.

C' 6:16 And *as many as will walk by this rule, peace be upon them*, and mercy and upon the *Israel of God*.

B' 6:17 Henceforth, let no man trouble me. For *I bear branded on my body the marks of Jesus*.

A' 6:18 The grace of our Lord Jesus Christ be with your *spirit, brothers*. Amen.

Gal 6:1-18 Chiastic Structure Table

A 6:1—brothers … spiritual … spirit	A' 6:18—brothers … spirit
B 6:2—bear on another's burdens and so fulfill the law of Christ	B' 6:17—I bear branded on my body the marks of Jesus
C 6:10—let us work … good toward all … household of the faith	C' 6:16—as many as walk by this rule … peace be upon them … Israel of God
D 6:12-13a—flesh … circumcised … cross of Christ … circumcision	D' 6:13b-15—flesh … circumcised … cross of our Lord Jesus Christ … circumcision

Commentary

The final chapter of Galatians is one chiastic literary unit. Both hemistiches of the A stich contain "brothers" and "spirit." The A hemistich also contains "spiritual." The B hemistich has "bear one another's burdens and so fulfill the law of Christ" matching "I bear branded on my body the marks of Jesus" in the B' hemistich. The C stich has three matching phrases in each hemistich. "Let us work" in the C hemistich matches "as many as will walk by this rule" in the C' hemistich. "Good toward all" in the C hemistich matches "peace be upon them" in the C' hemistich. "Household of the faith" in the C hemistich matches "Israel of God" in the C' hemistich. In the center D hemistich "flesh" is in both hemistiches; "circumcised" is in both hemistiches; "circumcision" is in both hemistiches; and "cross of Christ Jesus" is in the D hemistich while "cross of our Lord Jesus Christ" is in the D' hemistich.

Interpolations Gal 6:3-9, 11

O'Neill proposed that "and upon the Israel of God" in v. 6:16 is an interpolation.[17] That is possible in that the phrase seems unusual in the undisputed letters, but it leaves no match for "household of faith." As mentioned above O'Neill proposes that

---

17. O'Neill, *Galatians*, 71–72.

Part I | The Undisputed Letters

vv. 6:1–10 is an interpolation. Rhetorical analysis partially agrees with him, revealing that vv. 6:3–9 is an interpolation, but vv. 6:1, 2, 10 are the A, B, and C hemistiches respectively of a clear chiastic structure. The C', B', and A' hemistiches contain only forty-seven words, but the A, B, and C hemistiches, canonical vv. 6:1–11, contain one hundred fifty-five words, over one hundred words too many. By eliminating vv. 6:3–9 and 11 the A, B, and C hemistiches are reduced to fifty-one words, an acceptable balance.

Stiches	Words in first half	Words in second half	Words in interpolation
A, B, C	6:1–11–155	6:16–18–47	6:3–9, 11–104

7

LETTER TO THE PHILIPPIANS

Philippians 1

PHILIPPIANS CONTAINS SIX CHIASTIC literary units in its four chapters. Four of them have unusual center stiches. The unit at vv. 1:7–2:4 has an unusually long center E stich. The unit at vv. 3:1–20 has an FA, FB, FB,' FA;' F'A, F'B, F'B,' F'A' chiastic center stich. The unit at vv. 4:1–19 has a G, G,' G," G,'" G,"" G""" center stich. Finally the benediction at vv. 4:20–23 has a B, B,' B" center stich. Paul was very creative in designing the letter to the Philippians.

Phil 1:1–6

The letter is introduced by a short introductory parallel structure with three stiches.

  A 1:1a Paul and Timothy, servants of *Christ Jesus*,
  A' 1:1b to all the saints in *Christ Jesus* that are at Philippi with the bishops and deacons.
  A" 1:2 Grace to you and peace from God our father and the *Lord Jesus Christ*.
    B 1:3 I thank my God upon *every remembrance of you*
    B' 1:4a always in *every supplication of mine for all of you*
      C 1:4b making my supplication with joy 1:5 for your fellowship in the gospel *from the first day until now.*
      C' 1:6 Being confident of this very thing, that he who began a good work in you will perfect it *until the day of Jesus Christ.*

Phil 1:1–6 Parallel Structure Table

| A 1:1a – Paul and Timothy … Christ Jesus | A' 1:1b – bishops and deacons … Christ Jesus | A" 1:2- God our father … Lord Jesus Christ |

B 1:3—every remembrance of you	B' 1:4a—every supplication of mine for all of you
C 1:4b–5—from the first day until now	C' 1:6—until the day of Jesus Christ

Commentary

This is a short three-stich parallel structure. The A stich contains three elements while the B and C stiches contain only two. All three elements of the A stich mention Jesus Christ and two others. The A and A' elements have "Christ Jesus" and the A" element has "Lord Jesus Christ." As the second parallel wording, the A element has "Paul and Timothy," the A' element has "bishops and deacons," and the A" element has "God our father." Technically "God our father" is one person but Paul gives him two attributes to equal those in the other elements. Wolfgang Schenk proposed that Phil 1:1c is an interpolation, presumably "with the bishops and deacons" (*syn episkopois kai diakonois*).[1] Although the statement is unique in Paul's undisputed letters, the matching of this phrase with the other two in the A and A" elements assure the rhetorical analyst that Schenk is incorrect. In addition, Paul placed "bishops and deacons" after "Christ Jesus" whereas in the other two elements the additional personages are placed before "Jesus." This gives the parallel A stich a chiastic attribute. The B hemistich has "every remembrance of you" matching "every supplication of mine for all of you" in the B' stich. The C stich matches "from the first day until now" with "until the day of Jesus Christ."

Phil 1:7–2:4

This unit is a chiastic structure with a long center stich.

> A 1:7 Accordingly it is right *for me to think this way* about all of you, because I have you in my heart. In both my infirmity and in the defense and confirmation of the gospel you all are partakers with me of grace. 1:8 For God is my witness how I long for all of you in the *affection* of Christ Jesus. 1:9 And this I pray, that your *love* may excel yet more and more in knowledge and all understanding.
>
> B 1:10 So that you may approve the things that are excellent. That you may be sincere and blameless to the day of *Christ*. 1:11 Being filled with the fruit of righteousness that is through *Jesus Christ* to the glory and *praise of God*.
>
> C 1:12 Now I would have you know, brothers, that the things concerning me have turned out rather to the advancement of the *gospel*. 1:13 So that my

---

1. Schenk, *Philipperbriefe*, 78–82.

infirmity was revealed in *Christ* throughout the whole palace guard and to all the rest.

    D 1:14 And that most of the brothers in the Lord being confident because of my infirmity *dare to speak* the word fearlessly more vehemently.

        E 1:15 Some indeed *preach Christ* even of envy and strife, and some also of good will. 1:16 Some out of love knowing that I am appointed for the defense of the gospel. 1:17 But the others *proclaim Christ* of faction, not sincerely, thinking to raise up affliction for me in my infirmity. 1:18 For what? Only that in every way, whether in pretence or in truth, *Christ is proclaimed*, and therein I rejoice, yes, and will rejoice. 1:19 For I know that this will result in salvation for me, through your prayer and the support of the *spirit of Jesus Christ* 1:20a according to my eager expectation and hope.

        E' 1:20b So that I will not be ashamed of anything but with all boldness, as always, now also *Christ will be magnified* in my body, whether by life or by death. 1:21 For to me *to live is Christ* and to die is gain. 1:22 But if to live in the flesh, if this will bring fruit from my work, then what will I choose? I do not know. 1:23 But I am perplexed between the two, having the desire to *depart and be with Christ*. For it is very much better. 1:24 Yet to abide in the flesh is more necessary for your sake. 1:25 And having this confidence, I know that I will remain and continue with all of you for your progress and joy in the faith.

    D' 1:26 So that your *boasting* may excel in Christ Jesus in me through my coming to you again.

C' 1:27 Only conduct yourselves worthy of the *gospel* of *Christ*. So that whether I come and see you or being absent I may hear things concerning you. That you stand fast in one spirit with one mind striving for the faith of the *gospel*.

B' 1:28 And not being frightened by the opposition, which for them is proof of destruction, but for you *salvation and that from God*. 1:29 Because to you it has been granted concerning *Christ* not only to believe in him but also to suffer concerning him. 1:30 You have the same struggle that you saw in me and now hear of in me. 2:1a Therefore, if there is any encouragement in *Christ*, if any consolation of love, if any fellowship of the spirit,

A' 2:1b if any *affections* and compassions, 2:2 fulfill my joy. So that *you think alike*, having the same *love*, having one accord, of one mind. 2:3 Nothing through faction or through empty pride, but in humility each counting others better than himself, 2:4 not looking each of you to his own things but each of you also to the things of others.

Part I | The Undisputed Letters

Phil 1:7-2:4 Chiastic Structure Table

A 1:7-9—for me to think this way . . . affection . . . love	A' 2:1b—4—you think alike . . . affections . . . love
B 1:10-11—Christ . . . Christ . . . glory and praise of God	B' 1:28-2:1a—Christ . . . Christ . . . salvation and that from God
C 1:12-13—gospel . . . Christ	C' 1:27—gospel . . . Christ . . . gospel
D 1:14—dare to speak	D' 1:26—boasting
E 1:15-20a—preach Christ . . . proclaim Christ . . . Christ is proclaimed . . . spirit of Jesus Christ	E' 1:20b-25—Christ will be magnified . . . to live is Christ . . . to depart and be with Christ

Commentary

This literary unit has another rare mistake by Bishop Langdon in that the unit begins at 1:7 but is not completed until 2:4 extending into Phil 2. This unit has a chiastic structure, and it is without question that "for me to think this way" in 1:7 matches "you think alike" in 2:2. In addition, "affection" occurs in both 1:8 and 2:1. Finally "love" occurs in both 1:9 and 2:2, forming the A stich of the chiasm. The B hemistich has "Christ" twice as does the B' hemistich, but the second occurrence of "Christ" is not found until 2:1, solidifying the conclusion that this literary unit encompasses the first four verses of Phil 2. The B hemistich also has "glory and praise of God" matching "salvation and that from God" in the B' hemistich. The C hemistich contains "gospel" once while it occurs twice in the C' hemistich. "Christ" is also in both hemistiches. In the D hemistich "dare to speak" is a match for "boasting" in the D' hemistich. The long center E hemistich has four phrases "preach Christ," "proclaiming Christ," "Christ is proclaimed," and "spirit of Jesus Christ" that are parallel to "Christ will be magnified," "to live is Christ," and "to depart and be with Christ" in the E' hemistich.

Philippians 2

Phil 2:5-11

The first literary unit of Phil 2 is chiastic structure containing four stiches that does not begin until v. 2:5.

> A 2:5 *Have this mind in you,* which was also in *Christ Jesus.*
> B 2:6 Who, existing in the form of God, considered being *equal with God not a thing to be prized.*

C 2:7 But emptied himself, *having taken the form of a slave*, having been made in the likeness of men.

    D 2:8a And having been found in appearance as a man, he *humbled himself.*

    D' 2:8b Having become obedient to death, even the *death of the cross.*

C' 2:9 Therefore also *God highly exalted him* and gave to him the name which is above every name.

B' 2:10 In the name of Jesus *every knee should bow in Heaven and on Earth and under the Earth.*

A' 2:11 And that *every tongue should confess* that *Jesus Christ* is Lord to the glory of God the father.

Phil 2:5-11 Chiastic Structure Table

A 2:5 – have this mind in you . . . Christ Jesus	A' 2:11—every tongue should confess . . . Jesus Christ
B 2:6—equal with God not a thing to be prized	B' 2:10—every knee should bow in Heaven and on Earth and under the Earth
C 2:7—having taken the form of a slave	C' 2:9—God highly exalted him
D 2:8a—humbled himself	D' 2:8b—death of the cross

Commentary

This literary unit is the so-called Hymn of Philippians 2. Most scholars consider the hymn to be vv. 2:6–11. Recognizing that it has a chiastic structure demonstrates that the literary unit actually begins with v. 2:5 as the A hemistich "have this mind in you" is parallel to "every tongue should confess" and "Christ Jesus" is parallel to "Jesus Christ," being another Pauline chiasm within the chiastic structure. Naturally the tongue would confess what one has in mind. The B stich matches phrases to the opposite effect "equal with God not a thing to be prized" matching "every knee should bow in Heaven and on Earth." In the B' and A' hemistiches, vv. 2:10–11, Paul quotes Isa 45:23. The C stich is also a match of opposites with "having taken the form of a slave" in the C hemistich matching its opposite, "God highly exalted him" in the C' hemistich. This is not exactly a quote, but it is very reminiscent of Isa 52:13, the beginning of the song of the suffering servant. Finally, the center D stich matches "humbled himself with "death of the cross."

    Ernst Barnikol proposed that vv. 2:6–7 are an interpolation.[2] Rhetorical analysis demonstrates that this would eliminate the B and C hemistiches and destroy the entire chiastic structure. Barnikol is incorrect with regard to his proposal.

2. Barnikol, *Philipper*.

Phil 2:12-24

The second literary structure of Phil 2 is a parallel structure revealing an interpolation.

A 2:12a So then, my beloved, just as you have always obeyed, not as *in my presence* only,
A' 2:12b but now much more *in my absence*,
  B 2:12c *work out your own salvation* with fear and trembling.
  B' 2:13 For *it is God working in you* both to will and to work according to his good pleasure.
    C 2:14 Do all things without murmurings and arguments. 2:15a So that you may become *blameless and innocent children of God*,
    C' 2:15b unblemished in the midst of a *crooked and perverted generation* among whom you shine as lights in the world.

(2:16 Holding forth the word of life. So that I may boast in the day of Christ that I did not run in vain nor labor in vain.)

    D 2:17 But if I am offered upon the sacrifice and service of your faith, *I am glad and rejoice with all of you*.
    D' 2:18 And likewise also *you be glad and rejoice with me*. 2:19a But I hope in the Lord Jesus to send Timothy to you soon.
      E 2:19b That I also may be in good spirits *knowing the things about you*.
      E' 2:20 For I have no one likeminded who will *truly care for the things about you*.
        F 2:21 For *they all seek their own things* not the things of Jesus Christ.
        F' 2:22 But you know his character, that as a child serves a father, *he served with me in the gospel*.
          G 2:23 Therefore indeed *I hope to send him* after I see to the things concerning me immediately.
          G' 2:24 But I trust in the Lord that *I myself will also come soon*.

Phil 2:12-24 Parallel Structure Table

A 2:12a—in my presence	A' 2:12b—in my absence
B 2:12c—work out your own salvation	B' 2:13—it is God working in you
C 2:14-15—blameless and innocent children of God	C' 2:15b—crooked and perverted generation
D 2:17—I am glad and rejoice with all of you	D' 2:18-19a—you be glad and rejoice with me

E 2:19b—knowing the things about you	E' 2:20—truly care for the things about you
F 2:21—they all seek their own thing	F' 2:22—he served with me in the gospel
G 2:23—I hope to send him	G' 2:24—I myself will also come soon

Commentary

In the A stich "in my presence" is parallel to its opposite "in my absence." In the B stich "work out your own salvation" is parallel to "it is God working in you." The C stich matches opposites with "blameless and innocent children of God" matching "crooked and perverted generation." The D hemistich has "I am glad and rejoice with all of you" matching "you be glad and rejoice with me" in the D' hemistich. The E stich matches "knowing the things about you" with "truly care for the things about you." The F stich again matches opposites with "they all seek their own things" in the F hemistich with "he served with me in the gospel" in the F' hemistich. The final G stich matches "I hope to send him" with "I myself will also come soon."

Interpolation Phil 2:16

This parallel structure reveals an interpolation at v. 2:16 between the C' and D' hemistiches. All of the stiches in this literary unit contain only two hemistiches. Without considering the eighteen words in v. 2:16, the C and C' hemistiches both contain thirteen words. The D hemistich contains seventeen words and the D' hemistich contains eighteen words. Therefore, v. 2:16 over balances the structure and cannot be part of either the C' hemistich or the D hemistich. It also seems to be off topic and extraneous to Paul's message.

Stiches	Words in first half	Words in second half	Words in interpolation
C—D	2:14–16–30	2:17–18–49	2:16–18

Phil 2:25–30

This chiastic structure has uncharacteristically unbalanced hemistiches with the first half of the unit being longer than the second half.

> A 2:25 But I considered it necessary to send to you Epaphroditus, my brother and fellow worker and fellow soldier, and your messenger and *minister to my need*.
> B 2:26 Since he wanted to see all of you and was deeply distressed because you heard that he was ill. 2:27 And indeed *he was ill nearly to death*. But God had

mercy on him, and not only on him but on me also that I should not have sorrow upon sorrow.

    C 2:28 I have sent him therefore the more speedily that having seen him again you may *rejoice* and I may be less sorrowful.

    C' 2:29 Therefore, receive him in the Lord with all *joy* and hold him in such honor.

  B' 2:30a Because through the work of Christ *he came close to death*,

A' 2:30b disregarding his life to fulfill the deficit in your *service toward me*.

Phil 2:25-30 Chiastic Structure Table

A 2:25—minister to my need	A' 2:30b—service toward me
B 2:26-27—he was ill nearly to death	B' 2:30a—he came close to death
C 2:28—rejoice	C' 2:29—joy

Commentary

This is an unusual chiastic structure for Paul. It is short, containing only three stiches and there is an extreme imbalance in the B stich with the B hemistich containing thirty-five words and the B' hemistich containing only eight words. However, there is no occasion to find an interpolation in the B stich, unless it is 2:29b "and not only him, but on me also, that I should not have sorrow upon sorrow." That language seems to be typically Pauline and is probably original. The A stich matches "minister to my need" with "ministrations toward me." The B stich matches "he was ill nearly to death" with "he came close to death." The C stich matches "you may rejoice" with "joy."

Philippians 3

Philippians 3 has an unusual chiastic structure encompassing the entire chapter.

Phil 3:1-21

  A 3:1 Finally, my brothers, *rejoice in the Lord*. To write the same things to you to me indeed is not irksome, but for you it is safe.

    B 3:2 *Beware of the dogs, beware of the evil workers, beware of the mutilation.*

      C 3:3 For we are the circumcision those *worshiping the spirit of God and boasting in Christ Jesus* and not having put confidence in the *flesh*. 3:4 Though I have confidence even in the *flesh*. If any other person thinks to have confidence in the *flesh*, I more. 3:5 Circumcised the eighth day, of the nation of Israel, of the tribe of Benjamin, a Hebrew of Hebrews, according to the law, a Pharisee. 3:6 According to zeal persecuting the church, according to righteousness which is in the law *found blameless.*

   D 3:7 But *whatever things were a gain to me these I have considered a loss because of Christ.*

      E 3:8 But therefore, indeed, I count all things to be loss because of the superiority of *the knowledge of Christ Jesus* my Lord. For whom I suffered the loss of all things and consider them but rubbish *that I may gain Christ.*

         FA 3:9a And be found in him, not having a *righteousness* of my own

            FB 3:9b *that is of the law,*

            FB' 3:9c but *that through faith of Christ,*

         FA' 3:9d the *righteousness* which is of God by faith.

         F'A 3:10a To know him, and the power of his *resurrection*

            F'B 3:10b and the *fellowship of his sufferings,*

            F'B' 3:10c becoming *conformed to his death,*

         F'A' 3:11 if by any means I may attain to the *resurrection* from the dead.

      E' 3:12 Not that I have already obtained or am already have been perfected. But I press on if also *I may lay hold of that* for which also *I was laid hold of by Christ Jesus.*

   D' 3:13 Brothers, I do not consider myself to have taken hold. But one thing I do. *Forgetting the things that are behind and stretching forward to the things that are in front,*

C' 3:14 I press on toward the goal to the prize of *the high calling of God in Christ Jesus.* 3:15 Therefore as many as are perfect be like *minded.* And if in anything you are otherwise *minded*, this also God will reveal to you. 3:16 Nevertheless, whatever we have attained walk by that same rule, the same *mind.* 3:17 Brothers, be imitators together of me and observe those so walking as *you have us as a model.*

 B' 3:18 For many are walking of whom I often told you and now I say indeed even weeping, the *enemies of the cross of Christ.* 3:19 *Whose end is destruction, whose god is the belly, and glory is in their shame, who mind earthly things.*

A' 3:20 For our citizenship exists in Heaven from where also *we are waiting for a savior, the Lord Jesus Christ.* 3:21 Who will transfigure the body of our humiliation, conformed to the body of his glory, according to the working enabling him even to subject all things to himself.

Phil 3:1-21 Chiastic Structure Table

A 3:1—rejoice in the Lord	A' 3:20-21—we are waiting for a savior the Lord Jesus Christ
B 3:2—beware of the dogs beware of the evil workers beware of the mutilation	B' 3:18-19—enemies of the cross of Christ whose end is destruction whose god is the belly and glory is in their shame who mind earthly things
C 3:3-6—worshiping the spirit of God and boast in Christ Jesus … flesh … flesh … flesh … found blameless	C' 3:14-17—the high calling of God in Christ Jesus … minded … minded … mind … you have us as a model
D 3:7—whatever things were a gain to me these I have considered a loss because of Christ	D' 3:13—forgetting the things that are behind and stretching forward to the things that are in front
E 3:8—the knowledge of Christ Jesus … that I may gain Christ	E' 3:12—I was laid hold of by Christ Jesus … I may lay hold of that
FA 3:9a—righteousness	FA' 3:9d—righteousness
FB 3:9b—that is of the law	FB' 3:9c—that through faith
F'A 3:10a—resurrection	F'A' 3:11—resurrection
F'B 3:10b—fellowship of his suffering	F'B' 3:10c—conformed to his death

Commentary

This literary unit has a unique chiastic structure. The center F stich found at vv. 3:9-10 has two chiastic sub-stiches. Other than that unique feature the unit is a typical Pauline chiastic structure encompassing the entire chapter. The A stich matches "rejoice in the Lord" with "we are waiting for a savior, the Lord Jesus Christ." The B hemistich has "beware of the dogs, beware of the evil workers, beware of the mutilation" matching "enemies of the cross of Christ whose end is destruction whose god is the belly and glory is in their shame who mind earthly things" in the B' stich. In both hemistiches Paul is excoriating his rival apostles and warning the Philippians to ignore them. Both hemistiches of the C stich are long, but are balanced and the matching terms occur throughout both hemistiches. The first match is "worshiping the spirit of God and boast in Christ Jesus" in the C hemistich and "God in Christ Jesus" in the C' hemistich. The second set of matches is one of opposites "flesh" three times in the C hemistich and "mind, minded" three times in the C' hemistich. The third match in this long stich is a match of Paul bragging on himself. "Found blameless" in the C hemistich matches "you have us as a model."

The D stich makes an interesting match of "gain and loss" with "behind and forward." The D hemistich has "whatever things were a gain to me I have considered a loss because of Christ" matching "forgetting the things that are behind and stretching forward to the things that are in front." The E stich has two matches in each hemistich. The first is "the knowledge of Christ Jesus" in the D hemistich matching "I was laid hold of by Christ Jesus" in the D' hemistich. The second is "that I may gain Christ" matching "I may lay hold of that." As mentioned, the center F stich of Phil 3 is unique in Paul's letters in that each of the two hemistiches has a chiastic sub-stich. The first sub-stich is in an FA, FB, FB,' F'A' format. The FA and FA' sub-hemistiches both contain the word "righteousness" while the FB and FB' sub-hemistich contrast the law with faith with "that is of the law" matching "that through faith." The second sub-stich has an identical F'A, F'B, F'B,' F'A' format. The F'A and F'A' sub-hemistiches both contain the word "resurrection" while the F'B and F'B' sub-hemistiches parallel "fellowship of his suffering" with "conformed to his death."

Philippians 4

Phil 4:1–19

This literary unit has a chiastic structure with a six-element parallel center revealing an interpolation.

> A 4:1 Therefore my beloved and longed for brothers, my *joy and crown*, so stand firm in the *Lord*, beloved.
> > B 4:2 *I encourage Euodia, and I encourage Syntyche*, to be of the same mind in the Lord.
> > > C 4:3 Yes, I ask you also, true colleague, help these women for they *labored with me in the gospel* with Clement also and the rest of my fellow workers whose names are in the book of life.
> > > > D 4:4 *Rejoice* in the Lord always. Again I will say, *rejoice*. 4:5 Let your gentleness be known to all men. The Lord is near.
> > > > > E 4:6 In nothing be anxious But in everything by prayer and supplication with thanksgiving let your requests be made known to God. 4:7a And *the peace of God*, which passes all understanding
> > > > > > F 4:7b will guard your hearts and *your thoughts in Christ Jesus*.
> > > > > > > G 4:8a Finally, brothers, *what ever things are true,*
> > > > > > > G' 4:8b *what ever things are honorable,*
> > > > > > > G" 4:8c *what ever things are just,*
> > > > > > > G''' 4:8d *what ever things are pure,*
> > > > > > > G'''' 4:8e *what ever things are lovely,*
> > > > > > > G''''' 4:8f *what ever things are reputable,*
> > > > > > F' 4:8g if there be any virtue and if there be any praise *think on these things.*

E' 4:9 What also you learned and received and heard and saw in me, these things practice, and the *God of peace* will be with you.

D' 4:10 But I *rejoiced* in the Lord greatly that now at last you have revived your caring for me wherein you did indeed care but you lacked opportunity.

(4:11 Not that I speak in respect of want. For I have learned, in whatsoever state I am, therein to be content. 4:12 I know how to be abased, and I know also how to abound. In everything and in all things I have learned the secret both to be filled and to be hungry, both to abound and to be in want. 4:13 I can do all things in him that strengthens me. 4:14 Nevertheless you did well that you had fellowship with my affliction.)

C' 4:15 And you yourselves also know, you Philippians, that *in the beginning of the gospel*, when I departed from Macedonia no church but you had fellowship with me in the matter of giving and receiving.

(4:16 For even in Thessalonica you sent once and twice for my need. 4:17 Not that I seek for the gift. But I seek for the fruit that increases to your account. 4:18a But I have all things and excel.)

B' 4:18b I am filled, *having received from Epaphroditus* the things from you, an odor of a sweet smell, a sacrifice acceptable well-pleasing to God.

A' 4:19 And my God will supply all of your needs according to *his riches in glory* in *Christ Jesus*.

Phil 4:1–19 Chiastic Structure Table

A 4:1—joy and crown ... Lord			A' 4:19—his riches in glory ... Christ Jesus		
B 4:2—I encourage Euodia and I encourage Syntyche			B' 4:18b—having received from Epaphroditus		
C 4:3—labored with me in the gospel			C' 4:15—in the beginning of the gospel		
D 4:4–5—rejoice ... rejoice			D' 4:10—rejoice		
E 4:6–7a—the peace of God			E' 4:9—the God of peace		
F 4:7b—your thoughts in Christ Jesus			F' 4:8g—think on these things		
G 4:8a—what ever things are true	G' 4:8b—what ever things are honorable	G" 4:8c—what ever things are just	G'" 4:8d—what ever things are pure	G"" 4:8e—what ever things are lovely	G""' 4:8f—what ever things are reputable

Commentary

This literary unit has a chiastic structure and contains another unusual center stich. The A stich matches "joy and crown" with "his riches in glory." A second match in the A stich is "the Lord" with "Christ Jesus." The B stich has a match of proper names with "I encourage Euodia and I encourage Syntyche" in the B hemistich matching "having received from Epaphroditus" in the B' hemistich. The C stich matches "labored with me in the gospel" with "in the beginning of the gospel." Interestingly, this match in the C' hemistich is identical to the words at the beginning of Mark 1:1 (*archē tou euangeliou*). The D hemistich contains "rejoice" twice, and the D' hemistich contains "I rejoiced." The E stich has a mini chiasm with "the peace of God" (*hē eirēnē tou Theou*) matching "the God of peace" (*ho Theos tēs eirēnēs*). The F hemistich has "your thoughts in Christ Jesus" while the F' hemistich has "think on these things." The center G stich has Paul giving the Philippians an admonition to consider six parallel moral attributes to practice. In 1 Corinthians there are several chiastic structures with three-element center stiches, but this six-element center stich is unique in Paul's chiastic structures.

Interpolation 4:11–14

The chiastic structure reveals an interpolation at 4:11–14. The interpolation occurs between the D' and C' hemistiches. The D' and C' hemistiches contain ninety-two words while the C and D hemistiches contain only forty-four words. Removing 4:11–14 reduces the word count of the D' and C' hemistiches to forty-six words, a much better balance.

Stiches	Words in first half	Words in second half	Words in interpolation
C—D	4:3–5–44	4:10–15–92	4:11–14–46

Interpolation 4:16–18a

The chiastic structure also reveals an interpolation at 4:16–18a between the C' and B' hemistiches. The number of words in the B and C hemistiches is thirty-eight, but there are seventy-one words in the B' and C' hemistiches, almost twice as many. The interpolation seems to encompass vv. 4:16–18a that contain thirty-one words. Removing the interpolation makes the word count in the B' and C' hemistiches forty words, almost an exact balance.

Stiches	Words in first half	Words in second half	Words in interpolation
B–C	4:2–3–38	4:16–18 – 71	4:16–18a—31

Phil 4:20-23

The final literary unit in Philippians is a short two-stich chiastic benediction with a three-element center stich.

   A 4:20 Now to our *God and father* be the glory for ever and ever. Amen.
      B 4:21a *Greet every saint* in Christ Jesus.
      B' 4:21b The *brothers* that are with me *Greet you*.
      B" 4:22 *All the saints greet you*, especially they that are of Caesar's household.
   A' 4:23 The grace of the *Lord Jesus Christ* be with your spirit.

Phil 4:20-23 Chiastic Structure Table

A 4:20—God and father		A' 4:23—Lord Jesus Christ	
B 4:21a—greet every saint	B' 4:21b—brothers … greet you		B" 4:22—all the saints greet you

Commentary

The final structure of Phil 4 is a short benediction with a chiastic structure of only two stiches. The A stich matches "God and father" with "Lord Jesus Christ." The center B stich has three elements "Greet every saint," "brothers greet you," and "all the saints greet you."

8

First Letter To The Thessalonians

1 Thessalonians 1

THE FIRST LITERARY UNIT in 1 Thess is a parallel structure with four stiches encompassing the entire chapter.

1 Thess 1:1–10

> A 1:1 Paul, and Silvanus, and Timothy to the church of the Thessalonians in *God the father* and the *Lord Jesus Christ*. Grace to you and peace.
> A' 1:2 We give thanks to God always concerning all of you, making mention in our prayers, 1:3 remembering unceasingly your work of faith and labor of love and endurance of hope in our *Lord Jesus Christ* before our *God and father*.
>> B 1:4 Knowing, brothers beloved of God, your election 1:5 because our gospel did not come to you in *word* only but also in power and in the *Holy Spirit* and *much assurance*. Even as you know what we became among you for your sake.
>> B' 1:6 And you became imitators of us and of the Lord having received the *word* in *much affliction* with joy of the *Holy Spirit*.
>>> C 1:7 So that *you became an example* to all in *Macedonia and in Achaia* who believe.
>>> C' 1:8a For *from you has sounded forth the word of the Lord*, not only in *Macedonia and Achaia*, but in every place your *faith* in God has gone.
>>>> D 1:8b So that there is no need for us to say anything. 1:9 For they themselves report concerning us the kind of *reception* we had from you. And how you turned to God from idols to serve a *living* and true God.
>>>> D' 1:10 And to *await* his son from Heaven whom he *raised from the dead*, Jesus, delivering us from the wrath to come.

Part I | The Undisputed Letters

1 Thess 1:1–10 Parallel Structure Table

A 1:1—God the father ... Lord Jesus Christ	A' 1:2–3—God the father ... Lord Jesus Christ
B 1:4–5—word ... Holy Spirit ... much assurance	B' 1:6—word ... Holy Spirit ... much affliction
C 1:7—you became an example ... Macedonia and in Achaia ... believe	C' 1:8a—from you has sounded forth the word of the Lord ... Macedonia and Achaia ... faith
D 1:8b–9—reception ... living	D' 1:10—await ... raised from the dead

Commentary

This literary unit with a parallel structure encompasses the entire short chapter of only ten verses. The A stich has two matching phrases in each hemistich. The first match has "God the father" in the A hemistich and "God and father" in the A' hemistich. The B stich contains three matching phrases in each hemistich. "Word" is in both hemistiches. "Holy spirit" is also in both hemistiches. The third match of the B stich is one of opposites. "Much assurance" is in the B hemistich, and "much affliction" is in the B' hemistich. The C stich also has three matching phrases in each hemistich. "You became an example" in the C hemistich matches "for from you has sounded forth the word of the Lord" in the C' hemistich. "Macedonia and Achaia" are in both hemistiches. The third match of the C stich is "believe" (*pisteuousin*) in the C hemistich matching "faith" (*pistis*) in the C' hemistich, the verb matching the noun. In the final D stich "reception" (*eisodon*) in the D hemistich matches "await" (*anamenein*) in the D' hemistich. The second match in the final stich is "living" matching "raised from the dead." An attribute of 1 Thessalonians that is not found in any other undisputed letter of Paul is the statement found five times, near the end of each chapter, that Christians are waiting for Jesus to come to Earth from Heaven. First Thessalonians 1:10 has "await his son from Heaven;" v. 2:19 has "Lord Jesus is coming;" v. 3:13 has "the coming of our Lord Jesus;" 1 Thess 4 has it twice: v. 4:15 has "the coming of the Lord;" v. 4:16 has "the Lord himself will descend from Heaven" and v. 5:23 has "the coming of our Lord Jesus Christ." Apparently Bishop Landon divided the chapters of 1 Thessalonians such that each of those five statements came near the end of a chapter, but in typical fashion the chapters all end with the end of a literary unit.

First Letter To The Thessalonians

1 Thessalonians 2

1 Thess 2:1–18

The majority of 1 Thess 2 is a literary unit having a chiastic structure encompassing almost the entire chapter, revealing an interpolation that many scholars have recognized.

  A 2:1 For you know, brothers, *our coming to you* has not been in vain.
    B 2:2 But *having suffered* before and *having been mistreated* as you know *at Philippi*, we had boldness in our *God to speak to you of the gospel of God in much conflict*. 2:3 For our exhortation is not of error nor of uncleanness nor in guile.
      C 2:4 But even as we have been approved by *God* to be entrusted with the *gospel so we speak, not as pleasing men* but *God* who proves our hearts.
        D 2:5 For neither at any time were we found using *words of flattery* as you know nor a cloak of covetousness. *God* is witness.
          E 2:6 Nor seeking *glory* from men, neither from you nor from others when we might have claimed authority as *apostles of Christ*.
            F 2:7 But we were gentle in the midst of you as when a *nurse cherishes her own children*.
              G 2:8 Even so, being *affectionately desirous of you*, we were well pleased to impart to you not only the gospel of God but also our own souls because you were become very dear to us.
                H 2:9a For you remember, brothers, *our labor and travail*: working night and day.
                H' 2:9b So that we might not burden any of you *we preached to you the gospel of God*.
              G' 2:10 You are witnesses and God how holily and righteously and *without blame we behaved ourselves toward you* who believe.
            F' 2:11 As you know how we dealt with each one of you, as a *father with his own children*, exhorting you, and encouraging you, and testifying,
          E' 2:12 to the end that you should walk worthily of *God, who calls you* into his own kingdom and *glory*.
        D' 2:13a And for this cause we also *thank God without ceasing*
      C' 2:13b that, when you received from us the word of the *message of God, you did not accept the word of men*, but as it is in truth the *word of God*, which also works in you who believe.
    B' 2:14 For you, brothers, became imitators of the churches of *God* in *Judea* in Christ Jesus. For you also *suffered* the *same things of your own countrymen*, even as they did of the Jews; 2:15a who

(2:15b both killed the Lord Jesus and the prophets, and)

2:15c *drove us out* not pleasing *God* and

(2:15d are contrary to all men,)

2:16a *forbidding us to speak to the Gentiles that they may be saved.*

(2:16b to fill up their sins always. But the wrath is come upon them to the uttermost.)

A' 2:17 But we, brothers, having been separated from you for a short time, in presence not in heart, endeavored more exceedingly *to see your face with great desire,* 2:18 because *we wanted come to you,* I, Paul, not once but twice, and Satan hindered us.

1 Thess 2:1–18 Chiastic Structure Table

A 2:1—our coming to you	A' 2:17–18—we wanted to come to you . . . to see your face with great desire
B 2:2–3—having suffered . . . having been mistreated . . . at Philippi . . . God . . . to speak to you of the gospel of God in much conflict	B' 2:14–16 - suffered . . . drove us out . . . in Judea . . . God . . . God and forbidding us to speak to the Gentiles that they may be saved
C 2:4—so we speak not as pleasing men	C' 2:13b—you did not accept the word of men
D 2:5 - words of flattery . . . God	D' 2:13a—thank God without ceasing
E 2:6—glory . . . apostles of Christ	E' 2:12—glory . . . God who calls you
F 2:7—nurse cherishes her own children	F' 2:11—father with his own children
G 2:8—affectionately desirous of you	G' 2:10—without blame we behaved ourselves toward you
H 2:9a—our labor and travail	H' 2:9b—we preached to you

Interpolation 1 Thess 2:15a, 15c, 16b

Many exegetes including Walker have concluded that vv. 2:13–16 are an interpolation,[1] while others insist that it is not.[2] Fortunately, almost the entire second chapter of 1 Thessalonians has a chiastic structure. This excludes the last two verses of the chapter

---

1. Baur, *Paul,*.87–88; Pearson, "1 Thessalonians 2:13–16"; Schmidt, "1 Thess 2:13–16" 269–79; Koester, "I *Thessalonians,* 33–44; Walker, *Interpolations,* 210–20.

2. Collins, *Studies;* Jewett, *The Thessalonian Correspondence,* 36–42; Schlueter, *Filling up the Measure;* Still, *Conflict at Thessalonica;* Wanamaker, *The Epistles to the Thessalonians,* 29–33.

that repeat the idea expressed at the end of all five chapters of 1 Thessalonians that Christians are awaiting the arrival of Christ on Earth.

The A hemistich, v. 2:1, states "our coming to you." This is parallel to "to see your face with great desire" in v. 2:17 and "we wanted to come to you" found in v. 2:18, the A' hemistich. The parallel here is obvious. Paul begins the structure stating that his coming to Thessalonica was not in vain, and he ends the structure by apologizing for not coming sooner and saying he wants to come again and see their faces.

The B stich is the crucial one because if there are no parallels, vv. 2:14–16 might be an interpolation. However, there are parallel words and concepts. Under the assumptions of the rhetorical analysis technique, text containing appropriate parallels is original to Paul. The B hemistich is vv. 2:2–3, while the B' hemistich is quite long encompassing the entirety of vv. 2:14–2:16. For most stiches in this chiastic structure each hemistich is one verse long, basically a sentence. The excessive length of the B' hemistich raises the possibility of an interpolation. Here the text appears to change subject seven times alerting the reader that something may not be quite right with the B' hemistich.

Analyzing the text for parallel words and concepts in the B' stich, we find v. 2:2, contains "having suffered" parallel to "suffered" in v. 2:14. Then "having been mistreated," is parallel to "drove us out" in v. 2:15c. "At Philippi" is parallel to "in Judea," both being geographical locations. "God" is used twice in v. 2:2 and it is used twice in vv. 2:14–16 with the first use coming in the early part of v. 2:14. This implies that the beginning of v. 2:14 is the beginning of the B' hemistich. Since the beginning of v. 2:17 is the beginning of the A' hemistich, the B' hemistich must encompass vv. 2:14–16, assuming more parallel words and concepts are found in the hemistich.

In the B hemistich are the words "to speak to you of the gospel of God in much conflict." This contains three separate concepts: speaking, gospel of God, and conflict. All three of those concepts are found in the B' hemistich with "speak to the Gentiles," "they might be saved," and "forbidding us." Being saved is the objective of the gospel of God. Since these concepts in vv. 2:15–16 are not in exact reverse order from that found in v. 2:2, Paul did not intend them to be in separate stiches, therefore, rhetorical analysis demonstrates that vv. 2:14–16 is the second half of the B stich.

Before performing further analysis on the B stich, the analysis of the rest of the chiastic structure will be completed to make sure that the author intended a chiastic structure in this sequence of his work. As stated many exegetes believe vv. 2:13 is part of the interpolation. In the first half of the C stich, v. 2:4, is "we have been approved by God . . . the gospel, so we speak not as pleasing men, but God." The word order is "God, men, God." This hemistich also contains the concepts of speaking and the gospel. In the second half of the proposed C stich, v. 2:13b, there is "you received from us the word . . . message of God . . . word of men . . . word of God." In this hemistich we find the same word order "God, men, God." In addition "word of men" is parallel to speaking, and "message of God" is parallel to "gospel." It is clear that v. 2:13b is the

C' hemistich. This means that vv. 2:14–16 were designed by the author as the second half of the B stich, and v. 2:13b was designed as the second half of the C stich. Moving to the D hemistich "words of flattery . . . God" in v.2:5 is parallel to "thank God unceasingly" in v. 2:13a, the D' hemistich. Thanking one unceasingly would be a form of flattery. Therefore v. 2:13a is the D' hemistich. This demonstrates that those scholars who think v. 2:13 is part of an interpolation are incorrect.

In the E hemistich, v. 2:6, "glory" and "apostles of Christ" are parallel to "glory" and "God who calls you" in v. 2:12, the E' hemistich. Obviously "glory" in both halves is the same word while "apostles" meaning "sent out" is opposite to "calls you." It is clever to have "apostles of Christ" parallel to "God calls you" since an apostles of Christ is the method by which God calls you. "Christ" and "God" are clearly parallel. The F stich is obvious with "nursing mother cherishes her own children" in the first half of the stich, v. 2:7, being parallel to "a father with his own children" in v. 2:11, the second half. In the G hemistich, v. 2:8, "affectionately desirous of you . . . God" is parallel to "God . . . holy and righteously and without blame we behaved toward you who believed" in v. 2:10, the G' hemistich. Both halves of the stich contain the word "God" and mention the attitude Paul had toward the Thessalonians. The center H stich encompasses only one verse, v. 2:9, with v. 2:9a being the first half and v. 2:9b being the second half. The first half has "our labor and travail," while the second half has "burden . . . we preached to you the gospel of God." Paul's travail is a burden and his labor is preaching the gospel of God. Clearly vv. 2:1–18 has a chiastic structure and the closing of the chapter, vv. 2:19–20, looks forward to Christ's coming to Earth as in the other chapters.

Turning to a deeper analysis of the B stich, above it was noticed that the B' hemistich, vv. 2:14–16, seemed overly long for only one hemistich. The next task in the analysis is to compare the length of the various hemistiches in the structure in order to quantify suspicions about the excessive length of the B' hemistich. The B hemistich contains thirty-six words while the B' hemistich contains seventy-five words. This is definitely out of balance. The core of vv. 2:14–16 is original, but a great deal of text has probably been added to the original composition. In attempting to excise the words that may have been added by a redactor, one needs to insure that the words retained make sense and contain all of the parallel words of the first half of the B stich.

Canonical vv. 2:14–16 contain:

> 2:14 For you, brothers, became imitators of the churches of God in Judea in Christ Jesus. For you also suffered the same things of your own countrymen, even as they did of the Jews, 2:15 who both killed the Lord Jesus and the prophets, and drove us out, not pleasing God, and are contrary to all men, 2:16 forbidding us to speak to the Gentiles that they may be saved, to fill up their sins always. But the wrath is come upon them to the uttermost.

As an initial proposition those exegetes who believe that vv. 2:14–16 has been interpolated invariably note that one of the reasons for their skepticism of the passage is that it interrupts the narrative[3] and is uncharacteristically anti-Semitic.[4] A second reason is that the last phrase of the passage implies that the author was aware of the destruction of the Jerusalem and temple that occurred in 70 CE. The traditionally assumed date for Paul's death is approximately 62 CE. Therefore, the anti-Semitic and anachronistic parts should be excised first.

Verses 2:14–15 still make sense if "both killed the Lord Jesus and the prophets and" is removed. Secondly, "and are contrary to all men" can be excised and a sensible sentence remains. Next, the anachronistic and anti-Semitic phrase, "to fill up their sins always, but the wrath is come upon them to the uttermost" should be eliminated. Since the first half of the B stich contains "having been mistreated," "drove us out" must have been in the original second half of the B stich. In addition, it makes sense to retain who it was that drove Paul and the others out, so "even as they did of the Jews" should be retained. Since the first half of the B stich contains "speak to you of the gospel of God in much conflict," the parallel phrase "forbidding us to speak to the Gentiles that they may be saved" must be original.

Therefore, the original passage as written by Paul most probably was:

> 2:14 For you, brothers, became imitators of the churches of God in Judea in Christ Jesus. For you also suffered the same things of you own countrymen even as they did of the Jews; 2:15 who . . . drove us out, not pleasing God, 2:16 forbidding us to speak to the Gentiles that they may be saved.

This passage as amended now contains forty-nine words. It more reasonably compares with the C hemistich with its thirty-six words. In addition, it has been shown that v. 2:14 is also original and the interpolated words are limited to 2:15–16.

Paul writes that Jews, presumably the Jerusalem apostles and their community, hindered Gentiles in Judea from hearing Paul's message. He does not tell us how they did this, some use of force is implied. This is consistent with Paul's complaints against his opponents in 2 Corinthians and Galatians. Apparently, this event described by Paul inspired an anti-Semitic interpolation by a redactor. The redactor read Paul's complaint about being forbidden, apparently forcibly, from expounding his message to Gentiles in Judea, and decided to add further crimes allegedly committed by Jews. To make the interpolation seem to be Pauline, the redactor made reference to Paul's quote at Rom 11:3 of Elijah accusing Jews of killing the prophets based on 1 Kgs 19:10.

Stiches	Words in first half	Words in second half	Words in interpolation
B	2:2b–3–36	2:14–16–75	2:15b, d, 16b—26

---

3. Walker, *Interpolations*, 213.
4. Walker, *Interpolations*, 216–17.

Part I | The Undisputed Letters

1 Thess 2:19–20

This literary unit is a short chiastic structure with an unusual one-element center stich. This literary unit contains Paul's second iteration of a statement that Christ is coming to Earth.

>   A 2:19a For what is our hope, or *joy*,
>   B 2:19b or crown of *boasting*?
>   C 2:19c Is it not *you* before
>   D 2:19d our *Lord Jesus at his coming*?
>   C' 2:20a For *you* are
>   B' 2:20b our *glory* and
>   A' 2:20c our *joy*.

1 Thess 2:19–20 Chiastic Structure Table

A 2:19a—joy	A' 2:20c—joy
B 2:19b—boasting	B' 2:20b—glory
C 2:19c—you	C' 2:20a—you
D 2:19d our Lord Jesus at his coming	

Commentary

This short two-verse chiastic structure has an unusual one-element center stich that is Paul's main theme of 1 Thessalonians that Jesus Christ is coming to Earth. In the A stich both hemistiches contain "joy." The B hemistich has "boasting" and the B' hemistich has "glory." Both hemistiches of the C stich contain "you." The center D stich is the main theme of this letter "our Lord Jesus at his coming."

1 Thessalonians 3

This unit is an unusual one-stich structure encompassing the entire chapter. The same five words are found in each of the three elements of this structure.

1 Thess 3:1–13

>   A 3:1 Therefore *no longer enduring* we thought it best to be left behind at Athens alone. 3:2 And we sent Timothy, our brother and fellow worker of God in the gospel of Christ, to *strengthen* and to *encourage* you concerning your *faith* 3:3 that no one

be perturbed by these *afflictions*. For you yourselves know that we are destined for this. 3:4a And indeed *when we were with you*

A' 3:4b we were telling you beforehand that we are about to suffer *affliction*, even as it happened as you know. 3:5 Because of this when I could *no longer endure* I also sent in order to know your *faith*, lest somehow the tempter had tempted you and our labor would be in vain. 3:6 But presently Timothy came to us from you bringing us glad tidings of your *faith* and love, and that you have good memories of us always, *longing to see us*, even as we do you. 3:7a Because of this, brothers, we were *encouraged* concerning you

A" 3:7b in all our distress and *affliction* because your *faith*. 3:8 For now we live if you *persevere* in the Lord. 3:9 For what thanksgiving can we give to God concerning you in return for all the joy wherewith we rejoice for your sakes before our God, 3:10 night and day exceedingly praying that *we may see your face* and may perfect that which is lacking in your *faith*? 3:11 Now may our God and father himself and our Lord Jesus *direct our way to you*. 3:12 And the Lord make you to increase and excel in love toward one another and toward all even as we also are toward you. 3:13 In order to *strengthen* your hearts blameless in holiness before our God and father at the coming of our Lord Jesus with all his saints.

1 Thess 3:1–13 Parallel Structure Table

A 3:1–4a—no longer enduring . . . strengthen . . . encourage . . . faith . . . afflictions . . . when we were with you	A' 3:4b–7a—no longer endure . . . encourage . . . faith . . . faith . . . affliction . . . longing to see us	A" 3:7b–13—persevere . . . strengthen . . . faith . . . faith . . . affliction . . . we may see your face . . . direct our way to you

Commentary

This literary unit has an unusual construction. It appears to be divided into three sections, 3:1–4a, 3:4b–7a, and 3:7b–13. The first element contains fifty-three words. The second element contains seventy-two words. The third element contains one hundred twenty-three words. The elements become longer as the structure progresses. There are five phrases or concepts that appear in each element, but always in a different order. Each element has at least one of the phrases occurring twice. The five concepts are: 1 "no longer endure, persevere" (*mēketi stegontes, mēketi stegōn, stēkete*), 2 "encourage, strengthen" (*parakalesai, pareklēthēmen, stērixai*), 3 "faith" (*pisteōs, pistin*), 4 "affliction" (*thlipsesin, thlibesthai, thlipsei*), and 5 a phrase about Paul visiting the Thessalonians, "when we were with you" (*hote pros hymas ēmen*), "longing to see us" (*epipothountes hēmas idein*), "we may see your face" (*eis to idein hymōn to prosōpon*), and "direct our way to you" (*kateuthynai tēn hodon hēmōn pros hymas*).

With regard to the phrases that occur twice in each element, the first element repeats "encourage" "strengthen." The second element repeats "faith." The final element repeats "faith" and Paul visiting Thessalonica. The literary unit has a progression, and it ends with Paul's third statement about "the coming of our Lord Jesus."

1 Thessalonians 4

This unit is a parallel structure with an inclusio encompassing the entire chapter. The inclusio has two elements at the beginning of the unit. This is similar to the inclusios at Rom 2:17–24 and Gal 3:19–29.

1 Thess 4:1–18

A 4:1 Finally then, brothers, *we beseech and encourage you* in the *Lord Jesus*, that just as you received from us how you ought to walk and to please God even as you are walking so that you should excel more.

A' 4:2 For you know what *command we gave you* through the *Lord Jesus*.

  B 4:3 For this is the will of God your *sanctification*. Abstain from sexual immorality,
  B' 4:4 that each one of you know how to control his own vessel in *sanctification* and honor.

   C 4:5 *Not in the passion of lust* even as the Gentiles who do not know God,
   C' 4:6 *not to overreach and defraud his brother* in a transaction because the Lord is an avenger in all these things as we also told you before and so testified.

    D 4:7 For God has not called us for impurity, but in *holiness*.
    D' 4:8 Therefore he who is rejecting does not reject man but God who gives his *Holy Spirit* to you.

     E 4:9a But concerning *brotherly love* you have no need that I write to you.
     E' 4:9b For you yourselves are taught by God to *love* one another. 4:10 For indeed you do it toward all the *brothers* that are everywhere in Macedonia. But we encourage you, *brothers*, that you excel even more.

      F 4:11 And that you *strive earnestly* to be calm and attend to do your own business and to work with your hands as we commanded you.
      F' 4:12 So that you may *act appropriately* toward those who are outside and may have need of nothing.

       G 4:13 But we would not have you ignorant, brothers, concerning those *having fallen asleep*. That you should not be grieved, even as the rest who have no hope.
       G' 4:14 For if we believe that Jesus died and rose again, so also God will bring with him those *having fallen asleep* in Jesus.

G" 4:15 For this we say to you in the word of the Lord that we the living, remaining to the coming of the Lord, will not precede those *having fallen asleep.*

H 4:16 For the *Lord himself will descend from Heaven* with a shout with the voice of the archangel and with the trumpet of God. And the *dead in Christ will rise first.*

H' 4:17 Then we the living remaining *will be caught up in the clouds* together with them to meet the *Lord in the air.* And so we will forever be with the Lord.

A" 4:18 Therefore *encourage one another* with these words.

1 Thess 4:1-19 Parallel Structure Table

A 4:1—we beseech and encourage you . . . Lord Jesus	A' 4:2—command we gave you . . . Lord Jesus	A" 4:18—encourage one another
B 4:3—sanctification	B' 4:4—sanctification	
C 4:5—not in the passion of lust	C' 4:6—not to overreach and defraud his brother	
D 4:7—holiness	D' 4:8—his Holy Spirit	
E 4:9a—brotherly love	E' 4:9b-10—love . . . brothers . . . brothers	
F 4:11—strive earnestly	F' 4:12—act appropriately	
G 4:13—having fallen asleep	G' 4:14—having fallen asleep	G" 4:15—having fallen asleep
H 4:16—Lord himself will descend from Heaven . . . dead in Christ will rise first	H' 4:17—Lord in the air . . . will be caught up in the cloud	

Commentary

This literary unit has a parallel structure with an inclusio. The A and G stiches contain three elements while the others contain only two. The A stich is one of three inclusios in the undisputed letters that has two parallel elements at the beginning of the structure and then the closing element with the inclusio as the final element. The A element has "we beseech and encourage you" matching "command we gave you" in the A' element and "encourage one another" in the closing inclusio, the A" element. The A and A' elements both contain "Lord Jesus," not found in the A" element. Both hemistiches in the B stich contain "sanctification." The C stich matches "not in the passion of lust" with "not to overreach and defraud his brother." The D stich has "holiness" in the D hemistich and "his Holy Spirit" in the D' hemistich. The E stich matches "brotherly love" in the E hemistich with "love" and "brothers" found twice in the E' hemistich.

The F hemistich contains "strive earnestly" matching "act appropriately" in the F' hemistich. The G stich contains three elements all of which contain "having fallen asleep" meaning dying in this context. The H stich has two matches in each hemistich. The first match is "Lord himself will descend from Heaven" in the H hemistich matches "Lord in the air" in the H' hemistich. The second H stich match is "dead in Christ will rise first" matching "will be caught up in the clouds."

K. G. Eckart proposed that vv. 4:1–8 is an interpolation.[5] However, this section is a typical Pauline parallel structure with 4:1 providing the first half of an inclusio matching v. 4:18. Nothing revealed by rhetorical analysis suggests that vv. 4:1–8 is an interpolation. Eckart also proposed that vv. 4:10b–12 and 18 are interpolations. With respect to v. 4:18 it strains credulity to think that an interpolator realized that Paul created parallel literary structures defined by an inclusio and so executed that format when inserting his interpolations. With regard to vv. 4:10b–12 it is true that the E stich is unbalanced and eliminating v. 4:10b (everything after "Macedonia") from the E' hemistich would better balance the stich. However, v. 4:10b contains "brother" a parallel term to that found in v. 4:9a. Therefore, v. 4:10b was retained. Verses 4:11–12 make up the F stich and appear to be typically Pauline. Rhetorical analysis implies that vv. 4:11–12 are original to Paul.

1 Thessalonians 5

1 Thess 5:1–10

The first literary unit of 1 Thess 5 is a parallel structure with an inclusio.

  A 5:1 But concerning *the time and the season*, brothers, there is no need that anything be written to you.

    B 5:2 For you yourselves know perfectly that the *day of the Lord comes as a thief* in the night. 5:3a When they might say, "Peace and safety," then sudden destruction comes upon them

    B' 5:3b as labor pains upon a woman with child. And they will in no way escape. 5:4 But you, brothers, are not in darkness that *such day should overtake you as a thief*.

      C 5:5 For you are all sons of light and sons of the day. We are not of the night nor of darkness. 5:6 So then *we should not sleep* as the others, but *we should watch and be sober*.

      C' 5:7 For those *sleeping sleep at night*. And those becoming drunk get drunk at night. 5:8a But we being of the day *should be sober*,

        D 5:8b putting on the breastplate of faith and love, the helmet of the hope of *salvation*.

---

5. Eckart, "Thessalonicher" 30–44.

D' 5:9 For God has not destined us for wrath but for obtaining *salvation* through our Lord Jesus Christ,

A' 5:10 who died for us, so that whether we be *awake or asleep* we may live together with him.

1 Thess 5:1–10 Parallel Structure Table

A 5:1—the time and the season	A' 5:10—awake or asleep
B 5:2–3—the day of the Lord comes as a thief	B' 5:4—such day should overtake you as a thief
C 5:5–6—we should not sleep . . . we should watch and be sober	C' 5:7–8a—sleeping sleep at night . . . should be sober
D 5:8b—salvation	D' 5:9—salvation

Commentary

This literary unit has a parallel structure defined by an inclusio. The A hemistich, the first half of the inclusio has "the time and the season," while the A' hemistich and second half of the inclusio has "awake or asleep." The B stich matches "day of the Lord comes as a thief" with "such a day should overtake you as a thief." In the C stich "we should not sleep" matches "sleeping sleep at night." The second match of C stich is "we should watch and be sober" matching "should be sober." The D stich has "salvation" in both hemistiches.

Gerhard Friedrich proposed that vv. 5:1–11 is an interpolation.[6] This proposal encompasses the entire 1 Thess 5:1–10 literary unit, which is a typically Pauline parallel structure with an inclusio. There is no rhetorical analysis evidence that this literary unit is not from the hand of Paul. Verse 5:11 is the first verse in the next literary unit that also appears to be typically Pauline. Friedrich's suggestion would eliminate a match of the word "encourage" (*parakaleite*) with v. 5:14a. This is a word Paul uses often. Rhetorical analysis shows that verse 5:11 is original to Paul.

1 Thess 5:11–14

The second literary unit of 1 Thess 5 is a short parallel structure with only two stiches.

A 5:11 Therefore *encourage* one another and build up one another, just as also you are doing. 5:12a But we implore you, *brothers*,

---

6. Friedrich, "1 Thessalonischer 5:1–11," 288–315.

> B 5:12b to appreciate those who labor among you, and supervising you in the Lord and *admonishing* you.
>
> A' 5:13 And to esteem them highly in love because of their work. Be at peace among yourselves. 5:14a And we *encourage* you, *brothers*,
>
> > B' 5:14b *admonish* the disorderly, encourage the fainthearted, care for the weak, be patient toward all.

1 Thess 5:11–14 Parallel Structure Table

A 5:11—encourage … brothers	A' 5:13–14a—encourage … brothers
B 5:12—admonishing	B' 5:14b—admonish

Commentary

This short parallel structure contains only two stiches in an A, B, A,' B' format. Both hemistiches of the A stich contain "encourage" and "brothers." Both hemistiches of the B stich contain a form of "admonish."

1 Thess 5:15–22

The third literary unit of this chapter is a short chiastic structure with a six-element center stich.

> A 5:15a See that none render *evil* for *evil* to anyone.
> > B 5:15b But always pursue the *good*, toward one another, and toward all.
> > > C 5:16 *Always rejoice.*
> > > C' 5:17 *Unceasingly pray.*
> > > C" 5:18 *In everything give thanks.* For this is the will of God in Christ Jesus for you.
> > > C'" 5:19 *Do not quench the spirit.*
> > > C"" 5:20 *Do not despise prophesies.*
> > > C''''' 5:21a *Examine all things.*
> > B' 5:21b Hold tight that which is *good.*
> A' 5:22 Abstain from every form of *evil.*

1 Thess 5:15–22 Chiastic Structure Table

A 5:15a—evil … evil	A' 5:22—evil
B 5:15b—good	B' 5:21b—good

| C 5:16—always rejoice | C' 5:17 —unceasingly pray | C" 5:18—in everything give thanks | C''' 5:19—do not quench the spirit | C'''' 5:20—do not despise prophesies | C''''' 5:21—examine all things |

Commentary

This short chiastic structure is a series of admonitions from Paul to the Thessalonians. The A stich has one form of "evil" (*kakon, kakou*) in the A hemistich and another form of "evil" (*ponērou*) in the A' hemistich. Paul was covering all the bases. The B stich contrasts with that by containing two forms of "good" (*agathon* and *kalon*), again covering all bases. The center C stich has six elements, each containing a separate admonition.

Eckart also proposed that vv. 5:12–22 is an interpolation.[7] This proposal covers essentially two successive literary units that, while short, both exhibit Pauline attributes. These units were clearly written by Paul.

1 Thess 5:23–28

The final literary unit of 1 Thessalonians is a short chiastic structure benediction with Paul's final statement about Jesus coming to Earth.

> A 5:23 And the God of peace himself sanctify you completely. And may your spirit and soul and body be preserved entirely, blameless at the coming of *our Lord Jesus Christ*.
> B 5:24 Faithful is *he who calls you*, who will also do it.
> C 5:25 *Brothers*, pray for us.
> C' 5:26 Salute all the *brothers* with a holy kiss.
> B' 5:27 *I adjure you* by the Lord that this letter be read to all the brothers.
> A' 5:28 The grace of *our Lord Jesus Christ* be with you.

1 Thess 5:23–28 Chiastic Structure Table

A 5:23—our Lord Jesus Christ	A' 5:28—our Lord Jesus Christ
B 5:24—he who calls you	B' 5:27—I adjure you
C 5:25—brothers	5:26—brothers

---

7. Eckart, "Thessalonicher."

Commentary

The final literary unit of the letter is a benediction with a chiastic structure. The A hemistich contains the final statement about the future coming of Christ to Earth. "Our Lord Jesus Christ" is in both hemistiches of the A stich. The A stich seems out of balance, but v. 5:23a makes perfect sense as an introduction for this literary unit. There does not appear to be an interpolation into v. 5:23. The B hemistich has "he who calls you," Paul referring to himself, matching "I adjure you." Both hemistiches of the C stich contain "brothers." Eckart also proposed that v. 5:27 is an interpolation.[8] This is the B' hemistich of the chiastic structure and parallel to the B hemistich of v. 5:24. Eckart is also wrong about this proposal.

---

8. Eckart, "Thessalonicher."

9

Letter To Philemon

Phlm 1–25

THE ENTIRE LETTER TO PHILEMON is a dual chiastic/parallel structure with fifteen stiches in the chiastic structure and thirteen stiches in the parallel structure. The parallel structure has an inclusio identical to the A stich of the chiastic structure.

Chiastic Structure

    A 1:1a Paul, a prisoner of *Christ Jesus*,
      B 1:1b and *Timothy, our brother*, to *Philemon* our beloved and *fellow worker*,
        C 1:2 and to Apphia our sister, and to *Archippus our fellow soldier*, and to the church in your house.
          D 1:3 *Grace to you* and peace from God our father and the Lord Jesus Christ.
            E 1:4 I thank my God always, making mention of you in *my prayers*,
              F 1:5 hearing of your love and of the *faith* which you have toward the Lord Jesus and toward all the saints. 1:6a That the communion of your *faith* might become effective
                G 1:6b in the recognition of every good thing that is in us, *in Christ*.
                  H 1:7a For I had much *joy* and *encouragement* in your love, because the *hearts* of the saints
                    I 1:7b have been refreshed through you, *brother*. 1:8 Although I have much boldness in Christ to enjoin you that which is proper,
                      J 1:9a rather for love's sake I implore, being *as Paul* the old man
                        K 1:9b and now a prisoner also of *Christ Jesus*.
                          L 1:10 I implore you for *my child* whom I have begotten in chains *Onesimus*,
                            M 1:11 who once was useless to you, *but now is useful to both you and to me*.

N 1:12 I have sent back to you in person he who is *my very heart*.

    O 1:13 I was wishing to keep him with me so that *on your behalf* he might serve me in the chains of the gospel.

    O' 1:14a However, *without your consent* I would do nothing,

N' 1:14b so that *your goodness* should not be from necessity but of willingness.

M' 1:15 For perhaps he was therefore separated from you for a time, that *you might possess him in perpetuity*,

L' 1:16a no longer as a *slave* but above a *slave, a beloved brother*, especially to me.

K' 1:16b But how much more to you both in the flesh and in *the Lord*. 1:17 If then you consider me a partner, welcome him as you would me.

J' 1:18 But if he has wronged you at all or owes anything charge that to me. 1:19 *I, Paul*, write with my own hand, I will repay it. And I may not say to you that you yourself owe anything to me.

I' 1:20a Yes, *brother*,

H' 1:20b give me *help* in the Lord. *Refresh* my heart

G' 1:20c *in Christ*.

F' 1:21 Having *confidence* in your obedience I write to you, *knowing* that you will do even more than what I ask.

E' 1:22a But at the same time also prepare a lodging for me. For I hope that as a result of *your prayers*

D' 1:22b I will be *granted to you*.

C' 1:23 *Epaphras, my fellow prisoner* in Christ Jesus, greets you,

B' 1:24 as do Mark, *Aristarchus, Demas*, Luke, my *fellow workers*.

A' 1:25 The grace of our Lord *Jesus Christ* be with your spirit. Amen

1 Phlm 1-25 Chiastic Structure Table

A 1:1a—Christ Jesus	A' 1:25—Jesus Christ
B 1:1b—Timothy … Philemon … fellow worker	B' 1:24—Aristarchus … Demas … fellow workers
C 1:2—Archippus our fellow soldier	C' 1:23—Epaphras my fellow prisoner
D 1:3—grace to you	D' 1:22b—granted to you
E 1:4—my prayers	E' 1:22a—your prayers

F 1:5–6a—faith...faith	F' 1:21—confidence...knowing
G 1:6b—in Christ	G' 1:20c—in Christ
H 1:7a—joy...encouragement...hearts	H' 1:20b—refresh...help...heart
I 1:7b–8—brother	I' 1:20a—brother
J 1:9a—as Paul	J' 1:18–19—I Paul
K 1:9b—Christ Jesus	K 1:16b–17—the Lord
L 1:10—my child...Onesimus	L 1:16 a—beloved brother...slave...slave
M 1:11—but now is useful to both you and to me	M' 1:15—you might possess him in perpetuity
N 1:12—my very heart	N' 1:14b—your goodness
O 1:13—on your behalf	O' 1:14a—without your consent

Parallel Structure

The parallel structure has an inclusio which is identical to the A stich of the chiastic structure.

  A 1:1a Paul, a prisoner of *Christ Jesus*, and Timothy our brother,
    B 1:1b to *Philemon our beloved and fellow worker*,
    B' 1:2 and to Apphia our sister, and to *Archippus our fellow soldier*, and to the church in your house.
      C 1:3 Grace to you and peace from *God* our father and the Lord Jesus Christ.
      C' 1:4 I thank my *God* always, making mention of you in my prayers,
        D 1:5 hearing of your love, and of the *faith* which you have toward the Lord Jesus, and toward all the saints.
        D' 1:6 That the communion of your *faith* might become effective in the recognition of every good thing that is in us, in *Christ*.
          E 1:7a For *I had much joy and encouragement in your love* because the hearts of the saints
          E' 1:7b *I have been refreshed through you*, brother. 1:8 Although I have much boldness in Christ to enjoin you that which is proper.
            F 1:9 Rather *for love's sake I implore*, being as Paul the old man and now a *prisoner* also of Christ Jesus.
            F' 1:10 *I implore you for my child*, whom I have begotten *in chains*, Onesimus,
              G 1:11 who once was useless to you, but *now is useful to both you and to me*.

G' 1:12 I have sent back to you in person he who is my very heart. 1:13 I was *wishing to keep him with me* so that on your behalf he might serve me in the chains of the gospel.

   H 1:14a However, *without your consent* I would do nothing,

   H' 1:14b so that your goodness should not be from necessity *but of willingness*.

     I 1:15 For perhaps he was therefore separated from you for a time, that *you might possess him* in perpetuity,

     I' 1:16a no longer *as a slave, but above a slave*, a beloved brother, especially to me,

        J 1:16b but how much more to you, both in the flesh and in the Lord. 1:17 If then you consider me a partner, *welcome him as you would me*.

        J' 1:18 But if he has wronged you at all or owes anything charge that to me. 1:19 I, Paul, write with my own hand, *I will repay it*. And I may not say to you that you yourself owe anything to me.

           K 1:20a Yes, brother, *give me help in the Lord*.

           K' 1:20b *Refresh my heart in Christ*.

              L 1:21 Having confidence in your obedience I write to you, knowing that *you will do even more than what I ask*.

              L' 1:22 But at the same time also *prepare a lodging for me*. For I hope that as a result of your prayers I will be granted to you.

                 M 1:23 *Epaphras, my fellow prisoner* in Christ Jesus, greets you,

                 M' 1:24 as do Mark, *Aristarchus, Demas*, Luke, *my fellow workers*.

A' 1:25 The grace of our Lord *Jesus Christ* be with your spirit. Amen

Phlm 1–25 Parallel Structure Table

A 1:1—Christ Jesus	A' 1:25—Jesus Christ
B 1:1b—Philemon our beloved and fellow worker	B' 1:2—Archippus our fellow soldier
C 1:3—God	C' 1:4—God
D 1:5—faith . . . Lord Jesus	D' 1:6—faith . . . Christ
E 1:7a—I had much joy and encouragement in your love	E' 1:7b–8—I have been refreshed through you
F 1:9—for love's sake I implore . . . prisoner	F' 1:10—I implore you for my child . . . in chains
G 1:11—now useful to both you and to me	G' 1:12—wishing to keep him with me

H 1:14a—without your consent	H' 1:14b—but of willingness
I 1:15—you might possess him	I' 1:16a—as a slave but above a slave
J 1:16b-17—welcome him as you would me	J' 1:18-19—I will repay
K 1:20a—give me help in the Lord	K' 1:20b—refresh my heart in Christ
L 1:21—you will do even more than what I ask	L' 1:22—prepare a lodging for me
M 1:23—Epaphras my fellow prisoner	M' 1:24 - Aristarchus, Demas my fellow workers

Commentary

Chiastic Structure

This short letter with only twenty-five verses contains just one literary unit. It is extremely interesting that Paul would compose this letter with a complicated dual chiastic/parallel structure to his friend Philemon asking him to take back his runaway slave Onesimus. This suggests that when Paul was being taught to write he was taught to compose everything with a literary unit, whether parallel, chiastic, or a hybrid, and he may have done it almost unconsciously.

In the A stich "Christ Jesus" matches "Jesus Christ" in a now familiar chiasm within the chiastic structure. In the B stich Paul matches two proper names, "Timothy and Philemon" in the B hemistich with "Aristarchus and Demas" in the B' hemistich. When Paul uses proper names for a matching hemistich, he usually uses the same number of proper names as in Gal 1:18 matching Gal 2:1. However, in Phil 4:2 two proper names are a match with one proper name in Phil 4:18. It is my speculation that "Mark" and "Luke" are interpolations, but this is unprovable. It is curious that Onesimus, Aristarchus, Epaphras, Demas, Mark and Luke are all six mentioned in both Philemon and in Colossians.

The B stich also has "fellow worker" in both hemistiches. In the C stich "Archippus our fellow soldier" matches "Epaphras my fellow prisoner." The D hemistich has "Grace to you" (*charis hymin*) matching "granted to you" (*charisthēsomai hymin*) with the noun and verb having the same root. In the E stich "my prayers" matches "your prayers." The F hemistich has "faith" twice matching "confidence" and "knowing." If one has faith it gives him confidence and knowledge. Both hemistiches of the G stich contain "in Christ." "Joy" and "encouragement" in the H hemistich match "help" and "refresh" in the H' hemistich. Both hemistiches contain "heart." In the I stich both hemistiches contain "brother." The J stich matches "as Paul" with "I Paul." In the K stich "Christ Jesus" in the K hemistich matches "Lord" in the K' hemistich. In the L stich both hemistiches are referring to Onesimus. "My child" in the L hemistich matches "a beloved brother" in the L' hemistich. In addition, in the L stich "Onesimus" matches "slave" twice. "Onesimus" means "useful" and was a common slave name.[1]

Paul is making a play on words in the M stich when he refers to Onesimus as once being useless to Philemon but is now useful to both Philemon and Paul. The M hemistich has "useful to both you and me" matching "you might possess him in perpetuity" in the M' hemistich. The N stich matches "my very heart" with "your goodness." The center O stich matches "on your behalf" with "without your consent."

Parallel Structure

The A stich of the parallel structure is an inclusio with a chiastic format having "Christ Jesus" and "Jesus Christ." The B stich matches "Philemon our beloved and fellow worker" with "Archippus our fellow soldier." The C stich has "God" in both hemistiches. The D stich has "faith" in both hemistiches and "Lord Jesus" in the D hemistich and "Christ" in the D' hemistich. The E stich matches two ways Philemon has made Paul happy. The F stich has Paul "imploring" Philemon in both hemistiches and "prisoner" is in the F hemistich while "in chains" is in the F' hemistich. The G stich has two statements about the benefit the slave Onesimus would be to Paul with Paul making a pun in the G hemistich on the name "Onesimus" which means "useful." The H stich has Paul saying twice that he wants Philemon's permission to send Onesimus back to him. The I stich matches "you might possess him" in the I hemistich with "as a slave, but above a slave" in the I' hemistich. The J stich matches "receive him as you would me" with "I will repay it," both statements being about Philemon receiving something from Paul. The K stich matches "give me help in the Lord" with "refresh my heart in Christ." The L stich has "you will do even more than I ask" in the L hemistich matching "prepare a lodging for me" in the L' hemistich with Paul imposing on Philemon's generosity twice. The M stich matches "Epaphras my fellow-prisoner" with "Aristarchus, Demas my fellow workers."

---

1. Strong's Concordance, 3682.

10

Literary Units Of Paul

Attributes of Pauline Literary Units

After examining ninety-eight literary units in the undisputed letters it is clear that Baur's *hauptbriefe* theory is incorrect. All seven letters of the undisputed group were written by the same hand, presumably Paul as he identifies himself. As a result of the examination, the attributes of units authentically written by Paul can be identified.

1. Paul uses repetition and parallelism extensively. In the typical Pauline literary unit the repeated words and phrases make up a significant portion of the unit, estimated at 25 percent. Paul did not typically write many words without a repeated word, phrase, or abstract concept, whether the repetition is found in a chiastic format or in a parallel format.
2. Essentially half of Paul's literary units have a chiastic structure and half have a parallel structure.
3. Paul's literary structures exhibit a symmetry. Chiastic structures are inherently symmetric, and many of his parallel structures contain chiastic elements, and where there are stiches with multiple elements they are often placed in a symmetric pattern within the literary unit.
4. The undisputed letters all have multiple chiastic literary units except Philemon that contains only one dual chiastic/parallel unit encompassing the entire letter.
5. There is a definite beginning and ending of each literary unit. This is absolutely clear in a chiastic structure where the beginning A hemistich is parallel to the ending A' hemistich. This same definite demarcation applies to Paul's parallel structures that are defined by an inclusio. In addition, that same definite demarcation is found when a parallel structure has a chiastic structure preceding it and another chiastic structure following it. The only structures where this does not occur are in 2 Corinthians. In 2 Cor 9 there are two consecutive parallel units. However the first one has an A, B, C, D, A', B', C', D' format and the second one

is in an A, A,′ B, B,′ C, C′ format such that the beginning and ending of each is definite. The other place where Paul wrote two consecutive parallel literary units not defined by inclusios is at 2 Cor 12 and 13. The literary unit of 2 Cor 12 is in an A, A,′ B, B,′ C, C′ format and the literary unit of 2 Cor 13 is in that same format except that the beginning stich and the final stich both have three elements, setting off where one ends and the other begins.

6. Typically in Paul's literary units the parallel or repeated phrases rapidly follow one another. In other words, there is not an abundance of text between key matching phrases. Another way of looking at it is that the hemistiches or elements are relatively short.

7. Paul's literary units are relatively long. While there are short and transitional units, thirty-five of the sixty chapters in the undisputed letters (58 percent) are encompassed by only one literary unit.

8. Paul's literary units have a pleasing design. Of course, in writing his letters Paul intended that they be read aloud to a congregation, most of whom could not read. Therefore, he would have intended a pleasing aural design.

9. Paul is clever in his word usage. He frequently created chiasms within individual stiches. This is also shown by his use of puns and chiastic matches deprecating to his opponents.

10. The use of literary structures by Paul permeates every aspect of his writing. It appears that his academic training so thoroughly inculcated the use of literary structures when writing that even when writing a letter to his friend Philemon he created a rapid-fire dual chiastic/parallel structure for the entire letter including the address and closing.

Examination of Deutero-Pauline Letters

With the attributes of Paul's undisputed literary units in mind, the Deutero-Pauline letters can be examined with a view to investigating whether they contain the same attributes or are markedly different such that it can be determined that they were or were not written by Paul. Attributes to look for:

1. Definite beginnings and endings of literary units.
2. An equal balance of chiastic and parallel structures.
3. A density of repeated words and phrases.
4. A pleasing design and pattern to the parallel structures.
5. Relatively long literary units containing more than three or four stiches.

Most of the letters that follow show a clearly different style of literary structures, but there are some surprising aspects. The Deutero-Pauline letters will be discussed in the order of the most Pauline to the least Pauline rather than canonical order as in the previous part.

Part II

THE DEUTERO-PAULINE LETTERS

11

Second Letter To The Thessalonians

2 Thessalonians 1

2 Thess 1:1–12

This is a Pauline literary unit with a chiastic structure.

    A 1:1 Paul, and Silvanus, and Timothy to the church of the Thessalonians in *God our father and the Lord Jesus Christ*. 1:2 *Grace* to you and peace from *God the father and the Lord Jesus Christ*.

        B 1:3 We ought to thank God always concerning you just as it is fitting because your *faith* grows exceedingly, and the love of each one of you all toward one another is increasing.

            C 1:4a So that *we ourselves boast about you in the churches of God*

                D 1:4b for your endurance and faith in all the *persecutions of you and in the afflictions which you endure*. 1:5 A *sign of the righteous judgment of God*, showing you are worthy of the kingdom of God for *which you also suffer*.

                    E 1:6 If indeed it is righteous for *God to repay affliction to those who afflict you*. 1:7 And to *you that are being afflicted*, rest with us at the revelation of the *Lord Jesus* from Heaven with the angels of *his power in flaming fire*

                    E' 1:8 *inflicting vengeance on those who do not know God and to those who do not obey the gospel of our Lord Jesus,*

                D' 1:9 who will *suffer the penalty of eternal death* away from the presence of *the Lord and from the glory of his power*. 1:10 In that day when he will come to be glorified in his saints and to be marveled at in all those who believed because our testimony to you was believed.

            C' 1:11a For which *we also pray always for you that our God* may count you worthy of his call.

        B' 1:11b And he may fulfill every desire of goodness and work of *faith* with power.

A' 1:12 So that the name of our *Lord Jesus* may be glorified in you and you in him according to the *grace* of our *God* and the *Lord Jesus Christ*.

2 Thess 1:1–12 Chiastic Structure Table

A 1:1—God … Lord Jesus Christ … grace … God … Lord Jesus Christ	A' 1:12—God … Lord Jesus Christ … grace … Lord Jesus
B 1:3—faith	B' 1:11b—faith
C—1:4a we ourselves boast about you in the churches of God	C'—1:11 we also pray always for you that our God
D—1:4b–5 persecution of you and in the afflictions which you endure … sign of the righteous judgment of God … which you also suffer	D'—1:9–10 suffer the penalty of eternal death … the Lord and from the glory of his power
E—1:6–7 God to repay affliction to those who afflict you … you who are being afflicted … Lord Jesus	E'—1:8 inflicting vengeance on those who do not know God and to those who do not obey the gospel of our Lord Jesus

Commentary

The scholarly consensus is that 2 Thessalonians is a complete forgery.[1] However, 2 Thess 1 appears to be a Pauline literary unit. It has a five-stich chiastic structure. The B and C stiches are not quite balanced with the B and C hemistiches containing thirty-five words and the B' and C' hemistiches containing twenty-six words. However, the balance is reasonable.

One curious aspect is that the first twenty words of 2 Thess 1:1 are exactly the same as the first twenty words of 1 Thess 1:1. No undisputed letter of Paul has the exact same introduction as any other undisputed letter. They are similar and generally have the same idea but not the exact wording. However, every undisputed letter except 1 Thess contains "grace to you and peace from God our father and the Lord Jesus Christ." First Thessalonians contains only "grace to you and peace." Second Thessalonians 1:2 contains, "grace to you and peace from God *the* father and the Lord Jesus Christ." Some manuscripts have "God *our* father." Since 2 Thess 1:1 and the first four words of 1:2 are exactly the same as 1 Thess 1:1, it raises the question of whether the letter was originally written to some other church and a forger appropriated it with the purpose in mind to contradict 1 Thess about the parousia coming soon and introduce the concept of the anti-Christ into the Pauline corpus. In order to do that the forger may have redirected a genuine letter from Paul to some other church to Thessalonica.

---

1. Ehrman, *Forged*, 105–108.

Another curiosity in the wording of 2 Thessalonians is the use of a phrase containing the word "letter" (*epistolēs*). This is used four times, vv. 2:2, 15, 3:14, and 17. Second Thessalonians implies at v. 2:2 that 1 Thessalonians is a forgery; however, the references to "letters" at vv. 2:2; 15 and 3:14 are very similar in use to the references to the coming of Jesus Christ from Heaven in 1 Thess 1:10; 2:19; 3:13; 4:16; and 5:23. Therefore, while 2 Thessalonians implies that 1 Thessalonians is a forgery, in copying the introduction verbatim and the use of a phrase about a letter in each chapter, it copies unique characteristics of 1 Thessalonians. This copying of 1 Thessalonians characteristics in 2 Thessalonians seems to be working against the proposition that 1 Thessalonians is a forgery, and exposes 2 Thessalonians as the forgery.

2 Thessalonians 2

2 Thess 2:1–16

This section of 2 Thessalonians is not a Pauline literary unit. It contains a number of parallel phrases, but they are not in a Pauline pattern. It does seem to have a two-stich inclusio although the A" hemistich is not well executed.

> A 2:1 Now we implore you, brothers, concerning the *coming of our Lord Jesus Christ* and our gathering together to him.
>> B 2:2 So that you not be suddenly shaken out of your mind nor be troubled that the day of the Lord is at hand neither by spirit nor by word or by *letter as if from us*.
>>> C 2:3 No one should deceive you in any manner. For the apostasy comes first and *the man of sin be revealed, the son of destruction,*
>>> C' 2:4 the *one opposing and exalting himself* above all that is called God or that is worshipped so that he sits in the temple of God holding himself out as God. 2:5 Do you not remember that when I was yet with you I told you these things? 2:6 And now you know that which restrains. For *he is to be revealed* at the proper time.
>>> C" 2:7 For the mystery of lawlessness is already working. *Only one is restraining* it at present until he be taken away. 2:8a And then *will be revealed the lawless one,*
> A' 2:8b whom the *Lord Jesus* will slay with the breath of his mouth, and will annul by the *manifestation of his coming,* 2:9 whose coming is according to the working of Satan with all power and signs and false wonders,
>> D 2:10 and with all *deceit of unrighteousness* for those who perish because they did not receive the love of the truth that they be saved.
>>> E 2:11 And because of this God sends them a working of delusion that they believe a lie. 2:12a That they all might be judged not *believing the truth*

D' 2:12b but *delighting in unrighteousness.*
>F 2:13a But we ought to give thanks to God always concerning you, *brothers* beloved of the Lord,

E' 2:13b because God chose you from the beginning to salvation in sanctification of the spirit and *belief in the truth.* 2:14 Also he called you through our gospel to the obtaining of the glory of our Lord Jesus Christ.
>F' 2:15a So then, *brothers,* stand firm and hold the traditions which you were taught,

B' 2:15b whether by word or by *a letter of ours.*

A" 2:16 Now our *Lord Jesus Christ* himself and God our father who loved us and gave us eternal comfort and good hope through grace 2:17 encourage your hearts and strengthen them in every work and good word.

2 Thess 2:1–17 Structure Table

A 2:1—coming of the Lord Jesus Christ	A' 28b–9—manifestation of his coming . . . Lord Jesus	A" 2:16–17—Lord Jesus Christ
B 2:2—letter as if from us	B' 2:15b—a letter of ours	
C 2:3—the man of sin be revealed the son of destruction	C' 2:4–6—one opposing and exalting himself . . . he is to be revealed	C" 2:7–28a—only one is restraining . . . will be revealed the lawless one
D 2:10—deceit of unrighteousness	D' 2:12b—delighting in unrighteousness	
E 2:11–12a—believing the truth	E' 2:13–15a—belief in the truth	
F 2:13a—brothers	F' 2:15a—brothers	

Commentary

There are a number of parallel phrases in 2 Thess 2, but there is no apparent pattern. It is not Pauline in character. This structure bears a resemblance to the hybrid progressive structure of Rom 4, but there are important differences. First, the hemistiches and elements in 2 Thess 2 are not balanced as one would expect. The A and E stiches are relatively balanced, but the other stiches are not. Second, the progression from the C stich to the F stich is not based on single key words as they are in the progressive structures, Rom 4 and 2 Cor 2. It appears that a forger who knew Paul's penchant for parallelisms appropriated a letter from Paul, perhaps to congregants in Judea, retained the first literary unit, copying the introduction to 1 Thessalonians. Then he proceeded to contradict the message of 1 Thessalonians that Christ was coming to Earth soon, and he introduced the concept of an anti-Christ found no where else in Paul's letters. The use of the word "letter" in v. 2:2 looks as if the forger intended it to be near the end of the first literary unit in 2 Thessalonians just as "await his son from Heaven" at 1 Thess 1:10 is in the last hemistich of the first literary unit in 1 Thessalonians. Apparently he assumed no one would notice the first use of "letter" comes in the second literary unit. Verse 2:16 has been marked as the A" element but it lacks language about the coming of Christ that is found in the A and A' elements. Second Thessalonians 2 was not written by Paul.

2 Thessalonians 3

2 Thess 3:1–18

> A 3:1 Finally, brothers, pray for us that the word of the *Lord* may spread quickly and be glorified just as also with you. 3:2 And that we may be *delivered from unrighteous and evil men*. For not all have faith.
> A' 3:3 But the *Lord* is faithful who will strengthen you and *guard you from evil*.
>> B 3:4 And we are persuaded in the Lord concerning you that you both are doing and will do *the things that we command*.
>> B' 3:5 And the Lord direct your hearts into the love of God and into the steadfastness of Christ. 3:6a *Now we command you*, brothers, in the name of our Lord Jesus Christ
>>> C 3:6b that you avoid *every brother who walks disorderly* and not after the instruction which they received of us.
>>> C' 3:7 For yourselves know how you ought to imitate us. For we did not *behave disorderly* among you.
>>>> D 3:8 Neither *did we eat bread* from anyone without payment, but in labor and hardship, working night and day, that we might not burden any of you. 3:9 Not because we have not the right but to make ourselves an example to you that you should imitate us.
>> B" 3:10a For even when we were with you *this we commanded you*:
>>>> D' 3:10b If any will not work, neither *let him eat*.
>>> C" 3:11 For we hear of some that *walk among you disorderly*, that work not at all, but are busybodies.
>> B'" 3:12a Now such as *these we command* and encourage in the Lord Jesus Christ,
>>>> D" 3:12b that they work with quietness and *eat their own bread*.
>>>>> E 3:13 Now you, *brothers*, do not be weary in well-doing.
>>>>>> F 3:14 But if anyone does not obey *our word in this letter*, note this one that you have no association with him so that he may be ashamed.
>>>>> E' 3:15 But do not consider him as an enemy, but admonish him as a *brother*.
>>>>>> G 3:16a Now the *Lord of peace himself give you peace at all times in all ways*.
>>>>>> G' 3:16b The *Lord be with you all*.

F' 3:17 The greeting of me Paul with my own hand, which is the token in *every letter*. So I write.

G" 3:18 The grace of our *Lord Jesus Christ be with you all*.

2 Thess 3:1–18 Structure Table

A 3:1–2 – Lord . . . delivered from unrighteous and evil men		A' 3:3 – Lord . . . guard you from evil	
B 3:4 – things we command	B' 3:5–6a – we command you	B" 3:10a – this we commanded you	B'" 3:12a – these we command
C 3:6b – every brother who walks disorderly	C' 3:7 – behave disorderly among you	C" 3:11 – walk disorderly among you	
D 3:8–9 did we eat bread	D' 3:10b – let him eat	D" 3:12b – eat their own bread	
E 3:13 – brothers		E' 3:15 – brother	
F 3:14 – our word in this letter		F' 3:17 – every letter so I write	
G 3:16a – Lord of peace himself give you peace	G' 3:16b – Lord be with you	G" 3:18 – Lord Jesus Christ be with you all	

Commentary

Second Thessalonians 3 continues the same lack of a Pauline pattern that is found in 2 Thess 2. After the initial A, A', B, B', C, C' sequence that could be Pauline, the repeated phrases seem to be in an almost random order. There is no Pauline character and balance, although there are a number of repeated words and phrases. The forger seems to have used some ideas of not being a burden from 2 Cor 11 and excommunicating a wrong doer from 1 Cor 5. The forger also contrived to get the word "letter" in the text at v. 3:17, but it is un-Pauline in form coming in the middle of the benediction. Interestingly, v. 3:17 says that Paul greets the Thessalonians in his own hand which the token in every letter. However, it is only found in 1 Cor 16. Galatians 6 also mentions Paul writing large letters in his own hand, but that is shown to be an interpolation above. Second Thessalonians 3 was not written by Paul.

12

LETTER TO THE COLOSSIANS

COLOSSIANS IS ALMOST PAULINE. The forger did an admirable job copying Paul's literary style. The first eleven words that make up Col 1:1, plus the words of Col 1:2b appear to have been copied from 2 Corinthians 1:1a and 1:2a, much the same as 2 Thess 1:1 was copied from 1 Thess 1:1. Copying the introduction from 2 Corinthians is a mistake by the forger. No introductions of the undisputed letters are identical. Colossians 1:1–2 is an introduction that does not seem connected to the first literary unit found at Col 1:3–9b, an apparent chiastic structure. In Paul's undisputed letters the introductory sentence is always part of the first literary unit of the letter. It also appears that the author of Colossians copied the names of people from Philemon to give an air of authenticity to his letter.

Another un-Pauline characteristic of Colossians is the lack of chiastic structures. In the undisputed letters the fewest number of chiastic literary units is four, excepting Philemon which is one long chiastic literary unit. Colossians has one botched chiastic unit at Col 1:3–9. It could be said that Col 3:17–4:1 is a chiastic structure with a six-element B center stich, but it only has two stiches, too small a sample. Colossians does contain several Pauline type parallel structures. Parallel structures are more easily constructed because the repeated/matching phrases are closer. It appears that the writer of Colossians was familiar with Paul's parallelisms but did not quite grasp Paul's chiastic structures. The long sentences of Colossians with dependent clause following dependent clause, the lack of chiastic structures, and the simplicity of the ideas expressed rule out this letter having being written by Paul.

Colossians 1

Col 1:1–29

1:1 Paul, an apostle of Christ Jesus through the will of God, and Timothy, the brother,
1:2 To the saints and faithful brothers in Christ in Colossae. Grace to you and peace from God our father.

Part II | The Deutero-Pauline Letters

A 1:3 We give thanks to God the father of our Lord Jesus Christ, *praying always for you*,

  B 1:4 having *heard of your faith* in Christ Jesus, and of the love which you have toward all the saints,

    C 1:5 because of the hope which is laid up for you in the heavens, which *you heard of before in the word of the truth* of the gospel,

      D 1:6a which is come to you. Even as it is also in all the world *bearing fruit and increasing* as in you also,

    C' 1:6b since the day *you heard and knew the grace of God in truth*. 1:7 Even as you learned from Epaphras, our beloved fellow servant, who is a faithful minister of Christ on our behalf, 1:8 who also declared to us your love in the spirit.

  B' 1:9a For this cause *since the day we heard*

A' 1:9b *we also do not cease to pray and make request for you*, that you may be filled with the knowledge of his will in all spiritual wisdom and understanding,

      D' 1:10 to walk worthily of the Lord to all pleasing, *bearing fruit in every good work, and increasing* in the knowledge of God,

        E 1:11 *strengthened with all power*, according to the might of his glory, to all patience and longsuffering with joy, 1:12 giving thanks to the father, who enabled you to be partakers of the inheritance of the *saints in light*

        E' 1:13 who *delivered us from the authority of darkness* and translated us into the kingdom of his beloved son,

          F 1:14 in whom we have redemption, the forgiveness of our sins. 1:15a He is the image of the *invisible* God,

            G 1:15b the *firstborn of all creation*,

              H 1:16a for in him *all things were created* in the heavens and upon the Earth,

          F' 1:16b things visible and things *invisible*, whether thrones or dominions or rulers or authorities.

              H' 1:16c *All things have been created* through him and to him.

            G' 1:17 And he is before all things, and in him all things consist. 1:18 And he is the head of the body, the church, who is the beginning, the *firstborn from the dead*, so that in all things he might have the preeminence.

              I 1:19 For all fullness was pleased to dwell in him. 1:20a And through him to *reconcile all things to himself*, having made peace through the blood of his cross,

                J 1:20b through him, whether things upon the Earth, or *things in the heavens*.

              I' 1:21 And you, once being alienated and enemies in mind in evil deeds, 1:22 however now *he has reconciled in the body of his flesh* through death, to present you holy and without blemish and blameless before him.

J' 1:23a If indeed you continue in the faith, grounded and steadfast, and not moved away from the hope of the gospel which you heard, which was proclaimed in all *creation under Heaven*,

K 1:23b of which *I, Paul, was made a servant*. 1:24 Now I rejoice in my sufferings for your sake, and I am supplying that which is lacking of the tribulations of Christ in my flesh for his body's sake, which is the church,

K' 1:25 of which *I was made a servant*, according to the dispensation of God which was given me toward you to fulfill the word of God,

L 1:26 even the *mystery* which has been hidden from ages and generations. But *now has it been manifested to his saints*,

L' 1:27 to whom God desired to *make known* what is the riches of the glory of this *mystery among the Gentiles*,

M 1:28a which is Christ in you the hope of glory whom *we proclaim*,

N 1:28b *admonishing every man*

N' 1:28c and *teaching every man* in all wisdom,

N" 1:28d that we may *present every man perfect* in Christ;

M' 1:29 For this *I labor also, striving* according to his working, which works mightily in me.

Col 1:1-29 Structure Table

A 1:3—praying always for you	A' 1:9b—we also do not cease to pray and make request for you
B 1:4—heard of your faith	B' 1:9a—since the day we heard
C 1:5—you heard of before in the word of truth	C' 1:6b-8—you heard and knew the grace of God in truth
D 1:6a—bearing fruit and increasing	D' 1:10—bearing fruit in every good work and increasing
E 1:11-12—strengthened with all power . . . saints in light	E' 1:13—delivered us from the authority of darkness
F 1:14-15a—invisible	F' 1:16b—invisible
G 1:15b—firstborn of all creation	G' 1:17-18—firstborn from the dead
H 1:16a—all things have been created	H' 1:16c—all things have been created
I 1:19-20a—reconcile all things to himself	I' 1:21—he has reconciled in the body of his flesh

J 1:20b—things in Heaven		J' 1:23—creation under Heaven	
K 1:23b–24—I Paul was made a servant		K' 1:25—I was made a servant	
L 1:26—mystery ... now it has been manifested to his saints		L' 1:27—mystery among the Gentiles ... make known	
M 1:28a—we proclaim		M' 1:29—I labor also striving	
N 1:28b—admonishing every man	N' 1:28c—teaching every man		N" 1:28d—present every man perfect

Commentary

The chiastic structure at Col 1:3–9 has an uncharacteristic single element as the center stich at 1:6a, but the wording there "bearing fruit and increasing" is parallel to another element at v. 1:10. In addition, the literary unit did not end with the A' element as it would have if Paul had written it. The repetition of "bearing fruit and increasing" at v. 1:10 makes it clear that the literary unit has not ended. One definite attribute of Paul's writing is that there are clear endings and beginnings to his literary units. This attribute is not found in Colossians mainly because of its long sentences. Investigation was made into whether v. 1:10 is grossly out of order and should follow 1:6a, making it a proper Pauline chiastic structure, but if 1:10 is placed immediately after 1:6a the wording does not make sense. Investigation was also made into whether 1:6a should follow 1:9 and immediately precede 1:10, and that did not make sense either. Therefore, while it appears that there is a chiastic literary unit near the beginning of Colossians, close analysis shows that it is not Pauline in character.

There are fourteen stiches in this literary unit, each stich having two hemistiches except the N stich that has three elements. If Paul had written this literary unit it would have been two separate units with the second "bearing fruit and increasing" coming immediately after v. 1:6a and the sentence would have ended at the close of the A' hemistich at 1:9b. Within the botched chiastic structure the first anomaly is that vv. 1:1–2 are not part of the structure. The A stich is imbalanced with thirteen words in the A hemistich and twenty words in the A' hemistich. Next, there is an imbalance in the B stich with sixteen words in the B hemistich and eight words in the B' hemistich. The C stich is also out of balance with eighteen words in the C hemistich and thirty-seven words in the C' hemistich. Every stich in the chiastic structure is defective.

Following the close of the D stich is a balanced, parallel E stich. However, the F, G, and H stiches are anomalous. There is an extreme imbalance in the G stich and the H' hemistich would have followed the G' hemistich if Paul had written this literary unit. The rest of the literary unit has a reasonable Pauline appearance except the K stich is not balanced with thirty-two words in the K hemistich and eighteen words in the K' hemistich. Colossians 1:1–29 does not have the characteristics of a Pauline chiastic, parallel, or hybrid structure. The entirety of Col 1 appears to be written by a forger who had extensive appreciation of Paul's use of parallelisms and even an appreciation of Paul's chiastic structures, but he did not have Paul's talent for constructing clear literary units with chiastic or parallel structures.

Colossians 2

Col 2:1–19

A 2:1 For I would have you know how great a struggle I am having for you and for those at Laodicea and for as many as have not seen *my face* in the flesh,

A' 2:2a that *their hearts* may be comforted, they being knit together in love, and to all riches of the full assurance of understanding,

  B 2:2b that they may know the *mystery of God*, even Christ,

  B' 2:3 in whom are all the treasures of wisdom and *hidden knowledge*.

    C 2:4 This I say, *that no one may delude you with persuasiveness of speech.*

      D 2:5 For though I am absent in the flesh yet am I with you in the spirit, enjoying and beholding your order and the steadfastness of your *faith in Christ*.

      D' 2:6 As therefore you received *Christ Jesus the Lord* so walk in him, 2:7 rooted and built up in him, and established in your *faith*, even as you were taught, abounding in thanksgiving.

    C' 2:8 Take heed lest there shall *anyone who seduces you through his philosophy and vain deceit*, after the tradition of men, after the rudiments of the world, and not after Christ.

      E 2:9 For in him dwells all the *fullness* of the Godhead bodily,

      E' 2:10 and in him you are made *full*, who is the head of all principality and power.

        F 2:11a In whom you were also *circumcised* with a *circumcision* not made with hands,

        F' 2:11b in the putting off of the body of the flesh, in the *circumcision* of Christ,

          G 2:12 *having been buried with him in baptism*, wherein you were also raised with him through faith in the working of God, who raised him from the dead.

          G' 2:13 And you, *being dead through your trespasses* and the uncircumcision of your flesh, he made alive together with him, having forgiven us all our trespasses;

            H 2:14 *having blotted out the bond written* in ordinances that was against us, which was contrary to us. And he has taken it out that way nailing it to the cross,

            H' 2:15 *having despoiled the principalities* and the powers, he made a show of them openly triumphing over them in it.

I 2:16 *Let no man therefore judge you in meat*, or in drink, or in respect of a feast day or a new moon or a Sabbath day, 2:17 which are a shadow of the things to come, but the body is Christ's.

I' 2:18 *Let no man rob you of your prize* by a voluntary humility and worshipping of the angels, dwelling in the things which he has seen, vainly puffed up by his fleshly mind,

J 2:19a and not holding fast the head, from whom *all the body*, being supplied and knit together

J' 2:19b through the *joints and bands*, increasing with the increase of God.

Col 2:1–19 Parallel Structure Table

A 2:1—my face	A' 2:2a—their hearts
B 2:2b—mystery of God	B' 2:3—hidden knowledge
C 2:4—that no one may delude you with persuasiveness of speech	C' 2:8—anyone who seduces you through his philosophy and vain deceit
D 2:5—faith in Christ	D' 2:6–7—faith . . . Christ Jesus the Lord
E 2:9—fullness	E' 2:10—full
F 2:11a—circumcised . . . circumcision	F' 2:11b—circumcision
G 2:12—having been buried with him in baptism	G' 2:13—being dead through your trespasses
H 2:14—having blotted out the bond written	H' 2:15—having despoiled the principalities
I 2:16–17—Let no man therefore judge you in meat	I' 2:18—Let no man rob you of your prize
J 2:19a—all the body	J' 2:19b—joints and bands

Commentary

Colossians 2:1–19 is a Pauline literary unit with a parallel structure in the preferred Pauline format of A, A,' B, B,' C, C' if it can be assumed that v. 2:8 is out of original order and should follow v. 2:4. If that is done, the wording does make sense and may be the original version. There is an imbalance in the C stich with the C hemistich containing eight words and the C' hemistich containing twenty-seven. It is not inconceivable that Paul would have had a C, D, D,' C' chiastic sequence in the middle of a basically parallel literary unit. In fact, there are two sequences like this in 2 Cor 2 and six such sequences in 2 Cor 8. However, one such sequence appears to be a mistake and not a deliberate pattern.

While Colossians 1 beginning with 1:3 seems to be one long continuous un-Pauline sentence, Colossians 2 contains much shorter sentences. They seem to be somewhat longer than Paul's sentences found in the undisputed letters, but the first literary unit of Colossians 2 could conceivably have been written by Paul especially if v. 2:8 is out of order as the result of a scribal mistake. However, since vv. 1:10 and 4:1 also appear to be out of order, it is more probable that a forger did not quite get Paul's literary style correct rather than incompetent scribal copying.

Col 2:20–3:1a

A 2:20 *If you died with Christ* away from the principles of the world why, as though living in the world, do you subject yourselves to ordinances:
 B 2:21a *Do not handle,*
 B' 2:21b *nor taste,*
 B" 2:21c *nor touch*
  C 2:22 (*all which things are to perish* with the using) according to the precepts and doctrines of men?
  C' 2:23a *Which things have indeed an appearance of wisdom* in self imposed worship, and humility, and severity to the body,
A 2:23b but are not of any value against the indulgence of the flesh. 3:1a *If then you were raised with Christ,*

Col 2:20–3:1a Parallel Structure Table

A 2:20—If you died with Christ	A' 2:23b–3:1a—If then you were raised with Christ	
B 2:21a—Do not handle	B' 2:21b—nor taste	B" 2:21c—nor touch
C 2:22—all which things are to perish	C' 2:23a—Which things have indeed an appearance of wisdom	

Commentary

Colossians 2:20–3:1a is a strange literary unit. At first glance it appears to be a Pauline parallel structure defined by an inclusio with the closing A' hemistich at v. 3:1a, but the literary unit does not end there. The sentence continues and the literary unit continues, ending at v. 3:16 with vv. 3:1b–16 having a Pauline parallel structure. It is clear that v. 3:1a is thematically connected to the parallel unit at vv. 3:1b–16, but it seems to be the closing of the prior literary unit from a structural viewpoint. As stated previously, Paul had clear beginnings and endings to his literary units. There is nothing like this fuzzy ending of a literary unit in any of the undisputed letters. This unit has hallmarks of a Pauline literary unit, except for the botched ending created by the forger's penchant for long sentences.

Colossians 3

Col 3:1b–16

A 3:1b seek the *things that are above* where Christ is seated on the right hand of God.
A' 3:2 Set your mind on the *things that are above*, not on the things that are on the Earth.
　B 3:3 For you died, and *your life is hidden with Christ in God*.
　B' 3:4 When *Christ, our life, will be revealed* then you will also be revealed with him in glory.
　　C 3:5 Therefore put to death your members which are upon the Earth: *fornication, uncleanness, passion, evil desire, and covetousness, which is idolatry*, 3:6 for which things' sake comes the wrath of God upon the sons of disobedience,
　　C' 3:7 wherein you also once walked, when you lived in these things. 3:8 But now also put them all away: *anger, wrath, malice, railing, shameful speaking out of your mouth*.
　　　D 3:9 Do not lie one to another. Seeing that you have *put off the old man* with his doings
　　　D' 3:10 and have *put on the new man*, that is being renewed to knowledge after the image of him that created him.
　　　　E 3:11 Where there cannot be *Greek and Jew*, circumcision and uncircumcision, *barbarian, Scythian, bondman, freeman*, but Christ is all and in all.
　　　　E' 3:12 Put on therefore as God's elect, *holy and beloved*, a heart of *compassion, kindness, lowliness, meekness, longsuffering*. 3:13 Forbearing one another, and forgiving each other, if any man have a complaint against any, even as the Lord forgave you, so also do you.
　　　　　F 3:14 And above all these things love, which is the bond of perfection. 3:15 And *let the peace of Christ rule in your hearts*, to which also you were called in one body, and be thankful.
　　　　　F' 3:16 *Let the word of Christ dwell in you* richly, in all wisdom teaching and admonishing one another with psalms, hymns, spiritual songs, singing to God with *grace in your hearts*.

Col 3:1b–16 Parallel Structure Table

A 3:1b—things that are above	A' 3:2—things that are above
B 3:3—your life is hidden with Christ in God	B' 3:4—Christ, our life, will be revealed

C 3:5-6—fornication, uncleanness, passion, evil desire, and covetousness, which is idolatry	C' 3:7-8—anger, wrath, malice, railing, shameful speaking out of your mouth
D 3:9—put off the old man	D' 3:10—put on the new man
E 3:11—Greek and Jew .. barbarian, Scythian, bondman, freeman	E' 3:12-13—holy and beloved ... compassion, kindness, lowliness, meekness, longsuffering
H 3:14-15—let the peace of Christ rule in your hearts	H' 3:16—Let the word of Christ dwell in you grace in your hearts

Commentary

Except for the uncharacteristic beginning of this literary unit discussed in the previous section, it appears that Paul could have written it. There is one fairly long sentence in vv. 3:5-7, but otherwise the sentences are of a reasonable Pauline length. The E stich has some problems in not being quite parallel enough to be Pauline. It does look like the forger took the "old man" idea from Rom 6:6 and used it to make a parallelism in the D stich.

Col 3:17-4:1

A 3:17 And *whatever you do* in word or in deed all in the name of the *Lord Jesus*, giving thanks to God the father through him.
   B 3:18 *Wives*, be in subjection to your husbands as is fitting in the Lord.
   B' 3:19 *Husbands*, love your wives and do not be bitter against them.
   B" 3:20 *Children*, obey your parents in all things for this is well-pleasing in the Lord.
   B'" 3:21 *Fathers*, do not provoke your children so that they do not become discouraged.
   B"" 3:22 *Slaves*, in all things obey those who are your masters according to the flesh, not only when being watched, as men pleasers, but in singleness of heart, fearing the Lord.
   *B""' 4:1 *Masters*, render to your servants that which is just and equal, knowing that you also have a master in Heaven.
*A' 3:23 *Whatever you do*, work heartily, as to the Lord, and not to men; 3:24 knowing that from the Lord you will receive the recompense of the inheritance. You serve the *Lord Christ*. 3:25 For he who does wrong will be repaid for the wrong that he has done. And there is no favoritism.

Col 3:17-4:1 Chiastic Structure Table

A 3:17 whatever you do ... Lord Jesus			A' 3:23-25 whatever you do ... Lord Christ		
B 3:18—Wives	B' 3:19 —Husbands	B" 3:20 —Children	B'" 3:21—Fathers	B"" 3:22—Slaves	B""" 4:1 —Masters

Commentary

This is close to being a Pauline literary unit if it can be assumed v. 4:1 should fall in between vv. 3:22 and 23. If that is the result of a scribal error, it is a fairly gross error. There is a similar sequence at Eph 5:22–6:9 that is much wordier but does not have the admonition to masters out of order. It looks like the author of Ephesians copied Colossians to a great extent, and the fact that Eph 6:9 is not out of order may be evidence that originally Col 4:1 was in the proper order between Col 3:22 and 23. The A stich is not balanced with the A hemistich containing twenty-two words and the A' hemistich containing thirty-seven words, plus the A' hemistich contains several multisyllabic words, exacerbating the imbalance. It is also un-Pauline to have only two stiches with the B stich containing six elements. The chiastic literary unit at 1 Thess 5:15–22 has three stiches with the center C stich containing six elements, but this is unusual.

Colossians 4

Col 4:2–18

    A 4:2 *Continue steadfastly in prayer* watching therein with thanksgiving.
    A' 4:3 *At the same time praying for us* also that God may open to us a door for the word, to speak the mystery of Christ for which I am also in bonds,
        B 4:4 that I may make it manifest *as I ought to speak.* 4:5 Walk in wisdom toward those who are outside using the time wisely.
        B' 4:6 *Let your speech be always with grace* seasoned with salt that you may know how you ought to answer each one.
            C 4:7 *Tychicus will make known to you* all my affairs, the *beloved brother and faithful minister* and fellow servant in the Lord, 4:8 whom I have sent you for this very purpose that you may know our state and that he may comfort your hearts,
            C' 4:9 together with *Onesimus,* the *faithful and beloved brother,* who is one of you. They shall *make known to you* all things that are done here.
                D 4:10 *Aristarchus* my fellow prisoner *greets you,* and Mark, the cousin of Barnabas (touching whom you received commandments, if he come to you receive him), 4:11 and Jesus who is called Justus who are of the circumcision.

These only are my fellow workers to the kingdom of God, men that have been a comfort to me.

D' 4:12 *Epaphras* who is one of you, a servant of Christ Jesus, *greets you*, always striving for you in his prayers that you may stand perfect and fully assured in all the will of God.

D" 4:13 For I bear him witness that he has much labor for you and for them in Laodicea, and for them in Hierapolis. 4:14 Luke, the beloved physician, and *Demas greet you*.

E 4:15 Greet the brothers that are in *Laodicea*, and Nymphas, and the *church that is in her house*. 4:16a And when this *letter has been read among you*,

E' 4:16b cause that it be read also in the *church of the Laodiceans*; and that *you also read the letter* from Laodicea. 4:17 And say to Archippus, "Take heed to the ministry which you have received in the Lord, that you fulfill it." 4:18 The salutation of Paul in my own hand. Remember my bonds. Grace be with you.

Col 4:2–18 Parallel Structure Table

A 4:2—Continue steadfastly in prayer	A' 4:3—At the same time praying for us	
B 4:4–5—as I ought to speak	B' 4:6—Let your speech be always with grace	
C 4:7–8—Tychicus will make known to you . . . beloved brother and faithful minister	C' 4:9—Onesimus, the faithful and beloved brother . . . make known to you	
D 4:10–11—Aristarchus . . . greets you	D' 4:12—Epaphras . . . greets you	4:13–14—Demas greet you
E 4:15–16a—Laodicea . . . church that is in her house . . . epistle has been read among you	E' 4:16b–18—church of the Laodiceans . . . you also read the epistle	

Commentary

Colossians 4 is also a Pauline type literary unit. It is a straightforward parallel structure with two elements in each stich except for the three-element D stich. The curious thing about Col 4 is the names that are mentioned therein. Most of the names mentioned happen to be the exact same names that are mentioned in the last few verses of Philemon: Onesimus, Aristarchus, Mark, Epaphras, Luke, and Demas. Tychicus is the only person mentioned in Col 4 that is not mentioned in Phlm 1:22–25. Archippus is mentioned in Col 4 and is also mentioned in Phlm 1:2, rather than the closing. The other letters with persons' names mentioned at the end of the letter in greetings to the addressee congregation are Romans and 1 Corinthians. Neither of those has names in common with Colossians and Philemon. Another curious coincidence between

Colossians and Philemon is the phrase "church that is in her (your) house" (*kat' oikon autēs [sou] ekklēsian*). This phrase does not appear in any other letter of Paul. Its appearance in Philemon is understandable since the letter is addressed to Paul's friend, but it seems out of place in Colossians, which is addressed, to a separate congregation. The greeting section of Col 4:10–18 is too wordy for Paul. The wordy greeting section of Rom 16:17–19 was shown to be an interpolation.

13

Letter To The Ephesians

EPHESIANS CONTAINS A FEW sections that appear to mimic Paul's style, but they are not quite right. There are numerous large sections with no parallelisms or repetitions. Ephesians was not written by Paul. While it does contain several parallel structures, it only has two chiastic structures both of which are short. One is seven verses long, and the other is four verses long. The average length of chiastic structures in the undisputed letters is fourteen verses. It looks like the writer of Ephesians was aware of the literary structures Paul created in his undisputed letters and attempted to copy his style by using repeated/parallel words and phrases. However, the passages containing no repeated phrases get longer toward the end of the letter. Perhaps the author suffered from parallelism fatigue. That is, he got tired of expending the effort of trying to imitate Paul's literary style.

The author of Ephesians appears to have been copying and rewording Colossians. Alternatively, perhaps both letters were written by the same author. If that is the case, then perhaps Ephesians was his first attempt at imitating Paul's style, and he did a better job with Colossians, his second attempt.

As with Colossians, Ephesians contains extraordinarily long sentences, expressing simple ideas. Paul's undisputed letters contain complicated ideas expressed in short sentences. It seems as if the writer of Ephesians realized that Paul's ideas were complex and thought that if he wrote long sentences, the reader would think his ideas were complex also. It looks as if the author is attempting to make simple ideas appear complex.

The fact that there are only two short chiastic structures in six chapters, the lack of any chiastic structures more than seven verses, the five long passages without any repeated/parallel phrases, the unbalanced stiches in the chiastic and parallel structures that are present, the excessive wordiness within the chiastic and parallel structures, and the long sentences of Ephesians marks the letter as not being from the had of Paul. However, the author seems to have attempted to copy Paul's style.

PART II | THE DEUTERO-PAULINE LETTERS

Ephesians 1

Eph 1:1–3

  A 1:1a Paul, an apostle of *Christ Jesus* through the will of God,
  A' 1:1b to the saints being in Ephesus and the faithful in *Christ Jesus*.
    B 1:2 Grace to you and peace from *God our father* and the *Lord Jesus Christ*.
    B' 1:3 Blessed be the *God and father* of our *Lord Jesus Christ* who has blessed us with every spiritual blessing in the heavenly realms in Christ.

Eph 1:1–3 Parallel Structure Table

A 1:1a – Christ Jesus	A' 1:1b – Christ Jesus
B 1:2 – God our father ... Lord Jesus Christ	B' 1:3 – God and father ... Lord Jesus Christ

Commentary

The first section, vv. 1:1–3, could be a Pauline literary unit with an A, A,' B, B' format. However, no first literary unit of any of the undisputed letters is this short. The shortest first literary units in the undisputed letters are Romans with a six-verse chiastic structure and 1 Thessalonians with a ten-verse parallel structure. It appears that the writer of Ephesians copied the introduction to 2 Corinthians, with the exception that the first literary unit of 2 Corinthians has a parallel structure with an inclusio so that the second "Christ" in the A' hemistich occurs at the end of the unit. The writer of Ephesians also omitted the comment about Timothy. Among the undisputed letters of Paul no introduction is this similar to another introduction. The introduction of Colossians also seems to be copied from 2 Corinthians, leaving in the comment about Timothy. This is one of the reasons Ephesians seems to be a poor copy of Colossians.

    In the initial literary units of the undisputed letters "Jesus Christ" and "God" are typically parallel terms in the structure, but none of the undisputed letters have only those two parallel terms. It appears to be an accidental structure as the result of copying 2 Cor 1:1–3.

Eph 1:4–11

  A 1:4 Even as he chose us in him before the foundation of the world that we should be holy and without blemish before him in love. 1:5a Having *foreordained* us to adoption as sons through Jesus Christ to himself,
    B 1:5b *according to the good pleasure of his will,*

C 1:6 to the praise of the *glory of his grace*, which he freely bestowed on us in the beloved,

C' 1:7 in whom we have our redemption through his blood, the forgiveness of our trespasses, according to the *riches of his grace*,

B' 1:8 which he made to abound toward us in all wisdom and prudence, 1:9 making known to us the mystery *of his will, according to his good pleasure* which he purposed in him 1:10 to a dispensation of the fullness of the times to sum up all things in Christ, the things in the heavens, and the things upon the Earth in him,

A' 1:11 in whom also we were made a heritage, having been *foreordained* according to the purpose of him who works all things after the counsel of his will,

Eph 1:4-11 Chiastic Structure Table

A 1:4-5a—foreordained	A' 1:11 – foreordained
B 1:5b – according to the good pleasure of his will	B' 1:8-10 – of his will according to his good pleasure
C 1:6 – glory of his grace	C' 1:7 riches of his grace

Commentary

This section of Ephesians also has a Pauline flavor being a chiastic structure containing three stiches. In addition, in contrast to the attempted chiastic structure in Col 1, this chiastic structure has a two-hemistich center stich. On the other hand, there seems to be too much text in the A, B,' and C' hemistiches for Paul to have written it. The writer of Ephesians is much wordier than Paul. The B stich is grossly out of balance with the B' hemistich, vv. 1:8-10 being much longer than the B hemistich, v. 1:5b. There does not seem to be an interpolation into the B' hemistich since vv. 1:5b-14 is one long sentence. In the undisputed letters the repetitions and parallelisms are much more dense than those presented in Ephesians as a whole beginning with this section. From the basic design of the chiastic structure this section appears to be a Pauline literary unit; however, the sentence does not end with the conclusion of the A' stich as one would expect if Paul had written it. Just like the chiastic sub-structure found at Col 1:3-9, it continues into the next section.

Eph 1:12-14

A 1:12 to the end that we should be to the *praise of his glory*, we who had before hoped in Christ. 1:13a In whom you also, having heard the word of the truth, the gospel of your salvation,

A' 1:13b in whom, having also believed, you were sealed with the spirit of holy promise, 1:14 which is the guarantee of our inheritance, to the redemption of the possession, to the *praise of his glory*.

Eph 1:12–14 Parallel Structure Table

| A 1:12–13a—praise of his glory | A' 1:13b–14—praise of his glory |

Commentary

This section of Eph 1 is an extremely long one-stich structure having only one parallelism. It is almost as if this parallel stich is intended to be part of the previous chiastic structure, especially since it is part of the same sentence. This writer was attempting to copy Paul's style, but his repetitions/parallelisms lack the symmetry of the undisputed letters. There is too much text to only contain two three or four word parallel phrases. Paul's parallelisms are much more dense than that of the author of Ephesians.

Eph 1:15–23

1:15 For this cause I also, having heard of the faith in the Lord Jesus which is among you, and the love that you show toward all the saints, 1:16 do not cease to give thanks for you making mention of you in my prayers. 1:17 That the God of our Lord Jesus Christ, the father of glory, may give to you a spirit of wisdom and revelation in the knowledge of him, 1:18 having the eyes of your heart enlightened, that you may know what is the hope of his calling, what are the riches of the glory of his inheritance in the saints, 1:19 and what is the exceeding greatness of his power toward us who believe, according to that working of the strength of his might 1:20 which he worked in Christ, having raised him from the dead, and having set him at his right hand in the heavenly realms, 1:21 far above all principality, and authority, and power, and dominion, and every name that is named, not only in this age, but also in the coming one. 1:22 And he put all things under his feet, and gave him to be head over all things to the church, 1:23 which is his body, the fullness of him that fills all in all.

Commentary

This section of Eph 1 without any parallelisms cannot have been written by Paul, even though v. 1:22 copies 1 Cor 15:27. Perhaps the writer thought that if he copied an idea from 1 Corinthians he would be spared the work of creating parallelisms. Verses

1:15–1:21 are only one sentence. Rhetorical analysis concludes that Paul would never have written such a long sentence containing that many words without a parallelism.

Ephesians 2

Eph 2:1–9

> A 2:1 And you being *dead through your trespasses* and sins 2:2 in which you once walked according to the age of this world, according to the ruler of the powers of the air, of the spirit that now works in the sons of disobedience;
> A' 2:3 among whom we also all once lived in the lust of our flesh, doing the desires of the flesh and of the mind, and were by nature children of wrath even as the rest. 2:4 But God, being rich in mercy, for his great love with which he loved us, 2:5a even when we were *dead through our trespasses*,
>> B 2:5b made us alive together with *Christ* (*by grace you are saved*), 2:6 and raised us up with him, and seated us with him in the heavenly realms in *Christ Jesus*
>> B' 2:7 so that in the ages to come he might show the exceeding riches of his grace in kindness toward us in *Christ Jesus*. 2:8 For *by grace you are saved through faith*, and that not of yourselves. It is the gift of God, 2:9 not of works, that no man should boast.

Eph 2:1–9 Parallel Structure Table

A 2:1–2—dead through your trespasses	A' 2:3–5a—dead through your trespasses
B 2:5b–6—Christ ... by grace you are saved ... Christ Jesus	B' 2:7–9—by grace you are saved ... Christ Jesus

Commentary

Ephesians 2 begins with a parallel structure of two stiches, each of which has two hemistiches. This is similar to Eph 1:12–14. Once again the structure is superficially Pauline, in that it contains repeated phrases, but there is too much text for too few repetitions/parallelisms. The A stich, vv. 2:1–5a, contains eighty-eight words with only one parallelism. On the plus side, the ending of the literary unit coincides with the end of a sentence.

Eph 2:10–13

> A 2:10 For we are his workmanship, created in *Christ Jesus* for good works, that God prepared before hand so that we should walk in them.

PART II | THE DEUTERO-PAULINE LETTERS

   B 2:11a Therefore remember that once you, the *Gentiles*
      C 2:11b in the *flesh*,
         D 2:11c who are called *uncircumcision*
         D' 2:11d by those who are called *circumcision*,
      C' 2:11e in the *flesh* made by hands.
   B' 2:12a That you were at that time separate from Christ, alienated from the community of Israel and *strangers* to the covenants of the promise,
  A' 2:12b having no hope and without God in the world. 2:13 But now in *Christ Jesus* you that once were far off are made near in the blood of *Christ*.

Eph 2:10-13 Chiastic Structure Table

A 2:10—Christ Jesus	A' 2:12b-13—Christ Jesus . . . Christ
B 2:11a—Gentiles	B' 2:12a—strangers
C 2:11b—flesh	C' 2:11e—flesh
D 2:11c—uncircumcision	D' 2:11d—circumcision

Commentary

Ephesians 2:10–13 is a short four-stich chiastic structure containing only four verses that has Pauline characteristics. The B stich is a bit unbalanced with the B' hemistich having too much text. It does have the Pauline characteristic of a definite beginning and a definite ending. Every repetition in this literary unit is of one word only, Christ Jesus being considered one word. The writer of Ephesians apparently recognized Paul's love for chiasm, but was unwilling to put the work necessary into the creation of long chiastic units characteristic to Paul's writing. In Galatians, Philippians and 1 Thessalonians, letters of comparable size to Colossians and Ephesians, seventeen, or sixty-three percent, of the literary units have chiastic structures. In Colossians and Ephesians combined there are only three short chiastic structures.

Eph 2:14-22

  A 2:14 For he is our peace, having made both one and having broken down the middle wall of partition, 2:15 having *abolished in his flesh the enmity*, the law of commandments in ordinances; so that he might create in himself of the two one new man, making peace.
  A' 2:16 And might reconcile them both in one body to God through the cross, having *slain the enmity* thereby.
    B 2:17a And he came and proclaimed the gospel. *Peace to you who are far away*,

B' 2:17b and *peace to those who are near.*

C 2:18 For through him we both have access in *one spirit to the father.* 2:19 So then you are no longer strangers and sojourners, but you are fellow citizens with the saints, and of the household of God,

C' 2:20 having been built upon the foundation of the apostles and prophets, Christ Jesus himself being the chief corner stone, B' 2:21 in whom the whole building being framed together grows into a holy temple in the Lord, 2:22 in whom you also are built together for a habitation of *God in the spirit.*

Eph 2:14-22 Parallel Structure Table

A 2:14-15—abolished in his flesh the enmity	A' 2:16—slain in the enmity
B 2:17—a peace to you who are far away	B' 2:17b—peace to those who are near
C 2:19-19—one spirit to the father	C' 2:20-22—God in the spirit

Commentary

The last structure of Eph 2 is a three-stich parallel structure of nine verses. As usual in Ephesians there are too few parallelisms for so many words to be a Pauline creation. In this structure vv. 2:20-22 appear to be a restatement of 1 Cor 3:10-11. It appears that the writer is trying to appear to be Pauline by using ideas from other letters.

Ephesians 3

Eph 3:1-9

A 3:1 For this cause, I, Paul, the prisoner of Christ Jesus on behalf of you *Gentiles*,
   B 3:2 if indeed you have heard of the steward of that *grace* of God which was given me toward you,
      C 3:3 that by revelation was made *known to me the mystery*, as I wrote before in brief,
      C' 3:4 whereby when you read you can perceive *my understanding in the mystery* of Christ,
A' 3:5 which in other generations was not made known to the sons of men, as it has now been revealed to his holy apostles and prophets in the spirit. 3:6 That the *Gentiles* are joint heirs, and joint members of the body, and joint partakers of the promise in Christ Jesus through the gospel,
   B' 3:7 whereof I became a servant, according to the gift of that *grace* of God which was given me according to the working of his power.

B" 3:8a To me, the very least of all saints, this *grace* was given

A" 3:8b to preach to the *Gentiles* the unsearchable riches of Christ.

   C" 3:9 And to enlighten all to what is the *steward of the mystery* which has been hidden from the ages in God who created all things,

Eph 3:1–9 Parallel Structure Table

A 3:1—Gentiles	A' 3:5–6—Gentiles	A" 3:8b—Gentiles
B 3:2—steward of that grace	B' 3:7—gift of that grace	B" 3:8a—grace was given
C 3:3—known to me the mystery	C' 3:4—my understanding in the mystery	C" 3:9—steward of the mystery

Commentary

The first section of Eph 3, vv. 1–9, has three words and phrases that are each used three times in a random sort of pattern, "Gentiles," a phrase containing the word "grace," and a phrase containing the word "mystery." The phrases about "mystery" seem to echo Rom 16:25–26 and 1 Cor 2:7. It is not clear that the writer intended this section to end with the end of v. 3:9 since the sentence continues into v. 3:10 which appears to begin a new section because the repeated words are different. The lack of a definite demarcation between literary units exposes its un-Pauline nature. The mention of being a prisoner of Christ Jesus seems to be copying Plmn 1:1.

Eph 3:10–21

A 3:10 to the intent that now to the principalities and the powers in the heavenly places might be made known through the church the manifold wisdom of *God,*

   B 3:11 according to the eternal purpose which he purposed in *Christ Jesus* our Lord,

     C 3:12 in whom we have boldness and access in confidence through our *faith* in him. 3:13 Therefore I ask that you may not faint at my tribulations for you, which are your glory.

A' 3:14 For this cause I bow my knees to the *father,* 3:15 from whom every family in Heaven and on Earth is named, 3:16 that he would grant you according to the riches of his glory that you may be strengthened with power through his spirit in the inward man.

   B' 3:17a That *Christ* may dwell in your hearts

C' 3:17b through *faith*. To the end that you, being rooted and grounded in love, 3:18 may be strong to apprehend with all the saints what is the breadth and length and height and depth,

B" 3:19a and to know the love of *Christ* which passes knowledge.

A" 3:19b That you may be filled to all the fullness of *God*. 3:20 Now to him that is able to do exceeding abundantly above all that we ask or think, according to the power that works in us,

B"' 3:21 to him be the glory in the church and in *Christ Jesus* to all generations for ever and ever. Amen.

Eph 3:10-21 Parallel Structure Table

A 3:10—God		A' 3:14-16—father	A" 3:19b-20—God
B 3:11—Christ Jesus	B' 3:17a —Christ	B" 3:19a—Christ	B"' 3:21—Christ Jesus
C 3:12-13—faith		C' 3:17b—faith	

Commentary

The second half of Eph 3 is similar to the first half, but the repeated words, "God," "faith," and "Christ," are not used the same number of times as they are in the first half. This section starts out in an A, B, C, A,' B,' C' format and then changes the pattern. It is difficult to tell whether the writer intended the two halves to be connected or not. The second half structure begins in the middle of a sentence. There is no definite demarcation between the literary units as would be found in Paul's writing. The repetitions in this section consist of only one word, not typically Pauline. The large amount of text between repeated words also marks it an not being written by Paul.

Ephesians 4

Eph 4:1-3

4:1 I therefore, the prisoner in the Lord, beseech you to walk worthily of the calling wherewith you were called, 4:2 with all lowliness and meekness, with longsuffering, forbearing one another in love; 4:3 giving diligence to keep the unity of the spirit in the bond of peace.

Commentary

This three-verse section contains no parallels or repeated phrases. It does not seem to be connected to the prior structure or the following structure. There are a few short transitional structures in the undisputed letters such as 1 Cor 6:7b–8 and 1 Cor 7:9, but there were parallelisms in those transitional units. Paul did not write this section.

Eph 4:4-16

> A 4:4 *One body* and *one spirit*, even as also you were called in *one hope* of your calling.
> A' 4:5 *One Lord, one faith, one baptism,* 4:6 one God and father of all, who is over all, and through all, and in all.
>> B 4:7 But to each one of us was the grace given according to the measure of the gift of Christ. 4:8 Wherefore he says, when he *ascended* on high, he led captivity captive, and gave gifts to men.
>> B' 4:9 Now this, he *ascended,* what is it but that he also *descended* into the lower parts of the Earth?
>> B" 4:10 He that *descended* is the same also that *ascended* far above all the heavens that he might fill all things.
>>> C 4:11 And he gave some apostles. and some prophets, and some evangelists, and some pastors and teachers, 4:12 for the perfecting of the saints to the work of ministering to the building up of the *body of Christ*.
>>> C' 4:13 Till we all attain to the unity of the faith and of the knowledge of the son of God to a full grown man, to the measure of the stature of the *fullness of Christ*. 4:14 That we may be no longer children, tossed to and fro and carried about with every wind of doctrine by the sleight of men in craftiness after the wiles of error.
>>> C" 4:15 But speaking truth in love we may grow up in all things into him *who is the head, Christ*.
>>>> D 4:16a From whom *all the body* fitly framed and knit together through that which every joint supplies, according to the working in measure of each several part
>>>> D' 4:16b makes the *increase of the body* to the building up of itself in love.

Eph 4:4-16 Parallel Structure Table

A 4:4—one body . . . one spirit . . . one hope	A' 4:5—one Lord . . . one faith . . . one baptism

B 4:7–8—ascended	B' 4:9—ascended ... descended	B" 4:10—ascended ... descended
C 4:11–12—body of Christ	C' 4:13–14—fullness of Christ	C" 4:15—who is the head Christ
D 4:16a—all the body	D' 4:16b—increase of the body	

Commentary

This section of Eph 4 has a structure that is parallel in an A, A,' B, B,' B," C, C,' C," D, D' format. It does have a Pauline symmetry, but there is an excessive amount of text between the parallelisms. Verses 4:9–10 seem to have been inspired by Rom 10:6–7 that rhetorical analysis identified as an interpolation. Then vv. 4:11–12 seem to have been inspired by 1 Cor 12:28, but the author has added evangelists (*euangelistas*) and pastors (*poimenas*) to Paul's list of servants of the church. If by "evangelists" the writer is referring to the authors of the gospels, this may be a clue that Ephesians was written long after Paul's death. It seems to have been written after the interpolation was made into Rom 10.

Eph 4:17–21

4:17 This I say therefore and testify in the Lord, that you no longer walk as the Gentiles also walk in the vanity of their mind, 4:18 being darkened in their understanding, alienated from the life of God, because of the ignorance that is in them, because of the hardening of their heart, 4:19 who being past feeling gave themselves up to lasciviousness to work all uncleanness with greediness. 4:20 But you did not so learn Christ. 4:21 If indeed you have heard him and have been taught in him just as truth is in Jesus.

Commentary

For the second time in Eph 4 there is a long passage containing five verses without a parallelism. There is no section in the undisputed letters like these found in Ephesians. This one cannot have been written by Paul.

Eph 4:22–32

A 4:22 That you put away, as concerning your former manner of life, *the old man*, that waxes corrupt after the lusts of deceit.
A' 4:23 And that you be renewed in the spirit of your mind 4:24 and put on *the new man* that after God has been created in righteousness and holiness of truth.

B 4:25 Therefore, putting away falsehood, each one *speak truth with his neighbor* for we are members one of another.

B' 4:26a *Do not be angry,*

B" 4:26b *and do not sin.*

B''' 4:26c *Do not let the sun go down on your wrath.*

B'''' 4:27 *Neither give place to the devil.*

B''''' 4:28 Let him who stole *steal no more*. But rather let him labor, working with his hands the thing that is good, that he may have whereof to give to him that has need.

B'''''' 4:29 *Let no corrupt speech proceed out of your mouth,* but such as is good for edifying as the need may be, that it may give grace to them that hear.

B''''''' 4:30 And *do not grieve the Holy Spirit of God* in whom you were sealed to the day of redemption.

B'''''''' 4:31 *Let all bitterness, and wrath, and anger, and clamor, and railing, be put away from you* with all malice.

B''''''''' 4:32 And *be kind to one another,* tenderhearted, forgiving each other, even as God also in Christ forgave you.

Eph 4:22-32 Parallel Structure Table

With ten elements in the B stich the following table will show the B stich in two five-element rows.

A 4:22—the old man			A' 4:23-24—the new man	
B 4:25—speak truth with his neighbor	B' 4:26a—do not be angry	B" 4:26b—do not sin	B''' 4:26c—do not let the sun go down on your wrath	B'''' 4:27—neither give place to the devil
B''''' 4:28—steal no more	B'''''' 4:29—Let no corrupt speech proceed out of your mouth	B''''''' 4:30—do not grieve the Holy Spirit of God	B'''''''' 4:31—Let all bitterness and wrath and anger and clamor and railing be put away from you	B''''''''' 4:32—be kind to one another

Commentary

At v. 4:27 the writer uses the term "devil" (*diabolō*). Paul does not use that term in the undisputed letters. He invariably calls God's enemy "Satan." This unit is a two-stich structure that seems to have been inspired by Col 3:5-16, wherein the writer gives the Ephesians ten admonitions for good behavior, and using the metaphor of putting away the old man and putting on the new man also found in Colossians. The parallelisms that are found in this unit are the result of the unit giving moral admonitions to the Ephesians, not from a structural endeavor. The admonitions are very unbalanced. Once again, this section uses too many words to get the point across. Compare these admonitions with the poetry and economy of language found in Phil 5:8 and 1 Thess 5:16–21. Paul did not write this.

Ephesians 5–6

There is a structure encompassing the last third of Eph 5 and the first half of Eph 6. Bishop Langdon should have ended Eph 5 at v. 5:21 and started Eph 6 at v. 5:22.

Eph 5:1–13

> A 5:1 Therefore be imitators of *God* as beloved children. 5:2 And walk in love even as *Christ* also loved you and gave himself up for us, an offering and a sacrifice to God for an odor of a sweet smell.
>> B 5:3 But *fornication*, and all *uncleanliness*, or *covetousness*, let it not even be named among you as becomes saints, 5:4a nor filthiness, nor foolish talking, or jesting,
>> B' 5:4b which are not befitting, but rather giving of thanks. 5:5a For this you surely know, that no *fornicator*, nor *unclean* person, nor *covetous* man who is an idolater,
> A' 5:5b has any inheritance in the kingdom of *Christ* and *God*. 5:6 Let no man deceive you with empty words. For because of these things the wrath of God come upon the sons of disobedience.
>> C 5:7 Therefore do not be partakers with them. 5:8 For you were once *darkness* but are now *light* in the Lord. Walk as children of *light* 5:9 for the fruit of the *light* is in all goodness and righteousness and truth,
>> C' 5:10 proving what is well-pleasing to the Lord. 5:11 And have no fellowship with the unfruitful works of *darkness*, but rather even reprove them. 5:12 For the things which are done by them in secret it is a shame even to speak of. 5:13 But all things when they are reproved are made manifest by the *light*. For everything that is made manifest is *light*.

Eph 5:1–13 Parallel Structure Table

A 5:1–2—God . . . Christ	A' 5:5b–6—God . . . Christ
B 5:3–4—fornication . . . uncleanliness . . . covetousness	B' 5:4b–5a—fornicator . . . unclean . . . covetous

| C 5:7–9—darkness...light...light...light | C' 5:10–13—darkness...light...light |

Commentary

The first half of Eph 5 has a three-stich structure that has one chiastic section and one parallel section. The writer of Ephesians in v. 5:5 has introduced a new concept to the Pauline corpus with "the kingdom of Christ and God." In the undisputed letters Paul only mentions "the kingdom of God." The use of un-Pauline terms marks this as not being by Paul. The writer of Ephesians can only manage short literary units defined by parallelisms. Here again this is not in Paul's style, there being too much text compared to the parallelisms. The C hemistich contains "light" three times, but the C' hemistich has only two.

Eph 5:14–21

5:14 Therefore he says, awake, you who sleep, and arise from the dead, and Christ will shine upon you. 5:15 Look therefore carefully how you walk, not as unwise, but as wise, 5:16 redeeming the time, because the days are evil. 5:17 Therefore do not be foolish but understand what is the will of the Lord. 5:18 And do not be drunk with wine wherein is riot, but be filled with the spirit, 5:19 speaking one to another in psalms and hymns and spiritual songs, singing and making melody with your heart to the Lord, 5:20 giving thanks always for all things in the name of our Lord Jesus Christ to God, even the father; 5:21 subjecting yourselves one to another in the fear of Christ.

Commentary

This is an eight verse section without any parallelisms. This section is similar to the two sections without parallelisms found in Eph 4. This section also seems to have been inspired by 1 Thess 5:5–8. This was not written by Paul.

Ephesians 5:22—6:18

This seems to be another mistake by Bishop Langdon. This section of Ephesians is a parallel structure based upon Col 3:17–4:1 without the misplaced verse that is found in that literary unit. Ephesians 5:22–6:24 should have been all in one chapter.

> A 5:22 *Wives, be in subjection to your own husbands* as to the Lord.
>   B 5:23 For the husband is the head of the wife, and *Christ also is the head of the church,* himself the savior of the body.

B' 5:24a But as the *church is subject to Christ*,

A' 5:24b the *wives also be subject to their husbands* in everything.

   C 5:25a *Husbands, love your wives*,

B'' 5:25b even as *Christ also loved the church*, and gave himself up for it; 5:26 that he might sanctify it, having cleansed it by the washing of water with the word,

B''' 5:27 that *he might present the church* to himself glorious, not having spot or wrinkle or any such thing. But that it should be holy and without blemish.

   C' 5:28 Even so ought *husbands also to love their own wives* as their own bodies. He that loves his own wife loves himself.

B'''' 5:29 For no man ever hated his own flesh, but nourishes and cherishes it, even as *Christ also the church*, 5:30 because we are members of his body. 5:31 For this cause shall a man leave his father and mother, and shall cleave to his wife, and the two shall become one flesh.

B''''' 5:32 This mystery is great. But I speak in regard of *Christ and of the church*. 5:33 Nevertheless do you also severally love each one his own wife even as himself, and the wife that she fear her husband.

   D 6:1 *Children, obey your parents* in the Lord for this is right. 6:2 Honor your father and mother, which is the first commandment with promise. 6:3 That it may be well with you, and you may live long on the Earth.

   D' 6:4 And, you *fathers, do not provoke your children to wrath*, but nurture them in the chastening and admonition of the Lord.

     E 6:5 *Servants, be obedient to those who are your masters according to the flesh*, with fear and trembling, in singleness of your heart, as to Christ, 6:6 not in the way of eye service, as men-pleasers, but as servants of Christ, doing the will of God from the heart, 6:7 with good will doing service, as to the Lord, and not to men. 6:8 Knowing that whatever good thing each one does, he will receive the same again from the Lord, whether bond or free.

     E' 6:9 And, you *masters, do the same things to them, and forbear threatening*. Knowing that he who is both their master and yours is in Heaven, and there is no respect of persons with him.

        F 6:10 Finally, be strong in the Lord and in the strength of his might. 6:11 *Put on the whole armor of God, that you may be able to stand against the wiles of the devil*. 6:12 For our wrestling is not against flesh and blood, but against the principalities, against the powers, against the world-rulers of this darkness, against the spiritual of wickedness in the heavenly places.

        F' 6:13 *Therefore take up the whole armor of God that you may be able to withstand in the evil day*, and having done all, to stand.

           G 6:14a Stand therefore, *having girded your loins with truth*,

           G' 6:14b and *having put on the breastplate of righteousness*,

           G'' 6:15 and *having shod your feet with the preparation* of the gospel of peace,

G''' 6:16 besides all *taking up the shield of faith*, wherewith you shall be able to quench all the fiery darts of the evil one.

G'''' 6:17 And *take the helmet of salvation, and the sword of the spirit*, which is the word of God, 6:18 with all prayer and supplication praying at all seasons in the spirit, and watching thereto in all perseverance and supplication for all the saints.

Eph 5:22—6:18 Parallel Structure Table

A 5:22—wives be in subjection to your own husbands			A' 5:24b—wives also be subject to their husbands		
B 5:23—Christ also is head of the church	B' 5:24a—the church is subject to Christ	B" 5:25b—Christ also loved the church	B''' 5:27—he might present the church	B'''' 5:29-31—Christ also the church	B''''' 5:32-33—Christ and of the church
C 5:25a—husbands love your wives			C' 5:28—husbands also love their own wives		
D 6:1-3—Children obey your parents			D' 6:4—fathers do not provoke your children to wrath		
E 6:5-8—Servants be obedient to those who are your masters according to the flesh			E' 6:9—masters do the same things to them and forbear threatening		
F 6:10-12—put on the whole armor of God that you may be able to stand against the wiles of the devil			F' 6:13—take up the whole armor of God that you may be able to withstand the evil day		
G 6:14a—having girded your loins with truth	G' 6:14b—having put on the breastplate of righteousness	G" 6:15—having shod your feet with the preparation of the gospel	G''' 6:16—taking up the shield of faith	G'''' 6:17-18—take up the helmet of salvation and the sword of the spirit	

Commentary

This structure overlaps the last third of Eph 5 and the first half of Eph 6. It is a restatement of Col 3:17-4:1 using many more words and explanations of the admonitions being given. There does not seem to be any regularity or pattern to the parallelisms. The stiches are not balanced. This section is not in Paul's style and was not written by him. At v. 6:11 the author again uses the term "devil" instead of Paul's "Satan," clearly showing this was not written by Paul.

Eph 6:19–24

6:19 And on my behalf that utterance may be given to me in opening my mouth to make known with boldness the mystery of the gospel, 6:20 for which I am an ambassador in chains. That in it I may speak boldly, as I ought to speak. 6:21 But that you also may know my affairs, how I do, Tychicus, the beloved brother and faithful minister in the Lord, shall make known to you all things, 6:22 whom I have sent to you for this very purpose, that you may know our state, and that he may comfort your hearts. 6:23 Peace be to the brethren and love with faith from God the father and the Lord Jesus Christ. 6:24 Grace be with all them that love our Lord Jesus Christ in incorruptibility.

Commentary

The final section of Eph 6 is six verses containing no repetitions/parallelisms. This obviously was not written by Paul. Ephesians 6:21–22 seems to have been copied from Col 4:7–8.

14

First Letter To Timothy

First Timothy as a whole is definitely un-Pauline. The first chapter only contains one parallelism, and the second chapter contains none. There are no chiastic structures in 1 Timothy. There are seven stiches of parallels in 1 Tim 3, but that is the result of parallel admonitions to various groups. In 1 Tim 3:5 and 7 the writer uses the term "the devil" meaning Satan. As pointed out in the comments to Ephesians, Paul did not use the word "devil" in the undisputed letters. There are two parallelisms in 1 Tim 4 and several in 1 Tim 5 that also contains parallel admonitions. In v. 5:18 there is a quote of Deut 25:4 that Paul quoted at 1 Cor 9:9. There also seems to be a quote of Luke 10:7, clearly indicating a late composition for 1 Timothy. The author also introduces these quotes with "for scripture says" (*legei gar hē graphē*). Paul never used that phrase in the undisputed letters to introduce his quotes of the Old Testament. He used "as it is written" (*kathōs gegraptai*). There are four parallelisms in 1 Tim 6, three of them being the same word repeated. Rhetorical analysis supports the conclusion of critical scholars that 1 Timothy was not written by Paul.

1 Timothy 1

1 Tim 1:1–2

> A 1:1 Paul, an apostle of *Christ Jesus* according to the commandment of *God our savior, and Christ Jesus* our hope,
> A' 1:2 to Timothy, my true child in faith. Grace, mercy, peace, from *God the father and Christ Jesus our Lord.*

1 Tim 1:1–2 Parallel Structure Table

| A 1:1 – Christ Jesus . . . God our savior and Christ Jesus | A' 1:2 – God the father and Christ Jesus our Lord |

First Letter To Timothy

Commentary

This one-stich parallel could be an accident by the author since very often in the undisputed letters Paul repeated a phrase about Christ and about God in the introduction. The shortest literary structure in all the introductions to Paul's undisputed letters is the three-stich chiastic structure with a parallel center of Rom 1:1–6.

1 Tim 1:3–16

1:3 As I exhorted you to tarry at Ephesus when I was going into Macedonia that you might charge certain men not to teach a different doctrine. 1:4 Neither to give heed to fables and endless genealogies, which minister questionings, rather than a dispensation of God which is in faith. 1:5 But the end of the charge is love out of a pure heart and a good conscience and faith unfeigned. 1:6 from which things some having swerved have turned aside to vain talking, 1:7 desiring to be teachers of the law, though they understand neither what they say, nor whereof they confidently affirm. 1:8 But we know that the law is good if one uses it lawfully. 1:9 As knowing this, that law is not made for a righteous man but for the lawless and unruly, for the ungodly and sinners, for the unholy and profane, for murderers of fathers and murderers of mothers, for man slayers, 1:10 for fornicators, for abusers of themselves with men, for men stealers, for liars, for those false swearing, and if there be any other thing contrary to the sound doctrine, 1:11 according to the gospel of the glory of the blessed God, which was committed to my trust. 1:12 I thank him that enabled me, Christ Jesus our Lord, for that he counted me faithful, appointing me to service, 1:13 though I was before a blasphemer, and a persecutor, and injurious. However, I obtained mercy because I did it ignorantly in unbelief. 1:14 And the grace of our Lord abounded exceedingly with faith and love which is in Christ Jesus. 1:15 Faithful is the saying, and worthy of full acceptance, that Christ Jesus came into the world to save sinners, of whom I am chief. 1:16 However, for this cause I obtained mercy, that in me as chief might Jesus Christ show forth all his longsuffering for an example to those who will soon believe on him to eternal life. 1:17 But to the king of the ages, immortal, invisible, the only God, be honor and glory forever and ever. Amen. 1:18 This charge I commit to you, Timothy, my child, according to the prophecies which led the way to you, that by them you may fight the good fight, 1:19 holding faith and a good conscience, which some having thrust from them made a shipwreck of the faith, 1:20 among whom are Hymenaeus and Alexander, whom I delivered to Satan, that they might be taught not to blaspheme.

Commentary

This long discourse without a repeated word or phrase except "Christ Jesus" and "Jesus Christ" cannot be the work of Paul.

1 Timothy 2

1 Tim 2:1–10

2:1 I exhort therefore, first of all, that supplications, prayers, intercessions, thanksgivings, be made for all men. 2:2 For kings and all that are in high place. That we may lead a tranquil and quiet life in all godliness and gravity. 2:3 This is good and acceptable in the sight of God our savior, 2:4 who would have all men to be saved, and come to the knowledge of the truth. 2:5 For there is one God, one mediator also between God and men, the man, Christ Jesus, 2:6 who gave himself as a ransom for all, the testimony in its proper times. 2:7 There upon I was appointed a preacher and an apostle. I speak the truth, I do not lie, a teacher of the Gentiles in faith and truth. 2:8 I desire therefore that the men pray in every place lifting up holy hands without wrath and disputing. 2:9 In like manner, that women adorn themselves in respectable apparel, with modesty and self-control, not adorned with braided hair, and gold or pearls or costly raiment, 2:10 but (which becomes women professing godliness) through good works.

Commentary

This is another long discourse without a parallelism. The author copied Paul's frequent statement that he is not lying.

1 Tim 2:11–15

  A 2:11 Let a *woman learn in quietness with all subjection.*
  A' 2:12 But I do *not permit a woman to teach, nor to have authority over a man, but to be silent.*
    B 2:13 For *Adam was formed first, then Eve.*
    B' 2:14 And *Adam was not deceived, but the woman having been deceived* has fallen into transgression. 2:15 But she will be saved through her child-bearing, if they continue in faith and love and sanctification with self control.

1 Tim 2:11-14 Parallel Structure Table

A 2:11—woman learn in quietness with all subjection	A' 2:12—not permit a woman to teach nor to have authority over a man but to be silent
B 2:13—Adam was formed first then Eve	B' 2:14-15—Adam was not deceived but the woman having been deceived

Commentary

This short two-stich structure that contains two parallelisms is not well balanced and is not long enough to be a creation by Paul.

1 Timothy 3

1 Tim 3:1-16

A 3:1 Trustworthy is the saying, if a man seeks the office of a *bishop*, he desires a good work.
A' 3:2a The *bishop* therefore must be without reproach,
  B 3:2b the *husband of one wife*,
  B' 3:2c *temperate*,
  B'' 3:2d *sober-minded*,
  B''' 3:2e *orderly*,
  B'''' 3:2f *given to hospitality*,
  B''''' 3:2g *apt to teach*,
  B'''''' 3:3a *not a drunkard*,
  B''''''' 3:3b *not pugnacious*,
  B'''''''' 3:3c *but gentle*,
  B''''''''' 3:3d *not contentious*,
  B'''''''''' 3:3e *no lover of money*,
  B''''''''''' 3:4a *one that rules well his own house*,
  B'''''''''''' 3:4b *having children in subjection with all gravity*.
    C 3:5 (Now if a man does not know how to rule his own house, how shall he take care of the church of God?) 3:6 not a novice, lest being puffed up he fall into the *condemnation of the devil*.
    C' 3:7 Moreover he must have good testimony from those who are outside, lest he fall into reproach and the *snare of the devil*.
      D 3:8 Deacons in like manner *grave*, not double-tongued, not given to much wine, not greedy of filthy lucre, 3:9 holding the mystery of the faith in a pure

conscience. 3:10 And let these also first be proved, then let them serve as deacons, if they be blameless.

D' 3:11 Women in like manner *grave*, not slanderers, temperate, faithful in all things.

E 3:12a Let *deacons be husbands of one wife*,

E' 3:12b *ruling children and their own houses* well. 3:13 For they who have served well as deacons gain to themselves a good standing and great boldness in the faith which is in Christ Jesus.

F 3:14 These things write I to you hoping to come to you shortly. 3:15a But if I tarry long, that you may know how men ought to behave themselves in the *house of God*,

F' 3:15b which is the *church of the living God*, the pillar and ground of the truth. 3:16a And admittedly great is the mystery of godliness,

G 3:16b he who was *manifested in the flesh*,

G' 3:16c *justified in the spirit*,

G" 3:16d *seen of angels*,

G'" 3:16e *preached among the nations*,

G"" 3:16f *believed on in the world*,

G""" 3:16g *received up in glory*.

1 Tim 3:1-13 Parallel Structure Table

The B stich in this unit contains thirteen elements. Therefore, it is represented in the table below in two separate rows.

A 3:1—bishop			A' 3:2a—bishop			
B 3:2b—husband of one wife	B' 3:2c—temperate	B" 3:2d—sober minded	B'" 3:2e—orderly	B"" 3:2f—given to hospitality	B""" 3:2g—apt to teach	B"""" 3:3a—not a drunkard
B""""" 3:3b—Not pugnacious	B"""""" 3:3c—gentle	B""""""" 3:3d—not contentious	B"""""""" 3:3e—no lover of money	B""""""""" 3:4a—one that rules his own house well	B"""""""""" 3:4b—having children in subjection with all gravity	
C 3:5-6—condemnation of the devil			C' 3:7—snare of the devil			
D 3:8—grave, not doubled tongued, not given to much wine, not greedy of filthy lucre			D' 3:10—grave not slanderers temperate faithful in all things			
E 3:12a—be the husbands of one wife			E' 3:12b-13—ruling children and their own house			
F 3:14-15a—the house of God			F' 3:15b-16a—the church of the living God			

| G 3:16b—manifested in the flesh | G' 3:16c—justified in the spirit | G" 3:16d—seen of angels | G'" 3:16e—preached among the nations | G"" 3:16f—believed on in the world | G""' 3:16g—received up in glory |

Commentary

This is the longest structure in 1 Timothy. It is not well balanced and has a long three-verse sequence at vv. 3:13–15 without a parallelism. The parallelisms are a function of the rules being set forth for bishops, deacons, and women. The author in vv. 3:6–7 uses the term "devil" twice after using the name "Satan" in v. 1:20. The use of "Satan" in v. 1:20 may be the result of the author copying from 1 Cor 5:5. Paul was not the author of this literary unit.

1 Timothy 4

1 Tim 4:1–6

4:1 But the spirit says expressly that in later times some will fall away from the faith, giving heed to seducing spirits and doctrines of demons, 4:2 through the hypocrisy of men that speak lies, branded in their own conscience as with a hot iron, 4:3 forbidding to marry, commanding to abstain from meats, that God created to be received with thanksgiving by those who believe and know the truth. 4:4 For every creature of God is good, and nothing is to be rejected, if it be received with thanksgiving. 4:5 For it is sanctified through the word of God and prayer. 4:6 If you put the brethren in mind of these things, you will be a good minister of Christ Jesus, nourished in the words of the faith, and of the good doctrine which you have followed.

Commentary

This is a six-verse passage without a meaningful parallelism. Paul would never have written anything like this.

1 Tim 4:7–11

A 4:7 But refuse profane and old wives' fables. And exercise yourself to *godliness*.
A' 4:8 For bodily exercise is profitable for a little, but *godliness* is profitable for all things, having promise of the life which now is, and of that which is to come. 4:9 Trustworthy is the saying, and worthy of all acceptation.

> B 4:10 For to this end we labor and strive, because we have our hope set on the living God, who is the savior of all men, specially of *those who believe*.
> B' 4:11 These things command and teach. 4:12 Let no man despise your youth, but be an example to *those who believe*, in word, in manner of life, in love, in faith, in purity.

1 Tim 4:7-11 Parallel Structure Table

| A 4:7—godliness | A' 4:8–9 – godliness |
| B 4:10 – those who believe | B' 4:11—those who believe |

Commentary

This two-stich parallel structure is poorly balanced and has too much text without repetitions/parallelisms. This is not a Pauline literary unit.

1 Tim 4:13–16

4:13 Till I come give heed to reading, to exhortation, to teaching. 4:14 Do not neglect the gift that is in you, which was given to you by prophecy, with the laying on of the hands of the presbytery. 4:15 Be diligent in these things. Give yourself wholly to them that your progress may be manifest to all. 4:16 Take heed to yourself, and to your teaching. Continue in these things. For in doing this you will save both yourself and those who hear you.

Commentary

The last sequence in 1 Tim 4 is a four-verse passage without a parallelism. Paul did not write this.

1 Timothy 5

1 Tim 5:1–13

> A 5:1 Do not rebuke an *elder, but exhort him as a father*; the *younger men as brothers*,
> A' 5:2 the *elder women as mothers*; the *younger as sisters*, in all purity.
> B 5:3 Honor *widows* that are *widows indeed*.
> B' 5:4 But if any *widow* has children or grandchildren, let them learn first to show piety towards their own family, and to take care of their parents. For this is

acceptable in the sight of God. 5:5 Now she that is a *widow indeed*, and desolate, has her hope set on God, and continues in supplications and prayers night and day. 5:6 But she that gives herself to pleasure is dead while she lives. 5:7 These things also command, that they may be without reproach. 5:8 But if any provides not for his own and specially his own household, he has denied the faith, and is worse than an unbeliever.

> C 5:9a Let none be enrolled as a *widow under sixty years old*,
> C' 5:9b *the wife of one man*,
> C" 5:10a *well reported for good works*,
> C'" 5:10b *if she has brought up children*,
> C"" 5:10c *if she has practiced hospitality to strangers*,
> C""' 5:10d *if she has washed the saints' feet*,
> C""" 5:10e *if she has relieved the afflicted*,
> C"""" 5:10f *if she has diligently followed every good work*.
>> D 5:11 But younger widows refuse. For when they have waxed wanton against Christ, *they desire to marry*,
>> D' 5:12 having condemnation because *they have rejected their first pledge*.
>>> E 5:13a And at the same time they learn also to be *idle, going about from house to house*,
>>> E' 5:13b and not only *idle, but tattlers also and busybodies*, speaking things which they ought not.

1 Tim 5:1-13 Parallel Structure Table

The C stich in this unit contains eight elements and is represented in the table below in two rows.

A 5:1—elder but exhort him as a father . . . younger men as brothers		A' 5:2—elder women as mothers . . . younger as sisters	
B 5:3—widows . . . widows indeed		B' 5:4-8—widow . . . widow indeed	
C 5:9a—widow under sixty years old	C' 5:9b—wife of one man	C" 5:10a—well reported for good works	C'" 5:10b—if she has brought up children
C"" 5:10c—if she has practiced hospitality to strangers	C""' 5:10d—if she has washed the saints feet	C""" 5:10e—if she has relieved the afflicted	C"""" 5:10f—if she has diligently followed every good work
D 5:11—they desire to marry		D' 5:12—they have rejected their first pledge	
E 5:13a—idle going about from house to house		E' 5:13b—idle but tattlers also and busybodies	

PART II | THE DEUTERO-PAULINE LETTERS

Commentary

This parallel structure is not well balanced. There is a three verse passage at vv. 5:6–8 without any parallelisms. The B' hemistich is much longer than the B hemistich. Once again, this unit seems to contain parallelisms only because the writer is setting forth rules of conduct. The parallelisms do not seem intended to set forth and reinforce and argument as typically found in Paul's letters.

1 Tim 5:14–25

5:14 I desire therefore that the younger widows marry, bear children, rule the household, give no occasion to the adversary for reviling. 5:15 For already some are turned aside after Satan. 5:16 If any woman who believes has widows, let her render help to them, and do not let the church be burdened, so that it may render help to those who are truly widows. 5:17 Let the elders that rule well be counted worthy of double honor, especially those who labor in the word and in teaching. 5:18 For the scripture says, "You will not muzzle the ox when he treads out the corn. And the laborer is worthy of his hire." 5:19 Against an elder do not receive an accusation, unless there be two or three witnesses. 5:20 Reprove those who sin in the sight of all, so that the rest also may be in fear. 5:21 I charge in the sight of God and Christ Jesus and the elect angels, that you observe these things without prejudice doing nothing by partiality. 5:22 Do not lay hands on anyone hastily, neither be partaker of the sins of others. Keep yourself pure. 5:23 Do not be a water only drinker, but use a little wine for your stomach's sake and your frequent infirmities. 5:24 Some men's sins are evident, going before them to judgment. Some, however, they appear later. 5:25 In like manner also there are good works that are evident, and such as are otherwise cannot be hid.

Commentary

This long passage has many rules and admonitions, but they are not expressed in a Pauline style in parallel. Verse 5:18 quotes 1 Cor 9:9 and Luke 10:7, apparently referring to Luke as scripture. This implies a very late date for the writing of 1 Timothy and certainly not by Paul. It also reverts to the use of "Satan."

1 Timothy 6

1 Tim 6:1–8

A 6:1 Let as many as are slaves under the yoke count their own *masters* worthy of all honor that the name of God and the doctrine not be blasphemed.

A' 6:2a And they that have believing *masters*, let them not despise them because they are brethren. But rather let them serve them,

    B 6:2b because they that partake of the benefit are believing and beloved. These things *teach* and exhort.

    B' 6:3a If any man *teaches* a different doctrine and does not consent to sound words, the words of our Lord Jesus Christ,

        C 6:3b and to the doctrine which is according to *godliness*, 6:4a he is puffed up, knowing nothing, but doting about questionings and disputes of words,

        C' 6:4b whereof come envy, strife, railings, evil surmisings, 6:5 wranglings of men corrupted in mind and bereft of the truth, supposing that *godliness* is a way of gain.

        C" 6:6 But *godliness* with contentment is great gain. 6:7 For we brought nothing into the world for neither can we carry anything out. 6:8 But having food and clothing we will be content with these.

1 Tim 6:1–8 Parallel Structure Table

A 6:1—masters		A' 6:2a—masters	
B 6:2b—teach		B' 6:3a—teaches	
C 6:3b–4a—godliness	C' 6:4b–5—godliness	C" 6:6–8—godliness	

Commentary

This short three-stich structure has parallels of only one word in each hemistich or element. There is too much text that contains no parallel words or phrases. This is not a Pauline structure.

1 Tim 6:9–10

6:9 But they that are minded to be rich fall into a temptation and a snare and many foolish and hurtful lusts, such as drown men in ruin and destruction. 6:10 For the love of money is a root of all kinds of evil, which some reaching after have been led astray from the faith, and have pierced themselves through with many sorrows.

Commentary

It is difficult to know whether this two-verse passage should be considered as connecting the two parallel structures or should be separate. Having no repetitions or parallels, Paul did not write it.

1 Tim 6:11–12

A 6:11 But you, O man of God, flee these things, and *follow after righteousness, godliness, faith, love, patience, meekness.*
A' 6:12a *Fight the good fight of the faith,*
A" 6:12b *lay hold on the life eternal,* whereto you were called and did confess the good confession in the sight of many witnesses.

1 Tim 6:11–12 Parallel Structure Table

A 6:11—follow after righteousness faith love patience meekness	A' 6:12a—fight the good fight of the faith	A" 6:12b—lay hold on the life eternal

Commentary

As mentioned in the prior commentary section this one-stich structure may be intended to be part of the prior three-stich parallel structure. In any case the lack of a clear demarcation between literary units marks it as being un-Pauline.

1 Tim 6:13–21

6:13 I charge you in the sight of God, who gives life to all things, and of Christ Jesus, who before Pontius Pilate witnessed the good confession, 6:14 that you keep the commandment, without spot, without reproach, until the appearing of our Lord Jesus Christ, 6:15 which in its own times he shall show, who is the blessed and only sovereign, the king of kings, and Lord of Lords, 6:16 who only has immortality, dwelling in light unapproachable, whom no man has seen, nor can see, to whom be honor and power eternal. Amen. 6:17 Charge them that are rich in this present world, that they be not high minded nor have their hope set on the uncertainty of riches, but on God, who gives us richly all things to enjoy. 6:18 That they do good, that they be rich in good works, that they be ready to distribute, willing to communicate, 6:19 treasuring up for themselves a good foundation for the future, that they may take hold on that which is life indeed. 6:20 O Timothy, guard that which is committed to you, turning away from the profane babblings and oppositions of the knowledge which is falsely so called; 6:21 which some professing have erred concerning the faith. Grace be with you.

First Letter To Timothy

Commentary

This is a nine-verse passage with no repetitions or parallelisms to end the letter. The mention of Pontius Pilate once indicates that this was written after the gospels were published and is not from Paul's hand. There are no chiastic structures in the entire letter. The longest parallel structure in the letter contains only five stiches. There are seven parallel structures and seven unstructured passages. This letter was not written by Paul.

15

Second Letter To Timothy

THERE ARE PARALLELISMS IN 2 Tim 1 and the first part of 2 Tim 2. They cease half way through the chapter at 2:13. The remainder of the letter is then devoid of repetitions/parallels. There are no chiastic structures at all, similar to 1 Timothy. It appears the writer attempted to match Paul's style of parallel structures and gave up before he was half way through. The writer did not do a very good job of matching Paul's style in 2 Tim 1 and 2. The parallelisms have no regularity and no pleasing pattern. This letter was clearly not written by Paul.

2 Timothy 1

2 Tim 1:1–18

> A 1:1 Paul, an apostle of *Christ Jesus* through the will of *God*, according to the promise of the life which is in Christ Jesus,
> A' 1:2 to Timothy, my beloved child grace, mercy, peace, from *God* the father and *Christ Jesus* our Lord.
>> B 1:3 I thank God, whom I serve from my forefathers in a pure conscience, how unceasing is my *remembrance of you* in my supplications, night and day
>> B' 1:4 longing to see you, *remembering your tears*, that I may be filled with joy, 1:5 having been reminded of the unfeigned faith that is in you, which dwelt first in your grandmother Lois and your mother Eunice, and I am persuaded in you also.
>> B" 1:6 For which cause I put *you in remembrance* that you stir up the gift of God, which is in you through the laying on of my hands.
>>> C 1:7 For *God* did not give us a spirit of fearfulness but of *power and love* and discipline.
>>>> D 1:8a *Do not be ashamed* therefore of the testimony of our Lord nor of me his prisoner.
>>> C' 1:8b But suffer hardship with the gospel according to the *power of God*,

E 1:9 who saved us and called us with a holy calling, not according to our works, but according to his own purpose and grace, which was given us in *Christ Jesus* before times eternal.

E' 1:10 But has now been manifested by the appearance of our savior *Christ Jesus*, who abolished death, and brought life and immortality to light through the gospel, 1:11 to which I was appointed a preacher, and an apostle, and a teacher.

D' 1:12 For which cause I suffer also these things. Yet *I am not ashamed*. For I know him whom I have believed, and I am persuaded that he is able to guard that which I have committed to him against that day.

E" 1:13 Hold the pattern of sound words which you have heard from me, in faith and love which is in *Christ Jesus*. 1:14 That good thing which was committed to you guard through the Holy Spirit which dwells in us. 1:15 This you know, that all that are in Asia turned away from me, among whom are Phygelus and Hermogenes.

D" 1:16 The Lord grant mercy to the house of Onesiphorus. For he often refreshed me, and *was not ashamed* of my chain. 1:17 But, when he was in Rome, he sought me diligently, and found me. 1:18 The Lord grant to him to find mercy of the Lord in that day. And how much he served at Ephesus you know very well.

2 Tim 1:1-18 Parallel Structure Table

A 1:1—Christ Jesus . . . God		A' 1:2—Christ Jesus . . . God	
B 1:3—remembrance of you	B' 1:4-5—remembering your tears		B" 1:6—you in remembrance
C 1:7—God . . . power and love		C' 1:8b—power of God	
D 1:8a—do not be ashamed	D' 1:12—I am not ashamed		D" 1:16-18—was not ashamed
E 1:9—Christ Jesus	E' 1:10-11—Christ Jesus		E" 1:13-15—Christ Jesus

Commentary

There are only five stiches in this eighteen verse structure. There is too much text that does not contain repetitions/parallels for this to be a Pauline writing. The D and E stiches are not well balanced. In addition, after the initial A, A,' B, B,' B" format the repeated phrases seem to be in a random sort of order, not a pleasing pattern common to Pauline structures. The writer apparently used Rom 1:16 to compose the D stich about being ashamed. Paul did not compose this structure.

2 Timothy 2

2 Tim 2:1–13

A 2:1 You therefore, my child, be strengthened in the grace that is in *Christ Jesus*. 2:2a And the things that you have heard from me among many witnesses.
A' 2:2b Entrust these to faithful men who will be able to teach others also. 2:3 Suffer hardship with me as a good soldier of *Christ Jesus*.
   B 2:4a No serving *soldier* entangles himself in the affairs of life,
     B' 2:4b so that he may please him who enlisted him as a *soldier*.
        C 2:5 And *if also a man competes, he is not crowned unless he has competed lawfully.*
        C' 2:6 The *farmer that labors must be the first to partake of the fruits.* 2:7 Consider what I say. For the Lord will give you understanding in all things.
A" 2:8 Remember *Jesus Christ*, risen from the dead, of the seed of David, according to my gospel, 2:9 in which I suffer hardship even to chains, as an evil doer. But the word of God is not bound.
A'" 2:10 Therefore I endure all things for the sake of the elect that they also may obtain the salvation that is in *Christ Jesus* with eternal glory.
   D 2:11 Trustworthy is the saying, for *if we died with him, we shall also live with him.*
   D' 2:12a *If we endure, we will also reign with him.*
   D" 2:12b *If we deny him, he will also deny us.*
   D'" 2:13 *If we are faithless, he remains faithful.* For he cannot deny himself.

2 Tim 2:1–13 Parallel Structure Table

A 2:1–2a—Christ Jesus	A' 2:2b–3—Christ Jesus	A" 2:8–9—Jesus Christ	A'" 2:10—Christ Jesus
B 2:4a—soldier		B' 2:4b—soldier	
C 2:5—if also a man competes he is not crowned unless he has competed lawfully		C' 2:6—farmer who labors must be the first to partake of the fruits	
D 2:11—for if we died with him we shall also live with him	D' 2:12a—if we endure we will also reign with him	D" 2:12b—if we deny him he will also deny us	D'" 2:13—if we are faithless he remains faithful

Second Letter To Timothy

Commentary

This structure, encompassing the first half of 2 Tim 2, begins with an A, A,' B, B,' C, C' format common to many Pauline structures and then fails to follow through. It is not clear that the author intended the parallelism of the C and C' hemistiches. He was given the benefit of the doubt. This does not appear to have been written by Paul

2 Tim 2:14–26

2:14 Of these things put them in remembrance, charging in the sight of the Lord, that they strive not about words, to no profit, to the subverting of them that hear. 2:15 Give diligence to present yourself approved to God, a workman that needs not to be ashamed, handling aright the word of truth. 2:16 But shun profane babblings. For they will proceed further in ungodliness. 2:17 And their word will grow as does a gangrene. Or who are Hymenaeus and Philetus, 2:18 men who erred concerning the truth, saying that the resurrection has taken place. And they are overthrowing the faith of some. 2:19 However the firm foundation of God stands, having this seal, the Lord knows those who are his. And let every one that names the name of the Lord depart from unrighteousness. 2:20 Now in a great house there are not only vessels of gold and of silver, but also of wood and of earth; and some to honor, and some to dishonor. 2:21 If a man therefore purges himself from these, he shall be a vessel to honor, sanctified, useful for the master, prepared to every good work 2:22 after righteousness, faith, love, peace, with those who call on the Lord out of a pure heart. 2:23 But refuse foolish and ignorant questionings, knowing that they engender quarrels. 2:24 And the Lord's servant must not quarrel, but be gentle towards all, apt to teach, forbearing, 2:25 in meekness correcting those who oppose them, unless God gives them repentance to the knowledge of the truth, 2:26 and they recover themselves out of the snare of the devil, having been taken captive by him to his will.

Commentary

The second half of 2 Tim 2 has no repetitions/parallelisms that can be identified as defining a structure of passage. The author once again has use the word "devil" in v. 2:26, as did the author of 1 Timothy. This was not written by Paul.

2 Timothy 3

2 Tim 3:1–17

3:1 But know this, that in the last days grievous times shall come. 3:2 For men shall be lovers of self, lovers of money, boastful, haughty, railers, disobedient to parents, unthankful, unholy, 3:3 without natural affection, implacable, slanderers, without self-control, fierce, no lovers of good, 3:4 traitors, headstrong, puffed up, lovers of pleasure rather than lovers of God; 3:5 holding a form of godliness, but having denied the power therefore. From these also turn away. 3:6 For these are they that creep into houses, and take captive silly women laden with sins, led away by various lusts, 3:7 ever learning, and never able to come to the knowledge of the truth. 3:8 And even as Jannes and Jambres withstood Moses, so these also withstand the truth. Men depraved in mind, unapproved concerning the faith. 3:9 But they will proceed no further. For their folly will be evident to all men, as theirs also came to be. 3:10 But you closely followed my teaching, conduct, purpose, faith, longsuffering, love, patience, 3:11 persecutions, sufferings, the things that happened to me at Antioch, at Iconium, at Lystra. What persecutions I endured. And out of them all the Lord delivered me. 3:12 And all that would live godly in Christ Jesus will suffer persecution. 3:13 But evil men and impostors shall wax worse and worse, deceiving and being deceived. 3:14 But remain in the things that you have learned and have been assured of, knowing from whom you have learned them. 3:15 And that from a babe you have known the sacred writings which are able to make you wise to salvation through faith which is in Christ Jesus. 3:16 Every scripture inspired of God is also profitable for teaching, for reproof, for correction, for instruction which is in righteousness. 3:17 That the man of God may be complete, furnished completely to every good work.

Commentary

No structural repetitions/parallelisms can be detected in 2 Tim 3. This was not written by Paul.

2 Timothy 4

2 Tim 4:1–22

4:1 I charge in the sight of God, and of Christ Jesus who will judge the living and the dead, and by his appearing and his kingdom. 4:2 Preach the word. Be urgent in season, out of season, reprove, rebuke, encourage, with all longsuffering and teaching. 4:3 For the time will come when they will not endure the sound doctrine, but having itching ears, will heap to themselves teachers after their own lusts, 4:4 and will turn away their ears from the truth, and turn aside to fables. 4:5 But be sober in all things, suffer hardship, do the work of an evangelist, fulfill your ministry. 4:6 For I am already being offered, and the time of my departure is come. 4:7 I have fought the good fight. I have finished the course. I have kept the faith. 4:8 Henceforth there is laid up for me the crown of righteousness, which the Lord, the righteous judge, shall give to me at that day. And not to me only, but also to all them that have loved his appearing. 4:9 Try hard to come to me soon. 4:10 For Demas forsook me, having loved this present world, and went to Thessalonica, Crescens to Galatia, Titus to Dalmatia. 4:11 Only Luke is with me. Take Mark, and bring him with you, for he is useful to me for ministering. 4:12 But Tychicus I sent to Ephesus. 4:13 The cloak that I left at Troas with Carpus, bring when you come, and the books, especially the parchments. 4:14 Alexander the coppersmith did me much evil. The Lord will render to him according to his works. 4:15 Beware of him also. For he greatly withstood our words. 4:16 At my first defense no one took my part, but all forsook me. May it not be laid to their account. 4:17 But the Lord stood by me, and strengthened me. That through me the message might me fully proclaimed, and that all the Gentiles might hear. And I was delivered out of the mouth of the lion. 4:18 The Lord will deliver me from every evil work, and will save me to his heavenly kingdom to whom the glory forever and ever. Amen. 4:19 Salute Prisca and Aquila, and the house of Onesiphorus. 4:20 Erastus remained at Corinth, but Trophimus I left at Miletus sick. 4:21 Try hard to come before winter. Eubulus salutes you, and Pudens, and Linus, and Claudia, and all the brothers. 4:22 The Lord be with your spirit. Grace be with you.

Commentary

The last chapter of 2 Timothy also contains no structural repetitions/parallelisms. There were only two parallel structures in the entire letter, neither of which had Pauline characteristics. There were no chiastic structures in the letter. Interestingly the author mentions Mark and Luke implying that this letter was written after the gospels had been named in the mid second century. Second Timothy was not written by Paul.

16

Letter To Titus

TITUS IS CLEARLY NOT a writing by Paul. The parallel phrases that do exist are for the most part the result of a series of admonitions. There are no chiastic structures. In Titus 1 the author appears to be copying the admonitions found in 1 Tim 3. The author also has used the parallel phrases "God our savior" and "Christ Jesus our savior," three times, once in each chapter, reminiscent of repetitions of Jesus coming to Earth from Heaven in 1 Thessalonians and the repetitions of the word "letter" in 2 Thessalonians.

Titus 1

Titus 1:1–11

    A 1:1 Paul, a servant of God, and an apostle of Jesus Christ, according to the faith of God's elect, and the knowledge of the truth which is according to godliness, 1:2 in hope of eternal life, which God, who cannot lie, promised before times eternal. 1:3 But in his own seasons manifested his word in the message, with which I was entrusted according to the commandment of *God our savior*.
    A' 1:4 To Titus, my true child after a common faith. Grace and peace from God the father and *Christ Jesus our savior*. 1:5 For this cause left I you in Crete, that you should set in order the things that were wanting and appoint elders in every city as I charged you.
      B 1:6a If any man is *blameless*,
      B' 1:6b the *husband of one wife*,
      B" 1:6c *having children who believe*,
      B'" 1:6d who are *not accused of dissipation or insubordination*.
        C 1:7a For the bishop must be *blameless*, as God's steward;
        C' 1:7b *not self-willed*,
        C" 1:7c *not quick tempered*,
        C'" 1:7d *not a drinker to excess*,

C'''' 1:7e *not pugnacious*,
C''''' 1:7f *not greedy* for dishonest gain;
C'''''' 1:8a but *given to hospitality*,
C''''''' 1:8b a *lover of good*,
C'''''''' 1:8c *sober-minded*,
C''''''''' 1:8d *just*,
C'''''''''' 1:8e *holy*,
C''''''''''' 1:8f *self-controlled*;
C'''''''''''' 1:9a *holding to the faithful word* which is according to the teaching, that he may be able to exhort in the sound doctrine, and to convict the nay sayers.

   D 1:10 For there are many unruly men, vain talkers and deceivers, especially they of the circumcision, 1:11a *whose mouths must be stopped*.

   D' 1:11b Men who *overthrow whole houses*,

   D" 1:11c *teaching things which they ought not* for the sake of dishonest gain.

Titus 1:1–11 Parallel Structure Table

The C stich of this unit contains thirteen elements and is represented in the table below in two rows.

A 1:1–3—God our savior				A' 1:4—Christ Jesus our savior			
B 1:6a—blameless	B' 1:6b—husband of one wife			B" 1:6c—having children who believe	B'" 1:6d—not accused of dissipation or insubordination		
C 1:17a—blameless	C' 1:7b—not self willed	C" 1:7c—not quick tempered	C"' 1:7d —not a drinker to excess	C"" 1:7e —not pugnacious	C""' 1:7f—not greedy	C"""" 1:8a—given to hospitality	
C""""' 1:8b—lover of good	C"""""' 1:8c—sober minded	C""""""' 1:8d—just	C"""""""' 1:8e—holy		C""""""""' 1:8f—self-controlled	C"""""""""' 1:9a—holding to the faithful word	
D 1:10–11a—mouths must be stopped		D' 1:11b—overthrow whole houses		D" 1:11c—teaching things which they ought not			

Commentary

The parallelisms in Titus 1 are the result of the author listing admonitions rather than using parallelisms as a structural technique. The author appears to be copying the admonitions found in 1 Tim 3 about the quality of men chosen to be bishops. The A stich is extremely unbalanced. This is not a Pauline literary unit.

Titus 1:12–16

1:12 One of their own, a prophet, said, "Cretans are always liars, evil beasts, idle gluttons." 1:13 This testimony is true. For which cause reprove them sharply, that they may be sound in the faith, 1:14 not giving heed to Jewish fables, and commandments of men who turn away from the truth. 1:15 To the pure all things are pure. But to those who are defiled and unbelieving nothing is pure. But both their minds and their consciences are defiled. 1:16 They profess that they know God, but by their works they deny him, being abominable, and disobedient, and to every good work unapproved.

Commentary

The last five verses of Titus 1 contain no parallelisms and seem unconnected to the prior literary unit. This was not written by Paul.

Titus 2

Titus 2:1–3:2

   A 2:1 But speak about the things which are consistent with sound doctrine. 2:2a That *elderly men be temperate,*
A' 2:2b *grave,*
A" 2:2c *sober-minded,*
A'" 2:2d *sound in faith, in love, in patience.*
   B 2:3a that *elderly women likewise be reverent in demeanor,*
   B' 2:3b *not slanderers*
   B" 2:3c *nor enslaved to much wine,*
   B'" 2:3d *teachers of that which is good,*
     C 2:4a that they may *train the young women to love their husbands,*
     C' 2:4b to *love their children,*
     C" 2:5a to *be sober-minded,*
     C'" 2:5b *chaste,*
     C"" 2:5c *workers at home,*
     C""' 2:5d *kind,*
     C"""" 2:5e *being in subjection to their own husbands,*
     C""""' 2:5f *that the word of God not be blasphemed.*
        D 2:6 *Encourage the younger men likewise to be sober-minded.*
           E 2:7a *Show yourself in all things as an example of good works.*

E' 2:7b In your doctrine *show incorruptibility, gravity,* 2:8 *sound speech* that cannot be condemned, that he that is of the contrary part may be ashamed, having no evil thing to say of us.

D' 2:9 *Encourage servants to be in subjection to their own masters*, to be well-pleasing in all things, not nay saying, 2:10a not purloining, but showing all good fidelity,

F 2:10b that they may adorn the doctrine of *God our savior* in all things. 2:11 For the grace of God has appeared, bringing salvation to all men. 2:12 Instructing us to the intent that, denying ungodliness and worldly lusts, we should live soberly and righteously and godly in this present world,

F' 2:13 looking for the blessed hope and appearance of the glory of the great God and *our savior Jesus Christ*; 2:14 who gave himself for us, that he might redeem us from all iniquity, and purify to himself a people for his own possession, zealous of good works.

G 2:15 Speak these things and *encourage and reprove* with all authority. Let no man despise you.

G' 3:1 *Put them in mind* to be in subjection to rulers, to authorities, to be obedient, to be ready for every good work,

G" 3:2 *to speak evil of no man*, not to be contentious, to be gentle, showing all meekness toward all men.

Titus 2:1–3:2 Parallel Structure Table

A 2:1–2a—elderly men be temperate	A' 2:2b—grave		A" 2:2c—sober-minded		A'" 2:2d—sound in faith in love in patience		
B 2:3a—elderly women likewise be reverent in demeanor	B' 2:3b—not slanderers		B" 2:3c—nor enslaved to much wine		B'" 2:3d—teachers of that which is good		
C 2:4a—train the young women to love their husbands	C' 2:4b—love their children	C" 2:5a—be sober-minded	C'" 2:5b—chaste	C"" 2:5c—workers at home	C""' 2:5d—kind	C"""' 2:5e—being in subjection to their own husbands	C"""" 2:5f—that the word of God not be blasphemed
D 2:6—Encourage the younger men likewise to be sober-minded				D' 2:9–10a—encourage servants to be in subjection to their own masters			

E 2:7a—show yourself in all things as an example of good works	E' 2:7b–8—show incorruptibility gravity sound speech	
F 2:10b–12—God our savior	F' 2:13–14—our savior Jesus Christ	
G 2:15—encourage and reprove	G' 3:1—put them in mind	G" 3:2—speak evil of no man

Commentary

Once again the parallelisms of Titus 2 seem to be the result of a list of admonitions rather than a structural technique. The parallelism of "God our savior" and "our savior Jesus Christ" do not show up until the end of the literary unit. The parallelisms of the same quality seem to continue through the end of Titus 2 to v. 3:2. It is not clear where the end of literary unit is. Paul did not write this literary unit.

Titus 3

Titus 3:3–11

> A 3:3 For we also once were foolish, disobedient, deceived, serving diverse lusts and pleasures, living in malice and envy, hateful, hating one another. 3:4 But when the kindness of *God our savior* and his love toward man appeared,
> A' 3:5 not by works in righteousness, which we did ourselves, but according to his mercy he saved us, through the washing of regeneration and renewing of the Holy Spirit, 3:6 which he poured out upon us richly, through *Jesus Christ our savior*. 3:7 That being justified by his grace we might be made heirs according to the hope of eternal life.
> B 3:8 Trustworthy is the saying, and concerning these things I desire that you affirm confidently, to the end that they who have believed God may be careful to maintain good works. These things are good and profitable to men. 3:9 But *shun foolish questionings*, and genealogies, and strife, and fighting about law. For they are unprofitable and vain.
> B' 3:10 *Reject a factious man* after a first and second admonition, 3:11 knowing that such a one is perverted and sins, being self-condemned.

Titus 3:3–11 Parallel Structure Table

A 3:3–4—God our savior	A' 3:5–7—Jesus Christ our savior
B 3:8–9—shun foolish questioning	B' 3:10–11—reject a factious man

Commentary

In eleven verses there are only two pairs of parallel phrases. This seems to be the result of wanting to repeat the parallelism about "God our savior" and "Jesus Christ our savior" three times in the letter and the second parallelism is another admonition to Titus. It should be noted that the three parallelisms about saviors are all different. Each of the three has "God our savior," but the phrase about Jesus being our savior is different each time. This structure has too many words and too few parallelisms to have been written by Paul.

Titus 3:12–15

3:12 When I shall send Artemas to you, or Tychicus, give diligence to come to me to Nicopolis. For I have decided to winter there. 3:13 Diligently equip Zenas the lawyer and Apollos for their journey, so that nothing is lacking for them. 3:14 And let our people also learn to maintain good works for necessary uses, so that they are not unfruitful. 3:15 All that are with me greet you. Greet them that love us in faith. Grace be with you all.

Commentary

The last four verses of Titus contain no parallelisms. There were no chiastic structures in the letter. The parallel structures that exist in Titus are haphazard and not well formed. This letter was not written by Paul.

17

Conclusion

Rhetorical analysis can be used as a tool to expose forgery and interpolation in the Pauline corpus. The seven undisputed letters are organized into chiastic and parallel structured literary units. Imbalances in the stiches reveal interpolations by redactors who did not realize they were disrupting a carefully constructed composition. Paul's use of parallelism to emphasize the points he was making was not haphazardly included in his letters. They were carefully thought out and organized into coherent literary units. The consistent style of structural repetitions and parallelisms throughout the seven undisputed letters demonstrates that F.C. Baur's *hauptbriefe* theory is incorrect.

Interpolation

Many New Testament scholars have proposed various parts of the undisputed letters are interpolations. In his 2001 book on interpolation into Paul's letters, Walker listed sixty-two interpolations into Paul's undisputed letters that had been proposed by various scholars. In addition, in O'Neill's book on Romans, he proposed that about half of Romans is interpolation, including the last half of Rom 1, all of Rom 2, one-third of Rom 9, half of Rom 10, all of Rom 11, 12, and 13, plus other smaller sections. In his book on Galatians, O'Neill also proposed seventeen interpolations into Galatians including one that encompasses the last half of Gal 5 and the first half of Gal 6. Rhetorical analysis confirms a number of the interpolations that have been proposed by these scholars, but interpolations are not nearly as extensive as the literature would suggest. The method of rhetorical analysis utilized herein identifies that twenty-two of the ninety-eight literary units in the undisputed letters contain interpolations, with a total of thirty-five interpolations.

Some of the more important interpolations exposed by rhetorical analysis include Rom 10:6–7 which is the corrupted quote of Deut 30:12–13, the entire chapter of 1 Cor 8 that contradicts 1 Cor 10:19–33, 1 Cor 9:5–7 that speaks to brothers of the

Lord and Kephas being married, 1 Cor 11:3–16 which contains admonitions about the hair styles of men and women, 1 Cor 14:32–36 about women staying silent in church, 1 Cor 15:3–11 about apostles and brothers seeing the risen Christ and teaching the same doctrine of the death and resurrection of Christ, 1 Cor 15:29a and c about baptism of the dead, Gal 2:2b about Paul making sure his gospel met with the approval of the Jerusalem apostles, Gal 2:7b and 8b which call Kephas "Peter," and 1 Thess 2:15a, c and 16b, the anti-Semitic diatribe of 1 Thess 2. Rhetorical analysis also establishes that Rom 9–11 is not an interpolation and was written by Paul, that Rom 15–16 is not an interpolation, and that 1 Cor 12–14 is not an interpolation although the chapters are out of order in that 1 Cor 14 originally preceded 1 Cor 13.

Forgery

One traditional tool used by scholars in attempting to identify an interpolated passage or a forged letter is comparing word usage and grammar in the subject passage or letter with Paul's word usage and grammar elsewhere. The use of words or grammar in a passage being examined that are unusual with respect to the balance of Paul's writings is regarded as a clue that the passage may have been written by another person. Those are two elements of writing style. The use of repetition and parallels in patterns is another element of writing style that heretofore has not been adequately examined. The same type of analysis with respect to word usage and grammar applies to the use of parallelism, especially repetition. Paul's use of the repetition of words, phrases, and abstract concepts into clearly defined literary units is common to the seven undisputed letters but this quality is missing from the six other letters in the cannon that claim to have been written by Paul. It appears that 2 Thess 1 was written by Paul, perhaps to a church other than the one in Thessalonica, and it was hijacked by a forger who used it to promote his idea of an anti-Christ and to claim that 1 Thessalonians was a forgery.

Colossians has a number of parallel structures, even one with an inclusio. The first structure in the letter is the only chiastic structure and it lacks the Pauline attribute of a two-hemistich center unless there is an out of place verse. It appears that the author of Colossians was aware of Paul's use of repetition and even the chiastic format, but he did not copy Paul's style closely enough. If Paul had written Colossians, there would be clear demarcations between literary units and roughly half of those literary units would have a chiastic structure. Comparing Colossians with the shorter undisputed letters, Colossians has seven literary structures one of which is chiastic. Galatians has twelve literary units, seven of which have a chiastic structure. Philippians contains eight literary units six of which have a chiastic structure. Finally, 1 Thessalonians contains nine literary units five of which are chiastic. Colossians was not written by Paul.

The author of Ephesians also attempted to copy Paul's style, but was less adept than the author of Colossians. It is possible that Ephesians and Colossians were written by the same forger and Ephesians is his first attempt, doing a better job in Colossians. Either that or the author of Ephesians was copying Colossians and the similarity to Paul results from that endeavor. Ephesians contains two short chiastic structures that are superficially Pauline, but the repeated phrases are not as long as Paul's repeated phrases. Counting the long unstructured passages in Ephesians as separate literary units, Ephesians contains seventeen literary units and only two are chiastic. The author also used the un-Pauline terms "devil" and "evangelist." There are relatively long passages of Ephesians without any repeated words or phrases, marking it as definitively not by Paul. Ephesians was not written by Paul.

Both Colossians and Ephesians contain extremely long sentences that are not Paul's style as found in the undisputed letters. These long sentences result in confusing the beginnings and the endings of the literary units that are presented. In the undisputed letters Paul's literary units have clear beginnings and endings. The long sentences seem to be a crutch used by the author or authors of Colossians and Ephesians. In the undisputed letters Paul presents complicated ideas in rather simple sentences. In Colossians and Ephesians the author or authors present simple ideas in long, convoluted sentences, apparently hoping that the readers will think that the ideas presented are complicated. Colossians and Ephesians present no genuinely new ideas into the Pauline corpus. They are reiterations of the simplest ideas from the undisputed letters.

The pastoral letters, 1 and 2 Timothy and Titus, contain long stretches of text without any repeated phrases and are clearly not Pauline. There are no chiastic structures and the parallel structures show no regularity as one would expect if Paul had written them. These are without question forgeries.

Paul was a talented writer, well trained in argumentation by the use of chiastic and parallel structures, repeating his concepts to his readers in getting his point across. He varied his writing style to create hybrid and dual chiastic/parallel structures, and he used clever word play to keep his readers' attention. The writers of the Deutero-Pauline letters did not seem to have Paul's intellect or writing talent and were unable to successfully copy his style.

Bibliography

Bailey, Robert Arthur. *The Structure of Paul's Letters*. US: Xulon, 2010.

Barnikol, Ernst. "The Non-Pauline Origin of the Parallelism of the Apostles Peter and Paul. Galatians 2:7–8." *Journal of Higher Criticism*, 5 (1998) 285–300.

———. *Progelomena zur Neutestamentlichen Dogmengeschichte. II. Philipper . Der Marcionitische Ursprung des Mythos-Satzes Phil :-,* Forschungen zur Entstehung des Urchristentums des Neuen Testaments und der Kirche 7, Mühlau, Kiel (1932).

Baur, F.C. *Paul, the Apostle of Jesus Christ, His Life and Work, His Epistles and His Doctrine.* English Translation of 2nd ed. E. Zeller. London: Williams & Norgate, 1875–76; 2 vols, 2.87–88.

Britannica.com/biography/Ferdinand-Christian-Baur. Accessed 03/10/2021.

Britannica.com/art/parallelism-literature-and-rhetoric. Accessed 02/03/2021.

Bruce, F. F. *Romans: an Introduction and Commentary.* Tyndale New Testament Commentaries, Vol. 6. Downers Grove, IL: InterVarsity Press. (1985) 34.

Bultmann, Rudolf. "Glossen im Römenbrief." *Theolische Literarurzeitung* (1947) 197–202.

Collins, Raymond F. *Studies on the First Letter to the Thessalonians.* Bibliotheca EphemeridumTheologicarum Lovaniensium, 66, Leuven, Belgium: University Press (1984).

Cope, Lamar. "First Corinthians 8-10 Continuity or Contradiction?" *Anglican Theological Review Supp.* (1990) 114–23.

Dodd, C.H. *The Moffatt New Testament Commentary, The Epistle of Paul to the Romans.* London: Hodder & Staughton (1936).

Eckart, Karl G. "Der Zweite echte Brief des Apostel Paulus an die Thessalonicher." *Zeitschrift für Theologie und Kirche* 58 (1961) 30–44.

Ehrman, Bart D. *Forged.* New York: HarperCollins (2011).

———. *The Orthodox Corruption of Scripture*, NY: Oxford University Press (2011).

Fitzmeyer, Joseph A. *Romans.* The Anchor Bible. New York: Doubleday (1993).

Friedrich, Gerhard. "1 Thessalonischer 5:1–11, der apologetische Einschub eines Späteren." *Zeitschrift für Theologie und Kirche* 70 (1973).

Goodacre, Mark. "Dating Game II, Getting Paul's Letters in Order." NT Blog, Oct 14, 2008, https://ntweblog.blogspot.com/2008/10/dating-game-ii-getting-pauls-letters-in.html.

———. "Fatigue in the Synoptics." *New Testament Studies* 44 (1998) 45–58.

Hagen, Wayne H. "Two Deutero-Pauline Glosses in Romans 6." *The Expository Times* 92 (1981) 364.

Harrison, P.N. *Paulines and Pastorals.* London: Villiers, 1964.

Horn, Friedrich Wilhelm. "1 Korinther 15:56—ein exegetischer Stachel." *Zeitschrift für die Neutestamentliche Wissenschaft.* 82 (1991) 88–105.

BIBLIOGRAPHY

Jewett, Robert. *The Thessalonian Correspondence: Pauline Rhetoric and Millenarian Piety (Foundations and Facets).* Minneapolis: Fortress, 1986.

Keck, Leander E. "The Post-Pauline Interpretation of Jesus' Death in Rom 5:6–7." in *Theologie Crucis—Signum Crucis: Festerschrift für Eric Dinkler zum Gebustag.* Tübigen: J.C.B. Mohr [Paul Siebeck] (1979).

Knox, John. "The Epistle to the Romans, Introduction and Exegesis," *Interpreters Bible* IX New York: Abingdon-Cokesbury (1952).

Koester, Helmut. "I Thessalonians-Experiment in Christian Writing," in *Continuity and Discontinuity in Church History.* Edited by F. F. Church and T. George; Leiden: Brill (1979).

Lund, Nils W. *Chiasmus in the New Testament.* Chapel Hill, NC: U of NC Press (1942).

MacDonald, Dennis R. "A Conjectural Emendation of 1 Cor 15:31–32, Or the Case of the Misplaced Lion Fight." *Harvard Theological Review,* 73 (1980).

Magne, Jean. "Les paroles sur la coupe" in *Logia: Lesproles de Jésus—The Sayings of Jesus: Mémorial Joseph Coppens.* Bibliotheca Ephemeridum Theologicarum Lovaniensium Joël Delobel ed., 59. Leuven, Belgium: Leuven University Press (1982).

Metzger, B. *The Early Versions of the New Testament: Their Origin, Transmission and Limitations.* Oxford: Oxford University Press (1977).

Munro, Winsome. "Interpolations in the Epistles." *New Testament Studies* 36, 3 (1990) 431–43.

O'Neil, J. C. "Glosses and Interpolations in the Letters of St. Paul", *SE.* VII. *Papers Presented to the Fifth International Congress on Biblical Studies held at Oxford,* (Texte und Unterschugen, 126; Berlin Akademie-Verlag, 1982) 381–83.

———. *Paul's Letter to the Roman.* Middlesex, UK: Penguin Books. (1975).

———. *The Recovery of Paul's Letter to the Galatians.* London: S.P.C.K. (1972).

Pearson, Birger. "1 Thessalonians 2:13–16: A Deutero-Pauline Interpolation," HTR 64 (1971) 79–94.

Price, R.M. "1 Corinthians 15:3–11 as a Post-Pauline Interpolation," *Journal of Higher Criticism,* Vol. 2, No. 2 (Fall 1995) 60-99.

Refoule, Françoise."Unité de l'Epitre aux Romains et historie du salut," *Revue des Sciences Philosophiques et Théologiques,* 71, (1987) 219–42.

Schenk, Wolfgang, *Die Philipperbriefe des Paulus: Kommentar,* Stuttgart: W. Kohlhammer, 1984.

Schlueter, Carol. *Filling up the Measure,* Sheffield, UK: Sheffield Academic Press, 1994.

Still, Todd D. *Conflict at Thessalonica,* Journal for the Study of the New Testament Supplement Series 183, Sheffield, UK: Sheffield Academic Press, 1999.

Schmidt, Daryl. "1 Thess 2:13–16: Linguistic Evidence For An Interpolation" *Journal of Biblical Literature,* Vol 102, no 2, 269–79.

Schnelle, Udo. "1 Kor 6:14—Eine Nachpaulinische Glosse," *Novum Testamentum* 25 (1983) 217–19.

Slusser, Wayne T. "Chiasmus in the Pauline Writings?" No pages. Online http://www.chiasticstructures.com/iTodd__Moore_Vanity/Chiastic_Structures/Chiastic_Structures_files/Chiasmus_Slusser.pdf, 2002.

Smith, Christopher R. "Chapters and Verses: Who Needs Them?," *Bible Study Magazine* (July-Aug 2009): 46–47.

Smith, David Oliver. *Matthew, Mark, Luke, and Paul: The Influence of the Epistles on the Synoptic Gospels,* Eugene, OR: Wipf and Stock, 2011.

———. "*Unlocking the Puzzle: The Structure and Christology of the Original Gospel of Mark*, Eugene, OR: Wipf and Stock, 2016.
Strong, James. *The Exhaustive Concordance of the Bible*. No pages. Online http://biblehub.com/interlinear/htm.
Strugnell, John. "A Plea for Conjectural Emendation in the New Testament, with A Coda on 1 Cor 4:6," *Catholic Biblical Quarterly* Vol. 36 (1974) 543–58.
Talbert, C. H. "A Non-Pauline Fragment in Romans 3:24–26?" *Journal of Biblical Literature*, Vol. 85 (1966) 287–96.
Thomson, Ian H. *Chiasmus in the Pauline Letters*, JSNT Supp., Sheffield, UK: Sheffield Academic Press, 1995.
Van Manen, W.C. "Romans (Epistle)," in *Encyclopaedia Biblica*, New York: Macmillan, 4 Vols., 1899–1903, Vol. 4, 4127–4145.
Walker, William O. Jr. *Interpolations in the Pauline Letters*. Journal for the Study of the New Testament Supplement Series 213, Sheffield UK: Sheffield Academic Press, 2001.
Wanamaker, *The Epistles to the Thessalonians*, Grand Rapids, MI: Eerdmans, 1990.
Weiss, Johannes. *Der Erste Korintherbrief* (Kritisch-exegetischer Kommentar über das Neue Testament 5) Vandenhoek & Ruprecht, 9th Ed. (1910).
Welch, John W. "Chiasmus in Ancient Greek and Latin Literature," *Chiasmus in Antiquity*, Edited by John W. Welch, Hildesheim: Gerstenberg, 1981, 250–68.
———. "Chiasmus in the New Testament," *Chiasmus in Antiquity*, John W. Welch, ed., Hildesheim: Gerstenberg, 1981, 211–49.
Widmann, M. "1 Kor 2:6–16: Ein Einspruch gegen Paulus" *Zeitschrift für die Neutestamentliche Wissenschaft* 70 (1979) 47–48.
Zuntz Günter. The Text of the Epistles: A Disquisition Upon the Corpus Paulinum, Oxford UK: Oxford University Press, 1953.

www.ingramcontent.com/pod-product-compliance
Lightning Source LLC
Chambersburg PA
CBHW080724300426
44114CB00019B/2487